PENGUIN CLASSICS

TOTTEL'S MISCELLANY

The little book that kick-started the Golden Age of English litera-ture, *Songs and Sonnets*, commonly known as *Tottel's Miscellany*, is one of the most important landmarks of the poetic tradition. Published in 1557, and reissued many times in the Elizabethan period, it was the first major printed anthology of poetry in Eng-lish, introducing the new forms of the Renaissance to a popular audience for the first time. Though perhaps best known for its love poems, the *Miscellany* also contains a range of important elegies, nature poems, moral odes and a variety of other works. The first editions appeared at the peak of the persecution of Prot-estants under Queen Mary, and many of the poems can be read as responses to the tyranny and uncertainty of the age.

The two most important poets whose work was first popular-ized in the *Miscellany* are Henry Howard, Earl of Surrey (1517–47) and Sir Thomas Wyatt (1503–42). These were the major courtier-poets of the reign of Henry VIII. Surrey, a senior nobleman and soldier, invented the English sonnet and blank verse, the two forms which Shakespeare would later make the central mode of English literature. He was executed for treason in Henry VIII's last months. Wyatt, a diplomat and intimate of Anne Boleyn, remains one of the most enigmatic and influential characters of the English Renaissance. A wide range of anonymous, and often brilliant verse makes up the rest of the anthology.

AMANDA HOLTON is Visiting Fellow at the University of South-ampton, and a specialist in Old and Middle English literature and the English language. Her books include *The Sources of Chau-cer's Poetics* (2008).

TOM MACFAUL is Tutor in English at Merton College, University of Oxford. He is the author of *Male Friendship in Shakespeare and his Contemporaries* (2007), *Poetry and Paternity in Renais-sance England* (2010), and many articles on Renaissance poetry and drama.

Tottel's Miscellany

Songs and Sonnets of Henry Howard,
Earl of Surrey, Sir Thomas Wyatt
and Others

Edited with an Introduction and Notes by
AMANDA HOLTON *and* TOM MACFAUL

PENGUIN BOOKS

PENGUIN CLASSICS

Published by the Penguin Group
Penguin Books Ltd, 80 Strand, London WC2R 0RL, England
Penguin Group (USA) Inc., 375 Hudson Street, New York, New York 10014, USA
Penguin Group (Canada), 90 Eglinton Avenue East, Suite 700, Toronto, Ontario,
Canada M4P 2Y3 (a division of Pearson Penguin Canada Inc.)
Penguin Ireland, 25 St Stephen's Green, Dublin 2, Ireland
(a division of Penguin Books Ltd)
Penguin Group (Australia), 707 Collins Street, Melbourne, Victoria 3008, Australia
(a division of Pearson Australia Group Pty Ltd)
Penguin Books India Pvt Ltd, 11 Community Centre, Panchsheel Park,
New Delhi – 110 017, India
Penguin Group (NZ), 67 Apollo Drive, Rosedale, Auckland 0632, New Zealand
(a division of Pearson New Zealand Ltd)
Penguin Books (South Africa) (Pty) Ltd, Block D, Rosebank Office Park,
181 Jan Smuts Avenue, Parktown North, Gauteng 2193, South Africa

Penguin Books Ltd, Registered Offices: 80 Strand, London WC2R 0RL, England

www.penguin.com

This edition first published in Penguin Classics 2011

007

Introduction and editorial matter copyright © Amanda Holton and Tom MacFaul, 2011
All rights reserved

The moral right of the editors has been asserted

Set in Postscript Adobe Sabon
Typeset by Jouve (UK), Milton Keynes
Printed in England by Clays Ltd, Elcograf S.p.A.

ISBN: 978-0-141-19204-8

www.greenpenguin.co.uk

Contents

Acknowledgements

As with any editors, our first debt of gratitude is to the giant predecessors on whose shoulders our efforts stand: in particular, we owe thanks to Hyder E. Rollins, one of the greatest of all scholars in the field of literary studies; our debt to his work should be evident throughout. Other editors whose work we found indispensable include: Ruth Hughey, Richard Harrier, R. A. Rebholz, Emrys Jones, Kenneth Muir and Patricia Thomson. Paul A. Marquis's recent careful textual work has also been a valuable resource.

Work on this project was significantly enabled by the award of a Leverhulme Early Career Fellowship to Amanda Holton at the University of Reading, and we would like to thank the Leverhulme Trust and the School of English and American Literature for their support.

The British Library generously gave us permission to use their copy of the *Miscellany* as our base-text, and provided a superb working environment.

Introduction

RICHARD TOTTEL AND
THE PRINT TRADE

Richard Tottel (*c.* 1528–93) was primarily a publisher of legal texts, but history has indelibly associated his name with *Songes and Sonettes*, here styled *Tottel's Miscellany*. He was granted a patent by Edward VI in 1553 to produce common-law texts – a very lucrative monopoly which was renewed under Mary in 1556 and under Elizabeth in 1559. Tottel seems to have been well connected with London businessmen, lawyers and intellectuals, including both Catholics and Protestants in his circle. As a result, he was able to become one of the most successful publishers of his time. Later in his career, he was accused of profiteering in charging excessive prices for textbooks law students could not do without. He evidently knew his public and how to exploit them. The *Miscellany* may have been targeted mainly at Inns of Court students, who seem to have been as much in need of the flowers of courtly rhetoric and verse embodied therein as they were of legal textbooks.

Publishing was still a new trade, but its position amongst the London trade guilds was beginning to be entrenched. The Stationers' Company was incorporated in May 1557, a month before the *Miscellany*'s first edition. Tottel became a major player in the Company, contributing to royal loans on its behalf, and donating the profits from some of his most popular texts – including the *Miscellany* – to the relief of poorer Company members. The publication of the *Miscellany* may have been a way of testing the waters for a larger trade market: would poetry sell?

It did. There is a clear sense in Tottel's preface to the *Miscellany* that he is letting the general public in on works that had been hoarded, even kept secret, by the aristocracy. In some ways the process of publication of the poems here is similar to the publication of common-law texts, bringing the public in on something that had previously been kept from them. Yet the sense that the publisher is doing a public service is complicated by the idea of a market for entertainment: respectable publishers did not at this stage produce texts that were merely entertaining – they needed a strong sense of edification too.

Tottel's other literary publications have more obviously serious qualities; these include his involvement in the sumptuous publication of Thomas More's *Works* and, between the publication of the first and second editions of the *Miscellany*, Surrey's translation of Virgil's *Aeneid*, Books II and IV. The *Miscellany*'s admixture of an older mode of moralizing verse to more fashionable amorous verse may be an attempt to provide a leaven of edification, particularly given the positioning of moral poems towards the end of the collection's various sections.

Whether for its moral or for its erotic verse, the *Miscellany* evidently sold well. Its first edition was quickly followed by two separate printings of a second, with a significantly altered text. That second edition was the basis for at least seven further editions during the Elizabethan period; from the fifth edition onwards (that is, the second of the two editions published in 1559) the *Miscellany* was printed in octavo rather than quarto format: it seems that octavos were a more prestigious form of publication, despite their smaller size, as they could be more readily bound for preservation in libraries.[1] What had begun life as a relatively ephemeral form of publication had become accepted as something more permanent: volumes of poetry were now coming to be regarded as a significant part of the national culture.

MISCELLANIES

The name by which this collection came to be known, *Tottel's Miscellany*, indicates its membership of a particular genre of book, the poetic miscellany, or collection of poems by different people on a variety of subjects. Sixteenth-century printed poetic anthologies like Tottel's grew out of the tradition of commonplace books, volumes in which individuals or groups of people gathered material which was particularly interesting or useful to them personally or professionally. These manuscript books, characteristic of the medieval period and subsequent centuries, typically mixed lyric verse with other material like prose romances, recipes and prayers. Although in France manuscript books dedicated exclusively to lyric verse were common, in England this was not the case. However, a few manuscript poetic miscellanies are extant from the sixteenth century, the Arundel Harington MS being one of the best known. Other manuscript books were dedicated wholly or largely to the work of a particular individual; Egerton 2711, for instance, is mainly occupied by Sir Thomas Wyatt's work.

Through the first two centuries of printing in England, the older tradition of recording and circulating verse in handwritten manuscripts continued in parallel to print, and indeed, anthologies of poetry did not begin to be printed until surprisingly late, with the first edition of *Tottel's Miscellany* in 1557 a watershed. Marotti gives five reasons for the delay in the lyric anthology's penetration into print; (1) there was as yet no clear established vernacular lyric tradition in England for such publications to slot into; (2) the commercial and democratic connotations of print made it an unappealing outlet for poets of the aristocracy or gentry; (3) love poetry was regarded as frivolous and immoral; (4) love poetry was associated with privacy, and so was unsuitable for reading by the general public; (5) lyrics were regarded as essentially occasional, and hence ephemeral.[2] The fifth point has a direct bearing on the provision of titles for poems in *Tottel's Miscellany*. As Marotti notes, these titles attempt either to re-create the original social contexts for poems (as with poem 29), or to locate them within the context of a literary tradition (as with poem 48).[3]

Tottel's Miscellany was thus an immensely influential book which set a trend for putting into wider circulation lyrics which had previously been circulated only in manuscript. It led a cavalcade of printed poetic miscellanies including such works as *The Paradise of Dainty Devices* (1576) and *England's Helicon* (1600).

The *Miscellany* appears to be part of a triad which also includes two manuscripts mentioned above, Egerton, and the Arundel Harington MS. The latter was compiled by John Harington of Stepney and Sir John Harington of Kelston, and its contents span much of the sixteenth century, stretching from Wyatt to Sidney, Ralegh and Elizabeth I. Egerton probably came into the hands of John Harington at some point after the death of Wyatt (1542), and it is clear that it was used in the preparation of the Arundel Harington MS, which frequently follows it exactly, incorporating many of the corrections Wyatt made in Egerton, and some of the corrections Grimald made. It appears, however, that Tottel's editor sometimes consults Egerton rather than using Arundel Harington, binding the three texts even more firmly together.

LITERARY CONTEXT

The *Miscellany* draws from a variety of genres and literary traditions. There are elegies and epigrams, poems about fortune and friendship, riddles, moral odes and descriptions of battle. Many of the poems allude to or are versions of earlier works; Chaucer's influence is clear not only in the inclusion of his poem 'Truth' (207), but in the repeated echoes of his writing throughout the collection (see, for example, poem 48). The medieval period's interests in classical literature, particularly Ovid and Virgil, continues into this mid-sixteenth-century collection; but there is a distinctively humanist element too, particularly in Grimald's contributions (see below).

But above all, the *Miscellany* is a collection of love-lyrics, and love-lyrics drawing deeply on a tradition informed by Petrarch. It is no coincidence that a pair of poems about Petrarch lie near the centre of the collection (poems 188 and 189); the beginning of 188, 'O Petrarke hed and prince of poets al', expresses a key value in the collection. Many of the poems in the *Miscellany* are in fact close translations of Petrarch's poems, but even where textual relationships are less close, the love-poems in Tottel are characterized by behavioural and linguistic conventions which can be identified with Petrarchism.

A very important classical scholar, Francesco Petrarca (1304–74) is now most famous for his *Rime sparse* ('scattered rhymes'), a collection of love-poems about Laura, who may or may not have been a real woman. Petrarch worked on this collection for much of his life; the first version of it was circulated in 1359, and he continued to add to and rearrange the material until the end of his life.

The love-poems in the *Miscellany* follow Petrarch in being underpinned by a particular set of ideas about love, the lover and the beloved, characterized by the abject male speaker's pain and frustration at the inaccessibility of the woman he desires. The lover is a passive-aggressive cauldron of desire, pain, hope, puzzlement, resentment, blame and anger, all captured in recurrent tortuous paradoxes; many of these paradoxes are collected in poem 54, Wyatt's translation of Petrarch's *Rime*, 134. Here the lover is neither at peace nor at war; both burns and freezes; wishes both for death and health, '[a]nd my delight is causer of this strife' (line 14). The Petrarchan lady is typically presented as cruel, harsh, icy and deadly. In poem 98 and in its Petrarchan source, she conspires with Love against the speaker of the poem; in 100 she is the speaker's 'deare and cruel fo' (line 1). The lady manifests herself as a series of shocks or a sustained assault on the lover which give rise to an obsessive focus on the lover's own sensations; these are not poems about an individual beloved woman, but rather about the exquisite frustrated torture of the man. As Waller puts it, Petrarchan poetry is 'a theatre of the lover's desires alone'.[4]

The dynamic of idealized yet cruel lady and tormented lover

was not new to English poetry in the sixteenth century – and neither was it a dynamic Petrarch had invented. It had developed from the troubadour poetry of Provence in the late eleventh century, and was immensely important across European literature in the later Middle Ages. Medieval English poetry was saturated with what is now sometimes (problematically) called 'courtly love'; poems like Chaucer's *Troilus and Criseyde* are built around its conventions, and Chaucer was clearly fascinated by the power-play and covert intimidations within it. But for the sixteenth century, the tradition was refreshed through an icy injection of Petrarch.

THE MARIAN POLITICAL CONTEXT

The burning of Protestant 'heretics' peaked in the very month of the *Miscellany*'s publication. The reign of Mary has, retrospectively, come to be seen as a time of vigorous reaction to the Reformation and oppression of its adherents. England had a half-Spanish queen whose husband, Philip of Spain, was heir to the largest bloc of Catholic empire in Europe and the New World. Yet it is a mistake to think of this as a time of Catholic triumphalism. Philip was mostly an absentee, more interested in his Imperial possessions – particularly the Low Countries – than in begetting an heir to the English throne. By June 1557, England had finally been dragged into final preparations for an unpopular war with France – unpopular because it was felt that the war was mainly in Hapsburg interests. A collection of verse published at this time, and drawing most prominently on writings from earlier in the century, may well have concentrated current anxieties through reflection on the troubles of the earlier Tudor period, and perhaps also enabled readers to envision better times to come.

By 1557, the Queen was 41 years old, and her husband was out of the country; despite her own delusions, she was very unlikely to produce an heir of her own body. Her sister, Elizabeth Tudor, was the only possible heir. Several people associated with the *Miscellany*, most notably Sir John Harington, were also closely associated with Elizabeth, and were out of favour with the Marian regime or even imprisoned. They need not therefore have been ideologically committed Protestants to feel discontented in the present and hopeful for the succession; after all, Elizabeth herself was conforming – outwardly at least – to the restored Roman Catholic Church. Amatory verse was a particularly good resource in the circumstances: it both compensated for and focused their mixture of frustration and anticipation, all the more so when it was accompanied by a good deal of Horatian verse reflecting on the fickleness of fortune and the vanity of worldly success. Similar poetic modes would be used by later defeated poets and readers, such as out-of-favour Elizabethan courtiers like Philip Sidney and Walter Ralegh, and defeated Royalists in the 1650s. The fact that Wyatt and (particularly) Surrey had suffered under earlier Tudor regimes also made them attractive models for meditation on political discontent – a discontent that at times comes close to dissent, but which can never quite be pinned down as such.

Whoever compiled the *Miscellany* – Tottel himself, Nicholas Grimald, Harington or another courtly patron of the publisher[5] – knew that he had to be cautious in many respects. He could not present poems that attacked the present regime, but it is equally significant that he did not present poems that praised it. Indeed, one (poem 168) deliberately excludes praise of Mary that can be found in a manuscript version. It may also be significant that the *Miscellany* excludes one of Wyatt's most famous poems, 'Whoso list to hunt', given that its attitude to Anne Boleyn might be thought to reflect badly on her daughter Elizabeth. Though the *Miscellany* cannot be regarded as explicitly partisan, then, it is not and cannot be entirely neutral: by ending with a poem about the death of the humanist hero Cicero, it reflects on the endangerment of the arts under a tyrannic regime of any stamp.

SURREY

Henry Howard, Earl of Surrey, the only poet named in the title of the *Miscellany*, has often been more patronized than properly appreciated. It is easy to damn him with the apparently faint praise of having invented English poetry's two most enduring forms – blank verse and the 'Shakespearean' sonnet. Placing Surrey's poems first in the *Miscellany* may have much to do with the poet's social standing, but he deserves his prime position for poetic as well as snobbish reasons.

Surrey is a crucial mediating figure between medieval and Renaissance verse. His best works have the freshness and clarity of Chaucer and Langland while embracing the Italianate technical innovation that would drive the poets of the later sixteenth century. His aristocratically proud, feudal sensibility combines with elements of early modern individualism. By turns rebellious and fiercely loyal (on his own terms), he anticipates both the temper and the poetics of later courtiers such as Ralegh, Sidney and Essex.

Eldest son of the Duke of Norfolk, Surrey was the boyhood friend and brother-in-law of Henry VIII's illegitimate son, the Duke of Richmond, a friendship poignantly and pointedly celebrated in the so-called 'Windsor Elegy' (poem 15 in the *Miscellany*). Surrey was executed in 1547 on the pretext of having quartered the royal arms, but mainly because of fears that he and his father would be able to take charge of the kingdom as Protectors during Edward's minority (it was clear by that stage that Henry was on his last legs). Whatever the basis for the charge, Surrey's fault seems mainly to have been a mixture of pride and naivety; even his father called him 'my foolish son'. The chief practical reason for his tragedy was that he found himself opposed to the 'new men' such as Edward Seymour who came to dominate Henry's court; at least in his own mind, he represented an older aristocracy whose status was to be validated by martial rather than bureaucratic achievement. In fact, Surrey was not a great success as a soldier – being defeated in a near-disastrous skirmish while he was Lieutenant General of the King at Boulogne in 1546 – but his position as a love poet is always underpinned by a sense of his own chivalric identity.

A comparison of Surrey's 'Complaint of a lover rebuked' (poem 6) with Wyatt's 'The lover for shamefastnesse hideth his

desire within his faithfull hart' (poem 42), as they are versions
of the same Italian original, can give us a sense of the difference
between Tottel's two star poets. The poems' different rhythms
might, one imagines, capture the poets' different gaits as courtiers.
Surrey comes to court – his natural territory he thinks – with an
almost knowingly hubristic swagger; Wyatt sees the court as a
minefield, skittering around it while trying to preserve confi-
dence in his interior self. Surrey is affirmative; Wyatt ironic.
The twentieth century may have preferred the latter, but there
is much to be said for the former.

At his best, he has something of the piercing simplicity of
William Blake's lyrics, and he is a masterful constructor of indi-
vidual lines. A few examples may suffice: 'Nothing more good,
than in the spring the aire to fele a space' (poem 5); 'The rake-
hell life that longes to loves disporte' (poem 11); 'W.[yatt]resteth
here, that quick could never rest' (poem 35); 'No company so
pleasant as mine owne' (poem 39). None of these examples is
knotty or difficult, but they all pack in feeling with the energy
and tension of great verse. Such powerful compression is the
corollary of the formal experimentation discussed below. Surrey
carries forward two important medieval poetic devices, and
refreshes them. His alliteration is judicious rather than system-
atic, becoming a device for emphasis rather than a principle of
organization. His use of typification – e.g. describing himself 'As
one that beares flame in his brest' (poem 24, emphasis added) –
which was a favourite device of Dante – speaks for a common
humanity, and would be used in a similar way by Wordsworth.
As opposed to Wyatt's sense of the 'special' (poem 57), Surrey
speaks authoritatively for the general human condition.

Characteristically, Tottel's arrangement of Surrey's verse
attempts to present a narrative of the poet's life, putting poems
of youthful love first, and ending with poems that seem to have
been written just before his execution. The appeal to 'faith
more strong' in the final poem of the Surrey section gives a
pious turn to this narrative.

Surrey's Elizabethan reputation deserves some attention. As
he was the ancestor of the Catholic Howard faction, opponents

of the forward Protestants who included many of the most important Elizabethan poets and their patrons, Surrey was a dubious political figure even if his execution for treason could be ignored. The solution was to romanticize him, insisting on his love for 'Geraldine', to whom he in fact dedicated only one poem. This romantic version of Surrey was then subjected to brilliant irony in Nashe's *The Unfortunate Traveller*.

WYATT

Of the poets represented in the *Miscellany*, Sir Thomas Wyatt (*c.* 1503–42) is now the most famous and the one held in the highest regard. The most significant poet of Henry VIII's court, he also served at the court for most of his life, his diplomatic role being particularly important. His public life alternated success and political favour with failure and danger. His first diplomatic mission abroad was in 1526, and he was High Marshal of Calais in 1528–30. In May 1536, when Anne Boleyn and several men alleged to be her lovers were imprisoned and executed, Wyatt was himself imprisoned in the Tower of London, perhaps on suspicion of adultery with Anne Boleyn, or perhaps simply because his family had strong ties with hers. He may have owed his release in part to Thomas Cromwell, a consistent supporter of his. This episode did not prevent his further advancement, however. From 1537 to 1540 he was ambassador to the court of Charles V in Spain, his main task to prevent the French king and the emperor forming an allegiance to England's disadvantage. Inevitably, given the circumstances in Europe at the time, he failed in this, and in several marriage negotiations he was under instruction to manage. In 1538, Edmund Bonner, one of the men sent to assist (or spy on?) Wyatt, wrote to Cromwell accusing Wyatt of treason and misconduct. Cromwell protected Wyatt, but after his own fall from favour and execution in 1540 Bonner's accusations resurfaced, and in January 1541 Wyatt was again imprisoned and his possessions confiscated. He defended himself in writing to the Privy Council, and in March 1541 Catherine Howard, the then queen, interceded on his behalf, and he was released. He quickly regained favour, but died as a result of illness contracted during a diplomatic mission in October 1542.

Wyatt left a substantial and various body of work. He is best known for his lyrics, and in particular his early use of the sonnet; he also wrote a large number of short poems in ottava rima. He composed many stanzaic poems which may have been designed to be set to music; although no specific settings for any of his poems survive. He wrote epistolary satires in terza rima; also in terza rima is his 'Paraphrase of the Penitential Psalms', not included in *Tottel's Miscellany*.

The canon of Wyatt's verse is not fixed. The most authoritative source of his poems is the Egerton MS; this is because many of his poems are written there in his own hand, and there are corrections in his hand to poems copied by other scribes. Other manuscripts are more controversial; both the Blage MS and the Devonshire MS contain poems which are ascribed to Wyatt, and both also contain unascribed poems whose authorship by Wyatt has been a matter of heated debate. The *Miscellany* does not contain all poems known to have been written by Wyatt, but it does provide texts of fifteen of his poems which are not recorded elsewhere.

Wyatt wrote in a wide variety of forms, and the question of his use of metre is particularly interesting. If we take the poems in the Egerton MS as true representations of his composition, we can see that poems with shorter lines are composed of fairly regular iambic trimeters and tetrameters; the *Miscellany*'s poem 71, for instance, appears in Egerton (53) corrected in Wyatt's own hand, and is in almost totally regular iambic tetrameter. Wyatt's longer lines are metrically much more controversial. It seems clear that in some cases he is writing in iambic pentameter, either in individual lines or throughout entire poems. However, many of his longer lines seem to be informed by a different metrical expectation. This may be syllabic; Rebholz notes that of 921 long lines in Wyatt's own hand or subject to Wyatt's revisions in Egerton, 844 have ten syllables.[6] Or the metre may be governed primarily by the number of stresses: some poems seem to be characterized by four stresses per line; others,

like the famous poem which opens 'They flee from me, that
sometime did me seke' (poem 57), mix lines of four and five
stresses. Regardless of what Wyatt was himself trying to achieve
metrically, the *Miscellany*'s editor had a clear dislike of his
apparently irregular long lines, and frequently makes revisions
to tidy them into more regular iambic pentameter. 'There was
never ffile half so well filed' (Egerton 5), becomes 'Was never file
yet half so well yfiled' in the *Miscellany* (poem 44), for instance.

GRIMALD

Nicholas Grimald (1519/20–c. 1562) is an important figure in
Tottel's Miscellany for two reasons: first, some of his own
poems are included, and second, he may have been involved in
the editing of the volume.

Grimald was a humanist scholar whose life was intimately
affected by the fluctuations of power during the Edwardian
and Marian reigns. A Fellow of Christ Church, Oxford, with
responsibilities for lecturing on rhetoric, he disapproved of the
luxurious lives of Oxford-educated clerics, and reported Oxford
Catholics and Nonconformists to the authorities. He was a
protégé of Nicholas Ridley, Bishop of London, but Ridley was
imprisoned when Mary came to the throne, and Grimald may
have informed against him. Yet Grimald himself also eventu-
ally came under suspicion and was imprisoned, and it is possible
that he converted to Catholicism to save his life. After the pub-
lication of the *Miscellany* in 1557, he disappears from written
records.

Grimald wrote Latin drama; his best-known plays are *Chris-
tus redivivus* (1543) and *Archipropheta* (1548). He was also
the author of translations, versions and commentaries on a var-
iety of classical texts. Some but not all of these are extant.
Grimald, more clearly than anyone else involved in the *Miscel-
lany*, was a humanist. Humanism, an educational programme
that swept Europe in the fifteenth and sixteenth centuries,
entailed a belief in careful grammatical scholarship and an
emphasis on practical rhetoric designed to persuade rulers to

virtue, often finding itself in opposition to more militaristic aristocratic values. By the mid-Tudor period, it had become distinctly inflected by Protestantism: Grimald's translations of the Reformer Beza therefore have definite ideological meanings. His laments for the death of Cicero, the key hero of the humanists, and for the death of the scholarly Zoroas in battle, also constitute a lament for imperilled scholarship in an age when princely power was perceived as being abused.

He is now best known, however, for his contribution to the *Miscellany*. In the first edition, he was presented as the third named poet in the volume. His section, 'Songes written by Nicolas Grimald', which contained forty poems, followed on after Surrey's and Wyatt's. But his part in the second edition (the one presented in this volume) was very different. Grimald no longer occupies a prime place near the beginning of the book; instead his poems, reduced in number to ten, appear at the end, under the heading '*Songes written by N. G*'. His name is thus reduced to initials, and his contribution minimized. The poems which remain in the second edition are moral and/or on classical subjects. Grimald's more personal poems, such as the poem to his mother, are omitted after the first edition. It may be that these changes were made by Grimald himself, perhaps out of modesty, or Tottel may have decided that it was prudent to downplay Grimald's presence in the collection on the grounds of his apostasy. Interestingly, none of Grimald's poems is included in the Arundel Harington MS, unless they were on the pages which are now lost; Hughey suggests there may have been a connection between this surprising omission and the removal of so many of his poems from the second edition of the *Miscellany*.[7]

The identity of the editor of *Tottel's Miscellany* is unknown. The first edition of the book may well have been closely based on a manuscript in which some or most of the editorial activity usually associated with Tottel had already taken place. Rollins[8] believes that Tottel may have been his own editor, but Grimald has frequently been put forward as a likely candidate[9] on the grounds (1) of his being known to Tottel (who published Grimald's *Three Bokes of Duties*, a translation of Cicero's *De*

Officiis, in 1556), (2) the particularly intense editorial activity which took place around Grimald's own poems between the first and second edition; (3) the interest the editor took in metre, which may indicate he was a poet himself (if one insensitively occupied with metrical regularities at the expense of all else). Certainly many readings in the *Miscellany* are based on annotations which Grimald made on the Egerton MS (Wyatt's autograph MS), but whether Grimald was the editor of the *Miscellany* remains an open question.

UNCERTAIN AUTHORS

Manuscript evidence identifies some of the authors in this section (poems 138–270), whose names Tottel seemed so keen to keep dark. John Heywood (poem 168), Thomas Churchyard (poem 175 and probably several others), Lord Thomas Vaux (poems 181–2, 187 and possibly others nearby), Chaucer (poem 207), Sir Anthony St Leger (poem 223), Sir John Cheke (poem 234), William Gray (poem 239), and Thomas Norton (poems 242–3, possibly also 241 and 244). For brief discussions of those authors, see notes to the first poem attributed to each of them (for Churchyard, see below, as he may have been a major contributor). Perhaps the most important author in this section, though, is John Harington of Stepney (1517–82), given his family's association with manuscripts of so many of the poems in the *Miscellany*. It seems distinctly possible that his family were a major source for the poems in all sections here, and that he himself may have written many of these poems. Harington, having been involved in the younger Sir Thomas Wyatt's rebellion, was imprisoned in the Tower in 1554 alongside the future Queen Elizabeth I and others; he would become a significant and successful courtier in Elizabeth's reign (his son John, translator of *Orlando Furioso* and inventor of the flush toilet, was Elizabeth's godson). He was also an important champion of writing in English, writing thirty extant poems, and translating Cicero's *De Amicitia* (*On Friendship*, from a French version) as well as some stanzas of Ariosto.[10] The *Miscellany* may be a part of Harington's project to further

writing in English, as well as reflecting in many ways his polit-
ical and ideological commitments.

Thomas Churchyard (?1523–1604) was, as his life dates
imply, one of the great survivors of Tudor literary culture, des-
pite being something of a hack. Spenser, in *Colin Clouts Come
Home Againe* (1595), gives him a bit of affectionate mockery
as 'free from spight' and as one 'That sung so long untill quite
hoarse he grew' (lines 396–9). He was initially a soldier, first as
Surrey's page in 1543, later involving himself in most of the
mid-century campaigns. He continued to be patronized by
important men in the Elizabethan period, including Sidney, Sir
Christopher Hatton, Sir Walter Ralegh, and the seventeenth
Earl of Oxford. As he was a relentless self-publicist and brag-
gadocio, his self-proclaimed involvement in the *Miscellany*
may not have been as great as he suggested.

One thing of which we can be certain is that the compiler of
the *Miscellany* was not uncertain as to the authorship of at
least some of the poems by 'uncertain auctours'. The anonym-
ity of the poems' presentation may give the collection the air of
something mildly subversive. The majority of the authors we
can identify, as well as the subjects of the majority of the elegies
on specific figures, were associated with the Edwardian rather
than the Marian regime; they would, in many cases, become
more successful under Elizabeth.

The quality of the uncertain authors' poems is very varied. A
poem as bad as 218 is fortunately not common; a better flavour
of this section could be sampled by reading the following
poems: 143, 150, 154, 168, 175, 229, 234, 237–8, 242–3, 258
and 267. Nowhere else do we get as strong a sense of the
strengths of mid-Tudor verse, the platform on which the great
Elizabethans built.

FORM

The *Miscellany* was published under the title 'Songs and Son-
nets', and although 'sonnet' at this date could be used of any
short lyric, the fourteen-line form which has the name 'sonnet'

today is the dominant form in the collection. The sonnet form was developed in Italy in the thirteenth century, but although Chaucer was certainly reading Italian sonnets in the late fourteenth century, Wyatt and Surrey were the first writers of sonnets in English. There are more than fifty in the *Miscellany*, the vast majority by Surrey or Wyatt. Because of the way the collection is organized, sonnets have a particularly substantial and profile-raising presence; they are not only associated with the highest-status poets, but are also physically foregrounded at the beginning of the collection. The *Miscellany* was a vital promoter and disseminator of this form. It is a sonnet juggernaut which drives the form into the centre of English poetry and profoundly changes the subsequent poetic landscape.[11] Such is the collection's preoccupation with sonnets that even poems composed in other forms are rewritten into sonnets; three of Wyatt's rondeaux, for instance, are rendered as sonnets by Tottel's editor (poems 74, 75 and 107). The specific rhyming patterns which Wyatt and Surrey would have encountered in their Italian reading are not transferred directly into the English poems, however. The Italian sonnet is divided into an octave rhyming ABBAABBA, followed by a sestet which could have a variety of forms but which did not usually end with a couplet. Wyatt usually follows this octave pattern, but he has a strong attachment to closing the sestet with a couplet. Surrey, on the other hand, devised the form which came to be known as the English, or Shakespearean sonnet, consisting of three quatrains and a couplet (ABABCDCDEFEFGG). It is possible that the sequencing of material in the *Miscellany* may have contributed to the future popularity of the English form.[12]

The sonnet was not the only innovative and influential verse form used in the collection. Another Italian-derived form which is strongly represented is ottava rima (ABABABCC); Wyatt introduced this to English poetry and used it intensively, and it had a rich subsequent career (it is the stanza of Byron's *Don Juan*, for example). There are also two instances of blank verse, both by Grimald (poems 278 and 279); this was a new form in English, with Surrey's translations of the *Aeneid* in the 1530s or 1540s probably the earliest instance.

The sonnet, blank verse and ottava rima were forms with an important future before them, but another new form substantially witnessed in the *Miscellany* perished quickly: poulter's measure (alternating 12- and 14-syllable lines in rhyming couplets) was introduced by Wyatt, and used by Surrey and Grimald, although the majority of instances in the *Miscellany* are in the 'Uncertain Authors' section. This form (which Rollins calls 'perhaps the most ineffective meter in English',[13] shrivelled away after the sixteenth century.

However, the *Miscellany* is not only a mustering of new forms. Many older structures are also represented. Around fifty of the poems are written in some form of quatrains. There are some twenty instances of rhyme royal (ABABBCC), a favourite stanza of Chaucer. Rhyming couplets are well represented, with around twenty poems in the second edition, and the first edition had a further twenty, largely fourteener couplets by Grimald. However, there is an absence of the older song-forms like roundels and chansons.

THE *MISCELLANY* IN ELIZABETHAN
LITERARY CULTURE

In Shakespeare's *The Merry Wives of Windsor*, Abraham Slender says 'I had rather than forty shillings I had my Book of Songs and Sonnets here' – but he also wishes he had a 'Book of Riddles' (I. i. 198–202). The *Miscellany* may therefore have come to be seen as a somewhat yokelish accessory by the end of the century. On the other hand, it is likely to have been the major first reading of near-contemporary poets to which the young Shakespeare, Sidney, Edmund Spenser and John Donne were exposed. Donne's lyric poems, indeed, were posthumously published as *Songs and Sonnets*, showing the abiding currency of the term even if the title is not Donne's own. Though there are no extant editions of the *Miscellany* after 1585, it seems unlikely that none was printed. Steven W. May could be right that the *Miscellany* had had its day and done its job by the

1590s,[14] but its influence could still be felt in that turbulent and prolific decade. The mild aura of outdatedness surrounding the *Miscellany* could also be used to stunning effect by later authors: the artfully garbled appearance of poem 182 as the Gravedigger's song in *Hamlet* evokes a powerful nostalgia even as it enables the play's hero to reflect on his mortality and sense of lost potential.

Spenser's deliberately archaic diction and spelling harks back to the *Miscellany* as much as it does to Chaucer. Shakespeare's *Sonnets* often mimic turns or collocations of thought that can be found in the *Miscellany*. It is also notable that the six-line stanza rhyming ABABCC is so common in the *Miscellany*, as this was the form Shakespeare used for his first and most commercially successful published poem, *Venus and Adonis* (1593), after which the stanza would come to be known. Many of the *Miscellany*'s other common forms – notably poulter's measure – would not remain popular, however, even if George Chapman's use of fourteeners in his Homer translations may owe something to the *Miscellany*'s use of such long-line forms.

The *Miscellany*'s long-line poems are typical of a leisurely attitude that pervades many poets' contributions (Wyatt being a notable exception); however, late Elizabethan verse is generally rather more compressed, reflecting the effects of a growing professionalization of authorship even on those courtly poets who did not write for print publication. Yet if the *Miscellany*'s impact lessened at a local, attitudinal level, it remained powerful at a larger structural level: it created and sustained the idea of a coherent collection of verse that could, through its juxtaposition of differing modes and poetic stances, express a multi-stranded and complex response to the uncertain worlds of love and politics. Verse could remain a powerful monument, and a stay against impermanence: Wyatt and Surrey may have died in the 1540s, but their poems persisted through the time and tide of changing regimes, whether those regimes be amorous, poetic, religious or political.

NOTES

1. Arthur F. Marotti, *Literature and Culture in Early Modern London* (Cambridge: Cambridge University Press, 1995), p. 288.

2. Ibid., p. 210.

3. Ibid. pp. 218–19.

4. Gary Waller, *English Poetry of the Sixteenth Century* (London: Longman, 1986), p. 76.

5. Steven W. May, 'Popularizing Courtly Poetry: Tottel's Miscellany and its Progeny', in Mike Pincombe and Cathy Shrank (eds.), *The Oxford Handbook of Tudor Literature* (Oxford: Oxford University Press, 2009), pp. 418–33.

6. Sir Thomas Wyatt, *The Complete Poems*, ed. R. A. Rebholz, revised edn. (Harmondsworth: Penguin, 1997), pp. 49–50.

7. R. W. Hughey (ed.), *The Arundel Harington Manuscript of Tudor Poetry*, 2 vols. (Columbus: Ohio State University Press, 1960), vol. 1, p. 58.

8. *Tottel's Miscellany*, ed. Hyder Edward Rollins, 2 vols., revised edn. (Cambridge, Mass.: Harvard University Press, 1965), vol. 2, p. 93.

9. H. J. Byrom, 'The Case for Nicholas Grimald as Editor of Tottel's Miscellany', *Modern Language Review*, 27 (1932), pp. 125–43.

10. Ruth W. Hughey, *John Harington of Stepney, Tudor Gentleman: His Life and Works* (Columbus: Ohio State University Press, 1971).

11. The near-absence of sonnets from the miscellanies which followed the first editions of Tottel is notable, however; it was the ongoing presence of *Tottel's Miscellany* itself which kept the form in view until the taste for sonnet sequences developed towards the end of the century.

12. See Michael R. G. Spiller, *The Development of the Sonnet: An Introduction* (London: Routledge, 1992), p. 98 for a discussion.

13. *Tottel's Miscellany*, ed. Rollins, vol. 2, p. 103.

14. May, 'Popularizing Courtly Poetry', p. 432.

Further Reading

Betteridge, Thomas, *Literature and Politics in the English Reformation* (Manchester: Manchester University Press, 2004).

Blayney, Peter, *The Stationers' Company before the Charter 1403–1557* (London: Worshipful Company of Stationers & Newspapermakers, 2003).

Childs, Jessie, *Henry VIII's Last Victim: The Life and Times of Henry Howard, Earl of Surrey* (London: Jonathan Cape, 2006).

Duffy, Eamon, *Fires of Faith: Catholic England under Mary Tudor* (New Haven: Yale University Press, 2009).

Forster, Leonard Wilson, *The Icy Fire: Five Studies in European Petrarchism* (Cambridge: Cambridge University Press, 1969).

Fowler, Alastair, *Conceitful Thought: The Interpretation of English Renaissance Poems* (Edinburgh: Edinburgh University Press, 1975).

Haldane, Michael, ' "The Soote Season": Surrey and the Amatory Elegy', *English Studies*, 87 (2006), pp. 402–14.

Hamrick, Stephen, '*Tottel's Miscellany* and the English Reformation', *Criticism*, 44 (2002), pp. 329–61.

Harrier, R. C., *The Canon of Sir Thomas Wyatt's Poetry* (Cambridge, Mass.: Harvard University Press, 1975).

Heale, Elizabeth, *Wyatt, Surrey and Early Tudor Poetry* (London: Longman, 1998).

Howarth, Herbert, 'Wyatt, Spenser and the Canzone', *Italica*, 41 (1964), pp. 79–90.

Lewis, C. S., *English Literature in the Sixteenth Century, Excluding Drama* (Oxford: Clarendon Press, 1954).

Loach, Jennifer, Bernard, George, and Williams, Penry (eds.), *Edward VI* (New Haven: Yale University Press, 1999).

Loades, D. M., *The Reign of Mary Tudor: Politics, Government and Religion in England 1553–8* (London: Benn, 1979).

MacFaul, Tom, *Male Friendship in Shakespeare and his Contemporaries* (Cambridge: Cambridge University Press, 2007).

—— *Poetry and Paternity in Renaissance England: Sidney, Spenser, Shakespeare, Donne and Jonson* (Cambridge: Cambridge University Press, 2010).

Manley, Lawrence, *Literature and Culture in Early Modern London* (Cambridge: Cambridge University Press, 1995).

Marotti, Arthur F., *Manuscript, Print, and the English Renaissance Lyric* (Ithaca, NY: Cornell University Press, 1995).

Mason, H. A., *Editing Wyatt: An Examination of Collected Poems of Sir Thomas Wyatt together with Suggestions for an Improved Edition* (Cambridge: Cambridge Quarterly Publications, 1972).

—— *Sir Thomas Wyatt: A Literary Portrait* (Bristol: Bristol Classical Press, 1986).

Merrill, L. R., *The Life and Poems of Nicholas Grimald* (New Haven: Yale University Press, 1925).

Meyer-Lee, Robert J., *Poets and Power from Chaucer to Wyatt* (Cambridge: Cambridge University Press, 2007).

Muir, Kenneth, *Sir Thomas Wyatt and his Circle: Unpublished Poems Edited from the Blage Manuscript* (Liverpool: Liverpool University Press, 1961).

—— 'Surrey Poems in the Blage Manuscript', *Notes and Queries*, NS 7 (1960), pp. 368–70.

—— 'Unpublished Poems in the Devonshire Manuscript', *Proceedings of the Leeds Philosophical Society*, 6 (1947), pp. 253–82.

Neill, Michael, *Issues of Death: Mortality and Identity in English Renaissance Tragedy* (Oxford: Clarendon Press, 1997).

Nicolson, Adam, *Earls of Paradise: England and the Idea of Perfection* (London: HarperPress, 2008).

North, M. L., *The Anonymous Renaissance: Cultures of Discretion in Tudor-Stuart England* (Chicago: Chicago University Press, 2003).

Pigman, G. W., *Grief and Renaissance Elegy* (Cambridge: Cambridge University Press, 1985).

Sessions, W. A., *Henry Howard, the Poet Earl of Surrey: A Life* (Oxford: Clarendon Press, 1999).

Skura, Meredith Anne, *Tudor Autobiography: Listening for Inwardness* (Chicago: Chicago University Press, 2008).

Southall, Raymond, *The Courtly Maker: An Essay on the Poetry of Wyatt and his Contemporaries* (Oxford: Blackwell, 1964).

Spiller, Michael R. G., *The Development of the Sonnet: An Introduction* (London: Routledge, 1992).

Thomson, Patricia, *Sir Thomas Wyatt and his Background* (London: Routledge & Kegan Paul, 1964).

Walker, Greg, *Writing under Tyranny: English Literature and the Henrician Reformation* (Oxford: Oxford University Press, 2005).

Waller, Gary, *English Poetry of the Sixteenth Century* (London: Longman, 1986).

Whitelock, Anna, *Mary Tudor: England's First Queen* (London: Bloomsbury, 2009).

Note on the Text

Ten sixteenth-century editions of *Tottel's Miscellany* survive, as follows; corresponding identifiers in the edition by Hyder E. Rollins given in brackets:

Q1   5 June 1557 [Rollins's A]
Q2   31 July 1557 [Rollins's B]
Q3   31 July 1557 [Rollins's C]
Q4   1559 [Rollins's D]
Q5   1559 (octavo) [Rollins's D*]
Q6   1565 (octavo) [Rollins's E]
Q7   1567 (octavo) [Rollins's F]
Q8   1574 (octavo) [Rollins's G]
Q9   1585 (octavo) [Rollins's H]
Q10 1587 (octavo) [Rollins's I]

We have based our text on Q2, which was the essential basis for all subsequent Elizabethan editions; two copies of this are extant, in the British Library and the Huntingdon Library. The former is our copy-text, though we have also consulted the latter, which is available on EEBO, but is imperfect.

Major changes were made to the contents and arrangements of the *Miscellany* between Q1 and Q2; Q3 was based largely on Q2, but retains some readings from Q1; all subsequent editions are based on their immediate predecessor. We have recorded in the Notes some of the most interesting variants between Q1 and Q2, and some changes made in Q3 and Q4. For a full record of the Q1 and Q3 variants, see the edition by Paul A. Marquis. The greatest subsequent changes in wording occur in Q8; we have recorded instances of these changes, as this edition provides an important sample of how the *Miscellany* appeared in the mid-Elizabethan period; this was the edition in the Sidney family library at Penshurst, to take a significant example, which made it available to both Sidney, his siblings and possibly to Edmund Spenser; one may also imagine this edition or its successors in the hands of the young Shakespeare or Donne. Many of the changes we register as the readings of Q8 were first introduced in earlier editions, but we have taken Q8 as representative of the (sometimes creative) confusion involved in Elizabethan editions of the *Miscellany*.

Where Q2 prints lower-case w at the beginning of lines or in proper names, we print upper-case W; in the case of no other letter is this a feature of the text. Either Tottel had a shortage of upper-case Ws, or his compositors did not distinguish sharply between upper and lower cases.

At the beginning of most poems in Q2 there is a drop letter, followed by a capital. We have represented the drop letter as a capital and have decapitalized the following letter. In a few cases (following I or A as first word), the second letter capitalized begins a new word; in almost every case we have decapitalized this second letter, but where it is likely that the capitalization is intentional or at least significant we have preserved it.

Many titles of poems in Q2 contain words divided over a line by '–' or '='; we have silently tidied these up, as they often create unnecessary confusion.

We have modernized only i/j, u/v distinctions and contractions. There are one or two ambiguities over proper names, but these are easy enough to resolve: for example, the poem printed as being to lady 'I.S.' (A139) refers in its first line to 'Jane'. Only in the case of 'Troians' (poem 229, line 36) is there real doubt as to whether an 'i' or a 'j' is intended: in this case, we have preserved the reading of Q2.

We have silently corrected all inverted n and u forms, but have preserved all other compositorial errors and misprints, glossing where this may cause confusion.

For ease of reference, we have added poem numbers and section headings.

Tottel's Miscellany

To *the reder.*

That to have wel written in verse, yea and in small parcelles, deserveth great praise, the woorkers of divers Latines, Italians, & other, doe prove sufficiently. That our tong is able in that kinde to do as praise worthelye as the rest, the honorable stile of the noble earle of Surrey, and the weightinesse of the depewitted sir Thomas Wiat the elders verse, with several graces in sondry good Englishe writers, do show abundantly. It resteth now (gentle reder) that thou thinke it not evil don, to publishe, to the honor of the english tong, and for profit of the studious of Englishe eloquence, those workes which the ungentle horders up of such tresure have heretofore envied the. And for this point (good reder) thine own profit and pleasure, in these presentlye, & in moe hereafter, shal answer for my defence. If parhappes some mislike the statelinesse of stile removed from the rude skil of common eares: I aske help of the learned to defende their learned frendes, the authors of this woork: And I exhort the unlearned, by reding to learne to bee more skilfull, and to purge that swinelike grossenesse, that maketh the swete majerome not to smell to their delight.

2 *divers* various
11 *the* thee
19 *majerome* marjoram

HENRY HOWARD, EARL OF SURREY

(1517–47)

1. Descripcion of the restlesse state
of a lover, with sute to his
ladie, to rue on his diying
hart.

The sunne hath twise brought furth his tender grene,
Twise clad the earth in lively lustinesse:
Ones have the windes the trees despoiled clene,
And ones again begins their cruelnesse,
Sins I have hid under my brest the harm,
That never shal recover healthfulnesse.
The winters hurt recovers with the warm:
The parched grene restored is with shade.
What warmth (alas) may serve for to disarm
The frosen hart, that mine in flame hath made?   10
What cold againe is able to restore
My fresh grene yeres, that wither thus and fade?
Alas, I see nothing hath hurt so sore,
But time in time reduceth a returne:
In time my harm encreaseth more and more,
And semes to have my cure alwaies in scorne.
Strange kindes of death, in life that I do trie:
At hand to melt, farre of in flame to burne.
And like as time list to my cure apply,
So doth eche place my comfort cleane refuse.   20

1   3 *Ones* once
    5 *Sins* since
    14 *reduceth* brings back
    17 *trie* experience
    19 *list* pleases
    20 *cleane* completely

Al thing alive, that seeth the heavens with eye,
With cloke of night may cover, and excuse
It self from travail of the daies unrest,
Save I, alas, against all others use,
That then stirre up the tormentes of my brest,
And curse eche sterre as causer of my fate:
And when the sunne hath eke the dark opprest,
And brought the day, it doth nothing abate
The travailes of mine endlesse smart and pain.
For then as one that hath the light in hate,
I wish for night, more covertly to plain,
And me withdraw from every haunted place,
Lest by my chere my chaunce appere to plain:
And in my minde I measure pace by pace,
To seke the place where I my self had lost,
That day that I was tangled in the lace,
In semyng slack that knitteth ever most:
But never yet the travaile of my thought
Of better state coulde catch a cause to bost.
For if I found sometime, that I have sought,
Those sterres by whom I trusted of the port:
My sailes do fall, and I advance right nought,
As ankerd fast: my sprites do all resort
To stand agazed, and sink in more and more
The deadly harme which she doth take in sport.
Lo, if I seke, how I do finde my sore:
And if I flee, I cary with me still
The venomd shaft, which doth his force restore

23 *travail* labour
26 *sterre* star
27 *eke* also
31 *plain* complain
33 *chere* expression   *to* too
41 *by whom I trusted of the port* with whose aid I hoped to find the port
43 *sprites* spirits
44 *agazed* astonished

By haste of flight, and I may plaine my fill
Unto my self, unlesse this carefull song 50
Print in your hart some parcell of my tene.
For I, alas, in silence all to long,
Of mine old hurt yet fele the wound but grene.
Rue on my life: or els your cruel wrong
Shall well appere, and by my death be sene.

2. Description of Spring, wherin eche thing renewes, save onely the lover.

The soote season, that bud and blome forth brings,
With grene hath clad the hill, and eke the vale:
The nightingale, with fethers new she sings:
The turtle to her make hath tolde her tale:
Somer is come, for every spray now springs,
The hart hath hong his old hed on the pale:
The buck in brake his winter coate he flings:
The fishes flete with new repayred scale:
The adder all her slough away she slings:
The swift swallow pursueth the flies smalle: 10
The busybee her hony now she minges:
Winter is worne that was the flowers bale:
And thus I see among these pleasant things,
Eche care decayes, and yet my sorow springs.

50 *carefull* full of sorrows, troubles
51 *tene* woe
2 1 *soote* sweet, soft
2 *eke* also
4 *turtle* turtle dove   *make* mate
6 *hart* red deer stag   *hed* antlers   *pale* fence
7 *buck* male fallow deer   *brake* bracken
11 *minges* mixes/remembers
12 *bale* curse

3. Description of the restlesse state
of a lover.

When youth had led me half the race,
That Cupides scourge had made me runne:
I loked backe, to mete the place,
From whence my wery course begonne.
   And then I saw how my desire,
Misguidyng me, had led the way:
Mine eyen, to gredy of their hyre,
Had made me lose a better pray.
   For when in sighes I spent the day
And could not cloke my grief with game:
The boylyng smoke did still bewray
The persant heat of secrete flame.
   And when salt teares do bain my brest,
Where love his pleasant traines hath sowen:
Her beauty hath the frutes opprest,
Ere that the buds were sprong and blowne.
   And when mine eyen did styll pursue
The fliyng chace of their request
Their gredy lokes did oft renew
The hidden wound within my brest.
   When every loke these chekes might staine,
From deadly pale to glowyng red:
By outward signes appeared plaine,
To her for help my hart was fled.
   But all to late love learneth me,

---

3 3 *mete* measure, survey
   7 *Mine eyes, to gredy of their hyre* My eyes, too greedy for their wages
   8 *pray* prey
  10 *game* good humour
  11 *bewray* reveal
  12 *persant* piercing
  13 *bain* wash
  16 *Ere that* before
  25 *learneth* teaches

To paint all kinde of colors new:
To blinde their eyes that els should see
My specled chekes with Cupides hewe.
　　And now the covert brest I claime,
That worshipt Cupide secretely,   30
And nourished his sacred flame:
From whence no blasyng sparkes do flye.

4. Desciption of the fickle affections, panges, and sleightes of love.

Such waiward waies hath love, that most part in discord
Our willes do stand: whereby our harts but seldom do accord.
Deceit in his delight, and to begile, and mock
The simple hartes, whom he doth strike with froward divers
　　stroke.
　He causeth thone to rage with golden burning dart,
And doth alay with leaden cold again the other hart.
　　Whote glemes of burning fire, and easy sparkes of flame
In balaunce of unegal weight he pondereth by aime.
　　From easy ford, where I might wade and passe ful wel,
He me withdrawes, and doth me drive into a depe dark hel,   10
　　And me withholdes, wher I am cald, and offred place:
And willes me that my mortall foe I doe beseke of grace.
　　He lettes me to pursue a conquest welnere wonne,
To folow where my paines were lost, ere that my sute begonne.
　　So by this meanes I know how soone a hart may turne,
From warre to peace, from truce to strife, and so againe returne.

4　3　*in* misprint for 'is'
　4　*froward* backward, sullen　*divers* various
　5　*thone* the one
　7　*Whote glemes* hot gleams
　8　*by aime* deliberately
　13　*lettes me to* prevents me from　*welnere* very nearly
　14　*ere that* before

I know how to content my self in others lust:
Of litle stuffe unto my self to weave a web of trust:
And how to hide my harmes with soft dissembling chere,
20 When in my face the painted thoughtes would outwardly apere.
I know how that the blood forsakes the face for dred:
And how by shame it staines again the chekes with flaming red.
I know under the grene the serpent how he lurkes.
The hammer of the restles forge I wote eke how it workes.
I know and can by roate the tale that I would tel:
But oft the words come furth awrie of him that loveth wel.
I know in heat and cold the lover how he shakes:
In singing how he doth complain, in sleping how he wakes:
To languish without ache, sicklesse for to consume:
30 A thousand things for to devise, resolving all in fume.
And though he list to see his ladies grace full sore,
Such pleasures, as delight his eye, do not his health restore.
I know to seke the track of my desired foe:
And fear to finde that I do seke. But chiefly this I know,
That lovers must transforme into the thing beloved,
And live (alas who would beleve?) with sprite from life
    removed.
I know in harty sighes, and laughters of the splene,
At ones to change my state, my will, and eke my color clene.
I know how to deceave my self with others help:
40 And how the Lion chastised is by beating of the whelp.
In standing nere my fire, I know how that I freze:
Far of I burne: in both I wast: and so my life I leze.
I know how love doth rage upon a yelding minde:

17 *lust* desire
19 *chere* expression
24 *wote eke* know also
25 *can by roate* know by rote
29 *sicklesse for to consume* wither away without being ill
31 *list* pleases
38 *ones* once
40 *whelp* pup; see explanatory note
42 *of* off *leze* lose

How smal a net may take and meash a hart of gentle kinde:
    Or els with seldom swete to season heapes of gall:
Revived with a glimse of grace old sorowes to let fal,
    The hidden traines I know, and secret snares of love:
How soone a loke wil print a thought, that never may remove.
    The slipper state I know, the sodein turnes from wealth,
The doubtful hope, the certain woe, and sure despeire of
        health.

5. Complaint of a lover, that defied love, and was by love after the more tormented.

When sommer toke in hand the winter to assail,
With force of might, & vertue gret, his stormy blasts to quail,
    And when he clothed faire the earth about with grene,
And every tree new garmented, that pleasure was to sene:
    Mine hart gan new revive, and changed blood did stur
Me to withdrawe my winter woes, that kept within the dore.
    A brode, quod my desire: assay to set thy fote,
Where thou shalt finde the savour swete: for sprong is every
        rote.
    And to thy health, if thou were sick in any case,
Nothing more good, than in the spring the aire to fele a space.   10
    There shalt thou heare and se all kindes of birdes ywrought,
Well tune their voice with warble smal, as nature hath them
        tought.
    Thus pricked me my lust the sluggish house to leave:
And for my health I thought it best such counsail to receave.
    So on a morow furth, unwist of any wight,

45 *with seldom swete to season heapes of gall* to make up for much
    suffering with occasional happiness
49 *slipper* slippery, uncertain
5 4 *pleasure was to sene* it was a pleasure to see
   7 'Abroad!' said my desire, 'try to set your foot . . .'
  15 *unwist of any wight* without anyone knowing

I went to prove how well it would my heavy burden light.
  And when I felt the aire so pleasant round about,
Lord, to my self how glad I was that I had gotten out.
  There might I se how Ver had every blossom hent:
20 And eke the new betrothed birdes ycoupled how they went.
  And in their songes me thought they thanked nature much,
That by her licence all that yere to love their happe was such,
  Right as they could devise to chose them feres throughout:
With much rejoysing to their Lord thus flew they al about.
  Which when I gan resolve, and in my head conceave,
What pleasant life, what heapes of joy these litle birdes receave,
  And saw in what estate I wery man was brought,
By want of that they had at will, and I reject at nought:
  Lord how I gan in wrath unwisely me demeane.
30 I cursed love and him defied: I thought to turne the streame,
  But when I well beheld he had me under awe,
I asked mercy for my fault, that so transgrest his lawe.
  Thou blinded God (quod I) forgeve me this offence,
Unwittingly I went about, to malice thy pretence.
  Wherwith he gave a beck, and thus me thought he swore,
Thy sorowe ought suffice to purge thy fault, if it were more.
  The vertue of which sound mine hart did so revive,
That I, me thought, was made as whole as any man alive,
  But here I may perceive mine errour all and some,
40 For that I thought that so it was: yet was it still undone.
  And all that was no more but mine expressed minde,
That faine would have some good reliefe, of Cupide well assinde.
  I turned home forthwith, and might perceve it well,

19 *Ver* spring   *hent* seized
20 *birdes* birds/brides
22 *their happe was such* such was their good fortune
23 *feres* partners
28 *reject at nought* rejected as if valueless
29 *demeane* behave
34 *to malice thy pretence* to speak maliciously of your claim to power
35 *gave a beck* beckoned
37 *vertue* power
42 *faine would have* wished for   *of Cupide well assinde* generously given by Cupid

That he agreved was right sore with me for my rebell.
   My harmes have ever since, encreased more and more,
And I remaine without his help, undone for evermore,
   A mirror let me be unto ye lovers all:
Strive not with love, for if ye do, it will ye thus befall.

6. Complaint of a lover rebuked.

Love, that liveth, and raigneth in my thought,
That built his seat within my captive brest,
Clad in the armes, wherin with me he fought,
Oft in my face he doth his banner rest.
She, that me taught to love, and suffer payne,
My doutfull hope, and eke my hot desire,
With shamefast cloke to shadow and restraine,
Her smiling grace converteth straight to yre.
And coward love then to the hart apace
Taketh his flight, wheras he lurkes and plaines   10
His purpose lost, and dare not shew his face.
For my lordes gilt thus faultlesse bide I paines,
Yet from my lorde shall not my foote remove.
Swete is his death, that takes his end by love.

7. Complaint of the lover disdained.

In Ciprus, springes (where as dame Venus dwelt)
A Well so hotte is, that who tastes the same.
Were he of stone, as thawed yse should melt,
And kindeled finde his brest with fired flame.

6 6 *eke* also
  7 *shamefast* bashful, chaste
  8 *straight* straight away
10 *plaines* bemoans
12 *bide* suffer

Whose moist poyson dissolved hath my hart.
With crepyng fire my colde lyms ar supprest,
Feeleth the hart that harborde freedome smart,
Endlesse dispaire long thraldome hath imprest.
An other well of frosen yse is founde,
Whose chilling venome of repugnant kinde
The fervent heat doth quenche of Cupides wounde:
And with the spot of change infectes the minde:
Whereof my dere hath tasted, to my paine.
Wherby my service growes into disdaine.

8. Description and praise of his love Geraldine.

From Tuskane came my Ladies worthy race:
Faire Florence was sometime her auncient seate:
The Western yle, whose pleasant shore doth face
Wilde Cambers clifs, furst gave her lively heate:
Fostred she was with milke of Irishe brest:
Her sire, an Earle: her dame, of princes blood.
From tender yeres, in Britain did she rest,
With a kinges child, who tasteth ghostly food.
Honsdon did first present her to mine iyen:
Bright is her hewe, and Geraldine she hight.
Hampton me taught to wishe her first for mine:
And Windsor, alas, doth chase me from her sight.
Her beauty of kinde, her vertues from above,
Happy is he, that can obtaine her love.

7 10: *repugnant* the opposite/fighting against
8 9 *iyen* eyes
   10 *hight* is named
   13 *of kinde* from nature

9. *The frailtie and hurtfulnes*
of beautie.

Brittle beautie, that nature made so fraile,
Wherof the gift is small, and short the season,
Flowring to day, to morowe apt to faile,
Tickell treasure abhorred of reason,
Dangerous to dele with, vaine, of none availe,
Costly in keping, past not worthe two peason,
Slipper in sliding as is an eles taile,
Hard to attaine, once gotten not geason,
Jewel of jeopardie that perill doth assaile,
False and untrue, enticed oft to treason,   10
Enmy to youth: that most may I bewaile.
Ah bitter swete infecting as the poyson:
Thou farest as frute that with the frost is taken,
To day redy ripe, to morowe al to shaken.

10. *A complaint by night of the lover*
not beloved.

Alas so all things now do hold their peace:
Heaven and earth disturbed in nothing:
The beasts, the ayre, the birdes their song do cease:
The nightes chare the starres about doth bring:
Calme is the Sea, the waves worke lesse and lesse:
So am not I, whom love alas doth wring,
Bringing before my face the great encrease
Of my desires, whereat I wepe and sing,
In joy and wo, as in a doutfull ease.
For my swete thoughtes sometime do pleasure bring: 10

9 4 *Tickell* unstable
  6 *peason* peas
  8 *geason* extraordinary, rare
10 4 *chare* chariot

But by and by the cause of my disease
Geves me a pang, that inwardly doth sting.
When that I thinke what griefe it is againe,
To live and lacke the thing should ridde my paine.

11. How eche thing save the lover
in spring reviveth to
pleasure.

When Windsor walles susteyned my wearied arme,
My hand my chin, to ease my restles hed:
Yet pleasant plots revested green with warme,
The blossomd bowes with lusty Ver yspred,
The flowred meades, the wedded birdes so late
Mine eyes discover: and to my minde resorte
The joly woes, the hatelesse shorte debate,
The rakehell life that longes to loves disporte.
Wherewith (alas) the heavy charge of care
Heapt in my brest breakes forth against my will,
In smoky sighes, that overcast the ayre.
My vapord eyes suche drery teares distill,
The tender spring which quicken where they fall,
And I halfbent to throw me down withall.

12. Vow to love faithfullie howsoever
he be rewarded.

Set me wheras the Sunne do parche the grene,
Or where his beames do not dissolve the yse:
In temperate heat where he is felt and sene:
In presence prest of people madde or wise.

11 4 *Ver* spring
     8 *longes* belongs
     9 *care* sorrow, anxiety
12 4 *prest of* either pressed by or close by

Set me in hye, or yet in low degree:
In longest night, or in the shortest day:
In clearest skie, or where clowdes thickest be:
In lusty youth, or when my heares are gray.
Set me in heaven, in earth, or els in hell,
In hill, or dale, or in the foming flood: 10
Thrall, or at large, alive where so I dwell:
Sicke, or in health: in evyll fame, or good,
Hers will I be, and onely with this thought
Content my selfe, although my chaunce be nought.

13. Complaint that his ladie after she knew of his love kept her face alway hidden from him.

I never saw my Ladie laye apart
Her cornet blacke, in cold nor yet in heate,
Sith first she knew my griefe was growen so great,
Which other fansies driveth from my hart.
That to my selfe I do the thought reserve,
The which unwares did wounde my woful brest,
For on her face mine eyes mought never rest,
Sins that she knew I did her love and serve,
Her golden tresse is clad alway with blacke,
Her smiling lokes to hide thus evermore,   10
And that restraines which I desire so sore.
So doth this corner governe my alacke:
In somer, sunne: in winters breath, of frost:
Wherby the light of her faire lokes I lost.

11 *Thrall* imprisoned
13 1 *laye apart* take off
    2 *cornet* lady's headdress hanging over the ears
    3 *Sith* since
    8 *Sins* since
    12 *alacke* lack/woe

14. *Request to his love to joyne*
bountie with beautie.

The golden gift that nature did thee geve
To fasten frendes, and feede them at thy wyll,
With fourme and favour, taught me to beleve.
How thow art made to shew her greatest skill.
Whose hidden vertues are not so unknowen,
But lively domes might gather at the furst
Where beauty so her perfect seede hath sowen,
Of other graces folow nedes there must.
Now certesse Garret, sins all this is true,
That from above thy giftes are thus elect:
Do not deface them than with fansies newe,
Nor change of mindes let not thy minde infect:
But mercy him thy frende, that doth thee serve,
Who seekes alway thine honour to preserve.

15. *Prisoned in windsor, he recounteth*
his pleasure there
passed.

So cruell prison how could betide, alas,
As proude Windsor? where I in lust and joy,
With a kinges sonne, my childishe yeres did passe,
In greater feastes than Priams sonnes of Troy:
Where eche swete place returns a taste full sower,
The large grene courtes, where we were wont to hove,

14 6 *lively domes* quick judgements
   9 *sins* since
   10 *elect* chosen
   11 *than* then
15 6 *hove* wander

With eyes cast up into the maydens tower.
And easie sighes, such as folke drawe in love:
The stately seates, the ladies bright of hewe
The daunces short, long tales of great delight: 10
With wordes and lokes, that tigers could but rewe,
Where eche of us did pleade the others right:
The palme play, where, dispoiled for the game,
With dazed eies oft we by gleames of love,
Have mist the ball and got sight of our dame,
To baite her eies, which kept the leads above:
The gravell ground, with sleves tied on the helme:
On foming horse, with swordes and frendly hartes:
With cheare, as though one should another whelme:
Where we have fought, and chased oft with dartes,   20
With silver droppes the meade yet spred for ruth,
In active games of nimblenes, and strength,
Where we did straine, trained with swarmes of youth.
Our tender limmes, that yet shot up in length:
The secret groves, which oft we made resound
Of pleasaunt plaint, and of our ladies praise,
Recording oft what grace eche one had found,
What hope of spede, what dread of long delaies:
The wilde forest, the clothed holtes with grene:
With rains availed, and swift ybreathed horse,   30
With crie of houndes, and mery blastes betwene,
Where we did chase the fearfull hart of force,
The wide vales eke, that harborde us ech night,
Wherwith (alas) reviveth in my brest

13 *palme play* a form of handball
16 To entice her eyes which looked above the leads of the roof or gallery
19 *whelme* defeat
21 *ruth* pity
26 *plaint* poetic complaint, expressing injustice or sorrow
27 *Recording* recounting
33 *eke* also

The swete accord, such slepes as yet delight:
The pleasant dreames, the quiet bed of rest:
The secrete thoughtes imparted with such trust:
The wanton talke, the divers change of play:
The frenship sworne, eche promise kept so just:
40 Wherwith we past the winter nightes away.
And, with this thought, the bloud forsakes the face,
The teares beraine my chekes of deadly hewe:
The which as soone as sobbing sighes (alas)
Upsupped have, thus I my plaint renew:
O place of blisse, renuer of my woes,
Geve me accompt, where is my noble fere:
Whom in thy walles thou doest eche night enclose,
To other leefe, but unto me most dere.
Eccho (alas) that doth my sorow rewe,
50 Returns therto a hollow sound of plaint.
Thus I alone, where all my freedome grewe,
In prison pyne, with bondage and restraint,
And with remembrance of the greater griefe
To banish the lesse, I finde my chief reliefe.

16. *The lover comforteth himselfe*
with the worthinesse of
his love.

When raging love with extreme payne
Most cruelly distrains my hart:
When that my teares, as floods of rayne,
Beare witnes of my wofull smart:
When sighes have wasted so my breath,
That I lye at the point of death.
  I call to minde the navie great,

38 *wanton* careless   *divers* various
44 *Upsupped* drunk up
46 *fere* companion
48 *leefe* beloved

That the Grekes brought to Troye town:
And how the boysteous windes did beate
Their ships, and rent their sayles adown,   10
Till Agamemnons daughters blood
Appeasde the Gods, that them withstood.

   And how that in those ten yeres warre,
Full many a bloodie dede was done,
And many a lord, that came full farre,
There caught his bane (alas) to soone:
And many a good knight overron,
Before the Grekes had Helene won.

   Then thinck I thus: sithe such repaire,
So long time warre of valiant men,   20
Was all to winne a lady faire:
Shall I not learne to suffer then,
And thinck my life well spent to be,
Serving a worthier wight than she?

   Therfore I never will repent,
But paines contented still endure.
For like as when, rough winter spent,
The pleasant spring straight draweth in ure:
So after raging stormes of care
Joyfull at length may be my fare.   30

17. Complaint of the absence of her lover being upon the sea.

O happy dames, that may embrace
The frute of your belight,
Help to bewaile the wofull case,

16 16 *bane* lethal destiny   *to* too
   19 *sithe* since   *repaire* gathering of people at a place
   24 *wight* person
   28 *straight draweth in ure* suddenly comes into being
17 2 *belight* misprint for delight

And eke the heavy plight
Of me, that wonted to rejoyce
The fortune of my pleasant choyce:
Good ladies, help to fill my moorning voyce.
   In ship, freight with remembrance
Of thoughts, and pleasures past,
He sailes that hath in governance
My life, while it will last:
With scalding sighes, for lack of gale,
Furdering his hope, that is his sail
Toward me, the swete port of his avail.
   Alas, how oft in dreames I see
Those eyes that were my food,
Which somtime so delited me,
That yet they do me good.
Wherwith I wake with his returne,
Whose absent flame did make me burne.
But when I finde the lacke, Lord how I mourne?
   When other lovers in armes acrosse,
Rejoyce their chiefe delight:
Drowned in teares to mourne my losse,
I stand the bitter night,
In my window, where I may see,
Before the windes how the clowdes flee.
Lo, what a Mariner love hath made me.
   And in grene waves when the salt flood
Doth rise by rage of winde:
A thousand fansies in that mood
Assaile my restlesse minde.
Alas, now drencheth my swete fo,
That with the spoyle of my hart did go,
And left me but (alas) why did he so?
   And when the seas ware calme againe,

4 *eke* also
14 *avail* profit
36 *ware* misprint for 'waxe'

To chase fro me annoye.
My doutful hope doth cause me plaine:
So dread cuts of my joye.
Thus is my wealth mingled with wo,   40
And of eche thought a dout doth growe,
Now he comes, will he come? alas, no no.

18. Complaint of a diying lover refused upon his ladies injust mistaking of his writing.

In winters just returne, when Boreas gan his raigne,
  And every tree unclothed fast, as nature taught them plaine:
  In misty morning darke, as sheepe are then in holde,
I hyed me fast, it sat me on, my sheepe for to unfolde.
  And as it is a thing, that lovers have by fittes,
Under a palme I heard one cry, as he had lost his wittes.
  Whose voyce did ring so shrill, in uttering of his plaint,
That I amazed was to heare, how love could him attaint.
  Ah wretched man (quod he) come death, and ridde this wo:
A just reward, a happy end, if it may chaunce thee so.   10
  Thy pleasures past have wrought thy wo, without redresse.
If thou hadst never felt no joy, thy smart had bene the lesse,
  And retchlesse of his life, he gan both sighe and grone,
A rufull thing me thought, it was, to hear him make such mone,
  Thou cursed pen (sayd he) wo worth the bird thee bare,
The man, the knife, and all that made thee, wo be to their share.
  Wo worth the time, and place, where I so could endite.

37 To drive me away from misery
38 *plaine* to complain
39 *of* off
18 1 *gan* began
  4 *sat me on* obliged me
  7 *plaint* poetic complaint, expressing injustice or sorrow
  15 *wo worth* woe be upon
  17 *endite* compose poetry

And wo be it yet once againe, the pen that so can write.
   Unhappy hand, it had ben happy time for me,
20 If, when to write thou learned first, unjoynted hadst thou be.
   Thus cursed he himself, and every other wight,
Save her alone whom love him bound, to serve both day &
      night.
   Which when I heard, and saw, how he himself fordid,
Against the ground with bloody strokes, himself even ther
      to rid:
   Had ben my heart of flint, it must have melted tho:
For in my life I never sawe a man so full of wo.
   With teares, for his redresse, I rashly to him ran.
And in my armes I caught him fast, and thus I spake him than.
   What woful wight art thou, that in such heavy case
Tormentes thy selfe with such despite, here in this desert
30   place?
   Wherwith, as al agast, fulfild with ire, and dred,
He cast on me a staring loke, with colour pale, and ded.
   Nay, what art thou (quod he) that in this heavy plight,
Doest find me here, most wofull wretch, that life hath in
     despight?
   I am (quoth I) but poore, and simple in degre:
A shepardes charge I have in hand, unworthy though I be.
   With that he gave a sighe, as though the skie shold fall:
And lowd (alas) he shriked oft, and Shepard, gan he call,
   Come, hie the fast at ones, and print it in thy hart:
40 So thou shalt know, and I shall tell the, giltlesse how I smart.
   His back against the tree, sore febled al with faint,
With weary sprite he stretcht him up: and thus hee told his plaint.
   Ones in my hart (quoth he) it chaunced me to love
Such one, in whom hath nature wrought, her cunning for to
     prove.
   And sure I can not say, but many yeres were spent,

21 *wight* person
25 *tho* then
39 *ones* once
40 *the* thee

With such good will so recompenst, as both we were content
   Wherto then I me bound, and she likewise also,
The sunne should runne his course awry, ere we this faith
      forgo.
   Who joied then, but I? who had this worldes blisse?
Who might compare a life to mine, that never thought on this?   50
   But dwelling in this truth, amid my greatest joy,
Is me befallen a greater losse, then Priam had of Troy.
   She is reversed clene, and beareth me in hand,
That my deserts have geven her cause to breke this faithful
      band.
   And for my just excuse availeth no defence,
Now knowest thou all: I can no more, but shepheard hie the
      hence
   And geve him leave to dye, that may no lenger live:
Whose record lo I claime to have, my death, I do forgeve.
   And eke when I am gone, be bolde to speake it plaine:
Thou hast seen dye the truest man, that ever love did paine.   60
   Wherwith he turned him round, and gaspyng oft for breath,
Into his armes a tree he raught, and said welcome my death:
   Welcome a thousand folde, now dearer unto me,
Than should without her love to live, an emperour to be.
   Thus, in this wofull state, he yelded up the ghost:
And little knoweth his lady, what a lover she hath lost.
   Whose death when I beheld, no marvail was it, right
For pitye though my hart did blede, to se so piteous sight,
   My blood from heat to colde oft changed wonders sore:
A thousande troubles there I found I never knew before.   70
   Twene drede and dolour, so my sprites were brought in feare,
That long it was ere I could call to minde, what I did there.
   But, as ech thing hath end, so had these payns of myne:

48 *ere* before
53 *beareth me in hand* strings me along/tries to get me to believe/fobs me
   off with the excuse
58 *Whose record lo I claime to have* whose testimony I want to have that
59 *eke* also
62 *raught* grasped
69 *wonders* wondrously

The furies past, and I my wits restord by length of tyme.
    Then as I could devise, to seke I thought it best,
Where I might finde some worthy place, for such a corse to
      rest.
    And in my minde it came: from thence not far away,
Where Creseids love, king Priams sonne, the worthy Troilus
      lay.
    By him I made his tomb, in token he was true:
80 And as to him belongeth well, I covered it with blew.
    Whose soule by angels power, departed not so sone,
But to the heavens, lo it fled, for to receive his dome.

19. Complaint of the absence of
her lover being upon
the sea.

Good Ladies: ye that have your pleasures in exile,
    Step in your fote, come take a place, & moorne with me a
      while
And such as by their lordes do set but little price,
Let them sit still: it skilles them not what chance come on the
      dice.
    But ye whom love hath bound by order of desire,
To love your lords, whose good deserts none other wold
      require:
    Come ye yet once again, and set your fote by mine,
Whose wofull plight and sorowes great no tong may well define,
    My love and lorde alas, in whom consistes my wealth,
10 Hath fortune sent to passe the seas in hazarde of his health.
    Whom I was wont tembrace with well contented minde
Is now amid the fomyng floods at pleasure of the winde.
    Where God well him preserve, and sone him home me send,

82 *dome* judgement
19 4 *skilles them not* doesn't matter to them
  9 *wealth* well-being
  11 *tembrace* to embrace

Without which hope, my life (alas) were shortly at an end.
  Whose absence yet, although my hope doth tell me plaine,
With short returne he comes anone, yet ceaseth not my payne,
  The fearefull dreames I have, oft times do greve me so:
That when I wake, I lye in dout, where they be true, or no.
  Sometime the roaring seas (me semes) do grow so hye:
That my dere Lord (ay me alas) me thinkes I see him dye.   20
  An other time the same doth tell me: he is come:
And plaieng, where I shall him find with his faire little sonne,
  So forth I go apace to se that leefsom sight.
And with a kisse, me think, I say: welcome my lord, my knight:
  Welcome my swete, alas, the stay of my welfare.
Thy presence bringeth forth a truce atwixt me, and my care.
  Then lively doth he loke, and salueth me againe,
And saith: my dere, how is it now, that you have all this
      payne?
  Wherwith the heavy cares: that heapt are in my brest,
Breake forth, and me dischargen clene of all my huge unrest.   30
  But when I me awake, and find it but a dreme:
The anguish of my former wo beginneth more extreme:
  And me tormenteth so, that unneath may I find
Sum hidden place, wherein to slake the gnawing of my mind
  Thus every way you se, with absence how I burn:
And for my wound no cure I find, but hope of good return.
  Save whan I think, by sowre how swete is felt the more:
It doth abate som of my paines, that I abode before.
  And then unto my self I say: when we shal meete.
But litle while shal seme this paine, the joy shal be so sweete.   40
  Ye windes, I you conjure in chiefest of your rage,
That ye my lord safly sende, my sorowes to asswage:
  And that I may not long abide in this excesse.
Do your good wil, to cure a wight, that liveth in distresse.

18 *where* whether
23 *leefsom* agreeable, desirable
26 *care* sorrow, anxiety
27 *salueth* possibly 'salveth' – both words mean 'greets'
33 *unneath* with difficulty
44 *wight* person

20. A praise of his love: wherin he reproveth them that compare their Ladies with his.

Geve place ye lovers, here before
That spent your bostes and bragges in vaine:
My Ladies beawtie passeth more
The best of yours, I dare wel sayen,
Than doth the sonne, the candle light;
Or brightest day, the darkest night.
    And thereto hath a troth as just,
As had Penelope the faire.
For what she saith, ye may it trust,
As it by writing sealed were.
And vertues hath she many moe,
Than I with pen have skill to showe.
    I could reherse, if that I wold,
The whole effect of natures plaint,
When she had lost the perfite mould,
The like to whom she could not paynt:
With wringyng handes how she did cry,
And what she said, I know it, I.
    I know, she swore with ragyng minde:
Her kingdome onely set apart,
There was no losse, by lawe of kinde,
That could have gone so nere her hart.
And this was chefely all her paine:
She could not make the like againe.
    Sith nature thus gave her the praise,
To be the chefest worke she wrought:
In faith, me thinke some better wayes

10

20

20 7 *troth* fidelity
  11 *moe* more
  14 *plaint* complaint
  21 *kinde* nature
  25 *Sith* since

On your behalf might well be sought,
Then to compare (as ye have done)
To matche the candle with the sonne.   30

21. *To the ladie that scorned her lover.*

Although I had a check,
To geve the mate is hard,
For I have found a neck,
To kepe my men in gard.
   And you that hardy ar
To geve so great assay
Unto a man of war,
To drive his men away,
   I rede you take good hede,
And marke this folish verse,   10
For I will so provide,
That I will have your ferse,
   And when your ferse is had,
And all your war is done:
Then shall your self be glad
To end that you begon.
   For if by chance I winne
Your person in the felde:
To late then come you in
Your selfe to me to yeld.   20
   For I wil use my power,
As captain full of might,
And such I will devour,
As use to shew me spight.

21 3 *neck* a move to block check
  9 *rede* advise
 12 *ferse* queen (at chess)
 19 *to* too

And for because you gave
Me checke in such degre,
This vantage loe I have:
Now checke, and garde to the.
    Defend it, if thou may:
Stand stiffe, in thine estate.
For sure I will assay,
If I can give the mate.

22. *A warning to the lover how he is abused by his love.*

To dearely had I bought my grene and youthfull yeres,
    If in mine age I could not finde when craft for love apperes.
    And seldom though I come in court among the rest:
Yet can I judge in colours dim as depe as can the best.
    Where grefe tormentes the man that suffreth secret smart,
To breke it forth unto som frend it easeth well the hart.
    So standes it now with me for my well beloved frend,
This case is thine for whom I fele such torment of my mind.
    And for thy sake I burne so in my secret brest
That till thou know my hole disseise my hart can have no rest.
    I see how thine abuse hath wrested so thy wittes,
That all it yeldes to thy desire, and folowes the by fittes.
    Where thou hast loved so long with hart and all thy power.
I se thee fed with fained wordes, thy fredom to devoure.
    I know, (though she say nay, and would it well withstand)
When in her grace thou held the most, she bare the but in
        hand.
    I see her pleasant chere in chifest of thy suite:

28 *the* thee
22 1 *To* too
    12 *the* thee
    16 *she bare the but in hand* she was only stringing you along
    17 *chere* expression

Whan thou art gone, I se him come, that gathers up the fruite.
 And eke in thy respect I se the base degre
Of him to whom she gave the hart that promised was to the.   20
 I se (what would you more) stode never man so sure
On womans word, but wisedome would mistrust it to endure.

23. *The forsaken lover describeth*
& forsaketh love.

O lothsome place where I
Have sene and herd my dere,
When in my hert her eye
Hath made her thought appere,
By glisming with such grace
As fortune it ne would,
That lasten any space
Betwene us lenger should.
 As fortune did avance,
To further my desire: 10
Even so hath fortunes chaunce
Throwen al ammiddes the mire.
And that I have deserved
With true and faithfull hart,
Is to his handes reserved
That never felt the smart.
 But happy is that man,
That scaped hath the griefe
That love wel teche him can
By wanting his reliefe.   20
A scourge to quiet mindes
It is, who taketh hede,
A common plage that binds,

19 *eke* also
23 2 *hard* heard
 23 *plage* suffering, curse, plague

A travell without mede.
   This gift it hath also,
Who so enjoies it most,
A thousand troules grow
To vexe his weried ghost.
And last it may not long
The truest thing of all
And sure the greatest wrong
That is with in this thrall.
   But sins thou desert place
Canst give me no accompt
Of my desired grace
That I to have was wont,
Farewel thou hast me tought
To thinke me not the furst,
That love hath set aloft,
And casten in the dust.

24. *The lover describes his restlesse state.*

As oft as I behold and see
The soveraigne beauty that me bound:
The nyer my comfort is to me,
Alas the fressher is my wound.
   As flame doth quench by rage of fire,
And runnyng stremes consume by raine:
So doth the sight, that I desire,
Appease my grief and deadly payne.
   First when I saw those cristall streames,
Whose beauty made my mortall wound:
I little thought within her beames

24 *travell without mede* labour without reward
27 *troules* misprint for 'troubles'
28 *ghost* soul, spirit
32 *thrall* imprisonment
33 *sins* since

So swete a venom to have found.
   But wilfull will did prick me forth,
And blinde Cupide did whippe and guide:
Force made me take my grief in worth:
My fruteles hope my harme did hide.
   As cruel waves full oft be found,
Against the rockes to rore and cry:
So doth my hart full oft rebound
Against my brest full bitterly.   20
   I fall, and see mine owne decay,
As one that beares flame in his brest,
Forgets in payne to put away,
The thing that bredeth mine unrest.

25. *The lover excuseth himself of suspected change.*

Though I regarded not
The promise made by me,
Or passed not to spot
My faith and honestee:
Yet were my fancy strange,
And wilfull will to wite,
If I sought now to change
A falkon for a kite.
   All men might well disprayse
My wit and enterprise,   10
If I estemed a pese
Above a perle in prise:
Or judged the owle in sight
The sparehauke to excell,
Which flieth but in the night,

24 15 *take my grief in worth* be content with my grief
25 3 *passed not to spot*: didn't care about tainting
   6 *to wite* blameworthy
   11 *pese* pea

As all men know right well:
   Or if I sought to sayle
Into the brittle port,
Where anker hold doth faile,
To such as do resort.
And leave the haven sure,
Where blowes no blusteryng winde,
Nor fickelnesse in ure
So farforth as I finde.
   No, thinke me not so light,
Nor of so churlish kinde,
Though it lay in my might
My bondage to unbinde.
That I would leve the hinde
To hunt the ganders fo.
No no I have no minde
To make exchanges so:
   Nor yet to change at all,
For think it may not be
That I should seke to fall
From my felicitie,
Desirous for to win,
And loth for to forgo,
Or new change to begin:
How may all this be so?
   The fire it can not frese:
For it is not his kinde,
Nor true love can not lese
The constance of the minde.
Yet as sone shall the fire,
Want heat to blase and burn,
As I in such desire,
Have once a thought to turne.

23 *ure* customary practice
26 *kinde* nature
43 *lese* lose/lie

26. A carelesse man, scorning and describing, the suttle usage of women towarde their lovers.

Wrapt in my carelesse cloke, as I walkt to and fro:
I se, how love can shew, what force ther reigneth in his bow
    And how he shoteth eke, a hardy hart to wound:
And where he glanceth by againe, that litle hurt is found.
    For seldom is it sene, he woundeth hartes alike.
The tone may rage, when tothers love is often farre to seke.
    All this I see, with more: and wonder thinketh me:
How he can strike the one so sore, and leave the other free.
    I see, that wounded wight, that suffreth all this wrong:
How he is fed with yeas, and nayes, and liveth all to long.   10
    In silence though I kepe such secretes to my self:
Yet do I see, how she somtime doth yeld a looke by stelth:
    As though it seemd, ywys I will not lose thee so,
When in her hart so swete a thought did never truely grow.
    Then say I thus: alas, that man is farre from blisse:
That doth receive for his relief, none other gaine but this.
    And she, that fedes him so, I fele, and finde it plain:
Is but to glory in her power, that over such can reign.
    Nor are such graces spent, but when she thinkes, that he,
A weried man is fully bent, such fansies to let flie: 20
    Then to retain him still, she wrasteth new her grace,
And smileth lo, as though she would forthwith the man
        embrace.
    But when the proofe is made, to try such lookes withall:

26 *carelesse* free from sorrow, anxiety
  3 *eke* too
  6 *tone* one (as opposed to the other – 'tother')
  9 *wight* person
  10 *to* too
  13 *ywys* indeed
  21 *wrasteth new her grace* turns on the charm again

He findeth then the place all voyde, and freighted ful of gall.
　　Lord what abuse is this? who can such women praise?
That for their glory do devise, to use such craftie wayes.
　　I, that among the rest do sit, and marke the row,
Finde, that in her is greater craft, then is in twenty mo.
　　Whose tender yeres, alas, with wyles so well are sped:
30　What will she do, when hory heares are powdred in her hed?

27. An answer in the behalfe of a woman of an uncertain aucthor.

Girt in my giltles gowne as I sit here and sow,
I see that thinges are not in dede as to the outward show.
And who so list to looke and note thinges somewhat nere:
Shall finde wher plainesse semes to haunt nothing but craft
　　appere
For with indifferent eyes my self can well discerne,
How some to guide a ship in stormes seke for to take the
　　sterne.
Whose practise if were proved in calme to stere a barge,
Assuredly beleve it well it were to great a charge.
And some I see againe sit still and say but small,
10　That could do ten times more than they that say they can do all.
Whose goodly giftes are such the more they understand,
The more they seke to learn and know & take lesse charge in
　　hand.
And to declare more plain the time fleetes not so fast:
But I can beare full well in minde the song now soung and
　　past.
The authour whereof came wrapt in a crafty cloke:
With will to force a flaming fire where he could raise no
　　smoke,

28　*mo* more
30　*heares* hairs
27　3　*list* pleases
　8　*to* too

If power and will had joynde as it appeareth plaine,
The truth nor right had tane no place their vertues had ben
     vain.
So that you may perceive, and I may safely se,
The innocent that giltlesse is, condemned should have be.   20

28. *The constant lover lamenteth,*

Sins fortunes wrath envieth the wealth,
Wherein I raigned by the sight:
Of that that fed mine eyes by stelth,
With sower swete, dread and delight.
Let not my griefe move you to mone,
For I will wepe and waile alone.

   Spite drave me into Borias raigne,
Where hory frostes the frutes do bite,
When hilles were spred and every plaine:
With stormy winters mantle white.   10
And yet my dere such was my heate,
When others freze then did I sweate.

   And now though on the sunne I drive,
Whose fervent flame all thinges decaies,
His beames in brightnesse may not strive,
With light of your swete golden rayes,
Nor from my brest this heate remove,
The frosen thoughtes graven by love.

   Ne may the waves of the salt flood,
Quenche that your beauty set on fire,   20
For though mine eyes forbeare the foode,
That did releve the hot desire.
Such as I was such will I be,
Your own, what would ye more of me?

28 1 *Sins* since
   4 *sower* sour

29. A song written by the earle of Surrey
by a ladie that refused to
daunce with him.

Eche beast can chose his fere according to his minde,
 And eke can shew a frendly chere like to their beastly kinde.
 A Lion saw I late as white as any snow,
Which semed well to lead the race his port the same did show.
 Upon the gentle beast to gaze it pleased me,
For still me thought he semed wel of noble blood to be,
 And as he praunced before, still seking for a make,
As who wold say there is none here I trow will me forsake.
 I might perceive a Wolfe as white as whales bone,
10 A fairer beast of fresher hue beheld I never none.
 Save that her lookes were coy, and froward eke her grace,
Unto the which this gentle beast gan him advance apace.
 And with a beck full low he bowed at her feete,
In humble wise as who would say I am to farre unmeete.
 But such a scornefull chere wherewith she him rewarded,
Was never sene I trow the like to such as well deserved.
 With that she start aside welnere a foote or twaine,
And unto him thus gan she say with spite and great disdaine.
 Lion she sayd if thou hadst knowen my minde before,
20 Thou hadst not spent thy travail thus nor all thy paine forlore.
 Doway I let thee wete thou shalt not play with me,
Go range about where thou maiest finde some meter fere for
   thee.
 With that he bet his taile, his eyes began to flame,

29 *by* about
 1 *fere* mate
 2 *eke* also   *chere* expression, greeting
 4 *port* gait
 7 *make* mate
 11 *froward* unreasonable, awkward
 14 *unmeete* unworthy
 20 *travail* labour
 21 *Doway* go away   *I let thee wete* I'll have you know
 22 *meter fere* more suitable companion

I might perceive his noble hart much moved by the same.
    Yet saw I him refraine and eke his wrath aswage,
And unto her thus gan he say when he was past his rage.
    Cruell, you do me wrong to set me thus so light,
Without desert for my good will to shew me such despight.
    How can ye thus entreat a Lion of the race,
That with his pawes a crowned king devoured in the place: 30
    Whose nature is to pray upon no simple food,
As long as he may suck the flesh, and drink of noble blood.
    If you be faire and fresh, am I not of your hue?
And for my vaunt I dare well say my blood is not untrue.
    For you your self have heard it is not long agoe,
Sith that for love one of the race did end his life in woe
    In tower strong and hie for his assured truth,
Whereas in teares he spent his breath, alas the more the ruth.
    This gentle beast so dyed whom nothing could remove,
But willingly to lese his life for losse of his true love.   40
    Other there be whose lives do lingre still in paine,
Against their willes preserved ar that would have died faine.
    But now I do perceave that nought it moveth you,
My good entent, my gentle hart, nor yet my kinde so true,
    But that your will is such to lure me to the trade,
As other some full many yeres to trace by craft ye made.
    And thus behold our kindes how that we differ farre.
I seke my foes: and you your frendes do threaten still with
    warre.
    I fawne where I am fled: you slay that sekes to you,
I can devour no yelding pray: you kill where you subdue.   50
    My kinde is to desire the honour of the field:

25 *eke* also
26 *gan* began
36 *Sith* since
38 *ruth* pity
40 *lese* lose
42 *faine* willingly
44 *kinde* nature

And you with blood to slake your thirst on such as to you
      yeld.
   Wherefore I would you wist that for your coyed lookes,
I am no man that will be trapt nor tangled with such hookes.
   And though some lust to love where blame full well they
      might,
And to such beasts of currant sort that would have travail
      bright.
   I will observe the law that Nature gave to me,
To conquer such as will resist and let the rest go fre.
   And as a Faucon free that soreth in the ayre,
60 Which never fed on hand nor lure, nor for no stale doth care,
   While that I live and breath such shall my custome be,
In wildnes of the woods to seke my pray where pleaseth me.
   Where many one shall rue, that never made offence.
Thus your refuse against my power shall bote them no
      defence.
   And for revenge therof I vow and swere therto,
A thousand spoiles I shall commit I never thought to do.
   And if to light on you my lucke so good shall be,
I shall be glad to fede on that that would have fed on me.
   And thus farewell unkinde to whom I bent and bow,
70 I would ye wist the ship is safe that bare his sailes so low.
   Sith that a Lions hart is for a Wolfe no pray,
With bloody mouth go slake your thirst on simple shepe I say,
   With more dispite and ire than I can now expresse,
Which to my paine though I refrain, the cause you may wel
      gesse.
   As for because my self was aucthor of the game.
It bootes me not that for my wrath I should disturbe the same.

   53 *would you wist* will have you know
   56 *of currant sort* the running kind
   60 *stale* decoy
   64 *bote them no defence* do them no good as a defence
   70 *wist* knew
   71 *Sith that* since

30. *The faithfull lover declareth his paines and his uncertein joyes, and with only hope recomforteth somwhat his wofull heart.*

If care do cause men cry, why do not I complaine?
If eche man do bewaile his wo, why shew not I my paine?
   Since that amongst them all I dare well say is none,
So farre from weale, so full of wo, or hath more cause to
      mone.
   For all thinges having life sometime have quiet rest.
The bearing Asse, the drawing Oxe, and every other beast.
   The peasant and the post, that serves at all assayes,
The shipboy and the galley slave have time to take their ease,
   Save I alas whom care of force doth so constraine
To waile the day and wake the night continually in paine,   10
   From pensivenes to plaint, from plaint to bitter teares,
From teares to painfull plaint againe: and thus my life it weares.
   No thing under the sunne that I can heare or se,
But moveth me for to bewaile my cruell destenie.
   For where men do rejoyce since that I can not so,
I take no pleasure in that place, it doubleth but my wo.
   And when I heare the sound of song or instrument,
Me think eche tune there dolefull is and helps me to lament.
   And if I see some have their most desired sight,
Alas think I eche man hath weal save I most wofull wight.   20
   Then as the striken Dere withdrawes himselfe alone,
So do I seke some secrete place where I may make my mone.
   There do my flowing eyes shew forth my melting hart,
So that the stremes of those two welles right well declare my
      smart.
   And in those cares so colde I force my selfe a heat,

30 1 *care* sorrow, anxiety
  11 *plaint* poetic complaint, expressing injustice or sorrow
  20 *wight* person

As sick men in their shaking fittes procure them self to sweat,
   With thoughtes that for the time do much appease my paine,
But yet they cause a farther feare and brede my woe againe.
   Me thinke within my thought I se right plaine appere,
30 My hartes delight my sorowes leche mine earthly goddesse here,
   With every sondry grace that I have sene her have.
Thus I within my wofull brest her picture paint and grave.
   And in my thought I roll her bewties to and fro,
Her laughing chere her lovely looke my hart that perced so.
   Her strangenes when I sued her servant for to be,
And what she said and how she smiled when that she pitied me.
   Then comes a sodaine feare that riveth all my rest
Lest absence cause forgetfulnes to sink with in her brest.
   For when I think how far this earth doth us devide.
40 Alas me semes love throwes me downe I fele how that I slide,
   But then I think againe why should I thus mistrust,
So swete a wighte so sad and wise that is so true and just,
   For loth she was to love, and wavering is she not.
The farther of the more desirde thus lovers tie their knot.
   So in dispaire and hope plonged am I both up an doune,
As is the ship with wind and wave when Neptune list to froune,
   But as the watery showers delay the raging winde,
So doth good hope clene put away dispaire out of my minde.
   And biddes me for to serve and suffer paciently,
50 For what wot I the after weale that fortune willes to me.
   For those that care do know and tasted have of trouble,
When passed is their wofull paine eche joy shall seme them
      double.
   And bitter sendes she now to make me tast the better,
The plesant swete when that it comes to make it seme the
      sweter.
   And so determine I to serve until my breath.

30 *leche* remedy/doctor
34 *chere* expression
37 *riveth* takes away
44 *of* off
46 *list* pleases
50 *wot* know *weale* well-being, wealth

Ye rather die a thousand times then once to false my faithe.
    And if my feble corps through weight of woful smart,
Do faile or faint my wyll it is that still she kepe my hart.
    And when thys carcas here to earth shalbe refarde,
I do bequeth my weried ghost to serve her afterwarde.   60

31. *The meanes to attain*
happy life.

Martial, the thinges that do attain
The happy life, be these, I finde.
The richesse left, not got with pain:
The frutefull ground: the quiet minde:
The egall frend, no grudge, no strife:
No charge of rule, nor governance:
Without disease the healthful life:
The houshold of continuance:
The meane diet, no delicate fare:
Trew wisdom joyned with simplenesse: 10
The night discharged of all care,
Where wine the wit may not oppresse:
The faithfull wife, without debate:
Such slepes, as may begile the night:
Contented with thine own estate,
Ne wish for death, ne feare his might.

32. *Praise of meane and*
constant estate.

Of thy life, Thomas, this compasse wel mark:
Not aye with ful sailes the hye seas to beat:
Ne by coward dred, in shonning stormes dark,

31   5   *egall* tranquil, impartial, of equal status
     11   *care* anxiety
     14   *begile* while away
32   2   *aye* always

On shalow shores thy keel in peril freat.
Who so gladly halseth the golden meane,
Voide of daungers advisdly hath his home
Not with lothsome muck, as a den unclean:
Nor palacelike, wherat disdain may glome.
The lofty pyne the great winde often rives:
With violenter swey falne turrets stepe:
Lightnings assault the hie mountains, & clives,
A hart wel stayd, in overthwartes depe,
Hopeth amendes: in swete, doth feare the sowre.
God, that sendeth, withdraweth winter sharp.
Now il, not aye thus: once Phebus to lowre
With bowe unbent shal cesse, and frame to harp
His voice. In straite estate appere thou stout:
And so wisely, when lucky gale of winde
All thy puft sailes shal fill, loke well about:
Take in a ryft: hast is wast, profe doth finde.

33. Praise of certaine psalmes
of David, translated by
sir T. W. the elder

The great Macedon, that out of Persie chased
Darius, of whose huge power all Asie rong,
In the rich ark dan Homers rimes he placed,
Who fayned gestes of heathen princes song.
What holy grave? what worthy sepulture
To Wiattes Psalmes should Christians then purchase?
Where he doth paint the lively faith, and pure,
The stedfast hope, the swete returne to grace
Of just David, by perfite penitence.

4 *freat* wear away, graze
5 *halseth* embraces
11 *clives* cliffs
20 *ryft* a sheet of the sails
33 3 *dan* respectful term of address, particularly for a master poet
4 *gestes* deeds

Where rulers may see in a mirrour clere 10
The bitter frute of false concupiscence:
How Jewry bought Urias death full dere.
In princes harts Gods scourge imprinted depe,
Ought them awake, out of their sinfull slepe.

34. Of the death of the same
sir T. W.

Dyvers thy death do diversly bemone.
Some, that in presence of thy livelyhed
Lurked, whose brestes envy with hate had swolne,
Yeld Ceasars teares upon Pompeius hed,
Some, that watched with the murdrers knife,
With eger thirst to drink thy giltlesse blood,
Whose practise brake by happy end of life,
With envious teares to heare thy fame so good.
But I, that knew what harbred in that hed:
What vertues rare were temperd in that brest: 10
Honour the place, that such a jewell bred,
And kisse the ground, whereas thy corse doth rest,
With vapord eyes: from whence such streames avail,
As Pyramus did on Thisbes brest bewail.

35. Of the same.

W. resteth here, that quick could never rest:
    Whose heavenly giftes encreased by disdain,
And vertue sank the deper in his brest.
Such profit he by envy could obtain.
    A head, where wisdom misteries did frame:
Whose hammers bet still in that lively brain,
As on a stithe: where that some work of fame

34 1 *Dyvers* various people
35 1 *quick* alive
   7 *stithe* anvil

Was dayly wrought, to turne to Britaines gaine.
    A visage, stern, and mylde: where both did grow,
Vice to contemne, in vertue to rejoyce:
Amid great stormes, whom grace assured so,
To live upright, and smile at fortunes choyce.
    A hand, that taught, what might be said in rime:
That reft Chaucer the glory of his wit:
A mark, the which (unparfited, for time)
Some may approch, but never none shal hit.
    A toung, that served in forein realmes his king:
Whose courteous talke to vertue did enflame.
Eche noble hart: a worthy guide to bring
Our English youth, by travail, unto fame.
    An eye, whose judgement none affect could blinde,
Frendes to allure, and foes to reconcile:
Whose persing loke did represent a minde
With vertue fraught, reposed, void of gile.
    A hart, where dreade was never so imprest,
To hide the thought, that might the trouth avance:
In neither fortune loft, nor yet represt,
To swel in wealth, or yeld unto mischance,
    A valiaunt corps, where force, and beawty met:
Happy, alas, to happy, but for foes:
Lived, and ran the race, that nature set:
Of manhodes shape, where she the mold did lose.
    But to the heavens that simple soule is fled:
Which left with such, as covet Christ to know,
Witnesse of faith, that never shall be ded:
Sent for our helth, but not received so.
Thus, for our gilte, this jewel have we lost:
The earth his bones, the heavens possesse his gost.

15 *unparfited, for time* unfinished, for lack of time
20 *travail* labour, travel
21 *none affect* no desire
27 *loft* high
29 *corps* body
30 *to* too
33 *simple* innocent

36. Of the same.

In the rude age when knowledge was not rife,
    If Jove in Create and other were that taught,
Artes to convert to profit of our life,
Wend after death to have their temples sought,
If vertue yet no voide unthankfull time,
Failed of some to blast her endles fame,
A goodly meane both to deterre from crime:
And to her steppes our sequele to enflame,
In daies of truth if Wiates frendes then waile,
The only det that dead of quick may claime: 10
That rare wit spent employd to our availe.
Where Christ is taught we led to vertues traine.
His lively face their brestes how did it freat,
Whose cindres yet with envy they do eate.

37. Of Sardanapalus dishonorable
life, and miserable
death.

Thassirian king in peace, with foule desire,
And filthy lustes, that staind his regal hart
In warre that should set princely hartes on fire:
Did yeld, vanquisht for want of marciall art.
The dint of swordes from kisses semed strange:
And harder, than his ladies side, his targe:
From glutton feastes, to souldiars fare a change:
His helmet, farre above a garlands charge.
Who scace the name of manhode did retain,
Drenched in slouth, and womanish delight,   10
Feble of sprite, impacient of pain:

36 4 *wend* believed, intended
   13 *freat* torment
37 1 *Thassirian* the Assyrian

When he had lost his honor, and his right:
Proud, time of wealth, in stormes appalled with dred,
Murthered himself, to shew some manful dede.

38. How no age is content with his owne estate, and how the age of children is the happiest, if they had skill to understand it.

Layd in my quiet bed, in study as I were,
  I saw within my troubled head, a heape of thoughtes
     appere:
  And every thought did shewe so lively in myne eyes,
That now I sighed, & then I smilde, as cause of thought dyd
     rise.
  I saw the litle boy in thought, how oft that he
Did wish of god, to scape the rod, a tall yongman to be.
  The yongman eke that feles, his bones with paines opprest
How he would be a rich olde man, to lyve, and lye at rest.
  The rych oldman that sees his end draw on so sore,
10 How he would be a boy again, to live so much the more.
  Wherat full oft I smilde, to se, how all these three,
From boy to man, from man to boy, would chop & change
     degree.
  And musing thus I think, the case is very strange,
That man from welth, to live in wo, doth ever seke to change.
  Thus thoughtfull as I lay, I saw my witherd skyn,
How it doth show my dented chewes, the flesh was worne so
     thyn:
  And eke my tothelesse chaps, the gates of my rightway,
That opes and shuts, as I do speake, doe thus unto me say:
  Thy white and horish heares, the messengers of age,

38 7 *eke* also
  16 *chewes* jaws
  17 *chaps* cheeks

That shew, like lines of true belife, that this life doth asswage,   20
   Byds thee lay hand, and fele them hanging on thy chin:
The which do write two ages past, the third now comming in.
   Hang up therfore the bit of thy yong wanton time:
And thou that therin beaten art, the happiest life define,
   Wherat I sighed, and sayd, farewell, my wonted joy:
Trusse up thy pack, and trudge from me to every litle boy:
   And tell them thus from me, their time most happy is:
If, to their time, they reason had to know the trueth of this.

39. *Bonum est mihi quod*
humiliasti me.

The stormes are past these cloudes are overblowne,
And humble chere great rigour hath represt:
For the defaute is set a paine fore knowne,
And pacience graft in a determed brest.
And in the hart wher heapes of griefes were growne,
The swete revenge hath planted mirth and rest,
No company so pleasant as mine owne.
Thraldom at large hath made this prison fre,
Danger wel past remembred workes delight:
Of lingring doubtes such hope is sprong pardie,   10
That nought I finde displeasaunt in my sight:
But when my glasse presented unto me
The curelesse wound that bledeth day and night,
To think (alas) such hap shoud graunted be
Unto a wretch that hath no hart to fight,
To spill that blood that hath so oft bene shed,
For Britannes sake (alas) and now is ded.

39 *Bonum est . . . me* It is good for me that you have laid me low
  2 *chere* mood
 10 *pardie* by god
 14 *hap* chance, fortune

40. Exhortacion to learne by others trouble.

My Ratclif, when thy retchlesse youth offendes:
Receve thy scourge by others chastisement.
For such calling, when it workes none amendes:
Then plages are sent without advertisement.
Yet Salomon said, the wronged shall recure:
But Wiat said true, the skarre doth aye endure.

41. The fansie of a weried lover.

The fansy, which that I have served long,
That hath alway bene enmy to myne ease,
Semed of late to rue upon my wrong,
And bad me flye the cause of my misease.
And I forthwith did prease out of the throng,
That thought by flight my painfull hart to please
Som other way: tyll I saw faith more strong:
And to my self I said: alas, those daies
In vayn were spent, to runne the race so long.
And with that thought, I met my guyde, that playn
Out of the way wherin I wandred wrong,
Brought me amiddes the hilles, in base Bullayn:
Where I am now, as restlesse to remayn,
Against my will, full pleased with my payn.

SURREY.

40 4 *plages* sufferings, curses, plagues   *advertisement* warning
     6 *aye* for ever
41 10 *playn* completely
     12 *base Bullayn* low Boulogne

[SIR THOMAS WYATT (1503–42)]

42. The lover for shamefastnesse hideth his desire within his faithfull hart.

The long love, that in my thought I harber,
And in my hart doth kepe his residence,
Into my face preaseth with bold pretence,
And there campeth, displaying his banner.
She that me learns to love, and to suffer,
And willes that my trust, and lustes negligence
Be reined by reason, shame, and reverence,
With his hardinesse takes displeasure.
Wherwith love to the hartes forest he fleeth,
Leaving his enterprise with paine and crye,   10
And there him hideth and not appeareth.
What may I do? when my maister feareth,
But in the field with him to live and dye,
For good is the life, ending faithfully.

43. The lover waxeth wiser, and will not die for affeccion.

Yet was I never of your love agreved,
Nor never shall, while that my life doth last:

42 *shamefastnesse* modesty, propriety
  1 *harber* harbour, give shelter or quarters to
  3 pushes forward into my face making bold claims
  5 *learns* teaches *suffer* feel pain and also be patient
  6 *trust* confidence
  7 *reined* reined in or reigned
  8 *hardinesse* audacity
43 1 Until now I have never been injured by your love (or my love for you)

But of hating my self, that date is past,
And teares continuall sore hath me weried.
I will not yet in my grave be buried,
Nor on my tombe your name have fixed fast,
As cruel cause, that did my sprite sone hast.
From thunhappy boones by great sighes stirred,
Then if an hart of amorous faith and will
Content your minde withouten doing grief:
Please it you so to this to do relief,
If other wise you seke for to fulfyll
Your wrath: you erre, and shall not as you wene.
And you your self the cause therof have bene.

44. The abused lover seeth his folie, and entendeth to trust no more.

Was never file yet half so well yfiled,
To file a file for any smithes entent,
As I was made a filing instrument,
To frame other, while that I was begiled.
But reason loe, hath at my foly smiled,
And pardoned me, sins that I me repent
Of my last yeres, and of my time mispent.
For youth led me, and falshod me misguided.
Yet, this trust I have of great apparence:

7 *sprite* spirit   *hast* hasten away
8 *thunhappy boones* the unhappy bones
12–13 *If . . . wrath* if you seek to satisfy your anger in another way
13 *shall not as you wene* shall not achieve what you think you will
44 1 *file* a metal tool, but also perhaps a cunning person
  4 *To frame other* to make or shape another   *while* until or at the same time
  6 *sins* since
  9 *this trust I have of great apparence* this belief I have of great likelihood,
    i.e. I believe the following is very probably true

Sins that disceit is ay returnable,   10
Of very force it is agreable,
That therwithall be done the recompence.
Then gile begiled playnd should be never,
And the reward is little trust for ever.

45. The lover describeth his being striken with sight of his love.

The lively sparkes, that issue from those eyes,
Against the which there vaileth no defence,
Have perst my hart, and done it none offence,
With quaking pleasure, more then once or twise.
Was never man could any thing devise,
Sunne beames to turne with so great vehemence
To dase mans sight, as by their bright presence
Dased am I, much like unto the gise
Of one striken with dint of lightening,
Blinde with the stroke, and crying here and there,   10
So call I for helpe, I not when, nor where,
The paine of my fall paciently bearing.
For streight after the blase (as is no wonder)
Of deadly noyse heare I the fearfull thunder.

10 *ay* always
11 *Of very force* by true necessity *agreable* suitable
13 *begiled* deceived *playnd* complained about
45 2 *vaileth no defence* no defence is of any use
3 *perst* pierced
8 *gise* appearance, aspect
11 *I not* I know not

46. *The wavering lover willeth,*
and dreadeth, to move
his desire.

Such vain thought, as wonted to mislead me
In desert hope by well assured mone,
Makes me from company to live alone,
In folowing her whom reason bids me flee.
And after her my hart would faine begone:
But armed sighes my way do stop anone,
Twixt hope and dread lacking my libertie.
So fleeth she by gentle crueltie.
Yet as I gesse under disdainfull brow
One beame of ruth is in her cloudy looke:
Which comfortes the minde, that erst for feare shooke.
That bolded straight the way then seke I how
To utter forth the smart I bide within:
But such it is, I not how to begin.

47. *The lover having dreamed enjoying*
of his love, complaineth that
the dreame is not either
longer or truer.

Unstable dreame according to the place,
Be stedfast ones, or els at least be true.

46 *willeth* wishes   *move* advance
   1–2 Such empty thought as used to lead me astray with its confident
     moans into hope which turned out to be a desert.
   5 *faine* willingly
  10 *ruth* pity
  11 *erst* once, not long ago
  12 *bolded* emboldened, show self to be bold or big   *straight* immediately
  13 *bide* endure, suffer
  14 *not* do not know
47 1 *according to the place* appropriate to the setting
  2 *Be stedfast* endure, last   *ones* for once

By tasted swetenesse, make me not to rew
The soden losse of thy false fained grace.
By good respect in such a daungerous case
Thou broughtest not her into these tossing seas,
But madest my sprite to live my care tencrease,
My body in tempest her delight timbrace,
The body dead, the sprite had his desire.
Painlesse was thone, the other in delight.   10
Why then alas did it not kepe it right,
But thus returne to leape into the fire:
And where it was at wish, could not remaine?
Such mockes of dreames do turne to deadly paine.

48. *The lover unhappy biddeth happy lovers rejoice in Maie, while he waileth that month to him most unlucky.*

Ye that in love finde luck and swete abundance,
And live in lust of joyfull jolitie,
Arise for shame, doway your sluggardy:
Arise I say, do May some observaunce.
Let me in bed lye, dreaming of mischance.
Let me remember my mishappes unhappy,
That me betide in May most commonly:
As one whom love list little to advance.
Stephan said true, that my nativitie
Mischanced was with the ruler of May.   10
He gest (I prove) of that the veritie.

5 *respect* consideration
7 *sprite* spirit   *my care tencrease* to increase my sorrow, anxiety
8 *timbrace* to embrace
10 *thone* the one
13 *at wish* according to one's wish, at one's disposal
48 3 *doway* put off
8 *list* pleases
11 *gest* conjectured correctly

In May my wealth, and eke my wittes, I say,
Have stand so oft in such perplexitie.
Joye: let me dreame of your felicitie.

49. *The lover confesseth him in love*
with Phillis.

If waker care: if sodayn pale colour:
If many sighes, with litle speche to plaine:
Now joye, now wo: if they my chere distaine:
For hope of small, if much to feare therfore,
To haste, or slack: my pace to lesse, or more:
Be signe of love: then do I love againe.
If thou aske whom: sure sins I did refraine
Brunet, that set my welth in such a rore,
Thunfayned chere of Phillis hath the place,
That Brunet had: she hath, and ever shall:
She from my self now hath me in her grace:
She hath in hand my wit, my will, and al:
My hart alone wel worthy she doth stay,
Without whose helpe skant do I live a day,

10

50. *Of others fained sorrow, and*
the lovers fained
mirth.

Cesar, when that the traitour of Egipt
With thonorable hed did him present,

---

49 1 *waker care* unsleeping, watchful anxiety
    2 *to plaine* to complain (but perhaps with a pun on 'too plain')
    3 *chere* face, expression   *distaine* cause to look pale, discolour
    7 *sins* since   *refraine* give up
    8 *rore* confusion, disturbance
    9 The unfeigned face of Phillis has the position
    13 *stay* support
50 2 *thonorable* the honourable

Covering his hartes gladnesse, did represent
Plaint with his teares outward, as it is writ.
Eke Hannibal, when fortune him out shit
Clene from his reigne, and from all his entent,
Laught to his folke, whom sorow did torment,
His cruel despite for to disgorge and quit.
So chanceth me, that every passion
The minde hideth by colour contrary,   10
With fained visage, now sad, now mery.
Wherby, if that I laugh at any season:
It is because I have none other way
To cloke my care, but under sport and play.

51. Of change in minde.

Eche man me telth, I change most my devise:
And, on my faith, me thinke it good reason
To change purpose, like after the season.
For in eche case to kepe still one guise
Is mete for them, that would be taken wise.
And I am not of such maner condicion:
But treated after a divers fashion:
And therupon my diversnesse doth rise.
But you, this diversnesse that blamen most,
Change you no more, but still after one rate   10
Treat you me well: and kepe you in that state,

4 *Plaint* misery
5 *out shit* shut out
8 *despite* anger, defiance, chagrin
9 *chanceth me*: it happens to me
14 *care* sorrow, anxiety
51 1 *telth* tells *devise* intention, stratagem
    4 *guise* characteristic manner or appearance
    5 *mete* suitable
    7 *divers* variable
    8 *diversnesse* changeability, inconsistency
   10 *after one rate* in the same manner

And while with me doth dwell this weried gost,
My word nor I shall not be variable,
But alwaies one, your own both firme and stable.

52. How the lover perisheth in his delight, as the flie in the fire.

Some fowles there be that have so perfit sight,
Against the sunne their eies for to defend:
And some, because the light doth them offend,
Never appeare, but in the darke, or night.
Other rejoyce, to se the fire so bright,
And wene to play in it, as they pretend:
But find contrary of it, that they intend.
Alas, of that sort may I be, by right.
For to withstand her loke I am not able:
Yet can I not hide me in no dark place:
So foloweth me remembrance of that face:
That with my teary eyen, swolne, and unstable,
My desteny to behold her doth me lead:
And yet I know, I runne into the glead.

53. Against his tonge that failed to utter his sutes.

Because I stil kept thee fro lyes, and blame,
And to my power alwayes thee honoured,
Unkind tonge, to yl hast thou me rendred,

---

12 *gost* spirit
52 1 *fowles* flying creatures, including insects
   6 *wene* wish   *pretend* intend
   14 *glead* fire, live coal
53 *sutes* petitions, supplications
   3 *to yl* too ill/to ill

For such desert to do me wreke and shame.
In nede of succour most when that I am,
To aske reward: thou standst like one afraied,
Alway most cold: and if one word be said,
As in a dreame, unperfit is the same.
And ye salt teares, against my wyll eche nyght,
That are with me, when I would be alone: 10
Then are ye gone, when I shold make my mone.
And ye so ready sighes, to make me shright,
Then are ye slacke, when that ye should outstart.
And onely doth my loke declare my hart.

54. Description of the contrarious passions in a lover.

I finde no peace, and all my warre is done:
I feare, and hope: I burne, and frese like yse:
I flye aloft, yet can I not arise:
And nought I have, and all the world I season.
That lockes nor loseth, holdeth me in prison,
And holdes me not, yet can I scape no wise:
Nor lettes me live, nor dye, at my devise,
And yet of death it geveth me occasion.
Without eye I se, without tong I playne:
I wish to perish, yet I aske for helth: 10
I love another, and I hate my selfe.
I fede me in sorow, and laugh in all my paine.
Lo, thus displeaseth me both death and life.
And my delight is causer of this strife.

4 *desert* deserving   *wreke* punishment, harm
8 *unperfit* unskilled, defective
12 *shright* shriek
54 4 *season* fortify (but see explanatory note)
  5 *That lockes nor loseth* that which neither locks nor releases
  6 *no wise* by no means

55. *The lover compareth his state to a ship in perilous storme tossed on the sea.*

My galley charged with forgetfulnesse,
Through sharpe seas, in winter nightes doth passe,
Twene rocke, and rocke: and eke my fo (alas)
That is my lord, stereth with cruelnesse:
And every houre, a thought in readinesse,
As though that death were light, in such a case.
An endlesse wind doth teare the saile apace
Of forced sighes, and trusty fearefulnesse.
A rayne of teares, a clowde of darke disdaine
Have done the weried coardes great hinderance,
Wrethed with errour, and with ignorance.
The starres be hidde, that leade me to this payne.
Drownde is reason that should be my comfort:
And I remayne, dispearing of the port.

56. *Of doutful love.*

Avisyng the bright beames of those fayre eyes,
Where he abides that mine oft moistes and washeth:
The weried mynde streight from the hart departeth,
To rest within his worldly Paradise,
And bitter findes the swete, under his gise.
What webbes there he hath wrought, well he perceaveth
Whereby then with him self on love he plaineth,
That spurs with fire, and bridleth eke with yse.
In such extremitie thus is he brought:

55 1 *galley* boat propelled by sails and oars   *charged* loaded
    3 *eke* also
    7 *apace* quickly
56 1 *Avisyng* looking at, considering
    5 *gise* appearance
    8 *eke* also

Frosen now cold, and now he standes in flame: 10
Twixt wo and wealth: betwixt earnest and game:
With seldome glad, and many a divers thought:
In sore repentance of his hardinesse,
Of such a roote lo cometh frute frutelesse.

57. The lover sheweth how he is forsaken of such as he somtime enjoyed.

They flee from me, that sometime did me seke
With naked foote stalking within my chamber.
Once have I seen them gentle, tame, and meke,
That now are wild, and do not once remember
That sometime they have put them selves in danger,
To take bread at my hand, and now they range,
Busily seking in continuall change.
    Thanked be fortune, it hath been otherwise
Twenty times better: but once especiall,
In thynne aray, after a pleasant gise,   10
When her loose gown did from her shoulders fall,
And she me caught in her armes long and small,
And therwithall, so swetely did me kisse,
And softly sayd: deare hart, how like you this?
    It was no dreame: for I lay broade awaking.
But all is turnde now through my gentlenesse,
Into a bitter fashion of forsaking:
And I have leave to go of her goodnesse,
And she also to use newfanglenesse.

12 *divers* varying, contradictory
13 *hardinesse* audacity
57 9 *Twenty times better* more than twenty times   *once especiall* on one
particular occasion
    10 *after a pleasant gise* in a pleasant manner, with a pleasant appearance
    12 *small* slender
    15 *broade awaking* wide awake
    19 *newfanglenesse* love of novelty

20   But, sins that I unkindly so am served:
      How like you this, what hath she now deserved?

58. To a ladie to answer directlie
with yea or naie.

      Madame, withouten many wordes:
      Once I am sure, you will, or no.
      And if you will: then leave your boordes,
      And use your wit, and shew it so:
      For with a beck you shal me call.
      And if of one, that burns alway,
      Ye have pity or ruth at all:
      Answer him faier with yea, or nay.
      If it be yea: I shall be faine.
10   Yf it be nay: frendes, as before.
      You shall another man obtain:
      And I mine owne, and yours nomore.

59. To his love whom he
had kissed against
her will.

      Alas, Madame, for stealing of a kisse,
      Have I so much your minde therin offended?
      Or have I done so grevously amisse:
      That by no meanes it may not be amended?
      Revenge you then, the rediest way is this:
      Another kisse my life it shal have ended.

20 *sins* since
58 3 *boordes* jesting/mockery
   5 *beck* beckoning motion
   7 *ruth* pity, compassion
   8 *faier* fair
   9 *faine* happy

For, to my mouth the first my hart did suck:
The next shal clene out of my brest it pluck.

60. Of the Jelous man that loved
the same woman and espied
this other sitting
with her.

The wandring gadling, in the summer tide,
That findes the Adder with his rechlesse foote
Startes not dismaid so sodeinly aside,
As jealous despite did, though there were no boote,
When that he sawe me sitting by her side,
That of my health is very crop, and roote,
It plesed me then to have so faire a grace,
To stynge the hart, that would have had my place,

61. To his love from whom he had
her gloves.

What nedes these threatning woordes, and wasted wynd?
All this can not make me restore my pray.
To robbe your good ywis is not my mynde:
Nor causelesse your faire hand did I display,
Let love be judge: or els whom next we finde:
That may both hear, what you and I can say.
She reft my hart: and I a glove from her:
Let us se then if one be worth the other.

60 1 *gadling* wayfarer, vagabond   *summer tide* summertime
     2 *rechlesse* careless
     4 *despite* indignation, anger   *boote* remedy
61 1 *wynd* breath
     3 To steal your property indeed ('ywis') is not my intention
     7 *reft* took away

62. Of the fained frend.

Right true it is, and sayd full yore ago:
Take hede of him, that by the backe thee claweth.
For, none is worse, then is a frendly fo.
Though thee seme good, all thinge that thee deliteth:
Yet know it well, that in thy bosome crepeth.
For, many a man such fire oft times he kindleth:
That with the blase his berd him self he singeth.

63. The lover taught, mistrusteth allurementes.

It may be good like it who list:
But I do dout, who can me blame?
For oft assured, yet have I mist:
And now againe I feare the same.
The wordes, that from your mouth last came,
Of sodain change make me agast.
For dread to fall, I stand not fast.
    Alas I tread an endlesse mase:
That seke taccord two contraries:
And hope thus still, and nothing hase:
Imprisoned in liberties,
As one unheard, and still that cries:
Alwayes thirsty, and naught doth taste,
For dreade to fall, I stand not fast.
    Assured I dout I be not sure,
Should I then trust unto such suretie?

10

---

62 7 *singeth* singes, burns
63 1 *list* pleases
   3 *mist* missed, lost
   7 *fast* steadfast, steadily
   9 *seke taccord* attempt to accord, to reconcile
   10 *hase* (?) hazard (see explanatory note)

That oft have put the proofe in ure,
And never yet have found it trustie?
Nay syr in fayth, it were great folly.
And yet my life thus do I wast,   20
For dread to fall I stand not fast.

64. The lover complaineth that his love doth not pitie him.

Resownde my voyce ye woodes, that heare me plain:
Both hilles and vales causing reflexion,
And rivers eke, record ye of my paine:
Which have oft forced ye by compassion,
As judges lo to heare my exclamacion.
Among whom, ruth (I finde) yet doth remaine.
Where I it seke, alas, there is disdaine.
    Oft ye rivers, to heare my wofull sounde,
Have stopt your cours, and plainely to expresse,
Many a teare by moysture of the ground   10
The earth hath wept to heare my heavinesse:
Which causelesse I endure without redresse.
The hugy okes have rored in the winde,
Eche thing me thought complayning in their kind.
    Why then alas doth not she on me rew,
Or is her hart so hard that no pitie
May in it sinke, my joye for to renew?
O stony hart who hath thus framed thee
So cruell? that art cloked with beauty,

17 *put the proofe in ure* put the testing of the evidence into practice
64 1 *Resownde my voyce* resound with my voice
    2 *reflexion* echo, but perhaps also thought
    3 *eke* also
    6 *ruth* pity
    14 *in their kind* according to their nature
    15 *rew* take pity
    18 *framed* made

That from thee may no grace to me procede,
But as reward death for to be my mede.

65. The lover rejoyseth against fortune that by hindering his sute had happily made him forsake his folly.

In faith I wot not what to say,
Thy chaunces ben so wonderous,
Thou fortune with thy divers play
That makst the joyful dolourous,
And eke the same right joyous.
Yet though thy chaine hath me enwrapt
Spite of thy hap, hap hath wel hapt.
   Though thou hast set me for a wonder,
And sekest by change to do me paine:
Mens mindes yet maist thou not so order.
For honestie if it remaine,
Shal shine for all thy cloudy raine.
In vaine thou sekest to have me trapt,
Spite of thy hap, hap hath well hapt.
   In hindring me, me didst thou further,
And made a gap where was a stile.
Cruel willes ben oft put under.
Wening to lower, then didst thou smile.
Lord, how thy selfe thou didst begile,
That in thy cares wouldst me have wrapt?
But spite of hap, hap hath wel hapt.

21 *mede* reward
65 *sute* petition
1 *wot* know
3 *divers* variable
5 *eke* also
7 In spite of the bad luck [you have caused], the event has turned out well
12 *for all* despite
18 *Wening to lower* intending to scowl
19 *begile* deceive

66. A renouncing of hardly escaped love

Farewell the hart of crueltie.
Though that with paine my libertie
Deare have I bought, and wofully
Finisht my feareful tragedy,
Of force I must forsake such pleasure:
A good cause just, sins I endure
Therby my wo, which be ye sure,
Shal therwith go me to recure.
   I fare as one escapt that fleeth,
Glad he is gone, and yet still feareth   10
Spied to be caught, and so dredeth
That he for nought his paine leseth.
In joyfull paine rejoice my hart,
Thus to sustaine of ech a part.
Let not this song from thee astart,
Welcome among my pleasant smart.

67. The lover to his bed, with describing of his unquiet state.

The restfull place, renewer of my smart:
The labours salve, encreasing my sorow:
The bodies ease, and troubler of my hart:
Quieter of minde, mine unquiet fo:
Forgetter of paine, remembrer of my wo:
The place of slepe, wherin I do but wake:

66 *hardly* painfully, with difficulty
   5 *Of force* by necessity
   6 *sins* since
   8 *recure* restore to health
   12 *leseth* loses, wastes
   15 *astart* escape

Besprent with teares, my bed, I thee forsake.
   The frosty snowes may not redresse my heat:
Nor heat of sunne abate my fervent cold.
I know nothing to ease my paines so great.
Eche cure causeth encrease by twenty fold.
Renewing cares upon my sorowes old.
Such overthwart effectes in me they make.
Besprent with teares my bed for to forsake.
   But all for nought: I finde no better ease
In bed, or out. This most causeth my paine:
Where I do seke how best that I may please,
My lost labour (alas) is all in vaine.
My hart once set, I can not it refraine.
No place from me my griefe away can take.
Wherfore with teares, my bed I thee forsake.

68. Comparison of love to a streame falling from the Alpes.

From these hie hilles as when a spring doth fall,
It trilleth downe with still and suttle course,
Of this and that it gathers ay and shall,
Till it have just down flowed to streame and force:
Then at the foote it rageth over all.
So fareth love, when he hath tane a sourse.
Rage is his raine. Resistance vaileth none.
The first eschue is remedy alone.

67 7, 14 *Besprent* besprinkled
   13 *overthwart* adverse
68 2 *still* quiet/imperceptible
    3 *ay* always
    4 *force* waterfall
    7 *raine* rein, restraint   *vaileth* benefits, assists
    8 *first eschue* initial avoidance

69. *Wiates complaint upon Love,*
to Reason: with Loves
answere.

Mine old dere enmy, my froward maister,
Afore that Quene, I causde to be acited,
Which holdeth the divine part of our nature,
That, like as golde, in fire he mought be tried.
Charged with dolour, there I me presented
With horrible feare, as one that greatly dredeth
A wrongfull death, and justice alway seketh
    And thus I sayd: Once my left foote, Madame,
When I was yong, I set within his reigne:
Wherby other then firely burning flame   10
I never felt, but many a grevous pain.
Torment I suffred, angre, and disdain:
That mine oppressed pacience was past,
And I mine own life hated, at the last.
    Thus hitherto have I my time passed
In pain and smart. What waies profitable:
How many pleasant daies have me escaped,
In serving this false lyer so deceavable?
What wit have wordes so prest and forceable,
That may contain my great mishappynesse,   20
And just complaintes of his ungentlenesse?
    So small hony, much aloes, and gall,
In bitternesse, my blinde life hath ytasted.
His false semblance, that turneth as a ball:
With faire and amorous daunce, made me be traced,

69 1 *froward* unreasonable, awkward
   2 *acited* summoned
   5 *Charged with dolour* burdened with misery
  19 *prest* ready
  22 *aloes* bitter, nauseating medicine
  25 *traced* yoked

And, where I had my thought, and minde araced,
From earthly frailnesse, and from vain pleasure,
Me from my rest he toke, and set in errour:
   God made he me regardlesse, than I ought,
And to my self to take right litle hede:
And for a woman have I set at nought
All other thoughtes: in this onely to spede.
And he was onely counseler of this dede:
Whetting alwaies my youthly fraile desire
On cruell whetston, tempered with fire.
   But (Oh alas) where, had I ever wit?
Or other gift, geven to me of nature?
That sooner shalbe changed my weried sprite:
Then the obstinate will, that is my ruler.
So robbeth he my freedom with displeasure,
This wicked traytour, whom I thus accuse:
That bitter life hath turned in pleasant use.
   He hath me hasted, through divers regions:
Through desert woods, and sharp hye mountaines:
Through froward people, and through bitter passions:
Through rocky seas. and over hilles and plaines:
With wery travell, and with laborous paines:
Alwaies in trouble and in tediousnesse:
All in errour, and dangerous distresse.
   But nother he, nor she, my tother fo,
For all my flight, did ever me forsake:
That though my timely death hath been to slow
That me as yet, it hath not overtake:
The heavenly Gods of pitie do it slake.

30

40

50

26 *araced* torn up
32 *spede* be successful
36 *wit* wit, wisdom
42 *hath turned in pleasant use* has become a pleasant habit
43 *divers* various
44 *desert* deserted
47 *travell* labour, journey
50 *tother* other

And, note they this his cruell tiranny,
That feedes him, with my care, and misery.
 Sins I was his, hower rested I never,
Nor looke to do: and eke the waky nightes
The baneshed slepe may in no wise recover.
By guile, and force, over my thralled sprites,   60
He is ruler: sins which bell never strikes,
That I heare not as sounding to renue
My plaintes. Himself, he knoweth, that I say true.
 For never wormes old rotten stocke have eaten:
As he my hart, where he is resident
And doth the same with death dayly threaten,
Thence come the teares, and thence the bitter torment:
The sighes: the wordes, and eke the languishment:
That noy both me, and paraventure other.
Judge thou: that knowest the one, and eke the tother. 70
 Mine adversair, with such grevous reproofe,
Thus he began. Heare Lady, thother part:
That the plain troth, from which he draweth aloofe,
This unkinde man may shew, ere that I part.
In his yong age, I toke him from that art,
That selleth wordes, and makes a clattering knight:
And of my wealth I gave him the delight.
 Now shames he not on me for to complain,
That held him evermore in pleasant gaine,
From his desire, that might have been his pain.   80
 Yet therby alone I brought him to some frame:

56 *care* sorrow, anxiety
57 *Sins* since *hower* hour
58 *eke* also
60 *thralled sprites* imprisoned spirit, soul
63 *plaintes* poetic complaints, expressing injustice or sorrow
64 *stocke* wood, trunks
69 *noy* annoy, trouble, harm *paraventure* perhaps
70 *eke the tother* also the other
74 *ere that* before
76 *clattering* chattering
79 *gaine* probably a misprint for 'game'
81 *frame* advantage

Which now as wretchedes, he doth so blame:
And toward honour quicknd I his wit:
Whereas a daskard els he mought have sit
   He knoweth, how great Atride that made Troy freat,
And Hanniball, to Rome so troubelous:
Whom Homer honored, Achilles that great,
And Thaffricane Scipion the famous:
And many other, by much honour glorious:
Whose fame, and actes did lift them up above:
I did let fall in base dishonest love.
   And unto him, though he unworthy were:
I chose the best of many a Milion:
That, under sunne yet never was her pere,
Of wisdome, womanhod, and of discrecion:
And of my grace I gave her such a facion,
And eke such way I taught her for to teache,
That never base thought his hart so hye might reache.
   Evermore thus to content his maistresse,
That was his onely frame of honesty,
I stirred him still toward gentlenesse:
And causde him to regard fidelity.
Pacience I taught him in adversity.
Such vertues learned he in my great schoole:
Wherof repenteth now the ignorant foole.
   These were the same diceites, and bitter gall,
That I have used, the torment and the anger:
Sweter, then ever did to other fall,
Of right good sede yll fruite lo thus I gather.
And so shall he, that the unkinde doth further.
A Serpent nourish I under my wing:
And now of nature, ginneth he to sting.

90 (margin)
100 (margin)
110 (margin)

---

84 *daskard* dullard
85 *that made Troy freat* which destroyed Troy
88 *Thaffricane Scipion* the African Scipio, i.e. Scipio Africanus
96 *facion* appearance, manner
102 *regard* respect
112 *of nature* according to nature

And for to tell, at last, my great servise.
From thousand dishonesties have I him drawen:
That, by my meanes, him in no maner wise.
Never vile pleasure once hath overthrowen.
Where, in his dede, shame hath him alwaies gnawen:
Douting report, that should come to her eare:
Whom now he blames, her wonted he to feare.

What ever he hath of any honest custome: 120
Of her, and me: that holdes he every whit,
But, lo, yet never was there nightly fantome
So farre in errour, as he is from his wit.
To plain on us, he striveth with the bit,
Which may rule him, and do him ease, and pain:
And in one hower, make al his grief his gain,

But, one thing yet there is, above all other:
I gave him winges, wherwith he might upflie
To honour and fame: and if he would to higher
Then mortal thinges, above the starry skie: 130
Considering the pleasure, that an eye
Might geve in earth, by reason of the love:
What should that be that lasteth still above?

And he the same himself hath sayd ere this.
But now, forgotten is both that and I,
That gave her him, his onely wealth and blisse.
And, at this word, with dedly shreke and cry.
Thou gave her once: quod I, but by and by
Thou toke her ayen from me: that wo worth the.
Not I but price: more worth than thou (quod he.)   140

At last: eche other for himself, concluded:
I, trembling still: but he, with small reverence.
Lo, thus, as we eche other have accused:
Dere Lady: now we waite thine onely sentence.

115 *in no maner wise* in no way
118 *Douting* fearing   *to her eare* causing her suffering
119 *wonted* was accustomed
126 *hower* hour
139 *ayen* again   *that wo worth the* for that may woe come to thee

She smiling, at the whisted audience:
It liketh me (quod she) to have heard your question:
But, lenger time doth ask a resolucion.

70. *The lovers sorowfull state maketh him write sorowfull songes, but (Souche) his love may change the same.*

Marvell no more altho
The songes, I sing do mone:
For other life then wo,
I never proved none.
    And in my hart also,
Is graven with letters depe
A thousand sighes and mo:
A flood of teares to wepe.
    How may a man in smart
Finde matter to rejoyce?
How may a moorning hart
Set foorth a pleasant voyce.
    Play who so can, that part:
Nedes must in me appere:
How fortune overthwart
Doth cause my moorning chere.
    Perdy there is no man,
If he saw never sight:
That perfitly tell can

10

---

145 *whisted* silent
147 *lenger time doth ask a resolucion* more time is needed for a
    resolution
70 *Souche* such, but perhaps also (Mary) Souche; see explanatory note
4 *proved* experienced
6 *graven* engraved
15 *overthwart* hostile
16 *chere* mood
17 *Perdy* certainly

The nature of the light.   20
    Alas: how should I than,
That never taste but sowre:
But do, as I began,
Continually to lowre.
    But yet perchance some chance
May chance to change my tune:
And when (Souch) chance doth chance:
Then shall I thank fortune.
    And if I have (Souch) chance:
Perchance ere it be long: 30
For (Souch) a pleasant chance,
To sing some pleasant song.

71. The lover complaineth himself forsaken.

Where shall I have, at mine owne wyll,
Teares to complain? Where shall I fet
Such sighes? that I may sigh my fill:
And then againe my plaintes repete.
For, though my plaint shall have none end:
My teares cannot suffise my wo.
To mone my harm, have I no friend,
For fortunes friend is mishaps fo.
Comfort (God wot) els have I none:
But in the winde to wast my wordes,   10
Nought moveth you my deadly mone:
But still you turne it into bordes.
I speake not, now, to move your hart,

24 *lowre* look or be depressed
30 *ere* before
71 2 *fet* fetch
  5 *plaint* poetic complaint, expressing injustice or sorrow
  7 *To mone my harm* to bemoan my hurt
  9 *wot* knows
  12 *bordes* jests

That you should rue upon my pain:
The sentence geven may not revert:
I know, such labour were but vain.
But sins that I for you (my dere)
Have lost that thing, that was my best:
A right small losse it must appere,
To lese these wordes, and all the rest.
But, though they sparkle in the winde:
Yet, shall they shew your falsed faith:
Which is returned to his kinde:
For like to like: the proverb saith,
Fortune, and you did me avance.
Me thought, I swam, and could not drown:
Happiest of all, but my mischance
Did lift me up, to throw me down.
And you, with her, of cruelnesse,
Did set your foote upon my neck,
Me, and my welfare to oppresse:
Without offence your hart to wreck,
Where are your pleasant wordes? alas:
Where is your faith? your stedfastnesse?
There is no more: but all doth passe:
And I am left all comfortlesse.
But sins so much it doth you greve,
And also me my wretched life:
Have here my troth: Nought shall releve,
But death alone my wretched strife.

14 *rue* take pity
15 *revert* be reserved
17 *sins* since
20 *lese* lose
23 *kinde* nature
25 *avance* advance
29 *of cruelnesse* out of sheer cruelty
32 *wreck* gratify
39 *troth* promise

Therfore, farewell my life my death,
My gain, my losse: my salve my sore:
Farewell also, with you my breath:
For, I am gone for evermore.

72. Of his love that pricked
her finger with
a nedle.

She sat, and sowed: that hath done me the wrong:
Wherof I plain, and have done many a day:
And, whilst she heard my plaint, in piteous song:
She wisht my hart the samplar, that it lay.
The blinde master, whom I have served so long:
Grudging to heare, that he did heare her say:
Made her own weapon do her finger blede:
To fele, if pricking were so good in dede.

73. Of the same.

What man hath heard such cruelty before?
That, when my plaint remembred her my wo,
That caused it: she cruell more and more,
Wished eche stitche, as she did sit and sow,
Had prickt my hart, for to encrease my sore,
And, as I think, she thought it had been so.
For as she thought, this is his hart in dede:
She pricked hard: and made her self to blede.

42 *salve* healing ointment, remedy
72 1 *sowed* sewed
   2 *plain* complain, make a plaint
73 2 *plaint* complaint, expression of injustice or sorrow
   remembred her reminded her of

74. *Request to Cupide for revenge*
of his unkinde
love.

Behold, Love, thy power how she despiseth:
My grevous pain how litle she regardeth,
The solemne othe, wherof she takes no cure,
Broken she hath: and yet, she bydeth sure,
Right at her ease, and litle thee she dredeth.
Weaponed thou art, and she unarmed sitteth:
To thee disdainfull, all her life she leadeth:
To me spitefull, without just cause, or measure.
Behold Love, how proudly she triumpheth,
I am in hold, but if thee pitie meveth:
Go, bend thy bow, that stony hartes breaketh:
And with some stroke revenge the great displeasure
Of thee, and him that sorow doth endure,
And as his Lord thee lowly here entreateth.

75. *Complaint for true love*
unrequited.

What vaileth troth? or by it, to take payn
To strive by stedfastnesse, for to attain
How to be just: and flee from doublenesse?
Since all alyke, where ruleth carftinesse,
Rewarded is both crafty false, and plain.
Soonest he spedes, that most can lye and fayn.
True meaning hart is had in hie disdain.
Against deceit, and cloked doublenesse,

74 3 *wherof she takes no cure* which she does not care about
     8 *measure* moderation
    10 *in hold* imprisoned, captive *but if* unless
75 1 *What vaileth troth?* what is the point of faithfulness?
     4 *carftinesse* misprint for 'craftiness'
     5 *plain* straightforward
     6 *spedes* succeeds

What vaileth troth, or parfit stedfastnesse.
Deceaved is he, by false and crafty trayn,   10
That meanes no gile, and faithful doth remain
Within the trapt, without help or redresse.
But for to love (lo) such a sterne maistresse,
Where cruelty dwelles, alas it were in vain.

76. The lover that fled love, now folowes it with his harme.

Somtime I fled the fire, that me so brent,
By sea, by land, by water, and by wynde:
And now, the coales I folow, that be quent,
From Dover to Calas, with willing minde,
Lo, how desire is both forth sprong, and spent:
And he may see, that whilom was so blinde:
And all his labour, laughes he now to scorne,
Meashed in the breers, that erst was onely torne.

77. The lover hopeth of better chance.

He is not dead, that somtime had a fall.
The Sun returnes, that hid was under clowd.
And when Fortune hath spit out all her gall,
I trust, good luck to me shall be alowd.
For, I have seen a ship in haven fall,

10 *trayn* course of action
11 *gile* deception
12 *trapt* misprint for 'trap' (but could here imply 'within thee trapped')
76 *with his harme* to his injury
1 *Somtime* once *brent* burned
3 *quent* quenched, put out
6 *whilom* once
8 *Meashed in the breers* enmeshed in the briars *erst* before
77 1 *somtime* once
5 *in haven fall* come into safe harbour

After that storme hath broke both maste, & shroud,
The willow eke, that stoupeth with the winde,
Doth rise againe, and greater wood doth binde.

78. The lover compareth his hart to the overcharged gonne.

The furious goonne, in his most raging yre,
When that the boule is rammed into sore:
And that the flame cannot part from the fire,
Crackes in sunder: and in the ayer do rore
The shevered peces. So doth my desire,
Whose flame encreaseth ay from more to more.
Which to let out, I dare not loke, nor speake:
So inward force my hart doth all to breake.

79. The lover suspected of change praieth that it be not beleved against him.

Accused though I be, without desert:
Sith none can prove, beleve it not for true.
For never yet, since that you had my hert,
Intended I to false, or be untrue.
Sooner I would of death sustayn the smart,
Than breake one word of that I promised you
Accept therfore my service in good part.

6 *shroud* ropes, part of ship's rigging
7 *eke* also
78 *gonne* gun, cannon
   2 *boule* cannonball   *into sore* in too hard
   5 *shevered* shattered
   6 *ay* always
79 1 *desert* justification, deserving it
   2 *Sith* since

None is alyve, that can yll tonges eschew.
Hold them as false: and let not us depart
Our frendship old, in hope of any new.   10
Put not thy trust in such as use to fayn,
Except thou minde to put thy frend to payn.

80. *The lover abused renownseth love.*

My love to skorne, my service to retayne,
Therin (me thought) you used crueltie.
Since with good will I lost my libertie,
Might never wo yet cause me to refrain,
But onely this, which is extremitie,
To geve me nought (alas) nor to agree,
That as I was, your man I might remain.
But since that thus ye list to order me,
That would have bene your servant true & fast:
Displease you not: my doting time is past.   10
And with my losse to leave I must agree.
For as there is a certain time to rage:
So is there time such madnes to aswage.

81. *The lover professeth himself constant.*

Within my brest I never thought it gain,
Of gentle mindes the fredom for to lose
Nor in my hart sanck never such disdain,

8 *eschew* avoid
11 *use to fayn* are accustomed to deceive
12 *Except thou minde* unless you intend
80 8 *list* please
9 *fast* steadfast
10 *Displease you not* do not be displeased
81 2 to lose the detachment, *or* to take away the freedom of a civilized mind
3 *disdain* unpleasantness

To be a forger, faultes for to disclose.
Nor I can not endure the truth to glose,
To set a glosse upon an earnest pain.
Nor I am not in nomber one of those,
That list to blow retrete to every train,

82. *The lover sendeth his complaintes and teares to sue for grace.*

Passe forth my wonted cries,
Those cruel eares to pearce,
Which in most hatefull wyse
Doe stil my plaintes reverse.
Doe you, my teares, also
So wet her barrein hart:
That pitie there may grow,
And crueltie depart.
  For though hard rockes among
She semes to have bene bred:
And of the Tigre long
Bene nourished, and fed.
Yet shall that nature change,
If pitie once win place.
Whom as unknowen, and strange,
She now away doth chase.
  And as the water soft,
Without forcing or strength,
Where that it falleth oft,
Hard stones doth perse at length:
So in her stony hart

5 *glose* gloss over
8 That want to sound a retreat from every venture
82 1 *wonted* accustomed
3 *wyse* manner
4 *my plaintes reverse* turn away my complaints

My plaintes at last shal grave,
And, rygour set apart,
Winne graunt of that I crave.
   Wherfore my plaintes, present
Stil so to her my sute,
As ye, through her assent,
May bring to me some frute.
And as she shall me prove,
So bid her me regarde,   30
And render love for love:
Which is a just reward.

83. *The lovers case can not be hidden how ever he dissemble.*

Your lokes so often cast,
Your eyes so frendly rolde,
Your sight fixed so fast,
Alwaies one to behold.
Though hyde it fayn ye would:
It plainly doth declare,
Who hath your hart in hold,
And where good will ye bare,
   Fayn would ye finde a cloke
Your brennyng fire to hyde: 10
Yet both the flame, and smoke
Breakes out on every syde.
Yee can not love so guide,
That it no issue winnne.
Abrode nedes must it glide,

22 *grave* carve out, wear away
23 *rygour* harshness
29 *prove* test
83 1 *cast* turned aside

That brens so hote within.
   For cause your self do wink,
Ye judge all other blinde:
And secret it you think,
Which every man doth finde.
In wast oft spend ye winde
Your self in love to quit,
For agues of that kinde
Will show, who hath the fit.
   Your sighes you fet from farre,
And all to wry your wo:
Yet are ye neare the narre,
Men ar not blinded so.
Depely oft swere ye no:
But all those othes ar vaine.
So well your eye doth show,
Who puttes your hart to paine.
   Think not therfore to hide,
That still it selfe betraies:
Nor seke meanes to provide
To darke the sunny daies.
Forget those wonted waies:
Leave of such frowning chere:
There will be found no staies
To stoppe a thing so clere.

16 *brens so hote* burns so hot
22 *quit* acquit
25 *fet* heave/contrive
26 *wry* cover   *neare the narre* never the nearer
37 *wonted* accustomed
38 *chere* expression, mood
39 *staies* restraining ropes

84. *The lover praieth not be disdained,*
refused, mistrusted,
nor forsaken.

Disdaine me not without desert:
Nor leave me not so sodenly:
Since well ye wot, that in my hert
I meane ye not but honestly.
   Refuse me not without cause why:
For think me not to be unjust:
Sins that by lot of fantasy,
This carefull knot nedes knit I must.
   Mistrust me not, though some there be,
That faine would spot my stedfastnesse: 10
Beleve them not, sins that ye se,
The proofe is not, as they expresse.
   Forsake me not, till I deserve:
Nor hate me not, till I offend.
Destroy me not, till that I swerve.
But sins ye know what I intend:
   Disdaine me not that am your own:
Refuse me not that am so true:
Mistrust me not till all be known:
Forsake me not, now for no new.   20

84 1 *desert* deserving, justification
    3 *wot* know
    8 *carefull* full of worry, anxiety   *nedes knit I must* I must necessarily knit
  10 *That faine would spot* who would like to mar
  11 *sins* since

85. The lover lamenteth his estate
with sute for grace.

For want of will, in wo I plain:
Under colour of sobernesse.
Renewing with my sute my pain,
My wanhope with your stedfastnesse.
Awake therfore of gentlenesse.
Regard at length, I you require,
My swelting paines of my desire.
    Betimes who giveth willingly,
Redoubled thankes aye doth deserve.
And I that sue unfainedly,
In frutelesse hope (alas) do sterve.
How great my cause is for to swerve:
And yet how stedfast is my sute:
Lo, here ye see, where is the frute?
    As hound that hath his keper lost,
Seke I your presence to obtain:
In which my hart deliteth most,
And shall delight though I be slain.
You may release my band of pain.
Lose then the care that makes me cry,
For want of helpe or els I dye.
    I dye, though not incontinent,
By processe yet consumingly
As waste of fire, which doth relent.
If you as wilfull will deny.

85 *sute* petition
    1 *plain* complain
    4 *wanhope* despair, hopelessness
    5 *of gentlenesse* for the sake of your kindness/gentility
    7 *swelting* sweltering
    8 *Betimes* early
    9 *aye* always
    11 *sterve* die/starve
    20 *care* sorrow, anxiety
    22 *incontinent* straight away

Wherfore cease of such cruelty:
And take me wholy in your grace:
Which lacketh will to change his place.

86. The lover waileth his changed joyes.

If every man might him avaunt
Of fortunes friendly chere:
It was my selfe I must it graunt,
For I have bought it dere.
And derely have I held also
The glory of her name:
In yelding her such tribute, lo.
As did set forth her fame.
    Sometime I stoode so in her grace:
That as I would require,   10
Ech joy I thought did me embrace.
That furdered my desire.
And all those pleasures (lo) had I,
That fansy might support:
And nothing she did me deny,
That was unto my comfort.
    I had (what would you more perde?)
Ech grace that I did crave.
Thus fortunes will was unto me
All thing that I would have.   20
But all to rathe alas the while,
She built on such a ground:
In litle space, to great a guile
In her now have I found.

86 1 *avaunt* boast
    2 *chere* favour
    10 *require* ask
    17 *perde* indeed
    21 *to rathe* too hastily
    23 *In litle space* in a short time   *to* too

For she hath turned so her whele:
That I unhappy man
May waile the time that I dede fele
Wherwith she fed me than.
For broken now are her behestes:
And plesant lookes she gave:
And therfore now all my requestes,
From perill can not save.
   Yet would I well it might appere
To her my chiefe regard:
Though my desertes have been to dere
To merite such reward.
Sith fortunes will is now so bent
To plage me thus poore man:
I must my selfe therwith content:
And beare it as I can.

87. To his love that had geven him answere of refusell.

The answere that ye made to me my dere,
When I did sue for my poore hartes redresse:
Hath so appalde my countenance and my chere:
That in this case, I am all comfortlesse:
Sins I of blame no cause can well expresse.
   I have no wrong, where I can claime no right.
Nought tane me fro, where I have nothing had,
Yet of my wo, I can not so be quite.

27 *fele* experience
29 *behestes* promises
35 *my desertes* what I have deserved   *to dere* too precious
37 *Sith* since
37-8 *so bent / To plage me* so determined to make me suffer
87 3 *appalde* appalled and made pale   *chere* expression, mood
   5 *Sins* since
   7 *tane me fro* taken from me
   8 *quite* released

Namely, sins that another may be glad
With that, that thus in sorow makes me sad.   10
   Yet none can claime (I say) by former graunt,
That knoweth not of any graunt at all.
And by desert, I dare well make avaunt,
Of faithfull will, there is no where that shall
Beare you more truth, more ready at your call.
   Now good then, call againe that bitter word:
That toucht your friende so nere with panges of paine:
And say my dere that it was sayd in bord.
Late, or to sone, let it not rule the gaine,
Wherwith free will doth true desert retaine.   20

88. To his ladie cruel over her
yelden lover

Such is the course, that natures kinde hath wrought,
That snakes have time to cast away their stinges.
Ainst chainde prisoners what nede defence be sought:
The fierce lyon will hurt no yelden thinges:
Why should such spite be nursed then thy thought?
Sith all these powers are prest under thy winges:
And eke thou seest, and reason thee hath taught:
What mischief malice many wayes it bringes:
Consider eke, that spight availeth naught,
Therfore this song thy fault to thee it singes: 10
Displease the not, for saiyng thus (me thought.)

13 *desert* what I have deserved *avaunt* boast
14 *no where* no one
16 *call againe* recall, retract
18 *bord* jest
19 *let it not rule the gaine* don't let it cancel the advantage
20 *desert* deserving
88 1 *kinde* usual way of doing things
  3 *Ainst* against
  4 *yelden* surrendered
  6 *Sith* since *prest* pressed/ready
  7 *eke* also

Nor hate thou him from whom no hate forth springes,
For furies, that in hell be execrable.
For that they hate, are made most miserable.

89. *The lover complaineth that deadly sicknesse can not helpe his affeccion.*

The enmy of life, decayer of all kinde,
That with his cold withers away the grene:
This other night, me in my bed did finde:
And offerd me to ryd my fever clene.
And I dyd graunt: so did dispaire me blinde.
He drew his bowe, with arrowes sharpe and kene:
And strake the place, wher love had hit before:
And drave the first dart deper more and more.

90. *The lover rejoiceth the enjoying of his love.*

Once as me thought, fortune me kist:
And bade me aske, what I thought best:
And I should have it as me list,
Therewith to set my hart in rest.
    I asked but my ladies hart
To have for evermore myne owne:
Then at an end were al my smart:
Then should I nede no more to mone.
    Yet for all that a stormy blast
Had overturnde this goodly nay:
And fortune semed at the last,
That to her promise she said day.

89 1 *kinde* nature, natural things
90 3 *as me list* as it pleased me
   10, 12 *nay . . . day* the rhyme words have been mistakenly transposed

But like as one out of dispayre
To sodain hope revived I.
Now fortune sheweth her selfe so faire,
That I content me wondersly.
   My most desire my hand may reach:
My wyll is al way at my hand.
Me nede not long for to beseche
Her, that hath power me to commaunde.   20
   What earthly thing more can I crave?
What would I wishe more at my will?
Nothing on earth more would I have,
Save that I have, to have it styll.
   For fortune now hath kept her promesse,
In graunting me my most desire.
Of my soveraigne I have redresse,
And I content me with my hire.

91. *The lover complaineth the unkindnes*
of his love.

My lute awake performe the last
Labour that thou and I shal wast:
And end that I have now begonne:
And when this song is song and past:
My lute be stil for I have done.
   As to be heard where eare is none:
As lead to grave in marble stone:
My song may pearse her hart as sone.
Should we then sigh? or singe, or mone?
No, no, my lute for I have done.   10
   The rockes do not so cruelly
Repulse the waves continually,
As she my sute and affection:
So that I am past remedy,
Wherby my lute and I have done.
   Proude of the spoile that thou hast gotte
Of simple hartes through loves shot:

By whom unkind thou hast them wonne,
Thinke not he hath his bow forgot,
20   Although my lute and I have done.

Vengeaunce shall fall on thy disdaine
That makest but game on earnest payne.
Thinke not alone under the sunne
Unquit to cause thy lovers plain:
Although my lute and I have done.

May chance thee lie withered and olde,
In winter nightes that are so colde,
Plaining in vaine unto the mone:
Thy wishes then dare not be tolde.
30   Care then who list, for I have done.

And then may chance thee to repent
The time that thou hast lost and spent
To cause thy lovers sigh and swowne.
Then shalt thou know beaute but lent,
And wish and want as I have done.

Now cease my lute this is the last,
Labour that thou and I shal wast
And ended is that we begonne.
Now is this song both song and past,
40   My lute be still for I have done.

92. *How by a kisse he found both his life and death.*

Nature that gave the Bee so feate a grace,
To finde hony of so wondrous fashion:
Hath taught the spider out of the same place
To fetche poyson by strange alteracion.
Though this be strange, it is a straunger case,

91 24 *Unquit* unpunished   *plain* to complain
    26 *May chance thee* it may happen to be your fate to
    28 *mone* moon
    30 *list* pleases
92 1 *feate* nimble

With one kisse by secret operacion,
Both these at once in those your lipps to finde,
In change wherof, I leave my hart behinde.

93. The lover describeth his being
taken with sight of
his love.

Unwarely so was never no man caught,
With stedfast loke upon a goodly face:
As I of late: for sodainely me thought,
My hart was torne out of hys place.

Thorow mine eye the stroke from hers did slide,
And downe directly to my hart it ranne:
In helpe wherof the blood therto did glide,
And left my face both pale and wanne.

Then was I like a man for wo amased:
Or like the fowle that fleeth into the fier.   10
For while that I upon her beauty gased:
The more I burnd in my desire.

Anone the bloud start in my face againe,
Inflamde with heat, that it had at my hart.
And brought therwith through out in every vayne,
A quaking heate with pleasant smart.

Then was I like the straw, when that the flame
Is driven therin, by force, and rage of winde.
I can not tell, alas, what I shall blame:
Nor what to seke, nor what to finde.   20

But well I wot: the griefe doth hold me sore
In heat and cold, betwixt both hope and dreade:
That, but her helpe to health do me restore:
This restlesse life I may not lead.

8 *In change wherof* in exchange for which
93 14 *had at* got from
21 *wot* know
23 *but* unless

94. To his lover to loke upon him.

Al in thy loke my life doth whole depende.
Thou hydest thy self, and I must dye therfore.
But sins thou mayst so easily helpe thy frend:
Why dost thou stick to salve that thou madest sore?
Why do I dye? sins thou maist me defend:
And if I dye, thy lyfe may last no more.
For eche by other doth live and have reliefe,
I in thy loke, and thou most in my griefe.

95. The lover excuseth him of wordes wherwith he was unjustly charged.

Perdy I sayd it not:
Nor never thought to do.
As well as I ye wot:
I have no power therto,
And if I did, the lot,
That first did me enchayne:
May never slake the knot,
But strayght it to my payne.
    And if I did ech thing,
That may do harme or wo:
Continually may wring
My hart where so I go.
Report may alwayes ring

10

94 3 *sins* since
   4 *stick* hesitate
95 1 *Perdy* by God
   3 You know as well as I do
   5 *lot* fate, chance
   8 But tighten it to make me suffer more

Of shame on me for aye:
If in my hart did spring
The wordes that you do say
    And if I did ech starre,
That is in heaven above,
May frowne on me to marre
The hope I have in love.   20
And if I did such warre,
As they brought unto Troye,
Bring all my life as farre
From all his lust and joye.
    And if I did so say:
The beautie that me bounde,
Encrease from day to day
More cruel to my wounde:
With al the mone that may,
To plaint may turne my song: 30
My life may sone decay,
Without redresse by wrong.
    If I be cleare from thought,
Why do you then complayne?
Then is this thing but sought.
To turne my hart to payne,
Then this that you have wrought,
You must it now redresse,
Of ryght therfore you ought
Such rigour to represse.   40
    And as I have deserved:
So graunt me now my hire:
You know I never swarved.
You never founde me lier.
For Rachel have I served,
For Lea cared I never:
And her I have reserved
Within my hart for ever.

14 *for aye* for ever
24 *lust* pleasure
30 *plaint* poetic complaint, expressing injustice or sorrow

96. Of such as had forsaken him.

Lux, my faire fawlcon, and thy felowes all:
How well pleasant it were your libertie:
Ye not forsake me, that faire mought you fal.
But they that sometime liked my company:
Like lice away from deade bodies they crall.
Loe, what a proofe in light adversitie?
But ye my birdes, I sweare by all your belles,
Ye be my frendes, and very few elles.

97. A description of such a one as he would love.

A face that should content me wonderous wel,
Should not be faire, but lovely to behold:
Of lively loke, all griefe for to repel:
With right good grace, so would I that it should
Speake without word, such wordes as none can tel,
Her tresse also should be of crisped gold.
With wit, and these perchance I might be tride,
And knit againe with knot, that should not slide.

98. How unpossible it is to finde quiet in love.

Ever my hap is slack and slowe in comming
Desire encreasyng ay my hope uncertaine:
With doubtful love that but increaseth pain
For Tigre like so swift it is in parting.
Alas the snow black shal it be and scalding,

96 3 *that faire mought you fal* in order to have a happier fate
98 1 *hap* happiness, good fortune
    2 *ay* always

The sea waterles, and fishe upon the mountaine:
The Temis shal back retourne into his fountaine:
And wher he rose the sunne shal take his lodging.
Ere I in this finde peace or quietnesse.
Or that love or my lady rightwisely   10
Leave to conspire against me wrongfully.
And if I have after such bitternesse,
One drop of swete, my mouth is out of taste:
That al my trust and travell is but waste.

99. Of love, fortune, and the lovers minde.

Love, Fortune, and my minde which do remember
Eke that is now, and that that once hath bene:
Torment my hart so sore that very often
I hate and envy them beyonde al measure.
Love sleeth my hart while Fortune his depriver
Of all my comfort: the folishe minde than:
Burneth and plainth: as one that very sildam.
Liveth in rest. So styl in displeasure
My pleasant daies they flete away and passe.
And dayly doth myne yll change to the worse.   10
While more then halfe is runne now of my course.
Alas not of stele, but of brittle glasse,
I se that from my hand falleth my trust:
And all my thoughtes are dasshed into dust.

7 *The Temis* the River Thames
9 *Ere* before
10 *rightwisely* righteously
11 *Leave to conspire* leave off conspiring
14 *travail* labour
99 2 *Eke* both
  5 *sleeth* slays
  6 *than* then

100. *The lover praieth his offred hart to be received.*

How oft have I, my deare and cruel fo:
With my great pain to get som peace or truce,
Geven you my hart? but you do not use,
In so hie thinges, to cast your minde so low,
If any other loke for it, as you trow,
Their vaine weake hope doth greatly them abuse,
And that thus I disdaine, that you refuse.
It was once mine, it can no more be so.
If you it chase, that it in you can finde,
In this exile, no maner of comfort:
Nor live alone, nor where he is calde, resort,
He may wander from his naturall kinde.
So shall it be great hurt unto us twayne,
And yours the losse, and mine the deadly payne.

101. *The lovers life compared to the Alpes.*

Lyke unto these unmesurable mountaines,
So is my painefull life, the burden of yre.
For hye be they, and hye is my desire.
And I of teares, and they be full of fountaines.
Under craggy rockes they have barren plaines,
Hard thoughtes in me my wofull minde doth tire,
Small frute and many leaves their toppes do attire,
With small effect great trust in me remaines.
The boystous windes oft their hie boughes do blast:
Hote sighes in me continually be shed.

---

100 3 *you do not use* you are not accustomed
   5 *trow* believe
   9 If you chase my heart out, so that it can find in you
101 6 *tire* tear (as a falcon tears its prey)

Wilde beastes in them, fierce love in me is fed.
Unmoveable am I: and they stedfast.
Of singing birdes they have the tune and note:
And I alwaies plaintes passing through my throte.

102. *Charging of his love as unpetious and loving other.*

If amorous fayth, or if an hart unfained
A swete languor, a great lovely desire:
If honest will, kindled in gentle fire:
If long errour in a blind mase chained,
If in my visage ech thought distained:
Or if my sparkelyng voice, lower, or hier,
Which feare and shame, so wofully doth tyre:
If pale colour, which love alas hath stained:
If to have another then my self more dere,
If wailing or sighing continually,   10
With sorowfull anger feding busily
If burning farre of, and if frysing nere,
Are cause that I by love my selfe destroy:
Yours is the fault, and mine the great annoy.

103. *A renouncing of love.*

Farewell, Love, and all thy lawes for ever,
Thy bayted hookes shall tangle me no more.
Senec, and Plato call me from thy lore:
To parfit wealth my wit for to endever.

14 *plaintes* poetic complaints, expressing injustice or sorrow
102 *unpetious* pitiless
4 *errour* wandering
7 *tyre* dress/exhaust
12 *of* off
14 *annoy* pain, trouble

In blinde errour when I did parsever:
Thy sharp repulse, that pricketh aye so sore:
Taught me in trifles that I set no store:
But scape forth thence: since libertie is lever.
Therefore, farewell: go trouble yonger hartes:
And in me claime no more auctoritie.
With ydle youth go use thy propartie:
And theron spend thy many brittle dartes.
For, hitherto though I have lost my time:
Me list no lenger rotten bowes to clime.

104. *The lover forsaketh his unkinde love.*

My hart I gave thee, not to do it pain:
But to preserve, lo it to thee was taken.
I served thee not that I should be forsaken:
But, that I should receive reward again,
I was content thy servant to remain:
And not to be repayed on this fashion.
Now, since in thee there is none other reason:
Displease thee not, if that I do refrain.
Unsaciat of my wo, and thy desire.
Assured by craft for to excuse thy fault.
But, sins it pleaseth thee to fain default:
Farewell, I say, departing from the fire.
For, he, that doth beleve bearing in hand:
Ploweth in the water: and soweth in the sand.

103 6 *aye* always
     8 *lever* preferable
    13 *lost* wasted
    14 *Me list* I prefer
104 11 *sins* since
    13 *bearing in hand* stringing along

105. *The lover describeth his*
restlesse state.

The flaming sighes that boyle within my brest
Somtime breake forth and thei can well declare
The hartes unrest and how that it doth fare,
The pain therof the grief and all the rest.
The watred eyen from whence the teares do fall,
Do fele some force or els they would be dry:
The wasted flesh of colour ded can try,
And somtime tell what swetenes is in gall.
And he that lust to see and to disarne,
How care can force within a weried minde: 10
Come he to me I am that place assinde,
But for all this no force it doth no harme.
The wound alas happe in some other place:
From whence no toole away the skar can race.
   But you that of such like have had your part,
Can best bejudge. Wherfore my friend so deare:
I thought it good my state should now appeare.
To you and that there is no great desart.
And wheras you in weighty matters great:
Of fortune saw the shadow that you know,   20
For trifling thinges I now am striken so
That though I fele my hart doth wound and beat:
I sit alone save on the second day:
My fever comes with whom I spend my time,
In burning heat while that she list assigne.
And who hath helth and libertie alway:
Let him thank God and let him not provoke,
To have the like of this my painfull stroke.

105 10 *care* sorrow, anxiety
  12 *no force* it doesn't matter
  14 *race* erase
  25 *while that she list assigne* while it's her pleasure so to command
  26 *who* whoever

106. *The lover lamentes the death of his love.*

The piller perisht is wherto I lent,
The strongest stay of mine unquiet minde:
The like of it no man again can finde:
From East to West still seking though he went.
To mine unhappe for happe away hath rent,
Of all my joy the very bark and rinde:
And I (alas) by chance am thus assinde,
Dayly to moorne till death do it relent.
But sins that thus it is by desteny,
What can I more but have a wofull hart,
My penne, in plaint, my voyce in carefull cry:
My minde in wo, my body full of smart,
And I my self, my selfe alwaies to hate,
Till dreadfull death do ease my dolefull state.

107. *The lover sendeth sighes to mone his sute.*

Go burning sighes unto the frosen hart,
Go breake the yse with pities painfull dart.
Might never perce and if that mortall praier,
In heaven be heard, at lest yet I desire.
That death or mercy end my wofull smart.
Take with thee pain, wherof I have my part,
And eke the flame from which I cannot start.
And leave me then in rest, I you require:

106 2 *stay* support
    5 *happe* chance, fortune
    9 *sins* since
   11 *plaint* poetic complaint, expressing injustice or sorrow
       carefull full of sorrow, anxiety
107 4 *at lest* at least/at last
    7 *eke* also   *start* escape

Go burning sighes fulfill that I desire.
I must go worke I see by craft and art, 10
For truth and faith in her is laid apart:
Alas, I can not therfore now assaile her,
With pitefull complaint and scalding fier,
That from my brest disceivably doth start.

108. *Complaint of the absence of his love.*

So feble is the threde, that doth the burden stay,
Of my poore life: in heavy plight, that falleth in decay:
That, but it have elswhere some ayde or some succours:
The running spindle of my fate anone shall end his course.
For sins thunhappy hower, that did me to depart,
From my swete weale: one onely hope hath staied my
    life, apart:
Which doth perswade such wordes unto my sored minde:
Maintain thy self, O wofull wight, some better luck to
    finde.
For though thou be deprived from thy desired sight:
Who can thee tell, if thy returne be for thy more delight? 10
Or, who can tell, thy losse if thou mayst once recover?
Some pleasant hower thy wo may wrap: and thee
    defend, & cover
Thus in this trust as yet it hath my life sustained:
But now (alas) I see it faint: and I, by trust, am trayned.
The time doth flete, and I see how the howers, do bend
So fast: that I have scant the space to marke my comming
    end,

14 that leaps from my breast deceptively (i.e. it seems hot, but won't melt her)
108 1 *stay* support
    3 *but* unless
    5 *sins* since   *thunhappy* the unhappy
    6 *weale* well-being
    8 *wight* person
    14 *trayned* trapped

Westward the sunne from out the East scant shewes his
    light:
When in the West he hies him strayt, within the dark of
    night.
And comes as fast, where he began, his path awry.
From East to West, from West to East so doth his
20   journey lye.
The life so short, so fraile, that mortall men live here:
So great a weight, so heavy charge the bodies, that
    we bere:
That, when I think upon the distaunce, and the space:
That doth so farre devide me from my dere desired
    face:
I know not, how tattain the winges, that I require,
To lift me up: that I might flie, to folow my desire.
Thus of that hope, that doth my life some thing sustaine,
Alas: I feare, and partly fele: full litle doth remain.
Eche place doth bring me grief: where I do not behold
Those lively eyes: which of my thoughts wer wont
30   the keys to hold,
Those thoughts wer pleasant swete: whilst I enjoyed
    that grace:
My pleasure past, my present pain, when I might well
    embrace.
And, forbecause my want should more my wo encrease:
In watch, and slepe, both day and night, my will doth
    never cease
That thing to wish: wherof sins I did lese the sight:
Was never thing that mought in ought my wofull
    hart delight,
Thuneasy life, I lead, doth teach me for to mete

19 *path awry* oblique path
25 *tattain* to attain
35 *lese* lose
36 *mought in ought* might in any way
37 *Thuneasy* the uneasy   *mete* measure/dream, imagine

The floodes, the seas, the land, the hilles: that doth them
    entermete
Twene me, and those shene lightes: that wonted for
    to clere
My darked pangs of cloudy thoughts, as bright as Phebus
    spere   40
It teacheth me also, what was my pleasant state:
The more to fele, by such record, how that my wealth
    doth bate.
If such record (alas) provoke thenflamed minde:
Which sprong that day, that I did leave the best of me
    behinde:
If love forget himself, by length of absence let:
Who doth me guyde (O wofull wretch) unto this
    bayted net?
Where doth encrease my care: much better wer for me,
As dumme, as stone, all thing forgot, still absent for
    to be.
Alas: the clere christall, the bright transplendant glasse
Doth not bewray the colours hid, which underneth
    it hase: 50
As doth thaccumbred sprite the thoughtfull throwes
    discover,
Of feares delite, of fervent love: that in our hartes
    we cover.
Out by these eyes, it sheweth that evermore delight.
In plaint, and teares to seke redresse: and eke both
    day and night.

38 *entermete* place between
39 *shene* shining
42 *record* recollection   *bate* lessen, come to an end
43 *thenflamed* the enflamed
45 *let* obstructed
47 *care* sorrow, anxiety
49 *transplendant* brilliantly translucent
50 *bewray* reveal
51 *thaccumbred sprite* the encumbered soul/spirit   *throwes* throes
54 *plaint* poetic complaint, expressing injustice or sorrow   *eke* also

Those kindes of pleasures most wherein men so rejoyce,
To me they do redouble still of stormy sighes the voyce.
For, I am one of them, whom plaint doth well content:
It sits me well myne absent wealth me semes for to
    lament:
And with my teares, tassay to charge mine eyes twain:
60 Like as my hart above the brink is fraughted full of pain.
And forbecause, thereto, that those faire eyes to treate
Do me provoke: I will returne, my plaint thus to repeate.
For, there is nothing els, so toucheth me within:
Where they rule all: and I alone nought but the case,
    or skin.
Wherefore, I shall returne to them, as well, or spring:
From whom descendes my mortall wo, above all
    other thing.
So shall mine eyes in pain accompany my hart,
That were the guides, that did it lead of love to fele
    the smart.
The crisped gold, that doth surmount Apollos pride:
The lively streames of pleasant starres that under it
70   doth glide:
Wherein the beames of love do still encrease their heate:
Which yet so farre touch me so nere, in cold to make me
    sweate.
The wise and pleasant talk, so rare, or els alone:
That gave to me the curteis gift, that erst had never none:
Be farre from me, alas: and every other thing
I might forbeare with better will: then this that did
    me bring
With pleasant woord and chere, redresse of lingred pain:
And wonted oft in kindled will to vertue me to train.
Thus, am I forst to heare, and harken after newes.

59 *tassay* to try
73 *alone* unique
74 *curteis* courteous/welcome   *erst* before
76 *forbeare* tolerate the absence of
77 *chere* expression

My comfort scant, my large desire in doutfull trust
  renewes.   80
And yet with more delite to mone my wofull case:
I must complain those hands, those armes: that firmly
  do embrace
Me from my self: and rule the sterne of my poore life:
The swete disdaines, the pleasant wrathes, and eke
  the lovely strife
That wonted well to tune in temper just, and mete,
The rage: that oft did make me erre, by furour undiscrete.
All this is hid fro me, with sharp, and ragged hilles:
At others will, my long abode my depe dispaire fulfils.
And if my hope sometime rise up, by some redresse:
It stumbleth straite, for feable faint: my feare hath
  such excesse.   90
Such is the sort of hope: the lesse for more desyre:
And yet I trust ere that I dye to see that I require:
The resting place of love: where vertue dwelles and growes
There I desire, my wery life, somtime, may take repose.
My song: thou shalt attain to finde that pleasant place:
Where she doth live, by whom I live: may chance to
  have this grace
When she hath red, and sene the grief, wherin I serve:
Betwene her brestes she shall thee put: there, shall
  she the reserve.
Then, tell her, that I come: she shall me shortly see:
And if for waighte the body fayle, the soule shall
  to her flee.   100

85 *mete* fitting
86 *furour* rage
88 *my long abode my depe dispaire fulfils* my long wait fills up my deep
  despair
91 *sort* fate
92 *ere that* before
98 *the* thee

109. *The lover blameth his love for renting of the letter he sent her.*

Suffised not (madame) that you did teare,
My woful hart, but thus also to rent:
The weping paper that to you I sent.
Wherof eche letter was written with a teare.
Could not my present paines, alas suffise.
Your gredy hart? and that my hart doth fele,
Tormentes that prick more sharper then the stele,
But new and new must to my lot arise.
Use then my death. So shall your cruelty:
Spite of your spite rid me from all my smart,
And I no more such tormentes of the hart:
Fele as I do. This shall you gain thereby.

110. *The lover curseth the time when first he fell in love.*

When first mine eyes did view, and marke,
Thy faire beawtie to behold:
And when mine eares listned to harke:
The pleasant wordes, that thou me told:
I would as then, I had been free,
From eares to heare, and eyes to see.
And when my lips gan first to move,
Wherby my hart to thee was knowne:
And when my tong did talk of love,
To thee that hast true love down throwne:
I would, my lips, and tong also:
Had then bene dum, no deale to go.

---

109 2 *rent* tear
110 7 *gan* began
    12 *no deale to go* not to move at all

And when my handes have handled ought,
That thee hath kept in memorie:
And when my feete have gone, and sought
To finde and get thee companie:
I would, eche hand a foote had bene,
And I eche foote a hand had sene.
And when in minde I did consent
To folow this my fansies will:
And when my hart did first relent,
To taste such bayt, my life to spill:
I would, my hart had bene as thine:
Or els thy hart had bene, as mine.

111. *The lover determineth to serve faithfully.*

Synce love will nedes, that I shall love:
Of very force I must agree.
And since no chance may it remove:
In wealth, and in adversitie,
I shall alway my self apply
To serve and suffer paciently.
    Though for good will I finde but hate:
And cruelty my life to wast:
And though that still a wretched state
Should pine my daies unto the last:
Yet I professe it willingly,
To serve, and suffer paciently.
    For since my hart is bound to serve:
And I not ruler of mine owne:
What so befall, till that I sterve.
By proofe full well it shall be knowne:

20

10

13 *ought* anything
111 2 *Of very force* by necessity
  10 *pine* torment
  15 *sterve* die

That I shall still my selfe apply
To serve, and suffer paciently.
    Yea though my grief finde no redresse:
20 But still increase before mine eyes:
Though my reward be cruelnesse,
With all the harme, happe can devise:
Yet I professe it willingly
To serve and suffer paciently.
    Yea though fortune her pleasant face
Should shew, to set me up a loft:
And straight, my wealth for to deface,
Should writhe away, as she doth oft:
Yet would I still my selfe apply
30 To serve and suffer paciently.
    There is no grief, no smart, no wo:
That yet I feele, or after shall:
That from this minde may make me go,
And what so ever me befal:
I do professe it willingly
To serve and suffer paciently.

112. *The lover suspected blameth yll tonges.*

Mystrustfull mindes be moved
To have me in suspect.
The troth it shalbe proved:
Which time shall once detect.
    Though falshed go about
Of crime me to accuse:
At length I do not dout,

22 *happe* chance, fortune
27 *straight* immediately
112 4 *once* one day

But truth shall me excuse.
Such sawce, as they have served
To me without desart: 10
Even as they have deserved:
Therof God send them part.

113. *The lover complaineth and his ladie comforteth.*

Lover. It burneth yet, alas my hartes desire.
Ladye.   What is the thing, that hath inflamde thy hert?
Lover. A certain point, as fervent, as the fire.
Ladye.   The heate shall cease, if that thou wilt convert.
Lover. I cannot stop the fervent raging yre.
La.   What may I do, if thy self cause thy smart?
Lo.   Heare my request, and rew weping chere.
La.   With right good will, say on: lo, I thee here.
Lo.   That thing would I, that maketh two content.
La.   Thou sekest, perchance, of me, that I may not.   10
Lo.   Would god, thou wouldst, as thou maist, well
                 assent.
La.   That I may not, the grief is mine: God wot.
Lo.   But I it fele, what so thy wordes have ment.
La.   Suspect me not: my wordes be not forgot.
Lo.   Then say, alas: shall I have helpe? or no.
La.   I see no time to answer, yea, but no.
Lo.   Say ye, dere hart: and stand no more in dout.
La.   I may not grant a thing, that is so dere
Lo.   Lo, with delaies thou drieves me still about.
La.   Thou wouldest my death: it plainly doth appere.   20
Lo.   First, may my hart his blood, and life blede out

113 7 *chere* expression
  12 *wot* knows
  13 *what so* whatever
  17 *ye* yes

La.	Then for my sake, alas, thy will forbere.
Lo.	From day to day, thus wastes my life away.
La.	Yet, for the best, suffer some small delay.
Lo.	Now, good, say yea: do once so good a dede.
La.	If I sayd yea: what should therof ensue?
Lo.	An hart in pain of succour so should spede.
	Twixt yea, and nay, my doute shal still renew.
	My swete, say yea: and do away this drede.
La.	Thou wilt nedes so: be it so: but then be trew.
Lo.	Nought would I els, nor other treasure none,
	Thus, hartes be wonne, by love, request, and mone.

30 La.

114. Why love is blind.

Of purpose, love chose first for to be blinde:
For, he with sight of that, that I beholde,
Vanquisht had been, against all godly kinde.
His bow your hand, and trusse should have unfolde.
And he with me to serve had bene assinde.
But, for he blinde, and recklesse would him holde:
And still, by chance, his dedly strokes bestowe:
With such, as see, I serve, and suffer wo.

115. To his unkinde love.

What rage is this? what furor? of what kinde?
What power, what plage doth wery thus my minde:
Within my bones to rankle is assinde
What poyson pleasant swete?

27 *spede* succeed
114 3 *kinde* nature
   4 Your hand would have loosened his bow and his bundle of arrows
   6 Because he wanted to keep himself blind and free of worries
115 2 *plage* blow, suffering, plague

Lo, see, myne eyes flow with continuall teares:
The body still away slepelesse it weares:
My foode nothing my fainting strength repaires,
Nor doth my limmes sustain.
    In depe wide wound, the dedly stroke doth turne:
To cureles skarre that never shall returne.   10
Go to: triumph: rejoyce thy goodly turne:
Thy frend thou doest oppresse.
    Oppresse thou doest: and hast of him no cure:
Nor yet my plaint no pitie can procure.
Fierce Tigre, fell, hard rock without recure:
Cruel rebell to Love,
    Once may thou love, never beloved again:
So love thou styll, and not thy love obtain:
So wrathfull love, with spites of just disdain,
May thret thy cruell hart.   20

116. The lover blameth his instant desire.

Desire (alas) my master, and my fo:
So sore altered thy self how mayst thou see?
Sometime thou sekest, that drives me to and fro.
Sometime, thou leadst, that leadeth the and me.
What reason is to rule thy subjectes so?
By forced law, and mutabilitie.
For where by thee I douted to have blame:
Even now by hate again I dout the same.

13 *cure* care
14 *plaint*: poetic complaint, expression of injustice or sorrow
116 *instant* peremptory
 4 *the* thee
 7 *douted* feared

117. *The lover complaineth his estate.*

I see, that chance hath chosen me
Thus secertly to live in paine:
And to an other geven the fee
Of al my losse to have the gayn.
By chance assinde thus do I serve:
And other have, that I deserve.
   Unto my self sometime alone
I do lament my woful case.
But what availeth me to mone?
Since troth, and pitie hath no place
In them: to whom I sue and serve:
And other have, that I deserve.
   To seke by meane to change this minde:
Alas, I prove, it will not be.
For in my hart I cannot finde
Once to refraine, but styl agre,
As bound by force, alway to serve:
And other have that I deserve.
   Such is the fortune, that I have
To love them most, that love me lest:
And to my paine to seke, and crave
The thing, that other have possest.
So thus in vain alway I serve.
And other have, that I deserve.
   And tyll I may apease the heate:
If that my happe wyll happe so well:
To waile my wo my hart shal freate:

117 2 *secertly* misprint for 'secretly'
  13 *meane* any means
  14 *prove* discover
  26 *happe wyll happe* my fortune will come out
  27 *freate* waste away

Whose pensif pain my tong can tell.
Yet thus unhappy must I serve:
And other have, that I deserve.   30

118. Of his love called
Anna.

What word is that, that changeth not,
Though it be turned & made in twaine:
It is mine Anna god it wot.
The only causer of my paine:
My love that medeth with disdaine.
Yet is it loved what will you more,
It is my salve, and eke my sore.

119. That pleasure is mixed
with every
paine.

Venemous thrones that are so sharp and kene,
Beare flowers we se full fresh and faire of hue.
Poison is also put in medicine.
And unto man his helth doth oft renue.
The fier that all thinges eke consumeth cleane
May hurt and heale: then if that this be true.
I trust sometime my harme may be my health,
Sins every woe is joyned with some wealth.

118 3 *wot* knows
    5 *medeth* is rewarded
    7 *salve* remedy   *eke* also
119 1 *thrones* misprint for 'thorns', but see explanatory note
    5 *eke* also
    8 *Sins* since

120. A riddle of a gift geven by a Ladie.

A Lady gave me a gift she had not,
And I received her gift which I toke not,
She gave it me willingly, and yet she would not,
And I received it, albeit, I could not,
If she give it me, I force not,
And if she take it againe she cares not.
Conster what this is and tel not,
For I am fast sworne I may not.

121. That speaking or profering bringes alway speding.

Speake thou and spede where will or power ought helpth,
Where power doth want wil must be wonne by welth.
For nede will spede, where will workes not his kinde,
And gaine, thy foes thy frendes shall cause thee finde.
For sute and golde, what do not they obtaine,
Of good and bad the triers are these twaine.

122. He ruleth not though he raigne over realmes that is subject to his own lustes.

If thou wilt mighty be, flee from the rage
Of cruel will, and see thou kepe thee free
From the foule yoke of sensuall bondage,

120 5 *I force not* I don't care
7 *Conster* interpret
121 *speding* success
1 *spede* succeed   *ought* anything, in any way

For though thyne empyre stretche to Indian sea,
And for thy feare trembleth the fardest Thylee,
If thy desire have over thee the power,
Subject then art thou and no governour.
   If to be noble and high thy minde be meved,
Consider well thy ground and thy beginning:
For he that hath eche starre in heaven fixed,   10
And geves the Moone her hornes and her eclipsing:
Alike hath made the noble in his working,
So that wretched no way may thou bee.
Except foule lust and vice do conquer thee.
   All were it so thou had a flood of gold,
Unto thy thirst yet should it not suffice.
And though with Indian stones a thousand folde,
More precious then can thy selfe devise,
Ycharged were thy backe: thy covitise
And busy biting yet should never let,   20
Thy wretched life, ne do thy death profet.

123. *Whether libertie by losse of life, or life in prison and thraldom be to be preferred.*

Lyke as the birde within the cage enclosed,
The dore unsparred, her foe the Hawke without,
Twixt death and prison piteously oppressed,
Whether for to chose standeth in dout,
Lo, so do I, which seke to bring about,
Which should be best by determinacion,
By losse of life libertie, or life by prison.
   O mischiefe by mischiefe to be redressed.

122 8 *meved* moved
  15 *All were it so* even if
  18 *devise* imagine
  20 *let* cease
123 6 *determinacion* determining through thought

Where pain is best there lieth but litle pleasure,
By short death better to be delivered,
Than bide in painfull life, thraldome, and doler,
Small is the pleasure where much pain we suffer.
Rather therfore to chuse me thinketh wisdome,
By losse of life libertie, then life by prison.

    And yet me thinkes although I live and suffer,
I do but waite a time and fortunes chance:
Oft many thinges do happen in one houer.
That which opprest me now may me advance.
In time is trust which by deathes grevance
Is wholy lost. Then were it not reason,
By death to chuse libertie, and not life by prison.

    But death wer deliverance wher life lengths pain.
Of these two ylles let see now chuse the best:
This bird to deliver that here doth plain,
What say ye lovers? which shall be the best?
In cage thraldome, or by the Hawke opprest.
And which to chuse make plain conclusion,
By losse of life libertie, or life by prison.

124. *Against hourders of money.*

For shamfast harm of great, and hatefull nede:
In depe dispaire, as did a wretch go,
With ready corde, out of his life to spede:
His stumbling foote did finde an hoorde, lo,
Of gold, I say: where he preparde this dede:
And in eschange, he left the corde, tho.
He, that had hid the gold, and found it not:
Of that, he found, he shapte his neck a knot.

    16 *a* on
    24 *plain* complain
124 1 *shamfast* suffering from shame (here)
     6 *tho* then, there

125. *Discription of a gonne.*

Vulcane begat me: Minerva me taught:
Nature, my mother: Craft nourisht me yere by yere:
Thre bodies are my foode: my strength is in naught:
Anger, wrath, wast, and noyce are my children dere,
Gesse friend, what I am: and how I am wraught:
Monster of sea, or of land, or of els where.
Know me, and use me: and I may thee defend:
And if I be thine enmy, I may thy life end.

126. *Wiate being in prison, to Brian.*

Syghes are my foode: my drink are my teares.
Clinking of fetters would such musick crave.
Stink, and close ayre away my life it weares.
Poore innocence is all the hope I have.
Rain, winde, or wether judge I by mine eares.
Malice assaultes, that righteousnesse should have.
Sure am I, Brian, this wound shall heale again:
But yet alas, the skarre shall still remain.

127. *Of dissembling wordes.*

Throughout the world if it wer sought,
Faire wordes inough a man shall finde:
They be good chepe they cost right nought.
Their substance is but onely winde:
But well to say and so to mene,
That swete acord is seldom sene.

125 4 *noyce* annoyance/noise/uproar
127 3 *good chepe* bargains

128. *Of the meane and sure estate.*

Stond who so list upon the slipper wheele,
Of hye astate and let me here rejoyce.
And use my life in quietnesse eche dele,
Unknowen in court that hath the wanton toyes,
In hidden place my time shal slowly passe
And when my yeres be past withouten noyce
Let me dye olde after the common trace
For gripes of death doth he to hardly passe
That knowen is to all: but to him selfe alas,
He dyeth unknowen, dased with dreadfull face.

10

129. *The courtiers life*

In court to serve decked with fresh aray,
Of sugred meates feling the swete repast:
The life in bankets, and sundry kindes of play,
Amid the presse of worldly lookes to waste,
Hath with it joynde oft times such bitter taste.
That who so joyes such kinde of life to hold,
In prison joyes fettred with cheines of gold.

128 1 Let whoever wants to do so stand on the slippery/uncertain wheel
    3 *eche dele* all the time, every bit
    6 *noyce* annoyance
    7 *after the common trace* in the normal run of things
    8 *to* too *passe* suffer
129 1 *aray* clothing
    2 *meates* dishes
    3 *bankets* banquets
    4 *presse* crowd
    7 *joyes* feels joy

130. Of disapointed purpose by negligence.

Of Carthage he that worthy warriour
Could overcome, but could not use his chance
And I likewise of all my long endevour
The sharpe conquest though fortune did advance,
Ne could I use. The hold that is geven over,
I unposess, so hangeth now in balance
Of warre, my peace, reward of all my paine,
At Mountzon thus I restlesse rest in Spaine.

131. Of his returne from Spaine.

Tagus farewell that Westward with thy stremes
Turnes up the graines of gold already tried,
For I with spurre and saile go seke the temmes.
Gaineward the sunne that sheweth her welthy pride,
And to the town that Brutus sought by dreames,
Like bended mone that leanes her lusty side.
My king, my countrey, I seke for whom I live,
O mighty Jove the windes for this me give.

132. Of sodaine trusting.

Driven by desire I did this dede
To danger my self without cause why:

130 5 *hold* stronghold
131 2 *tried* sifted
   3 *temmes* Thames
   4 *Gaineward* in the opposite direction to
   6 *mone* moon

To trust thuntrue not like to spede,
To speake and promise faithfully:
But now the proofe doth verifie,
That who so trusteth ere he know,
Doth hurt himselfe and please his foe,

133. Of the mother that eat her childe at the seige of Jerusalem.

In doubtfull breast whiles motherly pity
With furious famine standeth at debate,
The mother sayth: O chyld unhappy
Returne thy bloud where thou hadst milke of late
Yeld me those limmes that I made unto thee,
And enter there where thou were generate.
For one of body against all nature,
To an other must I make sepulture.

134. Of the meane and sure estate writen to John Poins.

My mothers maides when they do sowe and spinne:
They sing a song made of the feldishe mouse:
That forbicause her livelod was but thinne,
Would nedes go se her townish sisters house,
She thought, her selfe endured to grevous paine,
The stormy blastes her cave so sore dyd sowse:
That when the furrowes swimmed with the raine:
She must lie colde, and wet in sory plight.

132 3 Trusting the untrue is not likely to prosper
     6 *ere* before
133 8 *sepulture* tomb
134 2 *feldishe mouse* fieldmouse, or country mouse
     3 *livelod* livelihood
     5 *endured* possibly a confusion with inured

And worse then that, bare meat there did remaine
To comfort her, when she her house had dight: 10
Sometime a barly corne: sometime a beane:
For which she laboured hard both day and night,
In harvest time, while she might go and gleane.
And when her store was stroyed with the floode:
Then weleaway for she undone was cleane.
Then was she faine to take in stede of fode,
Slepe if she might, her honger to begile.
My sister (quod she) hath a living good:
And hence from me she dwelleth not a mile.
In colde and storme, she lieth warme and dry,   20
In bed of downe: the durt doth not defile
Her tender fote, she labours not as I,
Richely she fedes, and at the richemans cost:
And for her meat she nedes not crave nor cry.
By sea, by land, of delicates the most
Her cater sekes, and spareth for no perell:
She fedes on boyle meat, bake meat, and on rost:
And hath therefore no whit of charge nor travell.
And when she list the licour of the grape
Doth glad her hart, tyll that her belly swell.   30
And at this journey makes she but a jape:
So forth she goes, trusting of all this wealth,
With her sister her part so for to shape:
That if she might there kepe her self in health:

9 *meat* food
10 *dight* put in order
14 *stroyed with* destroyed by
15 *weleaway* alas (with connotations of well-being [weal] having gone away)
   undone was cleane was completely destroyed
16 *faine* willing
17 *begile* distract
18 *quod* said
26 *cater* provisioner
28 *travell* labour
29 *list* pleases
31 *makes she but a jape* she considers it a mere trifle
33 To arrange to share with her sister

To live a Lady while her life doth last.
And to the dore nowe is she come by stealth:
And with her fote anone she scarpes full fast.
Thother for fear, durst not well scarse appeare:
Of every noyse so was the wretch agast.
40   At last, she asked softly who was there.
And in her language as well as she could,
Pepe (quod the other) sister I am here.
Peace (quod the towne mouse) why speakest thou so loude?
And by the hand she toke her faire and well.
Welcome (quod she) my sister by the rode.
She feasted her that joye it was to tell
The fare they hadde, they dranke the wine so clere:
And as to purpose now and then it fell:
She chered her, with how sister what chere?
50   Amid this joye be fell a sory chance:
That (weleaway) the stranger bought full dere
The fare she had. For as she lookt a scance:
Under a stole she spied two stemyng eyes
In a rounde head, wyth sharpe eares: in Fraunce
Was never mouse so ferde, for the unwise
Had not ysene such a beast before.
Yet had nature taught her after her gise,
To know her fo: and dread him evermore.
The townemouse fled: she knew whither to go:
60   The other had no shift, but wonders sore
Ferde of her life, at home she wisht her tho:
And to the dore (alas) as she did skippe:
The heaven it would, lo: and eke her chance was so:
At the threshold her sely fote did trippe:

37 *scarpes* probably a misprint for 'scrapes'
38 *Thother* the other
45 *rode* the Cross
55 *ferde* afraid
57 *after her gise* in her characteristic manner
60 *shift* stratagem   *wonders* wondrously
61 *tho* then
63 *The heaven it would* it was heaven's will that   *eke* also
64 *sely* unlucky, foolish

And ere she myght recover it againe:
The traitour cat had caught her by the hippe:
And made her there against her wyll remayne:
That had forgot her power, suerty and rest,
For seking welth, wherein she thought to raigne.
Alas (my Poyns) how men do seke the best,   70
And finde the worse, by errour as they stray,
And no marvell, when sight is so opprest,
And blindes the guide, anone out of the way
Goeth guide and all in seking quiet life.
O wretched mindes, there is no golde that may
Graunt that you seke, no warre, no peace, no strife.
No, no, although thy head were hoopt with golde,
Sergeant with mace, with hawbart, sword, nor knife,
Can not repulse the care that folow should.
Ech kinde of life hath with him his disease.   80
Live in delits, even as thy lust would:
And thou shalt finde, when lust doth most thee please:
It irketh straight, and by it selfe doth fade.
A small thing is it, that may thy minde appease.
None of you al there is, that is so madde,
To seke for grapes on brambles, or on bryers:
Nor none I trow that hath a wytte so badde,
To set his haye for coneies over rivers:
Nor ye set not a draggenet for an hare.
And yet the thing, that most is your desire,   90
You do misseke, with more travell and care.
Make plaine thine hart, that it be not knotted
With hope or dreade, and se thy wil be bare
From all affectes, whom vice hath never spotted.
Thy selfe content with that is thee assinde:

65 *ere* before
68 *power, suerty* poor safety (see explanatory note)
78 *hawbart* halberd (weapon combining spear and battle-axe)
79 *care* anxiety
81 *lust would* desire wishes
82 *lust* pleasure
83 *straight* immediately
88 *haye* net   *coneies* rabbits

And use it well that is to thee alotted,
Then seke no more out of thy selfe to finde
The thing that thou hast sought so long before.
For thou shalt feele it stickyng in thy minde.
100 Made, if ye list to continue your sore:
Let present passe, and gape on time to come,
And depe thy selfe in travell more and more.
Henceforth (my Poins) this shall be all and summe
These wretched foles shall have nought els of me:
But, to the great God and to his dome,
None other paine pray I for them to be:
But when the rage doth leade them from the right:
That loking backward, Vertue they may se,
Even as she is, so goodly fayre and bright.
110 And whilst they claspe their lustes in armes a crosse:
Graunt them good Lord, as thou maist of thy might,
To freat inwarde, for losyng such a losse.

135. Of the Courtiers life written to Jhon Poins.

Myne owne Jhon Poins: sins ye delite to know
The causes why that homeward I me draw,
And fle the prease of courtes, where so they go:
Rather then to live thrall under the awe,
Of lordly lokes, wrapped within my cloke,
To will and lust learning to set a law:
It is not that because I scorne or mocke
The power of them: whom fortune here hath lent
Charge over us, of ryght to strike the stroke.
10 But true it is that I have alwayes ment

100 *Made* (you are) mad *list* please
102 *depe* immerse *travell* work
105 *dome* judgement
112 *freat* fret
135 1 *sins* since
  3 *prease* crowd

Lesse to esteme them, then the common sort
Of outward thinges: that judge in their entent,
Without regarde, what inward doth resort.
I graunt, sometime of glory that the fire
Doth touch my hart. Me list not to report
Blame by honour, and honour to desire.
But how may I this honour now attaine?
That can not dye the colour blacke a lier.
My Poyns, I can not frame my tune to fayn:
To cloke the truth, for praise without desert,   20
Of them that list all vice for to retaine.
I can not honour them, that set their part
With Venus, and Bacchus, all their life long:
Nor holde my peace of them, although I smart.
I can not crouch nor knele to such a wrong:
To worship them like God on earth alone:
That are as wolves these sely lambes among.
I can not with my wordes complaine and mone,
And suffer nought: nor smart without complaynt:
Nor turne the word that from my mouth is gone,   30
I can not speake and loke like as a saint:
Use wiles for wit, and make disceyt a pleasure:
Call craft counsaile, for lucre still to paint.
I can not wrest the law to fill the coffer:
With innocent bloud to fede my selfe fatte:
And do most hurt: where that most helpe I offer.
I am not he, that can alow the state
Of hye Ceasar, and damne Cato to dye:
That with his death did scape out of the gate,
From Ceasars handes, if Livye doth not lye: 40

12 *entent* thinking
15–16 I don't want to speak disparagingly of the world of honours and
   preferment while still desiring them
21 *list* like
27 *sely* innocent
30 Nor put a spin on what I've said in the past
32 *wit* moral wisdom
37 *alow the state* tolerate the authority

And would not live, where libertie was lost,
So did his hart the common wealth apply.
I am not he, such eloquence to bost:
To make the crow in singyng, as the swanne:
Nor call the lyon of coward beastes the most.
That can not take a mouse, as the cat can.
And he that dieth for honger of the golde,
Call him Alexander, and say that Pan
Passeth Appollo in musike manifold:
50   Praise syr Topas for a noble tale,
And scorne the story that the knight tolde:
Praise him for counsell, that is dronke of ale:
Grinne when he laughes, that beareth al the sway:
Frowne, when he frownes: and grone when he is pale:
On others lust to hang both night and day.
None of these poyntes would ever frame in me.
My wit is nought, I can not learne the way.
And much the lesse of thinges that greater be,
That asken helpe of colours to devise
60   To joyne the meane with ech extremitie:
With nearest vertue ay to cloke the vice.
And as to purpose likewise it shall fall:
To presse the vertue that it may not rise.
As dronkennesse good fellowship to call:
The frendly foe, with his faire double face,
Say he is gentle and curties therewithall.
Affirme that favel hath a goodly grace,
In eloquence: And cruelty to name
Zeale of Justice: And change in time and place.
70   And he that suffereth offence without blame:

42 *apply* attach itself to
55 *lust* desires
56 *frame* succeed
59 *colours* rhetorical devices
61 *ay* always
62 In effect, what will turn out is this
66 *curties* courteous
67 *favel* a fraudulent and unattractive individual; see explanatory note

Call him pitifull, and him true and plaine,
That rayleth rechlesse unto ech mans shame.
Say he is rude, that can not lye and faine:
The letcher a lover, and tyranny
To be the right of a Princes raygne.
I can not I, no, no, it will not be.
This is the cause that I could never yet
Hang on their sleves, that weygh (as thou mayst se)
A chippe of chance more then a pounde of wit.
This maketh me at home to hunt and hauke: 80
And in fowle wether at my booke to sit:
In frost and snow, then with my bowe to stalke.
No man doth marke where so I ride or go.
In lusty leas at libertie I walke:
And of these newes I fele nor weale nor wo:
Save that a clogge doth hang yet at my heele.
No force for that, for it is ordred so:
That I may leape both hedge and dike full wele,
I am not now in Fraunce, to judge the wine:
With savery sauce those delicates to fele.   90
Nor yet in Spaine where one must him incline,
Rather then to be, outwardly to seme.
I meddle not with wyttes that be so fyne,
Nor Flaunders chere lettes not my syght to deme
Of blacke, and white, nor takes my wittes away
Wyth beastlinesse: such do those beastes esteme.
Nor I am not, where truth is geven in pray,
For money, poyson, and treason: of some
A common practise, used nyght and day.

71 *pitifull* contemptible
73 *rude* unpolished
79 *wit* wisdom
83 *go* walk
84 *lusty leas* pleasant meadows
87 *No force for that* let's not worry about that
88 *dike* ditch
90 *fele* sense
94 Food and drink such as one might meet with in Flanders does not
   cloud my judgement

100   But I am here in kent and christendome:
       Among the Muses, where I reade and ryme,
       Where if thou list myne owne Jhon Poyns to come:
       Thou shalt be judge, how I do spende my time.

             *136. How to use the court and him
                   selfe therin, written to sir
                        Fraunces Brian.*

       A spendyng hand that alway powreth out,
       Had nede to have a bringer in as fast.
       And on the stone that styll doth turne about,
       There groweth no mosse. These proverbes yet do last:
       Reason hath set them in so sure a place:
       That length of yeares their force can never waste.
       When I remember this, and eke the case,
       Wherin thou standst: I thought forthwith to write
       (Brian) to thee: who knowes how great a grace
10   In writyng is to counsayle man the right.
       To thee therfore that trottes styll up and downe:
       And never restes, but runnyng day and nyght,
       From realme to realme, from citie strete, and towne.
       Why doest thou weare thy body to the bones?
       And mightest at home slepe in thy bedde of downe:
       And drinke good ale so nappy for the nones:
       Fede thy selfe fatte, and heape up pounde by pound.
       Likest thou not this? No. Why? For swine so groines
       In stye, and chaw dung moulded on the ground.
20   And drivell on pearles with heade styll in the maunger,
       So of the harpe the asse doth heare the sound.

       136 6 *waste* reduce
            7 *eke* also
           16 *nappy* foaming *for the nones* a filler phrase (indeed), but with
              suggestions of a carefree manner
           18 *groines* grunts, digs with snout
           19 *chaw dung moulded on the ground* chew dung dropped on the ground

So sackes of durt be filde. The neat courtier
So serves for lesse, then do these fatted swine.
Though I seme leane and drye, withouten moyster:
Yet wyll I serve my prince, my lord and thyne.
And let them live to fede the paunch that list:
So I may live to fede both me and myne.
By God well said. But what and if thou wist
How to bring in, as fast as thou doest spende.
That would I learne. And it shal not be mist,   30
To tell thee how. Now harke what I intende.
Thou knowest well first, who so can seke to please,
Shall purchase frendes: where trouth shall but offend.
Flee therefore truth, it is both welth and ease.
For though that trouth of every man hath praise:
Full neare that winde goeth trouth in great misease.
Use vertue, as it goeth now a dayes:
In worde alone to make thy language swete:
And of thy dede, yet do not as thou saies.
Els be thou sure: thou shalt be farre unmete   40
To get thy breade, ech thyng is now so skant.
Seke styll thy profit upon thy bare fete.
Lend in no wise: for feare that thou do want:
Unlesse it be, as to a calfe a chese:
But if thou can be sure to winne a cant
Of halfe at least. It is not good to leese.
Learne at the ladde, that in a long white cote,
From under the stall, withouten landes or feese,
Hath lept into the shoppe: who knowes by rote
This rule that I have told thee here before.   50
Sometime also rich age beginnes to dote,
Se thou when there thy gaine may be the more.

26 *list* like to do so
28 *wist* knew
36 Truth sails close to the wind very uneasily
40 *unmete* unfit
45 *But if* unless   *cant* share
46 *leese* lose (with a possible pun on 'lie')
48 *feese* rents

Stay him by the arme, where so he walke or go:
Be nere alway, and if he coughe to sore:
What he hath spit treade out, and please him so.
A diligent knave that pikes his masters purse,
May please him so, that he withouten mo
Executour is. And what is he the wurse?
But if so chance, thou get nought of the man:
The wydow may for all thy paine disburse.
A riveld skynne, a stinkyng breath, what than?
A tothelesse mouth shall do thy lippes no harme.
The golde is good, and though she curse or banne:
Yet where thee list, thou mayest lye good and warme.
Let the olde mule bite upon the bridle:
Whilst there do lye a sweter in thy arme.
In this also se that thou be not idle:
Thy nece, thy cosyn, sister, or thy daughter,
If she bee faire: if handsome be her middle:
If thy better hath her love besought her:
Avaunce his cause, and he shall helpe thy nede.
It is but love, turne thou it to a laughter.
But ware I say, so gold thee helpe and spede:
That in this case thou be not so unwise,
As Pandar was in such a like dede.
For he the fole of conscience was so nice:
That he no gaine would have for all his paine.
Be next thy selfe for frendshyp beares no price.
Laughest thou at me, why? do I speake in vaine?
No not at thee, but at thy thrifty jest.
Wouldest thou, I should for any losse or gayne,
Change that for golde, that I have tane for best.
Next godly thinges: to have an honest name?
Should I leave that? then take me for a beast.
Nay then farewell, and if thou care for shame:

60 *disburse* pay
61 *riveld* wrinkled
63 *banne* curse, chide
73 Beware, I say, gold help you
82 *tane* taken

Content thee then with honest povertie:
Wyth free tong, what thee mislikes, to blame,
And for thy trouth sometime adversitie.
And therwithall this guift I shall thee give,
In this world now litle prosperitie: 90
And coyne to kepe: as water in a sive.

137. The song of Iopas unfinished.

When Dido feasted first the wandring Trojan knight:
Whom Junos wrath with storms did force in Libik sands
    to light
That mighty Atlas taught, the supper lasting long,
With crisped lockes on golden harpe, Iopas sang in song.
That same (quod he) that we the world do call and name:
Of heaven and earth with all contents, it is the very frame.
Or thus, of heavenly powers by more power kept in one
Repugnant kindes, in mids of whom the earth hath place
    alone:
Firme, round, of living thinges, the mother, place and
    nourse:
Without the which in egal weight, this heven doth hold
    his course   10
And it is cald by name, the first and moving heaven,
The firmament is placed next, conteining other seven,
Of heavenly powers that same is planted full and thicke:
As shining lightes which we call stars, that therin
    cleve & sticke.
With great swift sway, the first, and with his restlesse sours,
Carieth it self, and all those eyght, in even continuall cours.
And of this world so round within that rolling case,

137 2 *light* make landfall
     8 *Repugnant* contradictory
    10 *Without* around
    14 *cleve* adhere
    15 *sway* power/revolution   *sours* rising movement

Two points there be that never move, but firmly kepe
    their place.
The tone we see alway, the tother standes object
20   Against the same, deviding just the ground by line direct.
Which by imaginacion, drawen from the one to thother
Toucheth the centre of the earth, for way there is none
    other.
And these be calde the Poles, descryde by starres not
    bright.
Artike the one northward we see: Antartike thother
    hight,
The line, that we devise from thone to thother so:
As axel is, upon the which the heavens about do go
Which of water nor earth, of ayre nor fire have kinde,
Therefore the substance of those same were hard for man
    to finde.
But they bene uncorrupt, simple and pure unmixt:
And so we say been all those starres, that in those same
30   be fixt.
And eke those erring seven, in circle as they stray:
So calde, because against that first they have repugnant
    way:
And smaller bywayes to, skant sensible to man:
To busy worke for my poore harpe: let sing them he
    that can.
The wydest save the first, of all these nine above
One hundred yere doth aske of space, for one degree
    to move.
Of which degrees we make, in the first mooving heaven,

19 *tone* one   *tother* other   *object* opposite
20 *just* exactly   *the ground* the spheres
23 *descryde* marked out
24 *hight* is called
25 *devise* imagine   *thone* the one   *thother* the other
27 Which do not consist of the four elements of water, earth, air, and fire
31 *eke* also
32 *have repugnant way* move in the opposite direction
33 And smaller secondary movements too, barely noticeable by man
35 *The wydest* the sphere widest in diameter

Three hundred and threscore in partes justly devided
    even.
And yet there is another betwene those heavens two:
Whose moving is so sly so slack: I name it not for now.   40
The seventh heaven or the shell, next to the starry sky,
All those degrees that gatherth up, with aged pase so sly:
And doth performe the same, as elders count hath bene.
In nine and twenty yeres complete, and daies almost
    sixtene:
Doth carry in his bowt the starre of Saturne old:
A threatner of all living things, with drought and with
    his cold.
The sixt whom this conteins, doth stalke with yonger
    pase:
And in twelve yere doth somwhat more then thothers
    viage was.
And this in it doth beare the starre of Jove benigne,
Twene Saturns malice and us men, frendly defending
    signe.   50
The fift bears bloody Mars, that in three hundred daies,
And twise eleven with one full yere, hath finisht all those
    waies.
A yere doth aske the fourth, and howers therto sixe,
And in the same the daies eye the sunne, therin he stickes.
The third that governd is by that, that governs mee:
And love for love, and for no love provokes: as oft we see:
In like space doth performe that course, that did the tother.
So doth the next unto the same, that second is in order.
But it doth beare the starre, that cald is Mercury:
That many a crafty secrete steppe doth tread, as
    Calcars try.   60
That sky is last, and fixt next us, those waies hath gone,

40 *sly* stealthy
45 *bowt* orbit
57 *space* time
60 *Calcars* astrologers
61 *sky* sphere

In seven and twenty common daies, and eke the third
    of one:
And beareth with his sway, the divers Moone about:
Now bright, now brown, now bent, now ful, & now her
    light is out.
Thus have they of their own two movinges all these seven
One, wherein they be caried still, eche in his severall
    heaven.
An other of them selves, where their bodies be layd
In bywaies, and in lesser rowndes, as I afore have sayd.
Save of them all the Sunne doth stray lest from the
    streight,
The starry sky hath but one course, that we have cald
    the eight.
And all these moovinges eight are ment from West to East:
Although they seme to clime aloft, I say from East to west.
But that is but by force of the first moving sky:
In twise twelve houres from east to east that carieth them
    by & by
But marke we well also, these movinges of these seven,
Be not about the axell tree of the first moving heven.
For they have their two poles directly tone to the
    tother. &c.

T. WYATE the elder.

---

63 *sway* revolving motion   *divers* changeable
64 *brown* dark

SONGES AND SONETTES OF
UNCERTAIN AUCTOURS.

138. The complaint of a lover
with sute to his love
for pitie.

If ever wofull man might move your hartes to ruthe,
Good ladies here his woful plaint, whose deth shal try his truth
 And rightfull judges be on this his true report:
If he deserve a lovers name among the faithfull sort.
 Five hundred times the Sunne hath lodged him in the West:
Since in my hart I harbred first of all the goodlyest gest.
 Whose worthynesse to shew, my wits are all to faynt.
And I lack cunning of the scooles, in colours her to paynt.
 But this I briefly say in wordes of egall weight.
So void of vice was never none, nor with such vertues freight. 10
 And for her beauties prayse, no wight, that with her warres.
For, where she comes, she shewes her self as sun among the
   starres
 But Lord, thou wast to blame, to frame such parfitenesse:
And puttes no pitie in her hart, my sorowes to redresse.
 For if ye knew the paines, and panges, that I have past:
A wonder would it be to you, how that my life hath last.
 When all the Gods agreed, that Cupide with his bow
Should shote his arrowes from her eies, on me his might to show
 I knew it was in vain my force to trust upon:
And well I wist, it was no shame, to yelde to such a one. 20

138 1 *ruthe* pity
  2 *here* hear *plaint* poetic complaint, expression of injustice or sorrow
  6 *harbred* harboured, sheltered
  7 *to* too
  9 *egall* equal
  11 In praise of her beauty, there was no one to compete with her
  19 *force* strength
  20 *wist* knew

Then did I me submit with humble hart and mynde,
To be her man for evermore: as by the Gods assinde.
And since that day, no wo, wherwith love might torment,
Could move me from this faithfull band: or make me once
        repent.
Yet have I felt full oft the hottest of his fire:
The bitter teares, the scalding sighes, the burning hote desire.
And with a sodain sight the trembling of the hart:
And how the blood doth come, and go, to succour every part.
When that a pleasant looke hath lift me in the ayer:
30 A frowne hath made me fall as fast into a depe despayer.
And when that I ere this, my tale could well by hart:
And that my tong had learned it, so that no word might start:
The sight of her hath set my wittes in such a stay:
That to be lord of all the world, one word I could not say.
And many a sodayn cramp my hart hath pinched so:
That for the time, my senses all felt neither weale, nor wo.
Yet saw I never thing, that might my minde content:
But wisht it hers, and at her will, if she could so consent.
Nor never heard of wo: that did her will displease:
40 But wisht the same unto my self, so it might do her ease.
Nor never thought that fayre, nor never liked face:
Unlesse it did resemble her, or some part of her grace.
No distance yet of place could us so farre devide,
But that my hart, and my good will did still with her abide.
Nor yet it never lay in any fortunes powre,
To put that swete out of my thought, one minute of an howre.
No rage of drenching sea, nor woodnesse of the winde,
Nor cannons with their thundring cracks could put her from
        my minde
For when both sea and land asunder had us set:
50 My hole delite was onely then, my self alone to get.
And thitherward to looke, as nere as I could gesse:

31 *ere* before   *my tale could well by hart* I knew my tale well by heart
32 *start* shift from position
33 *stay* suspension of action, stasis
47 *woodnesse* madness

Where as I thought, that she was then, that might my wo
    redresse.
    Full oft it did me good, that waies to take my winde:
So pleasant ayre in no place els, me thought I could not
    finde.
    I saying to my self, my life is yonder way:
And by the winde I have her sent, a thousand sighes a day.
    And sayd unto the sunne, great giftes are geven thee:
For thou mayst see mine earthly blisse, where ever that she be.
    Thou seest in every place, would God I had thy might:
And I the ruler of my self, then should she know no night.   60
    And thus from wish to wish, my wits have been at strife:
And wanting all that I have wisht, thus have I led my life.
    But long it can not last, that in such wo remaines.
No force for that: for death is swete to him, that feles such
    paines.
    Yet most of all me greves: when I am in my grave,
That she shall purchase by my death a cruel name to have.
    Wherfore all you that heare this plaint, or shall it see:
Wish, that it may so perce her hart, that she may pitie mee.
    For and it were her will: for both it were the best,
To save my life, to kepe her name, and set my hart at rest.   70

139. Of the death of master Devorox
the lord Ferres
sonne.

Who justly may rejoyce in ought under the skye?
As life, or lands: as frends, or frutes: which only live to dye.
Or who doth not well know all worldly works are vaine?
And geveth nought but to the lendes, to take the same again.
For though it lift some up: as we long upward all:

    53 *winde* breath
    69 *and* if
139 1 *ought* anything
    4 *the* thee
    5 *long upward* yearn to go upward

Such is the sort of slipper welth: all thinges do rise to fall.
Thuncerteintie is such: experience teacheth so:
That what things men do covet most, them sonest they forgo.
Lo Devorox where he lieth: whose life men held so deare
10 That now his death is sorowed so, that pitie it is to heare.
His birth of auncient blood: his parents of great fame:
And yet in vertue farre before the formost of the same,
His king, and countrye both he served to so great gaine:
That with the Brutes record doth rest, and ever shall remaine.
No man in warre so mete, an enterprise to take:
No man in peace that pleasurde more of enmies frends to make.
A Cato for his counsell: his hed was surely such.
Ne Theseus frendship was so great, but Devorox was as much.
A graffe of so small grothe, so much good frute to bring:
20 Is seldome heard, or never sene: it is so rare a thing.
A man sent us from God, his life did well declare,
And now sent for by God again, to teach us what we are.
Death, and the grave, that shall accompany all that live,
Hath brought him heven, though somwhat sone, which life
          could never give
God graunt well all, that shall professe as he profest:
To live so well, to dye no worse: and send his soule good rest.

140. *They of the meane estate*
are happiest.

If right be rackt, and overronne:
And power take part with open wrong:
If feare my force do yelde to soone,
The lack is like to last to long.
     If God for goodes shalbe unplaced:

6 *sort* fate   *slipper* slippery, unstable
7 *Thuncerteintie* the uncertainty
15 *mete* suitable
19 *graffe* graft, plant shoot attached to another stock   *grothe* growth
140 1 *overronne* trampled
4 *to* too

If right for riches lose his shape:
If world for wisdome be embraced:
The gesse is great, much hurt may hap.

　　Among good thinges, I prove and finde,
The quiet life doth most abound:　　　　　　　　　10
And sure to the contented minde
There is no riches may be found.

　　For riches hates to be content:
Rule is enmy to quietnesse.
Power is most part impacient:
And seldom likes to live in pease.

　　I heard a herdman once compare:
That quiet nightes he had mo slept:
And had mo mery dayes to spare:
Then he, which ought the beastes, he kept.　　　　20

　　I would not have it thought hereby
The Dolphin swimme I meane to teache:
Nor yet to learne the Fawcon fly:
I row not so farre past my reache.

　　But as my part above the rest,
Is well to wish and well to will:
So till my breath shall fail my brest,
I will not ceasse to wish you still.

141. *Comparison of life and death.*

The life is long, that lothsomly doth last:
The dolefull dayes draw slowly to their date:
The present panges, and painfull plages forepast

9 *prove* test
17 *herdman* shepherd
18 *mo* more
20 Than the man who owned (ought) the beasts which the shepherd
　looked after
141 2 *date* end
　3 *plages* blows or evils

Yelde griefe aye grene to stablish this estate.
So that I feele, in this great storme, and strife,
The death is swete that endeth such a life.
    Yet by the stroke of this strange overthrow,
At which conflict in thraldom I was thrust:
The Lord be praised: I am well taught to know

10 From whence man came, and eke whereto he must:
And by the way upon how feble force
His terme doth stand, till death doth end his course.
    The pleasant yeres that seme, so swift that runne
The mery dayes to end, so fast that flete:
The joyfull nightes, of which day daweth so soone.
The happy howers, which mo do misse then mete,
Do all consume: as snow against the sunne:
And death makes end of all, that life begunne.
    Since death shall dure, till all the world be wast.

20 What meaneth man to drede death then so sore?
As man might make, that life should alway last.
Without regard, the lord hath led before
The daunce of death, which all must runne on row:
Though how, or when: the Lord alone doth know.
    If man would minde, what burdens life doth bring:
What grevous crimes to God he doth commit:
What plages, what panges, what perilles thereby spring:
With no sure hower in all his daies to sit:
He would sure think, as with great cause I do:

30 The day of death were better of the two.
    Death is a port, wherby we passe to joy.

---

4 *aye* always
10 *eke* also
11 *how feble force* what feeble power, vigour
12 *terme* period of duration, life
15 *daweth* dawneth
16 *which mo do misse then mete* which more people fail to take
    advantage of than is fitting
19 *dure* last
21 *As man might make* as if man could arrange it
23 *on row* in turn
25 *minde* bear in mind, remember

Life is a lake, that drowneth all in payn.
Death is so dere, it ceaseth all annoy.
Life is so leude, that all it yeldes is vayn.
And as by life to bondage man is braught:
Even so likewise by death was fredome wraught.
　　Wherfore with Paul, let all men wish and pray
To be dissolvde of this foule fleshly masse:
Or at the least be armde against the day:
That they be found good souldiers, prest to passe　　40
From life to death: from death to life again
To such a life, as ever shall remain.

142. The tale of Pigmalion with conclusion upon the beautie of his love.

In Grece somtime there dwelt a man of worthy fame:
To grave in stone his cunning was: Pygmalion was his name.
　　To make his fame endure, when death had him bereft:
He thought it good, of his own hand some filed worke
　　　　were left.
　　In secrete studie then such worke he gan devise,
As might his cunning best commend, and please the lookers
　　　　eyes.
　　A courser faire he thought to grave, barbd for the field:
And on his back a semely knight, well armd with speare &
　　　　shield:
　　Or els some foule, or fish to grave he did devise:
And still, within his wandering thoughtes, new fansies did arise.　　10
　　Thus varied he in minde, what enterprise to take:

34 *leude* ungodly, obscene
40 *prest* ready
142　1 *somtime* once, in the past
　2 *grave* engrave, carve　*cunning* skill
　3 *had him bereft* had taken him
　7 *courser* horse ridden in battle　*barbd* either equipped with barbs, or
　　clipped?

Till fansy moved his learned hand a woman fayre to make.
  Whereon he stayde, and thought such parfite fourme to
    frame:
Whereby he might amaze all Grece, and winne immortall name.
  Of yvorie white he made so faire a woman than:
That nature scornd her perfitnesse so taught by craft of man.
  Wel shaped were her lims, ful comly was her face:
Ech litle vain most lively coucht, eche part had semely grace.
  Twixt nature & Pigmalion, there might appere great strife,
20 So semely was this ymage wrought, it lackt nothing but life.
  His curious eye beheld his own devised work:
And, gasing oft thereon, he found much venome there to lurk.
  For all the featurde shape so did his fansie move:
That, with his idoll, whom he made, Pygmalion fell in love.
  To whom he honour gave, and deckt with garlandes swete,
And did adourn with jewels rich, as is for lovers mete.
  Somtimes on it he fawnd: somtime in rage would cry:
It was a wonder to behold, how fansy bleard his eye.
  Since that this ymage dum enflamde so wise a man:
30 My dere alas, since I you love, what wonder is it than?
  In whom hath nature set the glory of her name:
And brake her moulde, in great dispaire, your like she coulde
    not frame.

143. *The lover sheweth his wofull*
state, and praieth pitie.

    Lyke as the Larke within the Marlians foote
    With piteous tunes doth chirp her yelden lay:
    So sing I now, seyng none other boote,

    13, 32 *frame* shape
    18 *vain* vein   *coucht* inlaid
    26 *mete* suitable
    28 *bleard his eye* blurred his sight, i.e. deceived him
143 1 *Marlian* merlin (small falcon)
    2 *yelden lay* song of surrender
    3 *boote* remedy

My rendering song, and to your will obey.
Your vertue mountes above my force so hye.
And with your beautie seased I am so sure:
That there avails resistance none in me,
But paciently your pleasure to endure.
For on your will my fansy shall attend:
My life, my death, I put both in your choyce: 10
And rather had this life by you to end,
Than live, by other alwayes to rejoyce.
And if your crueltie do thirst my blood:
Then let it forth if it may do you good.

144. *Upon consideration of the state this life he wisheth death.*

The lenger lyfe, the more offence:
The more offence, the greater paine:
The greater pain, the lesse defence:
The lesse defence, the lesser gaine.
The losse of gayne long yll doth trye:
Wherefore come death, and let me dye.
    The shorter life, lesse count I finde:
The lesse account, the sooner made:
The count soon made, the merier minde:
The mery minde doth thought evade.   10
Short life in truth this thing doth trye:
Wherefore come death, and let me dye:
    Come gentle death, the ebbe of care,
The ebbe of care, the flood of lyfe,
The flood of life, the joyfull fare,

4 *rendering* surrendering
5 *force* strength
6 *seased* seized
144 5 *long yll doth trye* tests ability to cope with lengthy misfortunes
    7 *count* account
    5 *trye* ascertain
    13 *care* sorrow, anxiety

The joyfull fare, the end of strife.
The end of strife, that thing wishe I:
Wherefore come death, and let me dye.

*145. The lover that once disdained love
is now become subject beyng
caught in his snare.*

To thys my song geve eare, who list:
And mine intent judge, as you wyll:
The time is come, that I have mist,
The thyng, wheron I hoped styll,
And from the toppe of all my trust,
Myshap hath throwen me in the dust.
    The time hath bene, and that of late:
My hart and I might leape at large.
And was not shut within the gate
Of loves desire: nor toke no charge
Of any thing, that dyd pertaine
As touching love in any payn.
    My thought was free, my hart was light:
I marked not, who lost, who saught.
I playde by day, I slept by night.
I forced not, who wept, who laught.
My thought from all such thinges was free:
And I my self at libertee.
    I toke no hede to tauntes, nor toyes:
As leefe to see them frowne as smile:
Where fortune laught I scornde their joyes:

---

145 *subject* submissive, subjected to another's control
  1 *list* please
  3 *mist* failed to get
  5 *trust* confidence
 10 *toke no charge* did not care
 12 *in any payn* with any effort
 16 *I forced not* I did not care
 20 *leefe* happy

I found their fraudes and every wile.
And to my selfe oft times I smiled:
To see, how love had them begiled.
   Thus in the net of my conceit
I masked still among the sort
Of such as fed upon the bayt,
That Cupide laide for his disport.
And ever as I sawe them caught:
I them behelde, and therat laught.   30
   Till at the length when Cupide spied
My scornefull will and spitefull use
And how I past not who was tied,
So that my self might still live lose:
He set him self to lye in wait:
And in my way he threw a bait
   Such one, as nature never made,
I dare wel say save she alone.
Such one she was as would invade
A hart, more hard then marble stone.   40
Such one she is, I know, it right,
Her nature made to shew her myght.
   Then as a man even in a maze,
When use of reason is away:
So I began to stare, and gaze.
And sodeinly, without delay,
Or ever I had the wit to loke:
I swalowed up both bait, and hoke.
   Which dayly greves me more and more
By sondry sortes of carefull wo: 50
And none alive may salve the sore,
But onely she, that hurt me so.

---

26 *masked* attended masques
31 *at the length* in the end
33 *past not* didn't pay attention to
34 *lose* free
47 *Or* before
50 *carefull* full of sorrow, anxiety

In whom my life doth now consist,
To save or slay me as she list.
    But seing now that I am caught,
And bounde so fast, I cannot flee:
Be ye by my mine ensample taught,
That in your fansies fele you free.
Despise not them, that lovers are:
60   Lest you be caught within his snare.

146. Of Fortune, and fame.

The plage is great, where fortune frownes:
One mischiefe bringes a thousand woes
Where trumpets geve their warlyke sownes:
The weake sustain sharp overthrowes.
No better life they taste, and fele:
That subject are to fortunes whele.
    Her happy chance may last no time:
Her pleasure threatneth paines to come,
She is the fall of those, that clime:
10   And yet her whele avanceth some.
No force, where that she hates, or loves:
Her ficle minde so oft removes.
    She geves no gift, but craves as fast.
She soone repentes a thankful dede.
She turneth after every blast.
She helps them oft, that have no nede.
Where power dwelles, and riches rest:
False fortune is a common gest,
    Yet some affirme, and prove by skyl:
20   Fortune is not as fleyng Fame,
She neither can do good, nor yll.

146   1 *plage* evil
      3 *sownes* sounds
      4 *overthrowes* defeats
      11 *No force* no matter

She hath no fourme, yet beares a name.
Then we but strive against the streames,
To frame such joyes on fansies dreames.
　　If she have shape, or name alone:
If she do rule, or beare no sway:
If she have bodie, lief or none:
Be she a sprite I cannot say.
But well I wot, some cause there is:
That causeth wo, and sendeth blisse.　　　　　　30
　　The causes of thinges I wil not blame:
Lest I offend the prince of pease.
But I may chide, and braule with Fame:
To make her crye, and never cease.
To blow the trump within her eares:
That may apease my wofull teares.

147. Against wicked tonges.

O evyll tonges, which clap at every winde:
Ye slea the quick, and eke the dead defame:
Those that live well, some faute in them ye finde.
Ye take no thought, in sclandring their good name.
Ye put just men oft times to open shame.
Ye ryng so loude, ye sound unto the skyes:
And yet in proofe ye sowe nothing, but lies.
　　Ye make great war, wher peace hath been of long
Ye bring rich realmes to ruine, and decay.
Ye pluck down right: ye doe enchaunce the wrong.　　10

---

24 *frame* build
28 *sprite* spirit
29 *wot* know
147 1 *clap* talk loudly, clatter
　2 *Ye slea the quicke* you kill the living　*eke* also
　4 *sclandring* slandering
　8 *of long* for a long time
　10 *enchaunce* probably a misprint for 'enhance'

Ye turne swete myrth to wo, and wel away
Of myschiefes al ye are the grounde, I say.
Happy is he, that lives on such a sort:
That nedes not feare such tonges of false report.

148. Hell tormenteth not the damned ghostes so sore as unkindnesse the lover.

The restlesse rage of depe devouryng hell,
The blasing brandes, that never do consume,
The roryng route, in Plutoes den that dwell:
The fiery breath, that from those ymps doth fume:
The dropsy dryeth, that Tantale in the flood
Endureth aye, all hopelesse of relief:
He hongersterven, where fruite is ready food:
So wretchedly his soule doth suffer grief:
The liver gnawne of gylefull Promethus,
Which Vultures fell wyth strained talant tire:
The labour lost of weried Sisiphus:
These hellish houndes, with paines of quenchlesse
        fyre,
Can not so sore the silly soules torment,
As her untruth my hart hath all to rent.

11 *wel away* alas
12 *grounde* cause
148 2 *brandes* fires
  3 *route* group of people/rabble
  4 *ymps* evil spirits
  5 *dropsy dryeth* water-ridden thirst
  6 *aye* for ever
  7 *hongersterven* hunger-starved
  10 *fell* terrible   *talant* talon   *tire* tear
  11 *lost* wasted
  13 *silly* innocent
  14 *all to rent* entirely torn apart

149. Of the mutabilitie of
the worlde.

By fortune as I lay in bed, my fortune was to finde
Such fansies, as my careful thought had brought into my minde
And when eche one was gone to rest, ful soft in bed to lye:
I would have slept, but then the watch did folow stil mine eye
And sodeinly I saw a sea of wofull sorowes prest:
Whose wicked waies of sharp repulse bred mine unquiet rest.
I saw this world: and how it went, eche state in his degree:
And that from wealth ygraunted is, both life and libertee.
I saw, how envy it did rayne, and beare the greatest price:
Yet greater poyson is not founde within the Cockatrice.   10
I saw also, how that disdain oft times to forge my wo,
Gave me the cup of bitter swete, to pledge my mortall fo.
I saw also, how that desire to rest no place coulde finde
But still constrainde in endlesse payn to folow natures kinde.
I saw also most straunge of all how nature did forsake
The blood, that in her womb was wrought: as doth the lothed
        snake.
I saw, how fansie would retain no lenger then her lust:
And as the winde how she doth chaunge: and is not for to trust.
I saw, how stedfastnesse did fly with winges of often change:
A flying bird, but seldome seen, her nature is so strange.   20
I saw, how pleasant times did passe, as flowers do in the mede:
To day that riseth red as rose: to morow falleth ded.
I saw, my time how it did runne, as sand out of the glasse.
Even as eche hower appointed is from time, and tide to passe.
I saw the yeres that I had spent, and losse of all my gayn:

149 2 *careful* full of cares, anxious
      4 *watche* wakefulness
      8 *ygraunted* granted
      9 *rayne* reign
     10 *Cockatrice* serpent
     12 *pledge* drink with/to
     14 *natures kinde* nature's course
     17 *then her lust* than she wished

And how the sport of youthfull playes my foly did retain.
I saw, how that the litle Ant in somer still doth runne
To seke her foode, wherby to live in winter for to come,
I saw eke vertue, how she sat the threde of life to spinne.
30 Which sheweth the ende of every work, before it doth beginne.
And when all these I thus beheld with many mo pardy:
In me, me thought, ech one had wrought a parfite proparty.
And then I sayd unto my self: a lesson this shalbe
For other: that shall after come, for to beware by me.
Thus, all the night I did devise, which way I might constayn.
To forme a plot, that wit might work these branches in my
         brain.

150. *Harpalus complaint of Phillidaes love bestowed on Corin, who loved her not: and denied him, that loved her.*

Phylida was a fayre mayde,
As fresh as any flowre:
Whom Harpalus the herdman prayde
To be his paramour.
    Harpalus and eke Corin
Were herdmen both yfere:
And Phillida could twist and spin
And therto sing full clere.
    But Phillida was all to coy
10 For Harpalus to winne.

29 *eke* also
31 *mo* more   *pardy* certainly
32 *wrought a perfit proparty* done its characteristic business perfectly
35 *constayn* contrive (?); may be a misprint for 'constyrre' (= calculate)
36 *branches* lines of thought (but see explanatory note)
150 3 *herdman* shepherd
      5 *eke* also
      6 *yfere* together
      9 *to coy* too reserved, unresponsive

For Corin was her onely joy,
Who forst her not a pinne.
　　How often would she flowers twine
How often garlandes make:
Of Couslips and of Columbine,
And all for Corins sake.
　　But Corin he had Haukes to lure
And forced more the field:
Of lovers law he toke no cure
For once he was begilde.　　　　　　　　　　　20
　　Harpalus prevailed nought
His labour all was lost:
For he was fardest from her thought
And yet he loved her most.
　　Therefore waxt he both pale and leane
And dry as clot of clay:
His flesh it was consumed cleane
His colour gone away.
　　His beard it had not long be shave,
His hare hong all unkempt:　　　　　　　　　　30
A man most fit even for the grave
Whom spitefull love had spent.
　　His eyes were red and all forewatched
His face besprent with teares:
It semed unhap had him long hatched,
In mids of his dispaires.
　　His clothes were black and also bare
As one forlorne was he:
Upon his head alwaies he ware,
A wreath of wilow tree.　　　　　　　　　　　40
　　His beastes he kept upon the hill,

12 Who cared (forst) nothing for her
19 *toke no cure* cared nothing
20 *begilde* tricked
32 *spent* exhausted, consumed
33 *forewatched* weary with staying awake
34 *besprent* besprinkled
35 *unhap* bad luck　*hatched* brooded on

And he sate in the dale:
And thus with sighes and sorowes shrill,
He gan to tell his tale.
   O Harpalus (thus would he say,)
Unhappiest under sunne:
The cause of thine unhappy day
By love was first begunne.
   For thou wentest first by sute to seeke
A Tygre to make tame:
That sets not by thy love a leeke
But makes thy griefe her game.
   As easy it were, for to convert
The frost into the flame:
As for to turne a froward hert
Whom thou so fain wouldst frame.
   Corin he liveth carelesse
He leapes among the leaves:
He eates the frutes of thy redresse
Thou reapes, he takes the sheaves.
   My beastes a while your foode refrain
And harke your herdmans sound:
Whom spitefull love alas hath slain
Through girt with many a wound.
   O happy be ye beastes wilde
That here your pasture takes:
I see that ye be not begilde
Of these your faithfull makes.
   The hart he feedeth by the Hinde

50

60

---

49 *sute* petition, plea
51 Who values your love at nothing (a leek = something of very little value)
55 *froward* hostile, adverse
56 Who you so wish to succeed with
59 *redresse* proper wages
64 *Through girt* stricken through
67–8 *begilde / Of* deceived by
68 *makes* mates
69 *hart* stag   *Hinde* female (red) deer

The Buck hard by the Do,   70
The Turtle Dove is not unkinde
To him that loves her so.
    The Ewe she hath by her the Ramme
The yong Cow hath the Bull:
The Calf with many a lusty Lamme
Do fede their hunger full.
    But wellaway that nature wrought
Thee Phillida so faire:
For I may say that I have bought
Thy beauty all to deare.   80
    What reason is it that cruelty
With beauty should have part,
Or els that such great tyranny
Should dwell in womans hart.
    I see therfore to shape my death
She cruelly is prest:
To thende that I may want my breath
My dayes been at the best.
    O Cupide graunt this my request
And do not stoppe thine eares: 90
That she may feele within her brest
The paines of my dispaires.
    Of Corin that is carelesse
That she may crave her fee:
As I have done in great distresse
That loved her faithfully.
    But sins that I shall dye her slave
Her slave and eke her thrall:
Write you my frendes, upon my grave

77 *wellaway* alas
85 *shape* bring about
86 *prest* ready, eager
87 *to thende that* with the result (end) that   *want* lose
90 *stoppe* block
93 *is carelesse* cares nothing [for her]
94 *fee* reward/fealty
97 *sins* since

100 This chaunce that is befall.
        Here lieth unhappy Harpelus
     By cruell love now slaine:
     Whom Phillida unjustly thus
     Hath murdred with disdaine.

151. Upon sir James Wilfordes death.

Lo, here the end of man the cruell sisters three
The web of Wilfords life uneth had halfe ysponne,
When rash upon misdede they all accorded bee
To breake of vertues course ere half the race were ronne
And trip him on his way that els had won the game
And holden highest place within the house of fame.
    But yet though he be gone, though sence with him
            be past
Whych trode the even steppes that leaden to renowne
We that remaine alive ne suffer shall to waste
10   The fame of his desertes, so shall he lose but sowne,
The thing shall aye remaine, aye kept as fresh in store
As if his eares shold ring of that he wrought before.
    Waile not therefore his want sithe he so left the stage
Of care and wretched life, with joye and clap of handes
Who plaieth lenger partes may well have greater age
But few so well may passe the gulfe of fortunes sandes
So triedly did he treade ay prest at vertues beck
That fortune founde no place to give him once a check.
    The fates have rid him hence, who shal not after go,

151 2 *uneth* scarcely
     4 *of* off   *ere* before
     9 *suffer* allow
     10 *desertes* deserving, merit   *sowne* sound
     11 *aye* always
     13 *sithe* since
     14 *care* sorrow, anxiety
     17 *prest* ready   *beck* beckoning movement

Though earthed be his corps, yet florish shall his fame,   20
A gladsome thing it is that ere he stepte us fro,
Such mirrours he us left our life therby to frame,
Wherfore his praise shall last aye freshe in Brittons sight,
Till sunne shal cease to shine, and lende the earth his light.

152. Of the wretchednes in this world.

Who list to live upright, and hold himself content,
Shal see such wonders in this world, as never erst was sent.
Such gropyng for the swete, such tastyng of the sower
Such wandring here for worldly welth that lost is in one
    houre.
And as the good or badde, get up in hie degree,
So wades the world in right or wrong it may none other be.
And looke what lawes they make, ech man must them obay,
And yoke himselfe with pacient heart to drive and draw that
    way.
Yet such as long ago, great rulers wer assinde
Both lives & lawes are now forgot & worne clene out of
    minde   10
So that by this I se, no state on earth may last
But as their times appointed be, to rise and fall as fast.
The goodes that gotten be, by good and just desart,
Yet use them so that neady handes may help to spend the
    part
For loke what heape thou hordst, of rusty golde in store,
Thine enemies shall waste the same, that never swat
    therfore.

    21 *ere* before
152 1 *list* pleases
  2 *erst* before
  6 *wades* advances, proceeds
 13 *desart* deserving
 16 *swat* sweated

153. *The repentant sinner in durance and adversitie.*

Unto the living Lord for pardon do I pray,
From whom I graunt even from the shell, I have run stil astray.
And other lives there none (my death shall well declare)
On whom I ought to grate for grace, as faulty folkes do fare.
But thee O Lord alone, I have offended so,
That this smal scourge is much to scant for mine offence I know
I ranne without returne, the way the world liekt best
And what I ought most to regard, that I respected lest
The throng wherin I thrust, hath throwen me in such case
10 That Lorde my soule is sore beset without thy greater grace.
My giltes are growen so great, my power doth so appaire
That with great force they argue oft, and mercy much dispaire.
But then with faith I flee to thy prepared store
Wher there lieth helpe for every hurt, and salve for every sore.
My lost time to lament, my vaine waies to bewaile,
No day, no night, no place, no houre, no moment I shall faile
My soule shal never cease with an assured faith
To knock, to crave, to cal, to cry, to thee for helpe which sayth
Knocke and it shalbe heard, but aske and geven it is
20 And all that like to kepe this course, of mercy shall not misse
For when I call to minde how the one wandryng shepe,
Did bring more joye with his returne, then all the flocke did kepe.
It yeldes ful hope and trust my strayed and wandring ghost
Shalbe received and held more dere then those were never lost.
O Lord my hope beholde, and for my helpe make haste
To pardon the forpassed race that carelesse I have past.
And but the day draw neare that death must pay the det,

153 *durance* imprisonment
  4 *grate* weep, importune   *fare* do
  6 *to* too
 11 *appaire* deteriorate
 14 *salve* healing ointment
 26 *for passed* previously passed
 27 *but* unless

For love of life which thou hast lent and time of paiment set.
From this sharpe shower me shielde which threatened is at hand,
Wherby thou shalt great power declare & I the storme
      withstand   30
Not my will lord but thine, fulfilde be in ech case,
To whose gret wil & mighty power al powers shal once geve
      place
My fayth my hope my trust, my God and eke my guide
Stretch forth thy hand to save the soule, what so the body
      bide.
Refuse not to receive that thou so deare hast bought,
For but by thee alone I know all safetie in vaine is sought.
I know and knowledge eke albeit very late,
That thou it is I ought to love and dreade in ech estate.
And with repentant heart do laud thee Lord on hye,
That hast so gently set me straight, that erst walkt so awry.   40
Now graunt me grace my God to stand thine strong in sprite.
And let the world then work such waies, as to the world
      semes mete.

> ### 154. *The lover here telleth of his divers*
> ### *joyes and adversities in love*
> ### *and lastly of his*
> ### *ladies death.*

> Syth singyng gladdeth oft the harts
> Of them that fele the panges of love:
> And for the while doth ease their smarts:

33 *eke* also
34 *what so* whatever   *bide* endures
37 *knowledge eke* acknowledge too
40 *erst* before
41 *sprite* spirit
42 *mete* suitable
154 *divers* various
  1 *Syth* since

My self I shall the same way prove.
   And though that love hath smit the stroke,
Wherby is lost my libertie:
Which by no meanes I may revoke:
Yet shall I sing, how pleasantly.
   Ny twenty yeres of youth I past:
Which al in libertie I spent:
And so from first unto the last,
Ere aught I knewe, what loving ment.
   And after shal I syng the wo,
The paine, the greefe, the deadly smart:
When love this lyfe did overthrowe,
That hydden lyes within my hart.
   And then, the joyes, that I dyd feele.
When fortune lifted after this,
And set me hye upon her whele:
And changde my wo to pleasant blisse,
   And so the sodeyn fall agayne
From all the joyes, that I was in.
All you, that list to heare of payne,
Geve eare, for now I doe beginne.
   Lo, first of all, when love began
With hote desires my heart to burne:
Me thought, his might availde not than
From libertie my heart to turne.
   For I was free: and dyd not knowe,
How much his might mannes hert may greve.
I had profest to be his fo:
His law, I thought not to beleve.
   I went untied in lusty leas,
I had my wish alwaies at will:
Ther was no wo, might me displease:

  4 *prove* try
12 *Ere aught I knewe* before I knew anything about
23 *list* please
27 *availde not* did not have the power
33 *lusty leas* pleasant meadows

Of pleasant joyes I had my fill.
　　No paynfull thought dyd passe my hart:
I spilt no teare to wet my brest:
I knew no sorow, sigh, nor smart,
My greatest griefe was quiet rest.　　　　　　　　　　　40
　　I brake no slepe, I tossed not:
Nor dyd delite to syt alone.
I felt no change of colde and hote:
Nor nought a nightes could make me mone.
　　For al was joy that I did fele:
And of voide wandering I was free.
I had no clogge tied at my hele:
This was my life at libertie.
　　That yet me thinkes it is a blisse,
To thinke upon that pleasure past.　　　　　　　　　　50
But forthwithall I finde the misse,
For that it might no lenger last.
　　Those daies I spent at my desire,
Without wo or adversitie:
Till that my hart was set a fire,
With love, with wrath, and jelousie.
　　For on a day (alas the while)
Lo, heare my harme how it began:
The blinded Lord, the God of guile
Had list to end my fredome than.　　　　　　　　　　60
　　And through mine eye into my hart
All sodenly I felt it glide.
He shot his sharped fiery dart,
So hard, that yet under my side
　　The head (alas) doth still remaine,
And yet since could I never know,
The way to wring it out againe:
Yet was it nye three yere ago.
　　This soden stroke made me agast:
And it began to vexe me sore.　　　　　　　　　　　70

51 *forthwithall* immediately　*finde* realize　*misse* loss, lack
60 *than* then

But yet I thought, it would have past,
As other such had done before.
    But it did not that (wo is me)
So depe imprinted in my thought,
The stroke abode: that yet I see,
Me thinkes my harme how it was wrought.
    Kinde taught me streight that this was love
And I perceived it perfectly.
Yet thought I thus: Nought shall me move:
I will not thrall my libertie.
    And divers waies I did assay,
By flight, by force, by frend, by fo,
This firie thought to put away.
I was so lothe for to forgo
    My libertie: that me was lever,
Then bondage was, where I hard say:
Who once was bounde, was sure never
Without great paine to scape away.
    But what for that, there is no choice,
For my mishap was shapen so:
That those my dayes that did rejoyce,
Should turne my blisse to bitter wo.
    For with that stroke my blisse toke ende.
In stede wherof forthwith I caught,
Hotte burnyng sighes, that sins have brend,
My wretched hart almost to naught.
    And sins that day, O Lord my life,
The misery that it hath felt.
That nought hath had, but wo and strife,
And hotte desires my hart to melt.
    O Lord how sodaine was the change

80

90

100

77 *Kinde* Nature   *streight* immediately
81 *divers* various   *assay* try
85 *that me was lever* that was preferable to me
86 *hard* heard
93 *toke ende* was at an end
94 *forthwith* immediately
95 *sins* since   *brend* burned

From such a pleasant liberty?
The very thraldome semed straunge
But yet there was no remedy.
　　But I must yeld, and geve up all,
And make my guide my chefist fo.
And in this wise became I thrall,
Lo, love and happe would have it so.
　　I suffred wrong and held my peace,
I gave my teares good leave to ronne:　　　　　110
And never would seke for redresse,
But hopt to live as I begonne.
　　For what it was that might me ease,
He lived not that might it know,
Thus dranke I all mine owne disease:
And all alone bewailde my wo.
　　There was no sight that mighte me please,
I fled from them that did rejoyce,
And oft alone my hart to ease,
I would bewaile with wofull voyce　　　　　　120
　　My life, my state, my misery,
And curse my selfe & al my daies.
Thus wrought I with my fantasie,
And sought my helpe none other waies.
　　Save sometime to my selfe alone,
When farre of was my helpe God wot:
Lowde would I crye: My life is gone,
My dere, if that ye helpe me not.
　　Then wisht I streight, that death might end
These bitter panges, and al this grief　　　　130
For nought, methought, might it amend.
Thus in dispaire to have relief,
　　I lingred forth: tyl I was brought
With pining in so piteous case:

108 *happe* chance, fortune
112 *hopt* hoped
126 *of* off　*wot* knows
129 *streight* immediately

That al, that sawe me, sayd, methought:
Lo, death is painted in his face.
    I went no where: but by the way
I saw some sight before mine eyes:
That made me sigh, and oft times say:
My life, alas I thee despyse.

    This lasted well a yere, and more:
Which no wight knew, but onely I:
So that my life was nere for lore:
And I dispaired utterly.

    Til on a day, as fortune would:
(For that, that shalbe, nedes must fal)
I sat me down, as though I should
Have ended then my lyfe, and al.

    And as I sat to write my playnt,
Meanyng to shew my great unrest:
With quaking hand, and hart full faint,
Amid my plaintes, among the rest,

    I wrote with ynk, and bitter teares:
I am not myne, I am not mine:
Behold my life, away that weares:
And if I dye the losse is thine.

    Herewith a little hope I caught:
That for a whyle my life did stay.
But in effect, all was for naught.
Thus lived I styl: tyl on a day
As I sat staring on those eyes:
Those shining eyes, that first me bound:
My inward thought tho cryed: Aryse:
Lo, mercy where it may be found.

140

150

160

142 *no wight* no one
143 *nere for lore* nearly lost
145 *would* willed it
146 *fal* happen
149 *playnt* poetic complaint, expressing injustice or sorrow
158 *stay* sustain, support
163 *tho* then

And therewithall I drew me nere:
With feble hart, and at a braide,
(But it was softly in her eare)
Mercy, Madame, was all, I sayd.
　But wo was me, when it was told,
For therwithall fainted my breath: 170
And I sate still for to beholde,
And heare the judgement of my death.
　But Love nor Hap would not consent,
To end me then, but welaway:
There gave me blisse: that I repent
To thinke I live to se this day.
　For after this I plained styll
So long, and in so piteous wise:
That I my wish had at my will
Graunted, as I would it devise.   180
　But Lord who ever hard, or knew,
Of halfe the joye that I felt than?
Or who can thinke it may be true,
That so much blisse had ever man?
　Lo, fortune thus set me aloft:
And more my sorowes to releve,
Of pleasant joyes I tasted oft:
As much as love or happe might geve.
　The sorowes old, I felt before
About my hart, were driven thence: 190
And for ech griefe, I felt afore,
I had a blisse in recompence.
　Then thought I all the time well spent:
That I in plaint had spent so long.
So was I with my life content:
That to my self I sayd among.
　Sins thou art ridde of al thine yll:

166 *at a braide* in an outburst
173 *Hap* chance, fortune
174 *welaway* alas
181 *hard* heard
196 *among* at the same time, from time to time

To shewe thy joyes set forth thy voyce.
And sins thou haste thy wish at will:
My happy hart, rejoyce, rejoyce.
    Thus felt I joyes a great deale mo,
Then by my song may well be tolde:
And thinking on my passed wo,
My blisse did double many folde.
    And thus I thought with mannes blood,
Such blisse might not be bought to deare.
In such estate my joyes then stode:
That of a change I had no feare.
    But why sing I so long of blisse?
It lasteth not, that will away,
Let me therfore bewaile the misse:
And sing the cause of my decay.
    Yet all this while there lived none,
That led his life more pleasantly:
Nor under hap there was not one,
Me thought, so well at ease, as I.
    But O blinde joye, who may thee trust?
For no estate thou canst assure?
Thy faithfull vowes prove al unjust:
Thy faire behestes be full unsure.
    Good proofe by me: that but of late
Not fully twenty daies ago:
Which thought my life was in such state:
That nought might worke my hart this wo.
    Yet hath the enemy of myne ease,
Cruell mishappe, that wretched wight:
Now when my life did most me please:
Devised me such cruel spight.
    That from the hiest place of all,
As to the pleasing of my thought,

199 *haste* hast
201 *mo* more
211 *misse* loss
220 *behestes* promises
226 *wight* person

Downe to the deepest am I fall,
And to my helpe availeth nought,
   Lo, thus are all my joyes quite gone:
And I am brought from happinesse,
Continually to wayle, and mone.
Lo, such is fortunes stablenesse.

   In welth I thought such suertie,
That pleasure should have ended never.
But now (alas) adversitie,
Doth make my singyng cease for ever.   240

   O brittle joye, O welth unstable:
O fraile pleasure, O slidyng blisse,
Who feles thee most, he shall not misse,
At length to be made miserable.

   For all must end as doth my blisse:
There is none other certeintie.
And at the end the worst is his,
That most hath knowen prosperitie.

   For he that never blisse assaied,
May well away with wretchednesse: 250
But he shall finde that hath it sayd,
A pain to part from pleasantnesse:

   As I do now, for ere I knew
What pleasure was, I felt no griefe,
Like unto this, and it is true,
That blisse hath brought me all this mischiefe.

   But yet I have not songen, how
This mischiefe came: but I intend
With wofull voyce to sing it now:
And therwithall I make an end.   260

   But Lord, now that it is begoon,
I fele, my sprites are vexed sore.
Oh, geve me breath till this be done:

237 *suertie* confidence
242 *slidyng* transitory, unstable
243 *misse* fail
253 *ere* before

And after let me live no more.
Alas, the enmy of this life,
The ender of all pleasantnesse:
Alas, he bringeth all this strife,
And causeth all this wretchednesse.
For in the middes of all the welth,
That brought my hart to happinesse:
This wicked death he came by stelth,
And robde me of my joyfulnesse.
He came, when that I litle thought
Of ought, that might me vexe so sore:
And sodenly he brought to nought
My pleasantnesse for evermore.
He slew my joy (alas, the wretch)
He slew my joy, or I was ware:
And now (alas) no might may stretch
To set an end to my great care.
For by this cursed deadly stroke,
My blisse is lost, and I forlore:
And no helpe may the losse revoke:
For lost it is for evermore.
And closed up are those faire eyes,
That gave me first the signe of grace:
My faire swete foes, mine enemies,
And earth doth hide her pleasant face.
The loke which did my life uphold:
And all my sorowes did confound:
With which more blisse then may be told:
Alas, now lieth it under ground
But cease, for I will sing no more:
Since that my harme hath no redresse:
But as a wretche for evermore,
My life will waste with wretchednesse.
And ending this my wofull song,

270 *(line marker)*
280 *(line marker)*
290 *(line marker)*

274 *ought* anything
278 *or I was ware* before I was aware
280 *care* sorrow, anxiety

Now that it ended is and past:
I would my life were but as long:
And that this word might be my last. 300
  For lothsome is that life (men say)
That liketh not the livers minde:
Lo, thus I seke mine own decay,
And will, till that I may it finde.

155. Of his love named White.

Full faire and white she is, and White by name:
Whose white doth strive, the lillies white to staine:
Who may contemne the blast of blacke defame:
Who in darke night, can bring day bright againe.
The ruddy rose inpreaseth with cleare heew,
In lips and chekes, right orient to behold:
That the nerer gaser may that bewty reew,
And fele disparst in limmes the chilling cold:
For White, all white his bloodlesse face will be:
The asshy pale so alter will his cheare. 10
But I that do possesse in full degree
The harty love of this my hart so deare:
So oft to me as she presents her face,
For joy do feele my hart spring from his place.

156. Of the lovers unquiet
stare.

What thing is that which I both have and lacke,
With good will graunted, yet it is denyed

302 *liketh not* is not pleasing to
155 3 *contemne* disregard, disdain
  5 *inpreaseth* stains through
  6 *orient* brilliant, lustrous
  10 *cheare* countenance
156 *stare* misprint for 'state'

How may I be received and put abacke
Alway doing and yet unoccupied,
Most slow in that which I have most applied,
Still thus to seke, and lese all that I win,
And that was doon is newest to begin.
   In riches finde I wilfull povertie,
In great pleasure, live I in heavinesse.
In much freedome I lacke my libertie,
Thus am I both in joy and in distresse.
And in few wordes, if that I shall be plaine,
In Paradise I suffer all this paine.

157. *Where good will is, some proofe will appere.*

It is no fire that geves no heate,
Though it appeare never so hot:
And they that runne and can not sweate,
Are very leane and dry God wot,
   A perfect leche applieth his wittes,
To gather herbes of all degrees:
And fevers with their fervent fittes,
Be cured with their contraries.
   New wine will serch to finde a vent,
Although the caske be set so strong:
And wit will walke when will is bent,
Although the way be never so long.
   The Rabbets runne under the rockes:
The Snailes do clime the highest towers:
Gunpowder cleaves the sturdy blockes.
A fervent will all thing devowers.
   When wit with will and diligent

156 6 *lese* lose
157 4 *wot* knows
   5 *leche* physician
  15 *cleaves* splits
  17 *diligent* diligence

Apply them selves, and match as mates,
There can no want of resident,
From force defend the castell gates.   20
    Forgetfulnesse make litle haste,
And slouth delites to lye full soft:
That telleth the deaf, his tale doth waste,
And is full dry that craves full oft.

158. Verses written on the picture of sir James Wilford knight.

Alas that ever death such vertues should forlet,
As compast was within his corps, whose picture is here set.
Or that it ever lay in any fortunes might,
Through depe disdain to end his life that was so worthy a
        wight.
For sithe he first began in armour to be clad,
A worthier champion then he was, yet England never had.
And though recure be past, his life to have againe,
Yet would I wish his worthinesse in writing to remaine.
That men to minde might call how farre he did excell,
At all assayes to wynne the fame, which were to long to tell.   10
And eke the restlesse race that he full oft hath runne,
In painfull plight from place to place, where service was
        to don.
Then should men well perceive, my tale to be of trouth,
And he to be the worthiest wight that ever nature wrought.

23 *That* he that
24 *dry* thirsty
158 1 *forlet* release, leave to decay
  4 *wight* person
  5 *sithe* since
  7 *recure* remedy
  10 *assayes* attempts   *to* too
  11 *eke* also

159. *The ladie praieth the returne of*
her lover abiding on
the seas.

Shall I thus ever long, and be no whit the neare,
And shall I still complain to thee, the which me will not
     heare?
Alas say nay, say nay, and be no more so dome,
But open thou thy manly mouth, and say that thou wilt come.
Wherby my hart may thinke, although I see not thee,
That thou wilt come thy word so sware, if thou a lives man be.
The roaring hugy waves, they threaten my poore ghost,
And tosse thee up and downe the seas, in daunger to be lost.
Shall they not make me feare that they have swalowed thee,
10 But as thou art most sure alive, so wilt thou come to me.
Wherby I shall go see thy ship ride on the strand,
And think and say lo where he comes, and sure here will he
     land
And then I shall lift up to thee my litle hand,
And thou shalt think thine hart in ease, in helth to see me
     stand.
And if thou come in dede (as Christ thee send to do,)
Those armes which misse thee yet, shall then imbrace thee to.
Ech vain to every joynt, the lively blood shall spred,
Which now for want of thy glad sight, doth show full pale &
     dead.
But if thou slip thy trouth and do not come at all,
20 As minutes in the clocke do strike so call for death I shall.
To please both thy false hart, and rid my self from wo,
That rather had to dye in trouth then live forsaken so.

159 3 *dome* dumb
     6 *sware* sworn
     7 *ghost* spirit
    17 *vain* vein
    19 *slip thy trouth* break your promise, faith

160. *The meane estate is best.*

The doutfull man hath fevers strange
And constant hope is oft diseasde,
Dispaire cannot but brede a change,
Nor fleting hartes cannot be pleasde.
Of all these bad, the best I thinck,
Is well to hope, though fortune shrinck.
    Desired thinges are not ay prest,
Nor thinges denide left all unsought,
Nor new things to be loved best,
Nor all offers to be set at nought,   10
Where faithfull hart hath bene refusde,
The chosers wit was there abusde.
    The wofull ship of carefull sprite,
Fleting on seas of welling teares,
With sailes of wishes broken quite,
Hanging on waves of dolefull feares,
By surge of sighes at wrecke nere hand,
May fast no anker hold on land.
    What helps the dyall to the blinde,
Or els the clock without it sound.   20
Or who by dreames doth hope to finde,
The hidden gold within the ground:
Shalbe as free from cares and feares,
As he that holds a Wolfe by the eares.
    And how much mad is he that thinks
To clime to heaven by the beames,

160 *meane* low, poor
  1 *doutfull* uncertain, apprehensive
  7 *ay prest* always at hand
 13 *carefull* full of cares, anxieties
 14 *Fleting* floating
 19 *dyall* sundial

What joy alas, hath he that winks,
At Titan or his golden streames,
His joyes not subject to reasons lawes,
That joyeth more then he hath cause.
    For as the Phenix that climeth hye,
The sunne lightly in ashes burneth,
Againe, the Faulçon so quick of eye,
Sone on the ground the net masheth.
Experience therfore the meane assurance,
Prefers before the doutfull pleasance.

161. The lover thinkes no paine to great, wherby he may obtain his ladie.

Sith that the way to wealth is wo,
And after paine is pleasure prest,
Why should I than dispaire so,
Ay bewailing mine unrest:
Or let to leade my life in paine,
So worthy a lady to obtaine.
    The fisher man doth count no care,
To cast his nets to wrack or wast,
And in reward of eche mans share.
A gogen gift is much imbrast,
Should I than grudge it grief or gall,
That loke at length to whelm a Whall.
    The poore man ploweth his ground for grain,

27–8 *he that winks, / At* he who shuts his eyes to, looks away from
34 *masheth* enmeshes
161 1 *Sith* since
    2 *prest* at hand
    3 *than* then
    5 *let to leade* leave off leading
    7–8 The fisherman sees no difference when he casts his nets in them being
        destroyed or coming up empty
    10 *imbrast* appreciated
    12 *Whall* whale

And soweth his seede increase to crave,
And for thexpence of all his pain,
Oft holdes it hap his seede to save,
These pacient paines my part doth show,
To long for love ere that I know.
    And take no scorne to scape from skill,
To spend my sprites to spare my speche,   20
To win for welth the want of will.
And thus for rest to rage I reche,
Running my race as rect upright:
Till teares of truth appease my plight.
    And plant my plaint within her brest,
Who doutles may restore againe,
My harmes to helth, my ruthe to rest,
That laced is within her chaine,
For earst ne are the griefes so gret:
As is the joy when love is met.   30
    For who covets so high to clim,
As doth the bird that pitfoll toke,
Or who delightes so swift to swim,
As doth the fish that scapes the hoke,
If these had never entred wo:
How mought they have rejoysed so.
    But yet alas ye lovers all,
That here me joy thus lesse rejoyce,
Judge not amis what so befall.
In me there lieth no power of choyse,   40
It is but hope that doth me move:

15 *thexpence* the expense
16 *hap* propitious
18 *ere that* before
19 I see it as no shame to seem lacking in art
20 *sprites* vital powers
23 *rect* straight, righteous
25 *plaint* poetic complaint, expression of injustice or sorrow
27 *ruthe* distress
29 *earst* previously
32 *pitfoll toke* had been caught in a pitfall trap

Who standerd bearer is to love.
   On whose ensigne when I behold,
I see the shadow of her shape,
Within my faith so fast I fold:
Through drede I die, through hope I scape,
Thus ease and wo full oft I finde,
What will you more she knoweth my minde.

162. Of a new maried student that plaied fast or lose.

A studient at his boke so plast:
That welth he might have wonne,
From boke to wife did flete in hast,
From wealth to wo to runne.
Now, who hath plaied a feater cast,
Since jugling first begonne?
In knitting of him self so fast,
Him selfe he hath undonne.

163. The meane estate is to be accompted the best.

Who craftly castes to stere his boate
   and safely skoures the flattering flood:
He cutteth not the greatest waves,
   for why that way were nothing good.

43 *ensigne* heraldic arms
162 1 *plast* placed
  5 *feater* neater *cast* throw
163 *meane* middling
  1 *castes* contrives
  2 *skoures* passes rapidly over
  4 *for why* because

Ne fleteth on the crocked shore
   lest harme him happe awayting lest.
But wines away betwene them both,
   as who would say the meane is best.
Who waiteth on the golden meane,
   he put in point of sickernes: 10
Hides not his head in sluttish coates,
   ne shroudes himself in filthines.
Ne sittes aloft in hye estate,
   Where hatefull hartes envie his chance:
But wisely walkes betwixt them twaine,
   ne proudly doth himself avance
The highest tree in all the wood
   is rifest rent with blustring windes:
The higher hall the greater fall
   such chance have proude and lofty mindes.   20
When Jupiter from hye doth threat
   with mortall mace and dint of thunder
The hyest hilles bene batrid eft
   when they stand still that stoden under.
The man whose hed with wit is fraught
   in welth will feare a worser tide
When fortune failes dispaireth nought
   but constantly doth still abide.
For he that sendeth grisely stormes
   with whisking windes and bitter blastes   30
And fowlth with hayle the winters face,
   and frotes the soile with hory frostes:

6 Lest harm should happen to him that he least expected
7 *wines away* winds a way
10 *put in point* gives himself the best chance of   *sickernes* security
11 *sluttish coates* dirty garments
16 *himself avance* put himself forward
23 *batrid eft* battered repeatedly
26 *tide* occasion
31 *fowlth* makes ugly
32 *frotes* chafes

Even he adawth the force of cold
   the spring in sendes with somer hote:
The same full oft to stormy hartes
   is cause of bale: of joy the roote.
Not alwaies yll though so be now
   when cloudes ben driven, then rides the racke.
Phebus the fresh ne shooteth still,
   somtime he harpes his muse to wake.
Stand stif therfore, pluck up thy hart,
   lose not thy port though fortune faile.
Againe whan winde doth serve at will,
   take hede to hye to hoyse thy saile.

164. The lover refused, lamenteth his estate.

I lent my love to losse and gaged my life in vaine,
If hate for love and death for life of lovers be the gaine.
  And curse I may by course the place eke time and howre
That nature first in me did forme to be a lives creature.
  Sithe that I must absent my selfe so secretly
In place desert where never man my secretes shall discry:
  In doling of my dayes among the beastes so brute,
Who with their tonges may not bewray the secretes of my sute.
  Nor I in like to them may once to move my minde

33 *adawth* daunts
36 *bale* suffering
38 *rides* drifts *racke* mass of cloud
39 *ne shooteth still* does not always shoot
40 *harpes* plays on a harp
44 *take hede to hye to hoyse* beware of hoisting too high
164 1 *gaged* wagered, devoted
  3 *by course* as a consequence *eke* also
  4 *lives* living
  5 *Sithe* since
  6 *discry* discover
  7 *doling* grieving
  8 *bewray* disclose *sute* petition
  9 *in like* in a similar manner

40

But gase on them and they on me, as beastes are wont of kinde.   10
   Thus ranging as refusde, to reache some place of rest,
All ruff of heare, my nayles unnocht, as to such semeth best.
   That wander by their wittes, deformed so to be,
That men may say, such one may curse the time he first gan see
   The beauty of her face, her shape in such degree,
As God himself may not discerne, one place mended to be.
   Nor place it in like place, my fansy for to please,
Who would become a heardmans hyre, one howre to have of
     ease.
   Whereby I might restore, to me some stedfastnes,
That have mo thoughtes heapt in my hed then life may long
     disges   20
   As oft to throw me downe upon the earth so cold,
Wheras with teares most rufully, my sorowes do unfold.
   And in beholding them, I chiefly call to minde,
What woman could finde in her hart, such bondnge for to
     binde.
   Then rashly forth I yede, to cast me from that care,
Like as the bird for foode doth flye, and lighteth in the snare.
   From whence I may not meve, untill my race be roon,
So trained is my truth through her, that thinkes my life well
     woon.
   Thus tosse I to and fro, in hope to have reliefe,
But in the fine I finde not so, it doubleth but my griefe.   30
   Wherfore I will my want, a warning for to be,
Unto all men, wishing that they, a myrrour make of me.

---

10 *are wont of kinde* are accustomed to by nature
12 *heare* hair   *unnocht* uncut
16 *mended to be* that could be improved
18 *heardmans hyre* shepherd's boy
20 *mo* more   *disges* digest
24 *bondnge* misprint for 'bondage'
25 *yede* go   *care* sorrow, anxiety
26 *lighteth* alights
28 *trained* entrapped
30 *fine* end

165. The felicitie of a minde imbracing vertue,
that beholdeth the wretched desires
of the worlde.

When dredful swelling seas, through boisterous windy blastes,
So tosse the ships, that all for nought, serves ancor, sail, and
    mastes.
    Who takes not pleasure then, safely on shore to rest,
And see with drede and depe dispaire, how shipmen are
    distrest.
    Not that we pleasure take, when others felen smart,
Our gladnes groweth to see their harmes, and yet to fele no
    part.
    Delight we take also, well ranged in aray,
When armies meete to see the fight, yet free be from the fray.
    But yet among the rest, no joy may match with this,
10 Taspyre unto the temple hye, where wisdome troned is.
    Defended with the saws of hory heades expert,
Which clere it kepe from errours mist, that might the truth
    pervert
    From whence thou mayst loke down, and see as under
    foote,
Mans wandring wil & doutful life, from whence they take
    their roote.
    How some by wit contend, by prowes some to rise,
Riches and rule to gaine and hold, is all that men devise.
    O miserable mindes, O hartes in folly drent,
Why see you not what blindnesse in this wretched life is
    spent?
    Body devoyde of griefe, minde free from care and drede,
20 Is all and some that natute craves, wherwith our life to feede.
    So that for natures turne few thinges may well suffice,

165 7 *aray* martial order
    10 *Taspyre* to aspire   *troned* throned
    15 *prowes* prowess, martial skill
    17 *drent* drowned
    20 *natute* misprint for 'nature'

Dolour and grief clene to expell, and some delight surprice.
  Yea and it falleth oft, that nature more content
Is with the lesse, then when the more to cause delight is spent.

166. All worldly pleasures vade.

The winter with his griesly stormes ne lenger dare abide,
The plesant grasse, with lusty grene, the earth hath newly dide
The trees have leves, the bowes don spred, new changed is the
        yere
The water brokes are cleane sonk down, the plesant banks
        apere.
The spring is come, the goodly nimphes now daunce in every
        place
Thus hath the yere most pleasantly of late ychangde his face.
Hope for no immortalitie, for welth will weare away,
As we may learne by every yere, yea howers of every day.
For Zepharus doth molifie the cold and blustering windes:
The somers drought doth take away the spring out of our
        mindes   10
And yet the somer cannot last, but once must step aside,
Then Autumn thinks to kepe his place, but Autumn cannot
        bide.
For when he hath brought forth his fruits & stuft the barns
        with corn
Then winter eates and empties all, and thus is Autumn worn.
Then hory frosts possesse the place, then tempests work much
        harm,
Then rage of stormes done make all cold, which somer had
        made so warm
Wherfore let no man put his trust in that, that will decay,

23 *it falleth oft* it often happens
24 *then* than
166 *vade* fade
 2 *dide* dyed
 4 *water brokes* fast-flowing waters

For slipper wealth will not continue, pleasure will weare away.
For when that we have lost our life, and lye under a stone,
20 What are we then? we are but earth, then is our pleasure gone.
No man can tell what God almight of every wight doth cast,
No man can say to day I live, till morne my life shall last.
For when thou shalt before thy judge stand to receive thy dome,
What sentence Minos doth pronounce that must of thee
     become.
Then shall not noble stocke and bloud redeme the from his
     hands
Nor sugred talke with eloquence shall lose thee from his
     bandes.
Nor yet thy life uprightly lead, can help thee out of hell,
For who descendeth down so depe, must there abide and dwell.
Diana could not thence deliver chaste Hypolitus,
30 Nor Theseus could not call to life his frende Perithous.

167. A complaint of the losse of libertie
by love.

In seking rest, unrest I finde,
I finde that welth is cause of wo:
Wo worth the time that I inclinde,
To fixe in minde her beauty so.
   That day be darkned as the night,
Let furious rage it cleane devour:
Ne Sunne nor Moone therin give light,
But it consume with streame and shower.
   Let no small birds straine forth their voyce,
10 With pleasant tunes, ne yet no beast:

18 *slipper* transitory
21 *wight* person   *cast* allot, ordain
23 *dome* judgement
25 *the* thee
26 *lose* loose
167 3 Wo *worth* cursed be

Finde cause wherat he may rejoyce,
That day when chaunced mine unrest.
     Wherin alas from me was raught,
Mine own free choyce and quiet minde,
My life me death in balance braught
And reason rasde through barke and rinde.
     And I as yet in flower of age,
Both wit and will did still advance:
Ay to resist that burning rage:
But when I darte then did I glaunce.   20
     Nothing to me did seme so hye,
In minde I could it straight attaine:
Fansy perswaded me therby,
Love to esteme a thing most vaine.
     But as the bird upon the brier,
Doth pricke and proyne her without care:
Not knowing alas (poore foole) how nere
She is unto the fowlers snare.
     So I amid disceitfull trust,
Did not mistrust such wofull happe: 30
Till cruell love ere that I wist
Had caught me in his carefull trappe.
     Then did I fele, and partly know,
How litle force in me did raigne:
So soone to yelde to overthrow,
Do fraile to flit from joy to paine.
     For when in welth will did me leade

13 *raught* taken, snatched
16 *reason rasde through barke and rinde* cut my reason right through its
     bark and rind
20 *darte* dared
22 *straight* immediately
26 *pricke* trot *proyne* prance *care* anxiety
30 *happe* chance, fortune
31 *ere that I wist* before I knew it
32 *carefull* full of sorrows, anxieties
34 *force* power, control
36 *Do* misprint for either 'So' or 'To' (= too)

Of libertie to hoyse my saile:
To hale at shete and cast my leade,
40   I thought free choyce would still prevaile.
    In whose calme streames I sayld so farre,
No raging storme had in respect:
Untill I raysde a goodly starre,
Wherto my course I did direct.
    In whose prospect in doolfull wise,
My tackle failde, my compasse brake?
Through hote desires such stormes did rise,
That sterne and top went all to wrake.
    Oh cruell hap, oh fatall chaunce,
50 O Fortune why were thou unkinde:
Without regarde thus in a traunce,
To reve from me my joyfull minde.
    Where I was free now must I serve,
Where I was lose now am I bound:
In death my life I do preserve,
As one through girt with many a wound.

168. A praise of his Ladye.

Geve place you Ladies and be gone,
Boast not your selves at all:
For here at hand approcheth one:
Whose face will staine you all.
    The vertue of her lively lokes,
Excels the precious stone:
I wish to have none other bokes

39 *To hale at shete* to set the sail
    leade piece of lead suspended on string to test depth of water
43 *raysde* saw coming over the horizon
45 In the sight of which in a miserable way
52 *reve* steal
54 *lose* loose, free
56 *through girt* struck through
168 4 *staine* surpass, disgrace by comparison

To read or loke upon.
   In eche of her two cristall eyes,
Smileth a naked boye: 10
It would you all in hart suffice
To see that lampe of joye.

   I thinke nature hath lost the moulde,
Where she her shape did take:
Or els I doubt if nature could,
So faire a creature make.

   She may be well comparde
Unto the Phenix kinde:
Whose like was never sene nor heard,
That any man can finde.   20

   In life she is Diana chast,
In trouth Penelopey:
In word and eke in dede stedfast,
What wil you more we sey.

   If all the world were sought so farre,
Who could finde such a wight:
Her beuty twinkleth like a starre,
Within the frosty night.

   Her rosiall colour comes and goes,
With such a comely grace: 30
More redier to then doth the rose,
Within her lively face.

   At Bacchus feast none shall her mete,
Ne at no wanton play:
Nor gasyng in an open strete,
Nor gadding as a stray.

   The modest mirth that she doth use,
Is mixt with shamefastnesse:
All vice she doth wholy refuse,

18 *kinde* species
23 *eke* also
24 *What wil you more* what more could you ask for
26 *wight* person
29 *rosiall* roseate
38 *shamefastnesse* modesty, decency

40
    And hateth ydlenesse.
      O lord it is a world to see,
    How vertue can repaire:
    And decke in her such honestie,
    Whom nature made so faire.
      Truely she doth as farre excede,
    Our women now adayes:
    As doth the Jelifloure, a wede,
    And more a thousand waies.
      How might I do to get a graffe:

50
    Of this unspotted tree.
    For al the rest are plaine but chaffe,
    Which seme good corne to be.
      This gift alone I shal her geve,
    When death doth what he can:
    Her honest fame shall ever live,
    Within the mouth of man.

169. *The pore estate to be holden for best.*

Experience now doth shew what God us taught before,
Desired pompe is vaine, and seldome doth it last:
Who climbes to raigne with kinges, may rue his fate full sore.
Alas the woful ende that comes with care full fast,
Reject him doth renowne his pompe full low is caste.
Deceived is the birde by swetenesse of the call
Expell that pleasant taste, wherein is bitter gall.
    Such as with oten cakes in poore estate abides,
Of care have they no cure, the crab with mirth they rost,

---

    42 *repaire* come, be present
    47 *Jelifloure* gillyflower
    49 *graffe* graft, cutting
    51 *plaine but* nothing at all except/clearly nothing but
169 4 *care full* full of cares, anxiety
    9 *Of care have they no cure* they do not worry about burdensome cares

More ease fele they then those, that from their height
 down slides   10
Excesse doth brede their wo, they saile in Scillas cost,
Remainyng in the stormes tyll shyp and al be lost.
Serve God therefore thou pore, for lo, thou lives in rest,
Eschue the golden hall, thy thatched house is besT.

170. *The complaint of Thestilis*
amid the desert
wodde.

Thestilis a sely man, when love did him forsake,
In mourning wise, amid the wods thus gan his plaint to make
Ah woful man (quod he) fallen is thy lot to mone
And pyne away with careful thoughtes, unto thy love unknowen
Thy lady thee forsakes whom thou didst honor so
That ay to her thou were a frend, and to thy selfe a foe.
Ye lovers that have lost your heartes desired choyse,
Lament with me my cruell happe, & helpe my trembling voice.
Was never man that stode so great in fortunes grace:
Nor with his swete alas to deare possest so high a place. 10
As I whose simple hart aye thought him selfe full sure,
But now I se hie springing tides they may not aye endure.
She knowes my giltelesse hart, and yet she lets it pine,
Of her untrue professed love so feble is the twine.
What wonder is it than, if I berent my heares,
And carving death continually do bathe my selfe in teares,

11 *cost* coast
170 *desert wodde* deserted wood
 1 *sely* simple
 2 *wise* manner *plaint* poetic complaint, expression of injustice or sorrow
 4 *careful* full of sorrow, anxiety
 6 *ay* always
 8 *happe* fortune
 10 *to* too
 15 *berent my heares* tear my hair
 16 *carving* misprint for 'craving'

When Cresus king of Lide was cast in cruell bandes,
And yelded goodes and life also into his enemies handes.
What tong could tell his wo, yet was his griefe much lesse
Then mine: for I have lost my love whych might my woe
20   redresse.
Ye woodes that shroud my limes give now your holow sound,
That ye may helpe me to bewaile the cares that me
      confound.
Ye rivers rest a while and stay the streames that runne,
Rew Thestilis most woful man that lives under the sunne.
Transport my sighes ye windes unto my plesant foe,
My tricklyng teares shal witnesse beare of this my cruel woe.
O happy man wer I if all the goddes agreed:
That now the susters three should cut in twaine my fatall
      threde.
Till life with love shall ende I here resigne al joy:
Thy pleasant swete I now lament whose lacke bredes myne
30   anoy
Farewell my deare therfore farewell to me well knowne:
If that I die it shalbe said that thou hast slaine thine owne.

171. An answere of
comfort.

Thestilis thou sely man, why dost thou so complayne,
If nedes thy love wyll thee forsake, thy mourning is in vaine.
For none can force the streames against their course to ronne,
Nor yet unwilling love with teares or wailyng can be wonne.
Cease thou therefore thy plaintes, let hope thy sorowes ease,

18 *yelded* surrendered
21 *limes* limbs
23 *stay* halt
24 *Rew* pity
30 *anoy* suffering, trouble
171 1 *sely* simple, naive
  2 *If nedes thy love wyll thee forsake* if it must happen that your love will
    forsake you
  5 *plaintes* poetic complaints, expressing injustice or sorrow

The shipmen though their sailes be rent yet hope to scape the
      seas
Though straunge she seme a while, yet thinke she wil not
      chaunge
Good causes drive a ladies love, sometime to seme full straunge.
No lover that hath wit, but can forsee such happe,
That no wight can at wish or will slepe in his ladies lappe.   10
Achilles for a time faire Brises did forgo,
Yet did they mete with joye againe, then thinke thou maist do so.
Though he and lovers al in love sharpe stormes do finde,
Dispaire not thou pore Thestilis though thy love seme unkinde.
Ah thinke her graffed love cannot so sone decay,
Hie springes may cease from swelling styll, but never dry away
Oft stormes of lovers yre, do more their love encrease:
As shinyng sunne refreshe the fruites when raining gins to cease.
When springes are waxen lowe, then must they flow againe,
So shall thy hart advaunced be, to pleasure out of paine.   20
When lacke of thy delight most bitter griefe apperes,
Thinke on Etrascus worthy love that lasted thirty yeres,
Which could not long atcheve his hartes desired choice,
Yet at the ende he founde rewarde that made him to rejoyce.
Since he so long in hope with pacience did remaine,
Can not thy fervent love forbeare thy love a moneth or
      twaine?
Admit she minde to chaunge and nedes will thee forgo,
Is there no mo may thee delyght but she that paynes thee so?
Thestilis draw to the towne and love as thou hast done,
In time thou knowest by faythful love as good as she is
      wonne.   30
And leave the desert woodes and waylyng thus alone,
And seke to salve thy sore els were, if all her love be gone.

7 *straunge* cold
9 *happe* chance, fortune
10 *no wight* no one
15 *graffed* engrafted
28 *mo* more
32 *salve* heal   *els were* elsewhere

172. ¶The lover praieth pity showing that
nature hath taught his dog as it
were to sue for the same
by kissing his ladies
handes.

Nature that taught my silly dog god wat:
Even for my sake to like where I do love,
Inforced him whereas my lady sat
With humble sute before her fallyng flat.
As in his sorte he might her pray and move
To rue upon his lord and not forgete
The stedfast faith he beareth her and love,
Kissing her hand whom she could not remove.
A way that would for frowning nor for threte
As though he would have sayd in my behove.
Pity my lord your slave that doth remaine,
Lest by his death, you giltles slay us twaine.

173. Of his ring sent to
his ladie.

Since thou my ring mayst go where I ne may.
Since thou mayst speake, where I must hold my peace.
Say unto her that is my lives stay,
Graven within which I do here expresse:
That sooner shall the sunne not shine by day,
And with the raine the floods shall waxen lesse.

172 *sue* petition, beg
  1 *god wat* God knows
  4 *sute* petition, plea
  6 *rue* take pity
  10 *in my behove* for my benefit
173 1 *I ne may* I cannot
  3 *stay* support

Sooner the tree the hunter shall bewray,
Then I for change, or choyce of other love,
Do ever seke my fansy to remove.

174. *The changeable state of lovers.*

For that a restles hed must somwhat have in ure
Wherwith it may acquainted be, as falcon is with lure.
　　Fansy doth me awake out of my drowsy slepe,
In seing how the litle Mouse, at night begins to crepe.
　　So the desirous man, that longes to catch his pray,
In spying how to watch his time, lyeth lurking still by day,
　　In hoping for to have, and fearing for to finde
The salve that should recure his sore, & soroweth but the
　　　　minde.
　　Such is the guise of love, and the uncertain state,
That some should have their hoped hap, and other hard estate.　10
　　That some should seme to joy in that they never had,
And some againe shall frown as fast, where causeles they
　　　　be sad.
　　Such trades do lovers use when they be most at large,
That gide the stere when they themselves lye fettred in the
　　　　barge.
　　The grenesse of my youth cannot therof expresse
The processe, for by proofe unknowen, all this is but by gesse.
　　Wherfore I hold it best, in time to hold my peace,
But wanton will it cannot hold, or make my pen to cease.
　　A pen of no availe, a fruitles labour eke,

---

　　7 *bewray* expose
　　8 *Then* than
174 1 *must somwhat have in ure* must have something in recollection
　　8 *salve* healing ointment　*recure* cure
　　9 *guise* custom, practice
　　10 *hap* good fortune
　　14 *stere* rudder
　　19 *eke* also

My troubled hed with fansies fraught, doth paine it selfe
20   to seke.
    And if perhaps my wordes of none availe do pricke,
Such as do feele the hidden harmes, I wold not they shold kicke.
    As causeles me to blame which thinketh them no harme,
Although I seme by others fire, somtime my selfe to warme.
    Which clerely I deny, as giltles of that crime,
And though wrong demde I be therin, truth it will try in time.

175. A praise of Audley.

When Audley had run out his race, and ended wer his daies,
His fame stept forth & bad me write of him som worthi praise
What life he lad, what actes he did: his vertues and good name,
Wherto I calde for true report, as witnes of the same.
Wel born he was, wel bent by kinde, whose minde did never
        swerve
A skilfull head, a valiant hart, a ready hand to serve.
Brought up & trained in feates of war long time beyond
        the seas,
Cald home again to serve his prince, whom still he sought to
        please.
What tornay was there he refusde, what service did he shoon,
10   Where he was not nor his advice, what great exploit was doon?
In town a Lambe, in field full fierce, a Lion at the nede,
In sober wit a Salomon, yet one of Hectors seede,
Then shame it were that any tong shold now defame his dedes.
That in his life a mirrour was to all that him succedes.
No poore estate nor hie renowne his nature could pervart,
No hard mischance that him befell could move his constant
        hart.
Thus long he lived, loved of all, as one misliekt of none.
And where he went who cald him not the gentle Paragon.
But course of kinde doth cause eche fruite to fall when it is ripe,

175 5 *wel bent by kinde* well shaped by nature
     9 *tornay* tounament   *shoon* shun

And spitefull death will suffer none to scape his grevous gripe.   20
Yet though the ground received have his corps into her wombe,
This Epitaphe ygrave in brasse, shall stand upon his tombe.
Lo here he lies that hateth vice, and vertues life imbrast,
His name in earth, his sprite above, deserves to be well plast.

176. Time trieth truth.

Eche thing I see hath time, which time must try my truth,
Which truth deserves a special trust, on trust gret frendship
      groweth.
And frendship may not faile where faithfulnesse is sound,
And faithfulnesse is full of fruit, and frutefull thinges be sound.
And sound is good at proofe, and proofe is prince of praise,
And precious praise is such a pearle, as seldome ner decaies.
All these thinges time tries forth, which time I must abide,
How should I boldly credite crave till time my truth have tride.
For as I found a time to fall in fansies frame,
So I do wish a lucky time for to declare the same.   10
If hap may answere hope, and hope may have his hire,
Then shall my hart possesse in peace the time that I desire.

177. The lover refused of his love
imbraceth death.

My youthfull yeres are past,
My joyfull dayes are gone:
My life it may not last,

20 *gripe* grip
22 *ygrave* engraved
23 *imbrast* embraced
24 *sprite* soul   *plast* placed
176 3–4 *sound . . . sound* one of these is surely a misprint for 'found'
  6 *seldome ner* nearly never
  9 *frame* plan
 11 *hap* chance, fortune   *hire* payment

My grave and I am one.
   My mirth and joyes are fled,
And I a man in wo:
Desirous to be ded,
My mischiefe to forgo.
   I burne and am a colde,
I freze amids the fire:
I see she doth withold
That is my most desire.
   I see my help at hand,
I see my life also:
I see where she doth stand
That is my deadly fo.
   I see how she doth see,
And yet she will be blinde:
I see in helping me,
She sekes and will not finde.
   I see how she doth wry,
When I begin to mone:
I see when I come nye,
How faine she would begone.
   I see what will ye more
She will me gladly kill:
And you shall see therfore
That she shall have her will.
   I cannot live with stones
It is to hard a foode:
I will be dead at ones
To do my lady good.

10

20

30

177 21 *wry* turn away
   24 How she wishes to get away
   25 *what will ye more* what more do you want
   30 *to* too
   31 *ones* once

178. The picture of a lover.

Behold my picture here well portrayed for the nones.
With hart consumed and falling flesh, behold the very
    bones.
Whose cruell chance alas and desteny is such,
Onely because I put my trust in some folke all to much.
For sins the time that I did enter in this pine,
I never saw the rising sunne but with my weping eyen.
Nor yet I never heard so swete a voice or sound,
But that to me it did encrease the dolour of my wound.
Nor in so soft a bedde, alas I never lay,
But that it semed hard to me or ever it was day,   10
Yet in this body bare, that nought but life retaines,
The strength wherof clene past away the care yet still
    remaine.
Like as the cole in flame doth spend it self you se,
To vaine and wretched cinder dust till it consumed be.
So doth this hope of mine inforce my fervent sute,
To make me for to gape in vaine, whilst other eate the
    frute.
And shall do till the death doth geve me such a grace,
To rid this silly wofull sprite out of this dolefull case.
And then would God wer writ in stone or els in leade,
This Epitaphe upon my grave, to shew why I am dead.   20
Here lyeth the lover lo, who for the love he aught,
Alive unto his lady dere, his death therby he caught.
And in a shielde of blacke, loe here his armes appeares,

178 1 *for the nones* indeed
   3 *chance* fortune
   5 *sins* since   *pine* torment
 10 *or* before
 12 *care* sorrow, anxiety
 15 *sute* petition, plea
 18 *silly* pitiful, weak   *sprite* spirit   *case* casing
 19 *would God wer writ* I wish to God [my epitaph] were written
 21 *aught* bore/owed
 23 *armes* heraldic arms

With weping eyes as you may see, well poudred all with
    teares.
Loe here you may behold, aloft upon his brest,
A womans hand straining the hart of him that loved her
    best.
Wherfore all you that see this corps for love that starves,
Example make unto you all, that thanklesse lovers sarves.

179. *Of the death of Phillips.*

Bewaile with me all ye that have profest,
Of musicke tharte by touche of coarde or winde:
Lay down your lutes and let your gitterns rest.
Phillips is dead whose like you can not finde.
Of musicke much exceeding all the rest,
Muses therefore of force now must you wrest,
Your pleasant notes into an other sound,
The string is broke, the lute is dispossest.
The hand is cold, the body in the ground.
The lowring lute lamenteth now therfore.
Phillips her frende that can her touche no more.

180. *That all thing somtime finde*
ease of their paine, save
onely the lover.

I see there is no sort,
Of thinges that live in griefe:
Which at somtime may not resort,

24 *poudred* sprinkled
27 *corps* (live) body   *starves* dies
28 *that thanklesse lovers sarves* who serve as thankless lovers
179 2 *tharte* the art   *coarde* string   *winde* breath
   3 *gitterns* a gittern is a type of guitar
   6 *of force* by necessity
  10 *lowring* mourning, melancholy

Wheras they have reliefe.
   The striken Dere by kinde,
Of death that standes in awe:
For his recure an herbe can finde,
The arrow to withdrawe.
   The chased Dere hath soile,
To coole him in his heat: 10
The Asse after his wery toile,
In stable is up set.
   The Cony hath his cave,
The litle bird his nest:
From heate and cold them selves to save,
At all times as they list.
   The Owle with feble sight,
Lyes lurking in the leaves:
The Sparrow in the frosty night,
May shroude her in the eaves.   20
   But wo to me alas,
In sunne nor yet in shade,
I cannot finde a resting place,
My burden to unlade.
   But day by day still beares,
The burden on my backe:
With weping eyen and watry teares,
To hold my hope abacke.
   All thinges I see have place,
Wherein they bow or bende: 30
Save this alas my wofull case,
Which no where findeth ende.

180 5 *kinde* nature
     6 *awe* fear
     7 *recure* cure, healing
     13 *Cony* rabbit
     16 *list* please

181. Thassault of Cupide upon the fort where the lovers hart lay wounded and how he was taken.

When Cupide scaled first the fort,
Wherin my hart lay wounded sore:
The battry was of such a sort
That I must yelde or dye therfore.
    There saw I love upon the wall,
How he his banner did display:
Alarme alarme he gan to call,
And bad his souldiours kepe aray,
    The armes the which that Cupide bare,
Were pearced hartes with teares besprent:
In silver and sable to declare
The stedfast love he alwaies ment.
    There might you see his band all drest,
In colours like to white and blacke:
With powder and with pellets prest,
To bring the fort to spoile and sacke.
    Good will the master of the shot,
Stode in the rampyre brave and proud:
For spence of powder he sparde not,
Assault assault to cry aloud.
    There might you heare the cannons rore,
Eche pece discharged a lovers loke:
Which had the power to rent, and tore

---

181 *Thassault* the assault
  3 *battry* violent attack
  8 *kepe aray* stay in order
10 *besprent* besprinkled
11 *sable* black
15 *powder* gunpowder   *pellets* cannonballs   *prest* ready
18 *rampyre* rampart
19 He did not scrimp to save gunpowder
23 *rent* tear

In any place wheras they toke.
    And even with the trumpets sowne,
The scaling ladders were up set:
And beauty walked up and downe
With bow in hand and arrowes whet.
    Then first desire began to scale,
And shrowded him under his targe,   30
As on the worthiest of them all,
And aptest for to geve the charge.
    Then pushed souldiers with their pikes
And holbarders with handy strokes:
The hargabushe in flesh it lightes,
And dims the ayre with misty smokes.
    And as it is the souldiers use,
When shot and powder gins to want:
I hanged up my flagge of truce
And pleaded for my lives graunt.   40
    When fansy thus had made her breach,
And beauty entred with her band:
With bag and baggage sely wretch,
I yelded into beauties hand.
    Then beauty bad to blow retrete,
And every soldiour to retire.
And mercy wilde with spede to fet:
Me captive bound as prisoner.
    Madame (quoth I) sith that this day,
Hath served you at all assaies: 50

25 *sowne* sound
28 *whet* sharpened
30 *targe* light shield
31 *on the worthiest* one of the worthiest
34 *holbarders* halberds; weapon which is both spear and battle-axe
35 *hargabushe* harquebus, portable gun   *lightes* alights, lands on
37 *use* custom
38 *gins to want* begins to run out
43 *sely* pitiful, weak
47 *fet* fetch
49 *sith* since
50 *at all assaies* at every juncture

I yelde to you without delay,
Here of the fortresse all the kaies.
　　And sith that I have ben the marke,
At whom you shot at with your eye:
Nedes must you with your handy warke,
Or salve my sore or let me dye,

182. *The aged lover renounceth love.*

I lothe that I did love,
In youth that I thought swete:
As time requires for my behove,
Me thinkes they are not mete.
My lustes they do me leave,
My fansies all be fled:
And tract of time begins to weave,
Gray heares upon my hed.
　　For age with steling steps,
Hath clawed me with his crowch:
And lusty life away she leapes,
As there had bene none such.
　　My muse doth not delight
Me as she did before:
My hand and pen are not in plight,
As they have bene of yore.
　　For reason me denies,
This youthly idle rime:
And day by day to me she cries,
Leave of these toyes in time.

56 *Or salve my sore or* either heal my wound or
182 3 *behove* advantage
　4 *mete* suitable, fitting
　7 *tract* passing
　10 *crowch* crutch
　15 *in plight* in agreement, bound together

The wrinkles in my brow,
The furrowes in my face:
Say limping age will hedge him now,
Where youth must geve him place.
　　The harbinger of death,
To me I see him ride:
The cough, the cold, the gasping breath,
Doth bid me to provide.
　　A pikeax and a spade,
And eke a shrowding shete,   30
A house of clay for to be made,
For such a gest most mete.
　　Me thinkes I heare the clarke,
That knoles the carefull knell:
And bids me leave my wofull warke,
Ere nature me compell.
　　My kepers knit the knot,
That youth did laugh to scorne:
Of me that clene shalbe forgot,
As I had not bene borne.   40
　　Thus must I youth give up,
Whose badge I long did weare:
To them I yelde the wanton cup
That better may it beare.
　　Lo here the bared scull,
By whose balde signe I know:
That stouping age away shall pull,
Which youthfull yeres did sow.
　　For beauty with her band
These croked cares hath wrought: 50
And shipped me into the land,
From whence I first was brought.
　　And ye that bide behinde,

23 *hedge* restrict
30 *eke* also
33 *clarke* clergyman
34 *carefull* mournful
36 *Ere* before

Have ye none other trust:
As ye of claye were cast by kinde,
So shall ye waste to dust.

183. Of the ladie Wentworthes death.

To live to dye and dye to live againe,
With good renowne of fame well led before
Here lieth she that learned had the lore,
Whom if the parfect vertues wolden daine.
To be set forth with foile of worldly grace,
Was noble borne and match in noble race,
Lord Wentworthes wife, nor wanted to attaine,
In natures giftes her praise among the rest,
But that that gave her praise above the best
Not fame, her wedlocks chastnes durst distain,
Wherein with child deliveryng of her wombe,
Thuntimely birth hath brought them both in tomb
So left she life by death to live againe.

184. The lover accusing his love for her unfaithfulnesse, purposeth to live in libertie.

The smoky sighes the bitter teares,
That I in vaine have wasted:
The broken slepes, the wo and feares,
That long in me have lasted:
The love and all I owe to thee,
Here I renounce and make me free.
    Which fredome I have by thy guilt,

55 *kinde* nature
183 10 *durst distain* dared dishonour
    12 *Thuntimely* the untimely, premature

And not by my deserving,
Since so unconstantly thou wilt
Not love, but still be swering.   10
To leave me of which was thine owne,
Without cause why as shalbe knowen.
    The frutes were faire the which did grow,
Within thy garden planted,
The leaves were grene of every bough,
And moysture nothing wanted,
Yet or the blossoms gan fall,
The caterpiller wasted all.
    Thy body was the garden place,
And sugred wordes it beareth,   20
The blossomes all thy faith it was,
Which as the canker wereth.
The cater piller is the same,
That hath wonne thee and lost thy name.
    I meane thy lover loved now,
By thy pretented folye,
Which will prove like, thou shalt finde how,
Unto a tree of holly:
That barke and bery beares alwayes,
The one, birdes feedes, the other slayes.   30
    And right well mightest thou have thy wish
Of thy love new acquaynted:
For thou art lyke unto the dishe
That Adrianus paynted:
Wherin were grapes portraid so faire
That fowles for foode did there repaire.
    But I am lyke the beaten fowle
That from the net escaped,
And thou art lyke the ravening owle
That all the night hath waked.   40
For none intent but to betray

184 10 *swering* probably a misprint for 'swerving'
   11 *leave me of* abandon me
   17 *or* before
   41 *intent* intention

The slepyng fowle before the day.
  Thus hath thy love been unto me
As pleasant and commodious,
As was the fyre made on the sea
By Naulus hate so odious.
Therwith to train the grekish host
From Troyes return where they wer lost.

185. The lover for want of his desire, sheweth his death at hand.

As Cypres tree that rent is by the roote,
As branch or slippe bereft from whence it growes
As wel sowen seede for drought that can not sprout
As gaping ground that raineles can not close
As moules that want the earth to do them bote
As fishe on land to whom no water flowes,
As Thameleon that lackes the aier so sote,
As flowers do fade when Phebus rarest showes.
As Salamandra repulsed from the fire:
So wanting my wish I dye for my desire

186. A happy end excedeth all pleasures and riches of the world.

The shining season here to some,
The glory in the worldes sight,
Renowmed fame through fortune wonne
The glitteryng golde the eyes delight,

47 *train* trick, trap
185 1 *rent* torn up
    2 *slippe* cutting, shoot
    5 *bote* remedy
    7 *Thameleon* misprint for 'Chameleon'   *sote* sweet

The sensuall life that semes so swete,
The hart with joyful dayes replete,
The thyng wherto eche wight is thrall,
The happy ende exceadeth all.

187. *Against an unstedfast woman.*

O temerous tauntres that delights in toyes
Tumbling cockboat totring to and fro,
Janglyng jestres depravers of swete joyes,
Ground of the graffe whence al my grief
    doth grow,
Sullen serpent environned with dispite,
That yll for good at all times doest requite.

188. *A praise of Petrarke and of Laura his ladie.*

O Petrarke hed and prince of poets al,
Whose lively gift of flowing eloquence,
Wel may we seke, but finde not how or whence
So rare a gift with thee did rise and fal,
Peace to thy bones, and glory immortall
Be to thy name, and to her excellence.
Whose beauty lighted in thy time and sence:
So to be set forth as none other shall.
Why hath not our pens, rimes so parfit wrought
Ne why our time forth bringeth beauty such   10
To trye our wittes as golde is by the touche,

---

186 7 *wight* person
187 1 *temerous tauntres* rash taunting woman
   2 *cockboat* small light boat
   4 *Ground of the graffe* source of the grafted shoot
   5 *environned with dispite* envenomed with spite

If to the stile the matter aided ought.
But ther was never Laure more then one,
And her had Petrarke for his Paragone.

189. *That petrark cannot be passed*
but notwithstanding that
Lawra is far surpassed

With Petrarke to compare ther may no wight,
Nor yet attain unto so high a stile,
But yet I wote full well where is a file.
To frame a learned man to praise aright:
Of stature meane of semely forme and shap,
Eche line of just proporsion to her height:
Her colour fresh and mingled with such sleight:
As though the rose sate in the lilies lap.
In wit and tong to shew what may be sed,
To every dede she joynes a parfit grace,
If Lawra livde she would her clene deface.
For I dare say and lay my life to wed
That Momus could not if he downe discended,
Once justly say, Lo this may be amended.

190. *Against a cruel woman.*

Cruel unkinde whom mercy cannot move,
Herbour of unhappe wher rigours rage doth raigne,
Ground of my griefe where pitie cannot prove:

188 12 *ought* at all
189 1 No one may compare with Petrarch
    3 *wote* know
    5 *meane* moderate
    7 *sleight* skill
    11 *deface* make [her] look bad by comparison
    14 *amended* improved
190 2 *Herbour* abode   *unhappe* misfortune
    3 *Ground* source prove succeed

Trikle to trust of all untruth the traine,
Thou rigorous rocke that ruth cannot remove.
Daungerous delph depe dungeon of disdaine:
Sacke of selfe will the chest of craft and change,
What causeth the thus causels for to change?
   Ah piteles plante whom plaint cannot provoke.
Den of disceite that right doth still refuse,   10
Causles unkinde that cariest under cloke
Cruelty and craft me onely to abuse,
Stately and stubberne withstanding Cupides stroke,
Thou merveilouse mase that makest men to muse,
Solleyn by selfe wil, most stony stiffe and straunge,
What causeth thee thus causelesse for to change?
   Slipper and secrete where surety cannot sowe
Net of newelty, neast of newfanglenesse,
Spring of al spite, from whence whole fluddes do flow,
Thou cave and cage of care and craftinesse   20
Wavering willow that every blast doth blowe
Graffe without groth and cause of carefulnesse,
Heape of mishap of all my griefe the graunge,
What causeth thee thus causelesse for to chaunge.
   Hast thou forgote that I was thine infeft,
By force of love haddest thou not hart at all,
Sawest thou not other for thy love were left
Knowest thou unkinde, that nothing mought befall
From out of my hart that could have the bereft.
What meanest thou then at ryot thus to raunge,   30
And leavest thine owne that never thought to chaunge.

4 *Trikle* treacherous   *traine* trap
5 *ruth* pity
6 *delph* pit, ditch
9 *plaint* poetic complaint, expressing injustice or sorrow
15 *Solleyn* sullen, obstinate *straunge* cold
17 *slipper* slippery, deceitful
20 *care* sorrow, anxiety
22 *graffe* graft, grafted shoot
23 *graunge* barn, storehouse
25 *thine infeft* enfeoffed to you
29 *the* thee

191. The lover sheweth what he would have, if it were graunted him to have what he would wishe.

If it were so that God would graunt me my request,
And that I might of earthly thinges have that I liked best.
I would not wish to clime to princely hye astate,
Which slipper is and slides so oft, and hath so fickle fate.
Nor yet to conquere realmes with cruel sworde in hande,
And so to shed the giltlesse bloude of such as would withstand.
Nor I would not desire in worldly rule to raigne.
Whose frute is all unquietnesse, and breaking of the braine.
Nor richesse in excesse of vertue so abhorde,
10 I would not crave which bredeth care and causeth all discorde.
But my request should be more worth a thousand folde:
That I might have and her enjoye that hath my hart in hold.
Oh God what lusty life should we live then for ever,
In pleasant joy and perfect blisse, to length our lives together.
With wordes of frendly chere, and lokes of lively love,
To utter all our hotte desires, which never should remove.
But grose and gredie wittes which grope but on the ground.
To gather muck of worldly goodes which oft do them
      confounde,
Can not attaine to knowe the misteries devine
20 Of perfite love wherto hie wittes of knowledge do incline.
A nigard of his golde such joye can never have
Which gettes with toile and kepes with care and is his money
      slave,
As they enjoy alwayes that taste love in his kinde,
For they do holde continually a heaven in their minde.
No worldly goodes could bring my hart so great an ease,
As for to finde or do the thing that might my ladie please.
For by her onely love my hart should have al joye,

191 10 *care* sorrow, anxiety
     15 *chere* greeting
     22 *care* anxiety

And with the same put care away, and all that coulde annoy.
As if that any thing should chance to make me sadde,
The touching of her corall lippes would straightewaies make
      me gladde,   30
And when that in my heart I fele that dyd me greve
With one imbracing of her armes she might me sone releve:
And as the Angels al which sit in heaven hye
With presence and the sight of god have their felicitie,
So likewyse I in earth, should have all earthly blis,
With presence of that Paragon, my god in earth that is.

192. The lady forsaken of her lover, praieth his returne, or the end of her own life.

To love, alas, who would not feare
That seeth my wofull state,
For he to whom my heart I beare
Doth me extremely hate,
And why therfore I cannot tell,
He will no lenger with me dwell.
    Did you not sewe and long me serve
Ere I you graunted grace?
And will you this now from me swarve
That never did trespace?   10
Alas poore woman then alas,
A wery lyfe here must I passe.
    And shal my faith have such refuse
In dede and shall it so,
Is ther no choise for me to chuse
But must I leve you so?
Alas pore woman then alas,

30 *straightewaies* straight away
192 7 *sewe* sue, make a petition
  8 *Ere* before
  9 *this* thus   *swarve* go away

A werye life hence must I pas.
    And is there now no remedy
But that you will forget her?
Ther was a time when that perdy
You would have heard her better.
But now that time is gone and past,
And all your love is but a blast.
    And can you thus breake your behest
In dede and can you so?
Did you not sweare you loved me best,
And can you now say no?
Remember me poore wight in paine,
And for my sake turne once againe.
    Alas poore Dido now I fele
Thy present painful state,
When false Eneas did hym stele
From thee at Carthage gate.
And left thee slepyng in thy bed,
Regarding not what he had sed,
    Was never woman thus betrayed,
Nor man so false forsworne,
His faith and trouth so strongly tyed,
Untruth hath all totorne:
And I have leave for my good will
To waile and wepe alone my fyll.
    But since it will not better be,
My teares shal never blin:
To moist the earth in such degree,
That I may drowne therin:
That by my death al men may say,
Lo women are as true as they.
    By me al women may beware,

21 *perdy* without a doubt
25 *behest* promise
29 *wight* person
40 *totorne* torn apart
44 *blin* cease

That see my wofull smart, 50
To seke true love let them not spare,
Before they set their hart.
Or els they may become as I,
Which for my truth am lyke to dye.

*193. The lover yelden into his ladies
handes, praieth
mercie.*

In fredome was my fantasie
Abhorryng bondage of the minde,
But now I yelde my libertie,
And willingly my selfe I binde.
Truely to serve with al my hart,
Whiles life doth last not to revart.
    Her beauty bounde me first of all
And forst my will for to consent:
And I agree to be her thrall,
For as she list I am content. 10
My wyll is hers in that I may,
And where she biddes I wyll obey.
    It lieth in her my wo or welth,
She may do that she liketh best,
If that she list I have my helth,
If she list not in wo I rest.
Sins I am fast within her bandes.
My wo and welth lieth in her handes.
    She can no lesse then pitie me,
Sith that my faith to her is knowne, 20

193 1 My fancy was free/I fancied I was free
    6 *revart* turn away, leave
    9 *thrall* slave
    10 *list* pleases
    17 *Sins* since
    20 *Sith* since

It were to much extremitie,
With cruelty to use her owne.
Alas a sinnefull enterprise,
To slay that yeldes at her device.
  But I thinke not her hart so harde,
Nor that she hath such cruell lust:
I doubt nothing of her reward,
For my desert but well I trust,
As she hath beauty to allure,
30   So hath she a hart that will recure.

194. *That nature which worketh all thinges
for our behoofe, hath made women
also for our comfort
and delight.*

Among dame natures workes such perfite law is wrought,
That things be ruled by course of kind in order as thei ought.
  And serveth in their state, in such just frame and sort,
That slender wits may judge the same, and make therof
        report.
  Behold what secrete force the winde doth easely show,
Which guides the ships amid the seas if he his bellowes blow.
  The waters waxen wilde where blustering blastes do rise,
Yet seldome do they passe their bondes for nature that devise.
  The fire which boiles the leade, and trieth out the gold:
10 Hath in his power both help and hurt, if he his force unfold.
  The frost which kils the fruite, doth knit the brused bones:
And is a medecin of kinde, prepared for the nones.
  The earth in whose entrails the foode of man doth live,

21 *to* too
24 To kill him who yields at her instruction
26 *lust* wish, delight
28 *desert* deserving
194 *behoofe* benefit
2 *kind* nature
9 *trieth out* extracts/purifies
12 *for the nones* for that particular purpose

At every spring and fall of leafe, what pleasure doth she give?
  The ayre which life desires, and is to helth so swete,
Of nature yeldes such lively smelles, that comforts every
        sprete.
  The Sunne through natures might, doth draw away the dew,
And spredes the flowers wher he is wont his princely face to
        shew.
  The Moone which may be cald, the lanterne of the night,
Is halfe a guide to traveling men, such vertue hath her light.   20
  The sters not vertuelesse are beauty to the eyes,
A lodes man to the Mariner, a signe of calmed skyes.
  The flowers and fruitfull trees to man do tribute pay,
And when they have their duety done by course they fade
        away.
  Eche beast both fishe and foule, doth offer life and all,
To nourish man and do him ease, yea serve him at his call.
  The serpentes venemous, whose uglye shapes we hate,
Are soveraigne salves for sondry sores, and nedefull in their
        state.
  Sith nature shewes her power, in eche thing thus at large,
Why should not man submit himselfe to be in natures charge?   30
  Who thinkes to flee her force, at length becomes her thrall,
The wisest cannot slip her snare, for nature governs all.
  Lo, nature gave us shape, lo nature fedes our lives:
Then they are worse then mad I think, against her force that
        strives
  Though some do use to say, which can do nought but faine,
Women were made for this intent, to put us men to paine.
  Yet sure I thinke they are a pleasure to the minde,
A joy which man can never want, as nature hath assinde.

    16 *sprete* spirit
    22 *lodes man* guide
    24 *course* course of nature
    25 *foule* fowl
    28 *salves* cures, healing agents   *nedefull* necessary
    29 *Sith* since
    31 *force* power   *thrall* slave
    36 *intent* purpose

195. *When adversitie is once fallen,*
it is to late to beware.

To my mishap alas I finde
That happy hap is daungerous:
And fortune worketh but her kinde,
To make the joyfull dolorous.
But all to late it comes to minde,
To waile the want that makes me blinde.
   Amid my myrth and pleasantnesse,
Such chaunce is chaunced sodainly,
That in dispayre without redresse,
I finde my chiefest remedy.
No new kinde of unhappinesse,
Should thus have left me comfortlesse.
   Who would have thought that my
      request,
Should bring me forth such bitter frute:
But now is hapt that I feard lest:
And all this harme comes by my sute,
For when I thought me happiest
Even then hapt all my chiefe unrest.
   In better case was never none
And yet unwares thus am I trapt,
My chiefe desire doth cause me mone,
And to my harme my welth is hapt,
There is no man but I alone,
That hath such cause to sigh and mone.
   Thus am I taught for to beware
And trust no more such pleasant
      chance,

195 2 *hap* fortune
    3 *but her kinde* only according to her nature
    5 *to* too
    8 Such fortune happens suddenly
    16 *sute* petition, request

My happy hap bred me this care,
And brought my mirth to great mischance.
There is no man whom hap will spare,
But when she list his welth is bare.   30

196. Of a lover that made his onely
god of his love.

All you that frendship do professe,
And of a frende present the place:
Geve eare to me that did possesse,
As frendly frutes as ye imbrace.
And to declare the circumstaunce,
There were them selves that did avaunce:
To teach me truely how to take,
A faithfull friende for vertues sake.
    But I as one of litle skill,
To know what good might grow therby,   10
Unto my welth I had no will,
Nor to my nede I had none eye,
But as the childe doth learne to go,
So I in time did learne to know,
Of all good frutes the world brought forth,
A faithfull frende is thing most worth.
    Then with all care I sought to finde,
One worthy to receive such trust:
One onely that was riche in minde,
One secrete, sober, wise, and just.   20
Whom riches could not raise at all,
Nor povertie procure to fall:
And to be short in few wordes plaine,

27 *care* sorrow
30 *list* pleases
196 6 *avaunce* offer
  13 *go* walk
  20 *secrete* discreet, confidential

One such a frende I did attaine.
And when I did enjoy this welth,
Who lived Lord in such a case,
For to my frendes it was great helth,
And to my foes a fowle deface,
And to my selfe a thing so riche
30   As seke the world and finde none such.
Thus by this frende I set such store,
As by my selfe I set no more.

This frende so much was my delight,
When care had clene orecome my hart,
One thought of her rid care as quite,
As never care had causde my smart.
Thus joyed I in my frende so dere,
Was never frende sate man so nere,
I carde for her so much alone,
40   That other God I carde for none.

But as it doth to them befall,
That to them selves respect have none:
So my swete graffe is growen to gall,
Where I sowed mirth I reaped mone.
This ydoll that I honorde so,
Is now transformed to my fo.
That me most pleased, me most paines,
And in dispaire my hart remaines.

And for just scourge of such desart,
50   Thre plages I may my selfe assure,
First of my frende to lose my part,
And next my life may not endure,
And last of all the more to blame,
My soule shall suffer for the same.
Wherfore ye frendes I warne you all,
Sit fast for feare of such a fall.

34 *care* sorrow, anxiety   *orecome* overcome
35 *rid care as quite* banished anxiety as completely
43 *graffe* grafted shoot
49 *scourge* punishment   *desart* deserving
50 *plages* evils

197. Upon the death of sir Antony Denny.

Death and the king, did as it were contend,
Which of them two bare Denny greatest love.
The king to shew his love gan farre extende,
Did him advaunce his betters farre above.
Nere place, much welth, great honor eke him gave,
To make it known what powre gret princes have.
   But when death came with his triumphant gift,
From worldly cark he quite his weried ghost,
Free from the corps, and straight to heaven it lift,
Now deme that can who did for Denny most.   10
The king gave welth but fading and unsure,
Death brought him blisse that ever shall endure.

198. A comparison of the lovers paines.

Lyke as the brake within the riders hand,
Doth straine the horse nye wood with grief of
    paine,
Not used before to come in such a bande,
Striveth for griefe, although god wot in vain
To be as erst he was at libertie,
But force of force doth straine the contrary.
   Even so since band doth cause my deadly grief,
That made me so my wofull chaunce lament,

197 5 *eke* also
    8 *cark* trouble   *quite* set free   *ghost* spirit
198 1 *brake* bridle
    2 *nye wood* near madness
    4 *wot* knows
    5 *erst* before
    6 *force of force* force by necessity
    8 *chaunce* fortune, fate

Like thing hath brought me into paine & mischiefe,
Save willingly to it I did assent.
To binde the thing in fredome which was free,
That now full sore alas repenteth me.

199. Of a Rosemary branche sent.

Such grene to me as you have sent,
Such grene to you I sende againe:
A flowring hart that will not feint,
For drede of hope or losse of gaine:
A stedfast thought all wholy bent,
So that he may your grace obtaine:
As you by proofe have alwayes sene,
To live your owne and alwayes grene.

200. To his love of his constant hart.

As I have bene so will I ever be,
Unto my death and lenger if I myght,
Have I of love the frendly lokyng eye?
Have I of fortune favour or despite?
I am of rock by proofe as you may see:
Not made of waxe nor of no metall light,
As leefe to dye, by chaunge as to deceave,
Or breake the promise made. And so I leave.

199 5 *bent* directed
200 7 *leefe* willing

201. *Of the token which his love sent him.*

The golden apple that the Troyan boy,
Gave to Venus the fayrest of the thre,
Which was the cause of all the wrack of Troy,
Was not received with a greater joy,
Then was the same (my love) thou sent to me,
It healed my sore it made my sorowes free,
It gave me hope it banisht mine annoy:
Thy happy hand full oft of me was blist,
That can geve such a salve when that thou list.

202. *Manhode availeth not without good Fortune.*

The Cowerd oft whom deinty viandes fed,
That bosted much his ladies eares to please,
By helpe of them whom under him he led
Hath reapt the palme that valiance could not cease.
The unexpert that shores unknowen neare sought,
Whom Neptune yet apaled not with feare:
In wandring shippe on trustles seas hath tought
The skill to fele that time to long doth leare.
The sporting knight that scorneth Cupides kinde,
With fained chere the pained cause to brede: 10
In game unhides the leden sparkes of minde,

201 7 *annoy* suffering
   8 *blist* blessed
   9 *list* please
202 1 *viandes* food
   4 *cease* seize
   5 *unexpert* inexpert person   *neare* never
   6 *apaled* shocked/made white
   8 *to long* too long   *leare* teach
   10 *chere* expression   *brede* increase

And gaines the gole, where glowing flames shold spede,
Thus I see proofe that trouth & manly hart
May not availe, if fortune chaunce to start.

203. *That constancy of all vertues is most worthy.*

Though in the waxe a perfect picture made,
Doth shew as faire as in the marble stone,
Yet do we see it is estemed of none.
Because that fier or force the forme doth fade.
Wheras the marble holden is ful dere,
Since that endures the date of lenger dayes.
Of Diamondes it is the greatest praise,
So long to last and alwaies one tappere.
Then if we do esteme that thing for best,
10   Which in perfection lengest time doth last:
And that most vaine that turnes with every blast
What jewel then with tong can be exprest?
Like to that hart wher love hath framed such feth,
That can not fade but by the force of death.

204. *The uncertaine state of a lover.*

Lyke as the rage of raine.
Filles rivers with excesse,
And as the drought againe,
Doth draw them lesse and lesse.
So I both fall and clyme,
With no and yea sometime.
    As they swell hye and hye,

12 *spede* succeed
14 *start* abandon one
203 8 *tappere* to appear

So doth encrease my state,
As they fall drye and drye
So doth my wealth abate,   10
As yea is mixt with no.
So mirth is mixt with wo.
    As nothing can endure,
That lives and lackes reliefe,
So nothing can stande sure,
Where chaunge doth raigne as chiefe,
Wherefore I must intende,
To bowe when others bende.
    And when they laugh to smile,
And when they wepe to waile,   20
And when they craft, begile,
And when they fight, assaile,
And thinke there is no chaunge,
Can make them seme to strange.
    Oh most unhappy slave,
What man may leade this course,
To lacke he would faynest have,
Or els to do much worse.
These be rewardes for such,
As live and love to much.   30

205. *The lover in libertie smileth at them in thraldome, that sometime scorned his bondage.*

At libertie I sit and see,
Them that have erst laught me to scorne:
Whypt with the whip that scourged me

204 21 *craft* plot   *begile* deceive
    27 *faynest* most willingly
    30 *to* too
205 2 *erst* formerly

And now they banne that they were borne.
   I see them sit full soberlye,
And thinke their earnest lokes to hide:
Now in them selves they can not spye,
That they or this in me have spide.
   I see them sitting all alone,
Markyng the steppes ech worde and loke:
And now they treade where I have gone
The painfull pathe that I forsoke.
   Now I see well I saw no whit,
When they saw wel that now are blinde
But happy hap hath made me quit,
And just judgement hath them assinde.
   I see them wander all alone,
And treade full fast in dredfull dout:
The selfe same pathe that I have gone,
Blessed be hap that brought me out.
   At libertie all this I see,
And say no word but erst among:
Smiling at them that laught at me,
Lo such is hap, marke well my song.

206. A comparison of his love wyth the faithful and painful love of Troylus to Creside.

I read how Troylus served in Troy,
A lady long and many a day,
And how he bode so great anoy,
For her as all the stories say.
That halfe the paine had never man,

4 *banne* curse
8 *or* before
15 *hap* chance, fortune
206 3 *bode* endured

Which had this wofull Troyan than.
    His youth, his sport, his pleasant chere,
His courtly state and company,
In him so straungely altred were,
With such a face of contrary.   10
That every joy became a wo,
This poyson new had turnde him so.
    And what men thought might most him ease,
And most that for his comfort stode,
The same did most his minde displease,
And set him most in furious mode.
For all his pleasure ever lay,
To thinke on her that was away.
    His chamber was his comon walke,
Wherin he kept him secretly,   20
He made his bed the place of talke,
To heare his great extremity.
In nothing els had he delight.
But even to be a martyr right.
    And now to call her by her name
And straight therwith to sigh and throbbe:
And when his fansies might not frame,
Then into teares and so to sobbe,
All in extreames and thus he lyes,
Making two fountaines of his eyes.   30
    As agues have sharpe shiftes of fits
Of cold and heat successively:
So had his head like change of wits:
His pacience wrought so diversly.
Now up, now down, now here, now there,
Like one that was he wist not where.
    And thus though he were Priams sonne

6 *than* then
7 *chere* expression, manner
26 *straight* immediately afterwards
27 *frame* come to be a reality
36 *wist* knew

And comen of the kinges hye blood,
This care he had ere he her wonne.
Till she that was his maistresse good,
And lothe to see her servant so,
Became Phisicion to his wo.
        And toke him to her handes and grace,
And said she would her minde apply,
To helpe him in his wofull case,
If she might be his remedy.
And thus they say to ease his smart,
She made him owner of her hart.
        And truth it is except they lye,
From that day forth her study went,
To shew to love him faithfully,
And his whole minde full to content.
So happy a man at last was he,
And eke so worthy a woman she.
        Lo lady then judge you by this,
Mine ease and how my case doth fall,
For sure betwene my life and his,
No difference there is at all.
His care was great, so was his paine,
And mine is not the lest of twaine.
        For what he felt in service true
For her whom that he loved so,
The same I fele as large for you,
To whom I do my service owe.
There was that time in him no paine,
But now the same in me doth raigne.
        Which if you can compare and way,
And how I stand in every plight,
Then this for you I dare well say,
Your hart must nedes remorce of right
To graunt me grace and so to do,

39 *care* sorrow, anxiety   *ere* before
49 *except* unless
54 *eke* also

As Creside then did Troylus to.
　For well I wot you are as good,
And even as faire as ever was she,
And commen of as worthy blood,
And have in you as large pitie
To tender me your own true man,
As she did him her servant than.
　Which gift I pray God for my sake,
Full sone and shortly you me sende,   80
So shall you make my sorowes slake,
So shall you bring my wo to ende.
And set me in as happy case,
As Troylus with his lady was.

207. To leade a vertuous and honest life.

Flee from the prease and dwell with sothfastnes,
Suffise to thee thy good though it be small,
For horde hath hate, and climing ticklenes,
Praise hath envy, and weall is blinde in all,
Favour no more, then thee behove shall.
Rede well thy selfe that others well canst rede,
And trouth shall thee deliver, it is no drede.
　Paine thee not eche croked to redresse,
In hope of her that turneth as a ball,
Great rest standeth in litle businesse,   10
Beware also to spurne against a nall,
Strive not as doth a crocke against a wall,

　73 *wot* know
207　1 *prease* crowds　*sothfastnes* fidelity to truth
　3 *ticklenes* uncertainty
　4 *weall* well-being
　5 *then* than
　6 *Rede* advise
　12 *crocke* pot

Deme first thy selfe, that demest others dede,
And truth shall thee deliver, it is no drede.
    That thee is sent, receive in buxomnesse,
The wrestling of this world asketh a fall:
Here is no home, here is but wildernesse.
Forth pilgryme forth, forth beast out of thy stall,
Looke up on hye, geve thankes to God of all:
Weane well thy lust, and honest life ay leade,
So trouth shall thee deliver, it is no dreade.

20

208. *The wounded lover determineth*
to make sute to his lady
for his recure.

Sins Mars first moved warre or stirred men to strife,
Was never sene so fearce a fight, I scarce could scape
        with life.
Resist so long I did, till death approched so nye,
To save my selfe I thought it best, with spede away to flye.
In daunger still I fled, by flight I thought to scape
From my dere foe, it vailed not, alas it was to late.
For Venus from her campe brought Cupide with
        his bronde,
Who sayd now yelde, or els desire shall chace thee in every
        londe.
Yet would I not straight yelde, till fansy fiercely stroke,
Who from my will did cut the raines & charged me with
        this yoke.
Then all the daies and nightes mine eare might heare the
        sound,

10

13 *Deme* judge
15 *buxomnesse* obedience
20 *ay* always
208 1 *Sins* since
    6 *vailed not* did no good   *to* too
    7 *bronde* brand
    9 *straight* immediately

What carefull sighes my hart would steale, to feele it self so
      bound.
For though within my brest, thy care I worke (he sayde)
Why for good will didst thou behold her persing eye
      displayd,
Alas the fishe is caught, through baite that hides the hooke,
Even so her eye me trained hath, and tangled with her looke.
But or that it be long, my hart thou shalt be faine,
To stay my life pray her forththrow swete lokes when I
      complain.
When that she shall deny, to do me that good turne,
Then shall she see to asshes gray, by flames my body burne.   20
Deserte of blame to her, no wight may yet impute,
For feare of nay I never sought, the way to frame my sute.
Yet hap that what hap shall, delay I may to long,
Assay I shall for I heare say, the still man oft hath wrong.

209. *The lover shewing of the continuall paines that abide within his brest, determineth to die because he cannot have redresse.*

The dolefull bell that still doth ring,
The wofull knell of all my joyes:
The wretched hart doth perce and wring,
And fils mine eare with deadly noyes.
    The hongry Viper in my brest,
That on my hart doth lye and gnaw:
Doth dayly brede my new unrest,
And deper sighes doth cause me draw.
    And though I force both hand and eye,
On pleasant matter to attend: 10

12 *carefull* full of sorrow, anxiety
16 *trained* entrapped
17 *or* before   *be faine* desire
21 *no wight* no one

My sorowes to deceive therby,
And wretched life for to amend.
     Yet goeth the mill within my hart,
Which grindeth nought but paine and wo:
And turneth all my joy to smart,
The evil corne it yeldeth so.
Though Venus smile with yelding eyes,
And swete musicke doth play and sing:
Yet doth my sprites feele none of these,
The clarke doth at mine eare so ring.
     As smallest sparckes uncared for,
To greatest flames do sonest grow,
Even so did this mine inward sore,
Begin in game and end in wo.
     And now by use so swift it goeth,
That nothing can mine eares so fill:
But that the clacke it overgoeth,
And plucketh me backe into the mill.
     But since the mill will nedes about,
The pinne wheron the whele doth go:
I will assay to strike it out,
And so the mill to overthrow.

210. *The power of love over gods them selves.*

For love Apollo (his Godhed set aside)
Was servant to the king of Thessaley,
Whose daughter was so pleasant in his eye,
That both his harpe and sawtrey he defide:
And bagpipe solace of the rurall bride,
Did puffe and blow, and on the holtes hy,

209 19 *sprites* vital powers
     20 *clarke* church officer/cleric
     21 *uncared for* ignored
210 4 *sawtrey* psaltery (stringed instrument)
     6 *holtes* wooded hills

His cattell kept with that rude melody,
And oft eke him that doth the heavens gide,
Hath love transformed to shapes for him to base
Transmuted thus somtime a swan is he,   10
Leda taccoy, and eft Europe to please,
A milde white bull, unwrinckled front and face,
Suffreth her play till on his back lepeth she,
Whom in great care he ferieth through the seas.

211. *The promise of a constant lover.*

As Lawrell leaves that cease not to be grene,
From parching sunne, nor yet from winters threte
As hardened oke that feareth no sworde so kene,
As flint for toole in twaine that will not frete.
As fast as rocke, or piller surely set:
So fast am I to you, and ay have bene,
Assuredly whom I cannot forget,
For joy, for paine, for torment nor for tene.
For losse, for gaine, for frowning, nor for thret,
But ever one, yea both in calme and blast,   10
Your faithfull friende, and will be to my last.

212. *Against him that had slaundered*
a gentle woman with
him selfe.

False may be, and by the powers above,
Never have he good spede or lucke in love,

8 *eke* also
9 *to* too
11 *taccoy* to seduce   *eft* also   *Europe* Europa (see explanatory note)
12 *front* forehead
211 6 *ay* always
   8 *tene* misery
212 2 *good spede* success

That so can lye or spot the worthy fame,
Of her for whom thou R. art to blame.
For chaste Diane that hunteth still the chace,
And all her maides that sue her in the race.
With faire bowes bent and arrowes by their side,
Can say that thou in this hast falsely lide.
For never hong the bow upon the wall,
Of Dianes temple, no nor never shall.
Of broken chaste the sacred vow to spot,
Of her whom thou doste charge so large I wot,
But if ought be wherof her blame may rise,
It is in that she did not well advise
To marke thee right, as now she doth thee know
False of thy dede, false of thy talke also.
Lurker of kinde like serpent layd to bite,
As poyson hid under the suger white.
What daunger suche? So was the house defilde,
Of Collatine: so was the wife begilde.
So smarted she, and by a trayterous force,
The Cartage quene so she fordid her corse.
So strangled was the Rodopeian maide,
Fye traytour fye, to thy shame be it sayd,
Thou dunghill Crow that crokest against the rayne,
Home to thy hole, brag not with Phebe againe.
Carrion for thee, and lothsome be thy voyce,
Thy song is fowle, I weary of thy noyce.
Thy blacke fethers, which are thy wearing wede,
Wet them with teares, and sorow for thy dede.
And in darke caves, where yrkesome wormes
    do crepe,
Lurke thou all day, and flye when thou
    shouldest slepe.
And never light where living thing hath life,

6 *sue* follow
12 *wot* know
14 *advise* consider
17 *kinde* nature
29 *wede* clothing

But eat and drinke where stinche and filth is rife.
For she that is a fowle of fethers bright,
Admit she toke some pleasure in thy sight.
As fowle of state sometimes delight to take,
Fowle of mean sort their flight with them to make.
For play of wing, or solace of their kinde:
But not in sort as thou dost breake thy minde.   40
Not for to treade with such foule fowle as thou,
No no I sweare, and dare it here avow.
Thou never settest thy foote within her nest,
Boast not so broade then to thine owne unrest.
But blushe for shame, for in thy face it standes,
And thou canst not unspot it with thy handes.
For all the heavens against thee recorde beare,
And all in earth against thee eke will sweare,
That thou in this art even none other man,
But as the judges were to Susan than.   50
Forgers of that wherto their lust them prickt,
Bashe, blaser then the truth hath thee convict.
And she a woman of her worthy fame,
Unspotted standes, & thou hast caught the shame.
And there I pray to God that it may rest,
False as thou art, as false as is the best,
That so canst wrong the noble kinde of man,
In whom all trouth first floorisht and began.
And so hath stand, till now thy wretched part,
Hath spotted us, of whose kinde one thou art.   60
That all the shame that ever rose or may,
Of shamefull dede on thee may light I say.
And on thy kinde, and thus I wishe thee rather,
That all thy seede may like be to their father.
Untrue as thou, and forgers as thou art,
So as all we be blamelesse of thy part.
And of thy dede. And thus I do thee leave,
Still to be false, and falsely to deceave.

48 *eke* also
52 *Bashe, blaser* be ashamed, slanderer

213. *A praise of maistresse R.*

I heard when fame with thundring voice did sommon to
     appere,
The chiefe of natures children all that kinde hath
     placed here.
To view what brute by vertue got their lives could
     justly crave,
And bad them shew what praise by truth they worthy
     were to have.
Wherwith I saw how Venus came and put her selfe in place,
And gave her ladies leave at large to stand and pleade
     their case.
Ech one was calde by name a row, in that assemble there,
That hence are gone or here remaines, in court or other
     where.
A solemne silence was proclaimde, the judges sate and herd,
What truth could tell, or craft could fain, & who should be
10   preferd.
Then beauty stept before the barre, whose brest and neck
     was bare
With heare trust up, and on her hed a caule of gold she ware.
Thus Cupides thralles began to flock whose hongry eyes
     did say
That she had stayned all the dames, that present were
     that day.
For er she spake, with whispring words, the prease was fild
     throughout
And fansy forced common voyce, therat to give a shoute.
Which cried to fame take forth thy trump, & sound her
     praise on hy

213 2 *kinde* nature
   3 *brute* reputation
   7 *a row* in a line
  12 *heare* hair
  14 *stayned* surpassed
  15 *prease* crowd

That glads the hart of every wight that her beholdes
    with eye.
What stirre and rule (quod order than) do these rude people
    make,
We hold her best that shall deserve a praise for vertues sake.   20
This sentence was no soner said, but beauty therwith blusht,
The noise did cease, the hall was stil and every thing was
    whusht.
Then finenesse thought by training talke to win that
    beauty lost,
And whet her tonge with joly wordes, and spared for
    no cost:
Yet wantonnesse could not abide, but brake her tale in hast,
And pevish pride for Pecockes plumes would nedes be hiest
    plast.
And therwithall came curiousnesse and carped out of frame.
The audience laught to heare the strife as they beheld the
    same.
Yet reason sone apesdc the brute her reverence made and
    doon,
She purchased favour for to speake, and thus her tale begoon.   30
Sins bounty shall the garland weare, and crowned be by fame,
O happy judges call for her, for she deserves the same.
Where temperance governs beauties flowers & glory is not
    sought,
And shamefast mekenes mastreth pride, & vertu dwels in
    thought.
Bid her come forth and shew her face, or els assent eche one,
That true report shall grave her name in gold or marble stone.
For all the world to rede at will, what worthines doth rest,
In perfect pure unspotted life, which she hath here possest.
Then skill rose up and sought the prease to finde if that
    he might,

18 *every wight* everyone
19 *than* then
23 *training* deceptive
31 *Sins* since

A person of such honest name, that men should praise
40   of right.
This one I saw full sadly sit, and shrinke her self aside,
Whose sober lokes did shew what giftes her wifely grace
            did hide.
Lo here (quod skill, good people all) is Lucrece left alive,
And she shall most excepted be, that least for praise
            did strive.
No lenger fame could hold her peace, but blew a blast
            so hye,
That made an eckow in the aier and sowning through the
            skye.
The voice was loude & thus it said come .R. with happy
            daies,
Thy honest life hath wonne the fame & crowned thee with
            praies.
And when I heard my maistres name I thrust amids the
            throng,
And clapt my handes and wisht of god that she might
50   prosper long.

214. Of one unjustly
defamed.

I ne can close in short and cunning verse,
Thy worthy praise of bountie by desart:
The hatefull spite and slaunder to reherse.
Of them that see but know not what thou art,
For kind by craft hath wrought thee so to eye,
That no wight may thy wit and vertue spye.
But he have other fele then outward sight,
The lacke wherof doth hate and spite to trie

214 1 *I ne can close* I cannot enclose
     5 *kind* nature
     6 *no wight* no one
     7 *But* unless
     8 *doth* causes

Thus kind thy craft is let of vertues light:
See how the outward shew the wittes may dull: 10
Not of the wise but as the most entend,
Minerva yet might never perce their scull,
That Circes cup and Cupides brand hath blend.
Whose fonde affects now sturred have their braine,
So doth thy hap thy hue with colour staine.
Beauty thy foe thy shape doubleth thy sore,
To hide thy wit and shew thy vertue vaine,
Fell were thy fate, if wisdome were not more.
I meane by thee even G. by name,
Whom stormy windes of envy and disdaine,   20
Do tosse with boisteous blastes of wicked fame.
Where stedfastnesse as chiefe in thee doth raigne.
Pacience thy setled minde dothe guide and stere,
Silence and shame with many resteth there.
Till time thy mother list them forth to call,
Happy is he that may enjoye them all.

215. Of the death of the late countisse of Penbroke.

Yet once againe my muse I pardon pray,
Thine intermitted song if I repeate:
Not in such wise as when love was my pay,
My joly wo with joyfull verse to treate.
    But now (unthanke to our desert be geven,
Which merite not a heavens gift to kepe)
Thou must with me bewaile that fate hath reven,

9 *let* deprived
11 *as the most entend* those who look most intently; and see explanatory note
13 *blend* blinded
15 *hap* fortune
18 *Fell* terrible
25 *list* pleases
215 7 *reven* taken away

From earth a jewel laied in earth to slepe,
   A jewel yea a gemme of womanhed,
Whose perfect vertues linked as in chaine:
So did adorne that humble wivelyhed,
As is not rife to finde the like againe.
   For wit and learnyng framed to obey,
Her husbandes wil that willed her to use
The love he bare her chiefely as a staye,
For al her frendes that wold her furtherance chuse
   Wel said therfore a heavens gift she was,
Because the best are sonest hence bereft:
And though her self to heaven hence dyd passe,
Her spoyle to earth from whence it came
        she left.
   And to us teares her absence to lament,
And eke his chance that was her make by law:
Whose losse to lose so great an ornament,
Let them esteme which trueloves knot can draw.

216. *That eche thing is hurt of*
it self.

Why fearest thou thy outward fo,
When thou thy selfe thy harme dost fede,
Of grief, or hurt, of paine or wo,
Within eche thing is sowen the sede?
   So fine was never yet the cloth,
No smith so hard his yron did beate:
But thone consumed was with moth,
Thother with canker all to freate.
   The knotty oke and wainscot old,
Within doth eate the silly worme:

---

15 *staye* support
22 *eke* also   *make* mate, spouse
216 7 *thone* the one
  8 The other was all eaten up ('freate') by canker

Even so a minde in envy rold,
Alwaies within it self doth burne.
   Thus every thing that nature wrought.
Within it selfe his hurt doth beare:
No outward harme nede to be sought,
Where enemies be within so neare.

217. *Of the choise of a wife.*

The flickeryng fame that flieth from eare to eare,
And aye her strength encreaseth with her flight
Geves first the cause why men to heare delight,
Of those whome she doth note for beauty bright,
And with this fame that flieth on so fast,
Fansy doth hye when reason makes no hast.
   And yet not so content they wishe to see
And thereby know if fame have sayd aryght,
More trustyng to the triall of their eye,
Then to the brute that goes of any wight,   10
Wise in that point that lightly will not leve,
Unwise to seke that may them after greve,
   Who knoweth not how sight may love allure,
And kindle in the hart a hote desire:
The eye to worke that fame could not procure,
Of greater cause there commeth hotter fire.
For ere he wete him self he feleth warme,
The fame and eye the causers of his harme.
   Let fame not make her knowen whom
      I shal know,
Nor yet myne eye therin to be my guyde: 20
Sufficeth me that vertue in her grow,

217 2 *aye* always
  4 *note* make notable
  6 *hye* hurry
 10 *brute* reputation
 17 *ere he wete* before he knew it

Whose simple life her fathers walles do hide.
Content with this I leave the rest to go,
And in such choise shall stand my welth and wo.

218. Descripcion of an ungodly worlde.

Who loves to live in peace, and marketh every change,
Shall hear such news from time to time, as seme right
　　　wondrous strange,
　　Such fraud in frendly lokes, such frendship al for gaine:
Such cloked wrath in hatefull harts, which worldly men
　　　retayne.
　　Such fayned flattering fayth, amongs both hye and low:
Such great deceite, such subtell wittes, the pore to overthrowe.
　　Such spite in sugred tonges, such malice full of pride:
Such open wrong such great untruth, which cannot go
　　　unspide.
　　Such restlesse sute for roumes, which bringeth men to care:
Such sliding downe from slippry seates, yet can we not
10　　　beware.
　　Such barking at the good, such bolstring of the yll:
Such threatnyng of the wrathe of God, such vyce embraced
　　　still.
　　Such strivyng for the best, such climing to estate:
Such great dissemblyng every where, such love all mixt
　　　with hate
　　Such traines to trap the just, such prollyng faultes to pyke:
Such cruell wordes for speaking trouth, who ever hearde the
　　　lyke?
　　Such strife for stirring strawes, such discord dayly wrought,
Such forged tales dul wits to blind, such matters made of
　　　nought
　　Such trifles told for trouth, such credityng of lyes,

218 9 *roumes* estates or position　*care* sorrow, anxiety
　15 *such prollyng faultes to pyke* such prowling to detect crimes

Such silence kept when foles do speak, such laughyng at
      the wise.   20
  Such plenty made so scarce, such crying for redresse,
Such feared signes of our decay, which tong dares not
      expresse.
  Such chaunges lightly markt, such troubles still apperes,
Which never were before this time, no not this thousand
      yeres.
  Such bribyng for the purse, which ever gapes for more,
Such hordyng up of worldly welth, such kepyng muck in
      store.
  Such folly founde in age, such will in tender youth,
Such sundry sortes among great clarkes, & few that speake
      the truth
  Such falshed under craft, and such unstedfast wayes,
Was never sene within mens hartes, as is found now adayes.   30
  The cause and ground of this is our unquiet minde,
Which thinkes to take those goods away whiche wee must
      leve behinde.
  Why do men seke to get which they cannot possesse?
Or breake their slepes with careful thoughtes & all for
      wretchednes.
  Though one amonges a skore, hath welth and ease a
      while,
A thousand want which toyleth sore and travaile many
      a mile.
  And some although they slepe, yet welth falles in their lap,
Thus some be rich and some be pore as fortune geves
      the hap.
  Wherfore I hold him wise which thinkes him self at ease,
And is content in simple state both god and man to please.   40
  For those that live like gods and honored are to day,
Within short time their glory falles as flowers do fade away.
  Uncertein is their lives on whom this world wyl frowne,

28 *clarkes* clerics
34 *careful* full of sorrow, anxiety
38 *hap* chance

For though they sit above the starres a storme may strike
      them downe
  In welth who feares no fal, may slide from joy ful sone,
There is nothing so sure on earth but changeth as the Mone.
    What pleasure hath the rich, or ease more then the pore,
Although he have a pleasant house his trouble is the more.
    They bowe and speake him faire, which seke to suck his
      blood,
And some do wishe his soule in hell and al to have
50   his good.
    The covetyng of the goodes doth nought but dull
      the spirite,
And some men chaunce to tast the sower that gropeth for
      the swete
    The rich is still envied by those which eate his bred,
With fawning spech and flatteryng tales his eares are dayly
      fed,
    In fine I see and prove the rich have many foes,
He slepeth best and careth lest that litle hath to lose.
    As time requireth now who would avoyde much strife,
Were better live in pore estate then leade a princes life.
    To passe those troublesome times I see but little choise,
But helpe to waile with those that wepe & laugh when
60   they rejoise
    For as we se to day our brother brought in care,
To morow may we have such chance to fall with him
      in snare.
    Of this we may be sure, who thinkes to sit most fast,
Shal sonest fal like withered leaves that cannot bide a blast.
    Though that the flood be great, the ebbe as lowe doth
      ronne,
When every man hath playd his part our pagent shal be
      donne.
    Who trustes this wretched world I hold him worse then
      mad,

49 *speake him faire* speak pleasant flatteries to him
61 *care* sorrow, anxiety

Here is not one that fereth god the best is all to badde.
   For those that seme as saintes are devilles in their
      dedes,
Though that the earth brings forth some flowers it
      beareth many wedes.   70
   I se no present help from mischief to prevaile,
But flee the seas of worldly cares or beare a quiet saile.
   For who that medleth lest shall save him selfe from
      smart,
Who styrres an oare in every boate shal play a folish part.

219. The dispairing lover lamenteth.

Walkyng the pathe of pensive thought,
I askt my hart how came this wo.
Thine eye (quod he) this care me brought,
Thy mynde, thy witte, thy wyll also
Enforceth me to love her ever,
This is the cause joy shal I never.
   And as I walkt as one dismaide,
Thinkyng that wrong this wo me lent:
Right, sent me worde by wrath, which said,
This just judgement to thee is sent: 10
Never to dye, but dying ever,
Till breath thee faile, joy shalt thou never.
   Sith right doth judge this wo tendure,
Of health, of wealth, of remedy:
As I have done so be she sure,
Of faith and trouth untill I dye.
And as this paine cloke shal I ever,
So inwardly joye shal I never.
   Gripyng of gripes greve not so sore,

68 *to* too
219 3 *care* sorrow, anxiety
  13 *Sith* since *tendure* to endure

20 Nor serpentes styng causeth such smart,
Nothing on earth may payne me more,
Then sight that perst my woful hart.
Drowned with cares styll to persever,
Come death betimes joye shal I never,
  O libertie why dost thou swerve:
And steale away thus all at ones:
And I in prison like to sterve,
For lacke of foode do gnaw on bones.
My hope and trust in thee was ever,
30 Now thou art gone joy shall I never.
  But still as one all desperate,
To leade my life in misery:
Sith feare from hope hath lockt the gate,
Where pity should graunt remedy.
Despaire this lot assignes me ever,
To live in paine, joy shall I never.

220. The lover praieth his service to be accepted, and his defaultes pardoned.

Procryn that somtime served Cephalus,
With hart as true as any lover might,
Yet her betid in loving this unright.
That as in hart with love surprised thus,
She on a day to see this Cephalus,
Where he was wont to shrowde him in the shade,
When of his hunting he an ende had made.
Within the woods with dredfull foote forth stalketh.
So busily love in her hed it walketh.
10 That she to sene him may her not restraine.
This Cephalus that heard one shake the leaves

26 *ones* once
220 3 This undeserved misfortune in loving happened to her/The following happened to her in loving this unrighteous man

Uprist all egre thrusting after pray,
With darte in hand him list no further daine,
To see his love but slew her in the greaves,
That ment to him but perfect love alway.
　So curious bene alas the rites all,
Of mighty love that unnethes may I thinke,
In his high service how to loke or winke.
Thus I complaine that wretchedst am of all,
To you my love, and soveraine lady dere, 20
That may my hart with death or life stere
As ye best list. That ye vouchsafe in all
Mine humble service. And if me misfall,
By negligence, or els for lacke of wit.
That of your mercy you do pardon it,
And think that love made Procrin shake the leves
When with unright she slain was in the greves.

221. Descripcion and praise of his love.

Lyke the Phenix a birde most rare in sight,
That nature hath with gold and purple drest:
Such she me semes in whom I most delight,
If I might speake for envy at the least.
Nature I thinke first wrought her in despite,
Of rose and lilly that sommer bringeth first,
In beauty sure, exceding all the rest,
Under the bent of her browes justly pight:
As Diamondes, or Saphires at the least:
Her glistring lightes the darknesse of the night. 10
Whose litle mouth and chinne like all the rest.

13 *him list* it pleases him
14 *greaves* leg armour (or where such leg armour should be)
17 *unnethes* with difficulty
221 4 *for envy* despite the possibility of envy
　8 *pight* placed, pitched

Her ruddy lippes excede the corall quite.
Her yvery teeth where none excedes the rest,
Fautlesse she is from foote unto the waste:
Her body small and straight as mast upright,
Her armes long in just proporcion cast,
Her handes depaint with veines all blew & white.
What shal I say for that is not in sight?
The hidden partes I judge them by the rest.
20 And if I were the forman of the quest,
To geve a verdite of her beauty bright,
Forgeve me Phebus, thou shouldst be
     dispossest,
Which doest usurpe my ladies place of right.
Here will I cease lest envy cause dispite.
But nature when she wrought so faire
     a wight,
In this her worke she surely dyd entende,
To frame a thing that God could not amende.

222. *The lover declareth his paines to excede far the paines of hell.*

The soules that lacked grace,
Which lye in bitter paine:
Are not in such a place,
As foolish folke do faine.
  Tormented all with fire,
And boile in leade againe,
With serpents full of ire,
Stong oft with deadly paine.
  Then cast in frosen pittes:
10 To freze there certaine howers:

20 *quest* jury
25 *wight* person
27 *amende* improve

And for their painfull fittes,
Apointed tormentours.
　No no it is not so,
Their sorow is not such:
And yet they have of wo,
I dare say twise as much.
　Which comes because they lack
The sight of the godhed,
And be from that kept back
Where with are aungels fed　　　　　　20
　This thing know I by love
Through absence crueltie,
Which makes me for to prove
Hell pain before I dye.
　There is no tong can tell
My thousand part of care
Ther may no fire in hell,
With my desire compare.
　No boyling leade can pas
My scalding sighes in hete:　　　　　　30
Nor snake that ever was,
With stinging can so frete
　A true and tender hert,
As my thoughtes dayly doe,
So that I know but smart,
And that which longes thereto.
　O Cupid Venus son,
As thou hast showed thy might,
And hast this conquest woon,
Now end the same aright.　　　　　　40
　And as I am thy slave,
Contented with all this:
So helpe me soone to have
My parfect earthly blisse.

222 23 *prove* experience
　26 *care* sorrow, suffering
　36 *longes thereto* goes along with, belongs to that

223. *Of the death of sir Thomas Wiate the elder.*

Lo dead he lives, that whilome lived here,
Among the dead that quick go on the ground.
Though he be dead, yet doth he quick apere,
By lively name that death cannot confound
His life for ay of fame the trump shall sound.
Though he be dead, yet lives he here alive.
Thus can no death from Wiate, life deprive.

224. *That length of time consumeth all thinges.*

What harder is then stone, what more then
     water soft?
Yet with soft water drops, hard stones be
     persed softe.
What geves so strong impulse,
That stone ne may withstand?
  What geves more weake repulse,
Then water prest with hand?
  Yet weke though water be,
It holowith hardest flint:
By proofe wherof we see,
Time geves the greatest dint.

223 1 *whilome* formerly
  2 *go* walk
  3 *quick* alive
  5 *for ay* for ever
224 2 *soft* probably a misprint for 'oft'

225. *The beginning of the epistle of Penelope to Ulisses, made into verse.*

O lingring make Ulisses dere, thy wife lo sendes to thee,
Her driry plaint write not againe, but come thy selfe
    to me.
Our hatefull scourge that womans foe proud Troy
    now is fordon
We bye it derer, though Priam slaine, and all his
    kingdome won.
O that the raging surges great that lechers bane had
    wrought,
When first with ship he forowed seas, and Lacedemon
    sought,
In desert bed my shivering coarse then shold not have
    sought rest,
Nor take in griefe the cherefull sunne so slowly fall
    to west.
And whiles I cast long running nightes, how best I might
    begile,
No distaff should my widowish hand have weary made
    the while.   10
When dread I not more daungers great then are befall
    in dede:
Love is a carefull thing God wot, and passing full
    of drede.

225 1 *lingring make* dilatory spouse
   2 *write not againe* don't write in response to her sad poetic complaint
   5 *bane* appropriate doom
   7 *coarse* body
   9 *begile* while away
   12 *carefull* worrisome   *wot* knows

226. *The lover asketh pardon of his passed follie in love.*

You that in play peruse my plaint, and reade in rime the
        smart,
Which in my youth with sighes full cold I harbourd in my
        hart
Know ye that love in that fraile age, drave me to that
        distresse,
When I was halfe an other man, then I am now
        to gesse.
Then for this worke of wavering words where I now rage
        now rew
Tost in the toyes of troublous love, as care or comfort
        grew.
I trust with you that loves affaires by proofe have put
        in ure:
Not onely pardon in my plaint, but pitie to procure.
For now I wot that in the world a wonder have I be,
And where to long love made me blinde, to late shame
        makes me se.
Thus of my fault shame is the fruite, and for my youth
        thus past,
Repentance is my recompence, and this I learne
        at last.
Looke what the world hath most in price, as sure it is
        to kepe,
As is the dreame which fansie drives, while sence and
        reason slepe.

10

226 1 *plaint*: poetic complaint, expressing injustice or sorrow
  4 *then* than *to gesse* approximately
  6 *care* sorrow, anxiety
  7 I trust that experience has made you used to what love does
  9 *wot* know
  10 *to* too
  13 *Looke what* whatever

227. *The lover sheweth that he was striken by love on good friday.*

It was the day on which the sunne deprived of his light,
To rew Christs death amid his course gave place unto the night
When I amid mine ease did fall to such distemperate fits,
That for the face that hath my hart I was bereft my wits.
I had the bayte, the hooke and all, and wist not loves
       pretence,
But farde as one that fearde none yll, nor forst for no defence.
Thus dwelling in most quiet state, I fell into this plight,
And that day gan my secret sighes, when all folke wept in
      sight.
For love that vewed me voide of care, approcht to take his
      pray,
And stept by stelth from eye to hart, so open lay the way.   10
And straight at eyes brake out in teares, so salt that did
      declare,
By token of their bitter taste that they were forgde of care.
Now vaunt thee love which fleest a maid defenst with
      vertues rare,
And wounded hast a wight unwise, unweaponed and unware.

228. *The lover describeth his whole state unto his love, and promising her his faithfull good will: assureth himself of hers again.*

The Sunne when he hath spred his raies,
And shewde his face ten thousand waies.
Ten thousand thinges do then begin,

227 5 *wist* knew
    6 *forst* cared
    8 *gan* began
    9 *care* sorrow, anxiety
   11 *straight* immediately
   14 *wight* person

To shew the life that they are in.
The heaven shewes lively art and hue,
Of sundry shapes and colours new,
And laughes upon the earth anone.
The earth as cold as any stone,
Wet in the teares of her own kinde:
Gins then to take a joyfull minde.
For well she feeles that out and out,
The sunne doth warme her round about.
And dries her children tenderly,
And shewes them forth full orderly.
The mountaines hye and how they stand,
The valies and the great maine land,
The trees, the herbes, the towers strong,
The castels and the rivers long.
And even for joy thus of this heate,
She sheweth furth her pleasures great.
And sleepes no more but sendeth forth
Her clergions her own dere worth.
To mount and flye up to the ayre,
Where then they sing in order fayre.
And tell in song full merely,
How they have slept full quietly,
That night about their mothers sides.
And when they have song more besides,
Then fall they to their mothers breastes,
Where els they fede or take their restes.
The hunter then soundes out his horne,
And rangeth straite through wood and corne.
On hilles then shew the Ewe and Lambe,
And every yong one with his dambe.
Then lovers walke and tell their tale,
Both of their blisse and of their bale.

228 9 *of her own kinde* born from her own nature
     16 *maine* belonging to a demesne
     22 *clergions* choristers
     25 *merely* merrily

And how they serve, and how they do,
And how their lady loves them to.
Then tune the birdes their armonie.
Then flocke the foule in companie.   40
Then every thing doth pleasure finde,
In that that comfortes all their kinde.
No dreames do drench them of the night,
Of foes that would them slea or bite.
As Houndes to hunt them at the taile,
Or men force them through hill and dale.
The shepe then dreames not of the Woulf,
The shipman forces not the goulf.
The Lambe thinkes not the butchers knife,
Should then bereve him of his life.   50
For when the Sunne doth once run in,
Then all their gladnes doth begin.
And then their skips, and then their play
So falles their sadnes then away.
And thus all thinges have comforting,
In that that doth them comfort bring.
Save I alas, whom neither sunne,
Nor ought that God hath wrought and don,
May comfort ought, as though I were
A thing not made for comfort here.   60
For beyng absent from your sighte,
Which are my joy and whole delight
My comfort and my pleasure to,
How can I joy how should I do?
May sick men laugh that rore for paine?
Joy they in song that do complaine?
Are martirs in their tormentes glad?
Do pleasures please them that are mad?
Then how may I in comfort be,
That lacke the thing should comfort me.   70

38 *to* too
42 *kinde* nature
48 *forces not* doesn't worry about

The blind man oft that lackes his sight,
Complaines not most the lacke of light.
But those that knewe their perfectnes,
And then do misse ther blisfulnes,
In martirs tunes they syng and waile,
The want of that which doth them faile.
And hereof comes that in my braines,
So many fansies worke my paines
For when I wayghe your worthynes,
Your wisdome and your gentlnes,
Your vertues and your sundry grace,
And minde the countenaunce of your face,
And how that you are she alone,
To whom I must both plaine and mone.
Whom I do love and must do still.
Whom I embrace and ay so wil,
To serve and please you as I can,
As may a wofull faithful man.
And finde my selfe so far you fro.
God knowes what torment, and what wo,
My rufull hart doth then imbrace.
The blood then chaungeth in my face.
My synnewes dull, in dompes I stand.
No life I fele in fote nor hand,
As pale as any clout and ded,
Lo sodenly the blood orespred,
And gon againe it nill so bide.
And thus from life to death I slide
As colde sometymes as any stone,
And then againe as hote anone.
Thus comes and goes my sundry fits,
To geve me sundri sortes of wits.
Till that a sigh becomes my frende,

82 *minde* remember
86 *ay* always
89 *you fro* from you
97 *nill so bide* will not stay thus

And then to all this wo doth ende.
And sure I thinke that sigh doth roon,
From me to you where ay you woon.
For well I finde it easeth me,
And certes much it pleaseth me,
To think that it doth come to you,
As would to God it could so do.   110
For then I know you would soone finde,
By sent and savour of the winde.
That even a martirs sigh it is,
Whose joy you are and all his blis.
His comfort and his pleasure eke,
And even the same that he doth seke.
The same that he doth wishe and crave,
The same that he doth trust to have.
To tender you in all he may,
And all your likinges to obey,   120
As farre as in his powre shall lye:
Till death shall darte him for to dye.
But wealeaway mine owne most best,
My joy, my comfort, and my rest.
The causer of my wo and smart,
And yet the pleaser of my hart.
And she that on the earth above:
Is even the worthiest for to love.
Heare now my plaint, heare now my wo.
Heare now his paine that loves you so.   130
And if your hart do pitie beare,
Pitie the cause that you shall heare.
A dolefull foe in all this doubt,
Who leaves me not but sekes me out,
Of wretched forme and lothsome face,
While I stand in this wofull case:

106 *where ay you woon* wherever you live
115 *eke* also
123 *wealeaway* alas
129 *plaint*: poetic complaint, expressing injustice or sorrow

Comes forth and takes me by the hand,
And saies frende harke and understand.
I see well by thy port and chere,
And by thy lokes and thy manere,
And by thy sadnes as thou goest,
And by the sighes that thou outthrowest:
That thou art stuffed full of wo,
The cause I thinke I do well know.
A fantaser thou art of some,
By whom thy wits are overcome.
But hast thou red old pamphlets ought?
Or hast thou known how bokes have taught
That love doth use to such as thow,
When they do thinke them safe enow.
And certain of their ladies grace:
Hast thou not sene oft times the case,
That sodenly there hap hath turnde,
As thinges in flame consumde and burnde?
Some by disceite forsaken right.
Some likwise changed of fansy light.
And some by absence sone forgot.
The lottes in love, why knowest thou not?
And tho that she be now thine own:
And knowes the well as may be knowne.
And thinkes the to be such a one,
As she likes best to be her own.
Thinkes thou that others have not grace,
To shew and plain their wofull case.
And chose her for their lady now,
And swere her trouth as well as thow.
And what if she do alter minde?
Where is the love that thou wouldest finde?
Absence my frende workes wonders oft.

139 *port* gait, bearing   *chere* expression
145 *fantaser* lover
153 *there hap* their fortune
160 *the* thee

Now bringes full low that lay full loft.   170
Now turnes the minde now to and fro,
And where art thou if it were so?
If basence (quod I) be marveilous,
I finde her not so dangerous.
For she may not remove me fro,
The poore good will that I do owe
To her, whom unneth I love and shall.
And chosen have above them all,
To serve and be her own as far,
As any man may offer her.   180
And will her serve, and will her love,
As lowly as it shall behove.
And dye her own if fate be so.
Thus shall my hart nay part her fro.
And witnes shall my good will be,
That absence takes her not from me.
But that my love doth still encrease,
To minde her still and never cease.
And what I feele to be in me,
The same good will I think hath she.   190
As firme and fast to biden ay,
Till death depart us both away.
And as I have my tale thus rold,
Steps unto me with countenance bold:
A stedfast frende a counsellour,
And namde is Hope my comfortour.
And stoutly then he speakes and saies:
Thou hast sayde trouth withouten nayes.
For I assure thee even by othe,
And theron take my hand and trothe.   200
That she is one the worthiest,
The truest and the faithfullest.
The gentlest and the meekest of minde:

173 *basence* misprint for 'absence'
177 *unneth* with difficulty
193 *rold* possibly a misprint for 'told'; and see explanatory note

That here on earth a man may finde,
And if that love and trouth were gone,
In her it might be found alone.
For in her minde no thought there is,
But how she may be true iwis.
And tenders thee and all thy heale,
210   And wisheth both thy health and weale.
And loves thee even as farforth than,
As any woman may a man,
And is thine own and so she saies,
And cares for thee ten thousand waies.
On thee she speakes, on thee she thinkes,
With thee she eates, with thee she drinkes.
With thee she talkes, with thee she mones,
With thee she sighes, with thee she grones.
With thee she saies farewell mine own.
220   When thou God knowes full farre art gon.
And even to tell thee all aright,
To thee she saies full oft good night.
And names thee oft, her owne most dere,
Her comfort weale and al her chere.
And telles her pelow al the tale,
How thou hast doon her wo and bale,
And how she longes and plaines for the,
And saies why art thou so from me?
Am I not she that loves the best?
230   Do I not wish thine ease and rest?
Seke I not how I may the please?
Why art thou then so from thine ease?
If I be she for whom thou carest,
For whom in tormentes so thou farest:
Alas thou knowest to finde me here,
Where I remaine thine owne most dere,
Thine own most true thine owne most just,

208 *iwis* indeed
210 *weale* well-being
211 *as farforth than* as much, then

Thine own that loves the styl and must.
Thine own that cares alone for the,
As thou I thinke dost care for me.   240
And even the woman she alone,
That is full bent to be thine owne.
What wilt thou more? what canst thou crave?
Since she is as thou wouldest her have.
Then set this drivell out of dore,
That in thy braines such tales doth poore.
Of absence and of chaunges straunge,
Send him to those that use to chaunge.
For she is none I the avowe,
And well thou maiest beleve me now.   250
When hope hath thus his reason said,
Lord how I fele me well apaide.
A new blood then orespredes my bones,
That al in joy I stand at ones.
My handes I throw to heven above,
And humbly thank the god of love.
That of his grace I should bestow,
My love so well as I it owe.
And al the planets as they stand,
I thanke them to with hart and hand.   260
That their aspectes so frendly were,
That I should so my good will bere.
To you that are the worthiest,
The fairest and the gentillest.
And best can say, and best can do,
That longes me thinkes a woman to.
And therfore are most worthy far,
To be beloved as you ar.
And so saies hope in all his tale,

238 *the* thee
245 *drivell* driveller, dotard
249 *the* thee
254 *ones* once
260 *to* too
266 That is appropriate, I think, for a woman

270   Wherby he easeth all my bale.
For I beleve and thinke it true,
That he doth speake or say of you.
And thus contented lo I stand,
With that that hope beares me in hand:
That I am yours and shall so be,
Which hope I kepe full sure in me.
As he that all my comfort is,
On you alone which are my blis.
My pleasure chief which most I finde,
280   And even the whole joy of my minde.
And shall so be untill the death,
Shall make me yeld up life and breath.
Thus good mine own, lo here my trust.
Lo here my truth and service just.
Lo in what case for you I stand.
Lo how you have me in your hand.
And if you can requite a man,
Requite me as you finde me than.

229. *Of the troubled comon welth restored to quiet by the mighty power of god.*

The secret flame that made all Troy so hot,
Long did it lurke within the wooden horse.
The machine huge Troyans suspected not,
The guiles of Grekes, nor of their hidden force:
Till in their beds their armed foes them met,
And slew them there, and Troy on fire set.
  Then rose the rore of treason round about,
And children could of treason call and cry.
Wives wroung their hands, the hole fired town
        through out,

274 *beares me in hand* promises me
288 *than* then

When that they saw their husbands slain them by.   10
And to the Gods and to the skies they shright,
Vengeance to take for treason of that night.
   Then was the name of Sinon spred and blowne,
And wherunto his filed tale did tend.
The secret startes and metinges then were knowne,
Of Troyan traitours tending to this end.
And every man could say as in that case:
Treason in Anthenor and Eneas.
   But all to long such wisdome was in store,
To late came out the name of traytour than,   20
When that their king the aultar lay before
Slain there alas, that worthy noble man.
Ilium on flame, the matrons crying out,
And all the stretes in streames of blood about.
   But such was fate, or such was simple trust,
That king and all should thus to ruine roon,
For if our stories certein be and just:
There were that saw such mischief should be doon
And warning gave which compted were in sort,
As sad devines in matter but of sport.   30
   Such was the time and so in state it stoode,
Troy trembled not so careles were the men.
They brake the wals, they toke this hors for good,
They demed Grekes gone, they thought al surety then.
When treason start & set the town on fire,
And stroied Troians & gave Grekes their desire.
   Like to our time, wherin hath broken out,
The hidden harme that we suspected least.
Wombed within our walles and realme about,

229 10 When they saw their slain husbands near them
   11 *shright* shrieked
   14 *filed* polished, deceitful
   19 *to* too
   26 *roon* run
   29–30 They gave warnings which were regarded as solemn prophecies in
     trivial matters are
   36 *stroied* destroyed

40   As Grekes in Troy were in the Grekish beast.
      Whose tempest great of harmes and of armes,
      We thought not on, till it did noyse our harmes.
          Then felt we well the piller of our welth,
      How sore it shoke, then saw we even at hand,
      Ruin how she rusht to confound our helth,
      Our realme and us with force of mighty band.
      And then we heard how treason loud did rore:
      Mine is the rule, and raigne I will therefore.
          Of treason marke the nature and the kinde,
50   A face it beares of all humilitie.
      Truth is the cloke, and frendship of the minde,
      And depe it goes, and worketh secretly,
      Like to a mine that creepes so nye the wall,
      Till out breakes sulphure, and oreturneth all.
          But he on hye that secretly beholdes
      The state of thinges: and times hath in his hand,
      And pluckes in plages, and them againe unfoldes.
      And hath apointed realmes to fall and stand:
      He in the midst of all this sturre and rout,
60   Gan bend his browes, and move him self about.
          As who should say, and are ye minded so?
      And thus to those, and whom you know I love.
      Am I such one as none of you do know?
      Or know ye not that I sit here above,
      And in my handes do hold your welth and wo,
      To raise you now, and now to overthrow?
          Then thinke that I, as I have set you all,
      In places where your honours lay and fame:
      So now my selfe shall give you eche your fall,
70   Where eche of you shall have your worthy shame.
      And in their handes I will your fall shalbe,
      Whose fall in yours you sought so sore to see.
          Whose wisdome hye as he the same foresaw,
      So is it wrought, such lo his justice is.

57 *pluckes in plages* remits sufferings
70 *worthy* appropriate, fitting

He is the Lord of man and of his law,
Praise therfore now his mighty name in this,
And make accompt that this our case doth stand:
As Israell free, from wicked Pharaos hand.

230. The lover to his love: having forsaken him, and betaken her self to an other.

The bird that somtime built within my brest,
And there as then chief succour did receive:
Hath now els where built her another nest,
And of the old hath taken quite her leave.
To you mine oste that harbour mine old guest,
Of such a one, as I can now conceive,
Sith that in change her choise doth chiefe consist,
The hauke may check, that now comes fair to fiist.

231. The lover sheweth that in dissembling his love openly he kepeth secret his secret good will.

Not like a God came Jupiter to woo,
When he the faire Europa sought unto.
In other forme his godly wisdome toke,
Such in effect as writeth Ovides boke.
As on the earth no living wight can tell.
That mighty Jove did love the quene so well.
For had he come in golden garmentes bright,
Or so as men mought have starde on the sight:
Spred had it bene both through earth and ayre,
That Jove had loved the lady Europa fayre.   10

230 7 *Sith* since
231 5 *wight* person

And then had some bene angry at the hart,
And some againe as jelous for their part.
Both which to stop, this gentle god toke minde,
To shape him selfe into a brutish kinde.
To such a kinde as hid what state he was,
And yet did bring him what he sought to passe.
To both their joyes, to both their comfort soon,
Though knowen to none, til al the thing was don:
In which attempt if I the like assay,
20   To you to whom I do my selfe bewray:
Let it suffice that I do seke to be,
Not counted yours, and yet for to be he.

232. *The lover disceived by his love repenteth him of the true love he bare her.*

I that Ulysses yeres have spent,
To finde Penelope:
Finde well that folly I have ment,
To seke that was not so.
Since Troylous case hath caused me,
From Cressed for to go.
    And to bewaile Ulysses truth,
In seas and stormy skies,
Of wanton will and raging youth,
10   Which me have tossed sore:
From Scilla to Caribdis clives,
Upon the drowning shore.
    Where I sought haven, there found I hap,
From daunger unto death:
Much like the Mouse that treades the trap,
In hope to finde her foode,
And bites the bread that stops her breath,

20 *bewray* reveal
232 13 *hap* (bad) luck

So in like case I stoode.
   Till now repentance hasteth him
To further me so fast: 20
That where I sanke, there now I swim,
And have both streame and winde:
And lucke as good if it may last,
As any man may finde.
   That where I perished, safe I passe,
And finde no perill there:
But stedy stone, no ground of glasse,
Now am I sure to save,
And not to flete from feare to feare,
Such anker hold I have.   30

*233. The lover having enjoyed his love, humbly
thanketh the god of love: and avowing
his hart onely to her faithfully
promiseth, utterly to forsake
all other.*

Thou Cupide God of love, whom Venus thralles do serve,
I yeld thee thankes upon my knees, as thou dost well
    deserve.
By thee my wished joyes have shaken of despaire,
And all my storming dayes be past, and weather
    waxeth faire.
By thee I have received a thousand times more joy,
Then ever Paris did possesse, when Helen was in Troy.
By thee have I that hope, for which I longde so sore,
And when I thinke upon the same, my hart doth leap
    therefore.
By thee my heapy doubtes and trembling feares are fled,
And now my wits that troubled wer, with plesant thoughts
    are fed.   10

233 1 *thralles* servants/prisoners
   3 *of* off

For dread is banisht cleane, wherein I stoode full oft,
And doubt to speake that lay full low, is lifted now aloft.
With armes bespred abrode, with opende handes and
      hart,
I have enjoyed the fruite of hope, reward for all my
      smart.
The seale and signe of love, the key of trouth and trust,
The pledge of pure good will have I, which makes the
      lovers just
Such grace sins I have found, to one I me betake,
The rest of Venus derlinges all, I utterly forsake.
And to performe this vow, I bid mine eyes beware,
That they no straungers do salute, nor on their
20   beauties stare.
My wits I warn ye all from this time forth take hede,
That ye no wanton toyes devise my fansies new to fede.
Mine eares be ye shit up, and heare no womans voyce,
That may procure me once to smile, or make my
      hart rejoyce.
My fete full slow be ye and lame when ye should move,
To bring my body any where to seke an other love,
Let all the Gods above, and wicked sprites below,
And every wight in earth acuse and curse me where I go:
If I do false my faith in any point or case,
30 A sodein vengeance fall on me, I aske no better grace.
Away then sily rime, present mine earnest faith,
Unto my lady where she is, and marke thou what
      she saith.
And if she welcome thee, and lay thee in her lap,
Spring thou for joy, thy master hath his most desired hap.

12 *doubt* fear
17 *sins* since
23 *shit* shut
28 *every wight* everyone
34 *hap* fortune

234. *Totus mundus in maligno*
positus.

Complaine we may: much is amisse:
Hope is nye gone to have redresse:
These daies ben ill, nothing sure is:
Kinde hart is wrapt in heavinesse.
    The sterne is broke: the saile is rent:
The ship is geven to winde and wave:
All helpe is gone: the rocke present
That will be lost, what man can save?
    Thinges hard, therefore are now refused.
Labour in youth is thought but vaine: 10
Duty by (will not) is excused.
Remove the stop the way is plaine.
    Learning is lewd, and held a foole:
Wisdome is shent, counted to raile:
Reason is banisht out of schoole:
The blinde is bold, and wordes prevaile.
    Power, without care, slepeth at ease:
Will, without law, runth where he list:
Might without mercy can not please.
A wise man saith not, had I wist.   20
    When power lackes care and forceth not:
When care is feable and may not:
When might is slouthfull and will not:
Wedes may grow where good herbes cannot.
    Take wrong away, law nedeth not:
For law to wrong is bridle and paine.

---

234 *Totus mundus . . . positus* 'the whole world lieth in wickedness'
  2 The hope to put things right is nearly gone
 13 *lewd* unsophisticated
 14 *shent, counted to raile* disgraced, regarded as railing
 18 *list* pleases
 20 *had I wist* if only I'd known
 21 *forceth not* has no worries

Take feare away, law booteth not.
To strive gainst streame, it is but vaine.
        Wyly is witty: brainsicke is wise:
30   Trouth is folly: and might is right:
Wordes are reason: and reason is lies:
The bad is good: darknesse is light.
        Wrong to redresse, wisdome dare not.
Hardy is happy, and ruleth most.
Wilfull is witlesse, and careth not,
Which end go first, till all be lost.
        Few right do love, and wrong refuse.
Pleasure is sought in every state.
Liking is lust: there is no chuse.
40   The low geve to the hye checke mate.
        Order is broke in thinges of weight.
Measure and meane who doth not flee?
Two thinges prevaile: money, and sleight.
To seme is better then to be.
        The bowle is round, and doth downe slide,
Eche one thrusteth: none doth uphold.
A fall failes not, where blinde is guide.
The stay is gone: who can him hold?
        Folly and falshed prayeth apace.
50   Trouth under bushell is faine to crepe.
Flattry is treble, pride singes the bace.
The meane the best part scant doth pepe.
        This firy plage the world infectes.
To vertue and trouth it geves no rest:
Mens harts are burnde with sundry sectes,
And to eche man his way is best.
        With floods and stormes thus be we tost,
Awake good Lord, to thee we crye.
Our ship is almost sonk and lost.

27 *booteth not* does no good
39 *chuse* choice (i.e. discrimination amongst men, or possibly choice for
      women)
50 *faine* apt
53 *plage* evil, plague

Thy mercy help our miserye.   60
    Mans strength is weake: mans wit is dull:
Mans reason is blinde. These thinges tamend,
Thy hand (O Lord) of might is full,
Awake betime, and helpe us send.
    In thee we trust, and in no wight:
Save us as chickens under the hen.
Our crokednesse thou canst make right,
Glory to thee for aye. Amen.

235. The wise trade of lyfe.

Do all your dedes by good advise,
Cast in your minde alwaies the end.
Wit bought is of to dere a price.
The tried, trust, and take as frend,
For frendes I finde there be but two:
Of countenance, and of effect.
Of thone sort there are inow:
But few ben of the tother sect.
Beware also the venym swete
Of crafty wordes and flattery.   10
For to deceive they be most mete,
That best can play hypocrisy.
Let wisdome rule your dede and thought:
So shall your workes be wisely wrought.

62 *tamend* to amend
65 *wight* person
68 *for aye* for ever
235 3 Wisdom bought by experience is too expensive
  4 Trust and befriend those whom you have tried
  5–6 I find there are only two kinds of friend – friends in appearance and
     friends in deed
  7–8 There are plenty of the former sort and few of the latter group
  11 *mete* fitting, capable

236. *That few wordes shew wisdome, and work much quiet.*

Who list to lead a quiet life,
Who list to rid him self from strife:
Geve eare to me, marke what I say,
Remember wel, beare it away.
Holde backe thy tong at meat and meale,
Speake but few wordes, bestrow them well.
By wordes the wise thou shalt espye,
By wordes a foole sone shalt thou trye.
A wise man can his tong make cease,
A foole can never holde his peace,
Who loveth rest of wordes beware.
Who loveth wordes, is sure of care.
For wordes oft many have ben shent:
For silence kept none hath repent.
Two eares, one tong onely thou hast,
Mo thinges to heare then wordes to wast.
A foole in no wise can forbeare:
He hath two tonges and but one eare.
Be sure thou kepe a stedfast braine,
Lest that thy wordes put thee to paine.
Words wisely set are worth much gold:
The price of rashnesse is sone told.
If time require wordes to be had,
To hold thy peace I count thee mad.
Talke onely of nedefull verities:
Strive not for trifling fantasies.
With sobernesse the truth boult out,
Affirme nothing wherin is dout.
Who to this lore will take good hede,

236   1 *list* wishes
      12 *care* sorrow, anxiety
      13 *shent* disgraced
      16 *Mo* more

And spend no mo words then he nede,   30
Though he be a fole and have no braine,
Yet shall he a name of wisdome gaine
Speake while time is or hold thee still.
Words out of time do oft things spyll.
Say well and do well are thinges twaine,
Twise blest is he in whom both raigne.

237. The complaint of a hot woer, delayed with doutfull cold answers.

A kinde of coale is as men say,
    Which have assaied the same:
That in the fire will wast away,
    And outward cast no flame.
Unto my self may I compare,
    These coales that so consume:
Where nought is sene though men do stare,
    In stede of flame but fume.
They say also to make them burne,
    Cold water must be cast: 10
Or els to ashes will they turne,
    And half to sinder wast.
As this is wonder for to se,
    Cold water warme the fire,
So hath your coldnesse caused me,
    To burne in my desire.
And as this water cold of kinde,
    Can cause both heat and cold,
And can these coales both breake and binde,
    To burne as I have told.   20
So can your tong of frosen yse,
    From whence cold answers come:
Both coole the fire and fire entice,
    To burne me all and some.

Like to the corne that standes on stake,
    Which mowen in winter sunne:
Full faire without, within is black:
    Such heat therin doth runne.
By force of fire this water cold,
30   Hath bred to burne within,
Even so am I, that heat doth hold,
    Which cold did first begyn.
Which heat is stint when I do strive,
    To have some ease sometime:
But flame a fresh I do revive,
    Wherby I cause to clime.
In stede of smoke a sighing breath:
    With sparkes of sprinkled teares,
That I should live this livyng death,
40   Which wastes and never weares.

238. The answer.

Your borrowd meane to move your mone, of fume
    withouten flame
Being set from smithy smokyng coale: ye seme so
    by the same.
To shew, what such coales use is taught by such as
    have assayd,
As I, that most do wish you well, am so right well
    apayd.
That you have such a lesson learnd, how either to
    maintaine,
Your fredome of unkindled coale, upheaped all in vaine:
Or how most frutefully to frame, with worthy
    workmans art,

237 25–6 Like corn left standing on its stalks, which is then mown in winter
    sunshine
238 1 *meane* simile

That cunnyng pece may passe there fro, by help of
    heated hart.
Out of the forge wherin the fume of sighes doth mount
    aloft,
That argues present force of fire to make the metall soft,   10
To yelde unto the hammer hed, as best the workman
    likes.
That thiron glowyng after blast in time and temper strikes.
Wherin the use of water is, as you do seme to say,
To quenche no flame, ne hinder heat, ne yet to wast away:
But, that which better is for you, and more deliteth me,
To save you from the sodain waste, vaine cinderlike to be.
Which lastyng better likes in love, as you your semble ply,
Then doth the baven blase, that flames and fleteth by
    and by.
Sith then you know eche use, wherin your coale may be
    applide:
Either to lie and last on hoord, in open ayre to bide,   20
Withouten use to gather fat by fallyng of the raines,
That makes the pitchy jucye to grow, by sokyng in
    his veines,
Or lye on fornace in the forge, as is his use of right,
Wherin the water trough may serve, and enteryeld
    her might
By worke of smithes both hand and hed a cunnyng
    key to make,
Or other pece as cause shall crave and bid him undertake:
Do as you deme most fit to do, and wherupon may grow,
Such joy to you, as I may joy your joyfull case to know.

8 *passe there fro* escape from there
12 *thiron* the iron
17 *your semble ply* develop your simile
18 *baven* brushwood faggot
19 *Sith* since
20–21 Either to lie unburned in a heap, becoming greasy by rainfall
22 *jucye* probably misprint for 'juyce'
24 *enteryeld* transfuse

239. An epitaph made by .W. G. lying on
his death bed, to be set upon
his owne tombe.

Lo here lieth G. under the ground
 Among the gredy wormes,
Which in his life time never found
 But strife and sturdy stormes.
And namely through a wicked wife,
 As to the world apperes:
She was the shortnyng of his life
 By many dayes and yeres.
He might have lived long, god wot:
 His yeres, they were but yong:
Of wicked wives this is the lot,
 To kill with spitefull tong.
Whose memory shall still remayne
 In writing here with me,
That men may know whom she hath slayne,
 And say this same is she.

240. An answer.

If that thy wicked wife had spon the thread,
 And were the weaver of thy wo:
Then art thou double happy to be dead,
 As happely dispatched so.
If rage did causelesse cause thee to complayne,
 And mad moode mover of thy mone:
If frensy forced on thy testy braine:
 Then blist is she to live alone.
So, whether were the ground of others grefe,

239 9 *wot* knows
240 9 *whether* which of the two

Because so doutfull was the dome: 10
Now death hath brought your payne a right relefe,
    And blessed be ye both become:
She, that she lives no longer bound to beare
    The rule of such a froward hed:
Thou, that thou livest no lenger faine to feare
    The restlesse ramp that thou hadst wed,
Be thou as glad therfore that thou art gone,
    As she is glad she doth abide:
For so ye be a sonder, all is one:
    A badder match can not betide.   20

241. *An epitaph of maister Henry Williams.*

From worldly wo the mede of misbelefe,
From cause of care that leadeth to lament,
From vaine delight the ground of greater grefe,
From feare for frendes, from matter to repent,
From painefull pangs last sorowe that is sent,
From dred of death sith death doth set us free:
With it the better pleased should we be.
    This lothsome life where likyng we do finde,
Thencreaser of our crimes, doth us bereve
Our blisse that alway ought to be in minde.   10
This wily world whiles here we breath alive,
And flesh our fayned fo, do stifly strive
To flatter us, assuryng here the joy,

10 *dome* judgement
14 *froward* contrary, perverse, argumentative
15 *faine* disposed
16 *ramp* wanton or tomboyish woman
241 1 *mede* reward
    2 *care* sorrow, anxiety
    5 *last* possibly a misprint for 'salt'
    6 *sith* since
    9 *Thencreaser* the increaser

Where we, alas, do finde but great annoy.
    Untolde heapes though we have of worldly wealth,
Though we possesse the sea and frutefull ground,
Strength, beauty, knowledge, and unharmed health,
Though at a wish all pleasure do abound.
It were but vaine, no frendship can be found,
When death assalteth with his dredfull dart.
No raunsome can stay the home hastyng hart.
    And sith thou cut the lives line in twaine,
Of Henry, sonne to sir John Williams knight,
Whose manly hart and prowes none could staine,
Whose godly life to vertue was our light,
Whose worthy fame shall florish long by right.
Though in this life so cruell mightest thou be,
His spirite in heaven shall triumph over thee.

242. *An other of the same.*

Stay gentle frend that passest by,
And learne the lore that leadeth all:
From whence we come with hast to hye,
To live to dye, and stand to fall.
    And learne that strength and lusty age,
That wealth and want of worldly woe,
Can not withstand the mighty rage,
Of death our best unwelcome foe.
    For hopefull youth had hight me health,
My lust to last till time to dye,
And fortune found my vertue wealth:
But yet for all that here I lye.
    Learne also this, to ease thy minde:
When death on corps hath wrought his spite,
A time of triumph shalt thou finde,

242 3 *hast to hye* too great haste
     9 *hight* promised
     10 *lust* pleasure

With me to scorne him in delight.
　For one day shall we mete againe,
Maugre deathes dart in life to dwell.
Then will I thanke thee for thy paine,
Now marke my wordes and fare thou well.   20

243. *Against women, either good or bad.*

A man may live thrise Nestors life,
Thrise wander out Ulisses race:
Yet never finde Ulisses wife.
Such change hath chanced in this case.
　Lesse age will serve than Paris had,
Small pein (if none be small inough)
To finde good store of Helenes trade.
Such sap the rote doth yelde the bough.
　For one good wife Ulisses slew
A worthy knot of gentle blood: 10
For one yll wife Grece overthrew
The towne of Troy: Sith bad and good
Bring mischief: Lord let be thy will,
To kepe me free from either yll.

244. *An answer.*

The vertue of Ulisses wife
Doth live, though she hath ceast her race,
And farre surmountes old Nestors life:
But now in moe than then it was.
Such change is chanced in this case.
　Ladies now live in other trade:

18 *Maugre* despite
19 *paine* effort
243 12 *Sith* since
244 4 *moe* more

Farre other Helenes now we see,
Than she whom Troyan Paris had.
As vertue fedes the roote, so be
The sap and rote of bough and tre.
   Ulisses rage, not his good wife,
Spilt gentle blood. Not Helenes face,
But Paris eye did raise the strife,
That did the Troyan buildyng race.
Thus sith ne good, ne bad do yll:
Them all, O Lord maintain my wyll,
To serve with all my force and skill.

245. *Against a gentilwoman by whom he was refused.*

To false report and flying fame,
Whilist my minde gave credit light,
Belevyng that her bolstred name
Had stuffe to shew that praise did hight.
I finde well now I did mistake,
Upon report my ground to make.
   I heard it said such one was she,
As rare to finde as parragon,
Of lowly chere, of hart so free,
As her for bounty could passe none.
Such one were faire though forme and face,
Were meane to passe in second place.
   I sought it neare, and thinkyng to finde
Report and dede both to agree:
But chaunge had tried her suttle minde:
Of force I was enforced to see,
That she in dede was nothing so:

14 *race* raze
15 *sith* since
245 4 *hight* adorn
   9 *chere* expression
   12 *meane* a means

Which made my will my hart forgo.
   For she is such, as geason none.
And what she most may boast to be: 20
I finde her matches mo then one,
What nede she so to deale with me?
Ha fleryng face, with scornefull hart,
So yll reward for good desert?
   I will repent that I have done,
To ende so well the losse is small:
I lost her love, that lesse hath won,
To vaunt she had me as her thrall.
What though a gillot sent that note,
By cocke and pye I meant it not.   30

246. *The answere.*

Whom fansy forced first to love,
Now frensy forceth for to hate:
Whose minde erst madnesse gan to move,
Inconstance causeth to abate.
No minde of meane, dut heat of braine
Bred light love: like heate, hate againe
   What hurld your hart in so great heat?
Fansy forced by fayned fame.
Belike that she was light to get.
For if that vertue and good name   10
Moved your minde, why changed your will,
Sithe vertue the cause abideth still.

19 *as geason none* as is no rarity
21 *mo* more
23 *fleryng* mocking
27 *lesse* a lesser man
29 *gillot* loose woman
246 3 *erst* before *gan* began
  5 *meane* moderation *dut* misprint for 'but'
  9 *light to get* easy to obtain
  12 *Sithe* since

Such, Fame reported her to be
As rare it were to finde her peere,
For vertue and for honestie,
For her free hart and lowly cheere.
This laud had lied if you had sped,
And fame bene false that hath ben spred.
   Sith she hath so kept her good name.
Such praise of life and giftes of grace,
As brute self blusheth for to blame,
Such fame as fame feares to deface:
You sclaunder not but make it plaine,
That you blame brute of brutish traine.
   If you have found it looking neere,
Not as you toke the brute to be.
Bylike you ment by lowly cheere,
Bountie and hart that you call free,
But lewd lightnesse easy to frame,
To winne your will against her name.
   Nay she may deme your deming so,
A marke of madnesse in his kinde,
Such causeth not good name to go:
As your fond folly sought to finde.
For brute of kinde bent ill to blase,
Alway sayth ill, but forced by cause.
   The mo there be, such as is she,
More should be gods thank for his grace.
The more is her joy it to see.
Good should by geason, earne no place,
Nor nomber make nought, that is good.
Your strange lusting hed wants a hoode.
   Her dealing greveth you (say ye)

16 *cheere* expression
21 *brute self* rumour itself/even a brute
24 You accuse rumour of beastly behaviour
27–9 Perhaps you construed meek behaviour, generosity and a free heart
    as being only naive/lascivious lightness that is easily conquered
37 *mo* more
40 *geason* rarity

Byside your labour lost in vaine.
Her dealing was not as we see,
Sclaunder the end of your great paine,
Ha lewd lieng lips, and hatefull hart,
What canst thou desire in such desart.
 Ye will repent, and right for done.
Ye have a dede deserving shame.   50
From reasons race farre have ye ronne.
Hold your rayling, kepe your tong tame.
Her love, ye lye, ye lost it not.
Ye never lost that ye never got.
 She reft ye not your libertie,
She vaunteth not she had your thrall.
If ought have done it, let it lye,
On rage that reft you wit and all.
What though a varlets tale you tell:
By cock and pye you do it well.   60

247. The lover dredding to move his sute for dout of deniall, accuseth all women of disdaine and ficklenesse.

To walke on doutfull ground, where daunger is unsene,
Doth double men that carelesse be in depe dispaire I wene.
For as the blinde doth feare, what footing he shall finde:
So doth the wise before he speake, mistrust the straungers
 minde.
For he that blontly runnes, may light among the breers,
And so be put unto his plunge where danger least apperes:
The bird that selly foole, doth warne us to beware,

49 *right for done* would be right to do so
55–6 She didn't take away your liberty; she doesn't boast that she had you
 as a prisoner/slave
247 *dout* fear
 2 Puts careless men twice as much into deep peril, I believe
 7 *selly* innocently happy

Who lighteth not on every bush, he dreadeth so the
    snare.
The Mouse that shons the trap, doth shew what harme
    doth lye:
Within the swete betraying bait, that oft disceives the eye.
The fish avoydes the hooke, though hunger bids him bite,
And hovereth still about the worme, whereon is his delite.
If birdes and beastes can see, where their undoing lies:
How should a mischief scape our heades, that have both
    wit & eyes?
What madnesse may be more, then plough the
    barreyn fielde:
Or any frutefull wordes to sow, to eares that are unwild.
They heare and than mislike, they like and then they lothe,
They hate, thei love, thei scorn, thei praise, yea sure
    thei can do both
We see what falles they have, that clime on trees
    unknowne:
As they that trust to rotten bowes, must nedes be
    overthrowne.
A smart in silence kept, doth ease the hart much more,
Than for to playn where is no salve, for to recure the sore.
Wherfore my grief I hide, within a holow hart:
Untill the smoke thereof be spred, by flaming of the smart.

248. *An answere.*

To trust the fayned face, to rue on forced teares,
To credit finely forged tales, wherin there oft appeares
    And breathes as from the brest a smoke of kindled smart,
Where onely lurkes a depe deceit within the hollow hart,
    Betrayes the simple soule, whom plaine deceitlesse minde
Taught not to feare that in it selfe, it selfe did never finde.

16 *unwild* unwilling to hear
17 *than* then
248 6 *that* that which

Not every trickling teare doth argue inward paine:
Not every sigh doth surely shew the sigher not to faine:
Not every smoke doth prove a presence of the fire:
Not every glistring geves the gold, that gredy folke desire: 10
Not every wayling word is drawen out of the depe:
Not grief for want of graunted grace enforceth all to wepe.
Oft malice makes the minde to shed the boyled brine:
And envies humor oft unlades by conduites of the eyen.
Oft craft can cause the man to make a seming show,
Of hart with dolour all distreined, where grief did never
      grow.
As cursed Crocodile most cruelly can tole,
With truthlesse teares, unto his death, the silly pitying soule.
Blame never those therfore, that wisely can beware
The guilefull man, that sutly sayth himselfe to dread
      the snare.   20
Blame not the stopped eares against the Syrenes song:
Blame not the minde not moved with mone of falsheds
      flowing tong.
If guile do guide your wit by silence so to speake,
By craft to crave and faine by fraude the cause that you
      wold break.
Great harme your suttle soule shall suffer for the same:
And mighty love will wreke the wrong, so cloked with his
      name.
But we, whom you have warnde, this lesson learne
      by you:
To know the tree before we clime, to trust no rotten bowe,
To view the limed bushe, to looke afore we light,
To shunne the perilous bayted hooke, and use a further
      sight.   30

14 *envies* envious, dishonest
17 *tole* deceive
18 *silly* naive
20 *sayth himselfe* tells himself
24 *break* advance
26 *wreke* revenge
29 *limed* tied up with bird-lime traps

As do the mouse, the birde, the fish, by samply fitly
        show,
    That wily wits and ginnes of men do worke the
        simples wo:
    So, simple sithe we are, and you so suttle be,
    God help the Mouse, the birde, the fish, & us your
        sleightes to fle.

249. *The lover complaineth his fault, that with ungentle writing had displeased his lady.*

Ah love how waiward is his wit what panges do perce
    his brest
Whom thou to wait upon thy will hast reved of his rest.
The light, the darke, the sunne, the mone, the day &
    eke the night,
His dayly dieng life, him self, he hateth in despight,
Sith furst he light to looke on her that holdeth him
    in thrall,
His moving eyen his moved wit he curseth hart and all,
From hungry hope to pining feare eche hap doth hurle
    his hart,
From panges of plaint to fits of fume from aking into smart.
Eche moment so doth change his chere not with
    recourse of ease,
But with sere sortes of sorrowes still he worketh as
10   the seas.

31 *by samply* for example
32 *ginnes* traps
33 *sithe* since
249 2 *reved* deprived
    3 *eke* also
    5 *Sith* since   *light* happened
    7 *hap* vicissitude of fortune
    8 *plaint* misery
    9 *chere* expression
    10 *sere* various

That turning windes not calme returnde rule in unruly
    wise,
As if their holdes of hilles uphurld they brasten out
    to rise.
And puffe away the power that is unto their king assignde
To pay that sithe their prisonment they deme to be
    behinde.
So doth the passions long represt within the wofull wight,
Breake downe the banks of all his wits & out they gushen
    quite.
To rere up rores now they be free from reasons rule and
    stay,
And hedlong hales thunruled race his quiet quite away.
No measure hath he of his ruth, no reason in his rage,
No bottom ground where stayes his grief, thus weares
    away his age   20
In wishing wants, in wayling woes. Death doth he
    dayly call,
To bring release when of relief he seeth no hope at all.
Thence comes that oft in depe despeire to rise to better
    state,
On heaven and heavenly lampes he layeth the faute of
    al his fate.
On God and Gods decreed dome cryeth out with cursing
    breath,
Eche thing that gave and saves him life he damneth of his
    death.
The wombe him bare, the brests he suckt, ech star that
    with their might,
Their secret succour brought to bring the wretch to
    worldly light

12 *brasten* burst
15 *wight* person
18 headlong hail razes/erases his quiet quite away
19 *No measure hath he of his ruth* he has no moderation in his distress/
remorse
25 *dome* judgement, destiny

Yea that to his soules perile is most haynous harme of all,
30   And craves the cruellest revenge that may to man befall:
Her he blasphemes in whom it lieth in present as she
            please,
To dampne him downe to depth of hell, or plant in
            heavens ease.
Such rage constrainde my strained hart to guide
            thunhappy hand
That sent unfitting blots to her on whom my life
            doth stand.
But graunt O God that he for them may beare the
            worthy blame
Whom I do in my depe distresse finde guilty of the same,
Even that blinde boy that blindly guides the fautles to
            their fall,
That laughes when they lament that he hath throwen
            into thral.
Or Lord, save louring lookes of her, what penance els
            thou please
40   So her contented will be wonne I count it all mine ease.
And thou on whom doth hang my will, with hart, with
            soul & care,
With life and all that life may have of well or evell fare:
Graunt grace to him that grates therfore with sea of
            saltish brine
By extreme heat of boylyng brest distilled through
            his eyen.
And with thy fancy render thou my self to me againe,
That dayly then we duely may employ a painelesse paine.
To yelde and take the joyfull frutes that herty love
            doth lend,
To them that meane by honest meanes to come to
            happy end.

33 *thunhappy* the unhappy
39 *Or* oh   *louring* threatening, angry
43 *grates* weeps/wails

250. *The lover wounded of Cupide,*
wisheth he had rather ben
striken by death.

The blinded boy that bendes the bow,
To make with dint of double wound:
The stowtest state to stoupe and know:
The cruell craft that I have found.
    With death I would had chopt a change,
To borow as by bargain made:
Ech others shaft when he did range,
With restlesse rovyng to invade,
    Thunthralled mindes of simple wightes,
Whose giltlesse ghostes deserved not: 10
To fele such fall of their delightes,
Such panges as I have past God wot.
    Then both in new unwonted wise,
Should death deserve a better name,
Not (as tofore hath bene his guise)
Of crueltie to beare the blame.
    But contrary be counted kinde,
In lendyng life and sparyng space:
For sicke to rise and seke to finde,
A way to wish their weary race   20
    To draw to some desired end,
Their long and lothed life to rid.
And so to fele how like a frend,
Before the bargain made he did.
    And love should either bring againe,
To wounded wightes their owne desire:

---

250 9 The unenthralled minds of ordinary people
  10 *ghostes* spirits
  12 *past* suffered   *wot* knows
  15 *tofore* until now   *guise* custom
  19 *sicke* sick people

A welcome end of pinyng payne,
As doth their cause of ruthe require:
Or when he meanes the quiet man,
A harme to hasten him to grefe:
A better dede he should do then,
With borrowd dart to geve relefe.

That both the sicke well demen may,
He brought me rightly my request:
And eke the other sort may say,
He wrought me truely for the best.

So had not fancy forced me,
To beare a brunt of greater wo:
Then leaving such a life may be,
The ground where onely grefes do grow.

Unlucky likyng linkt my hart,
In forged hope and forced feare:
That oft I wisht the other dart,
Had rather perced me as neare.

A fayned trust, constrayned care,
Most loth to lack, most hard to finde:
In sunder so my judgement tare,
That quite was quiet out of minde.

Absent in absence of mine ease,
Present in presence of my paine:
The woes of want did much displease,
The sighes I sought did greve againe.

Oft grefe that boyled in my brest,
Hath fraught my face with saltish teares,
Pronouncyng proves of mine unrest,
Whereby my passed paine appeares.

My sighes full often have supplied,
That faine with wordes I wold have said:

28 *ruthe* pity
35 *eke* also
36 *wrought* worked on
58 *faine* willingly

My voice was stopt, my tong was tyed,
My wits with wo were overwayd.   60
    With tremblyng soule and humble chere,
Oft grated I for graunt of grace:
On hope that bounty might be there,
Where beauty had so pight her place.
    At length I found, that I did fere,
How I had labourde all to losse,
My self had ben the carpenter,
That framed me the cruell crosse.
    Of this to come if dout alone,
Though blent with trust of better spede: 70
So oft hath moved my minde to mone,
So oft hath made my hart to blede.
    What shall I say of it in dede,
Now hope is gone mine olde relefe:
And I enforced all to fede,
Upon the frutes of bitter grefe?

251. Of womens changeable will.

I wold I found not as I fele,
Such changyng chere of womens will,
By fickle flight of fortunes whele,
By kinde or custome, never still.
    So shold I finde no fault to lay,
On fortune for their movyng minde,
So should I know no cause to say
This change to chance by course of kinde.

61 *chere* expression
62 *grated* wept/wailed
64 *pight* pitched
70 *blent* blinded
251 2 *chere* expression, mood
  4 *kinde* nature

So should not love so work my wo,
To make death surgeant for my sore,
So should their wittes not wander so,
So should I reck the lesse therfore.

252. The lover complayneth the losse of his ladye.

No joy have I, but live in heavinesse,
My dame of price bereft by fortunes cruelnesse,
My hap is turned to unhappinesse,
Unhappy I am unlesse I finde relesse.
My pastime past, my youthlike yeres are gone,
My mouthes of mirth, my glistring daies of
        gladsomnesse:
My times of triumph turned into mone.
Unhappy I am unlesse I finde relesse.
My wonted winde to chaunt my cherefull chaunce,
Doth sigh that song somtime the balades of my lesse:
My sobbes, my sore and sorow do advaunce.
Unhappy I am unlesse I finde relesse.
I mourne my mirth for grefe that it is gone,
I mourne my mirth wherof my musing mindefulnesse:
Is ground of greater grefe that growes theron,
Unhappy I am unlesse I finde relesse.
No joy have I: for fortune frowardly:
Hath bent her browes hath put her hand to cruelnesse:
Hath rest my dame, constrayned me to crye,
Unhappy I am unlesse I finde relesse.

10 *surgeant* surgeon
12 *reck* care
252 2 *dame of price* valuable lady
3 *hap* good luck, happiness
10 *lesse* loss
17 *frowardly* in opposition
19 *rest* misprint for 'reft'

253. Of the golden meane.

The wisest way, thy bote, in wave and winde to guie,
Is neither still the trade of middle streame to trie:
Ne (warely shunnyng wrecke by wether) aye to nie,
          To presse upon the perillous shore,
Both clenely flees he filthe: ne wonnes a wretched
   wight,
In carlish coate: and carefull court aie thrall to spite,
With port of proud astate he leves: who doth delight,
         Of golden meane to hold the lore.
Stormes rifest rende the sturdy stout pineapple tre.
Of lofty ruing towers the fals the feller be.   10
Most fers doth lightenyng light, where furthest we
   do se.
         The hilles the valey to forsake.
Well furnisht brest to bide eche chanses changing
   chear,
In woe hath chearfull hope, in weal hath warefull fear,
One self Jove winter makes with lothfull lokes appear,
         That can by course the same aslake.
What if into mishap thy case now casten be?
It forceth not such forme of luck to last to thee.
Not alway bent is Phebus bow: his harpe and he,
         Ceast silver sound sometime doth raise. 20

---

253 1 *guie* steer
   3 *aye to nie* all too near
   5 *ne wonnes a wretched wight* does not live as a wretched person
   6 *carlish coate* vulgar hovel *carefull* full of anxiety *aie thrall to spite*
     always subject to spite
   7 *port* gait
  10 *ruing* probably a misprint for 'rising' (see explanatory note)
  11–12 Lightning strikes most fiercely where the hills rise furthest above
     the valley
  13 A breast well equipped to endure the changing moods of chance
  15 *One self Jove* the same god Jove
  18 *It forceth not* it doesn't matter

In hardest hap use helpe of hardy hopefull hart.
Seme bold to beare the brunt of fortune overthwart.
Eke wisely when forewinde to full breathes on thy part,
          Swage swellyng saile, and doubt
          decayes.

254. The praise of a true frende.

Who so that wisely weyes the profite and the price,
Of thinges wherin delight by worth is wont to rise.
Shall finde no jewell is so rich ne yet so rare,
That with the frendly hart in value may compare.
   What other wealth to man by fortune may befall,
But fortunes changed chere may reve a man of all.
A frend no wracke of wealth, no cruell cause of wo,
Can force his frendly faith unfrendly to forgo.
   If fortune frendly fawne, and lend thee welthy store,
Thy frendes conjoyned joy doth make thy joy the more.
If frowardly she frown and drive thee to distresse,
His ayde releves thy ruthe, and makes thy sorowe lesse.
   Thus fortunes pleasant frutes by frendes encreased be,
The bitter sharp and sowre by frendes alayde to thee.
That when thou doest rejoyce, then doubled is thy joy,
And eke in cause of care, the lesse is thy anoy.
   Aloft if thou do live, as one appointed here,
A stately part on stage of worldly state to bere:
Thy frende as only free from fraud will thee advise,
To rest within the rule of mean as do the wise.

10

20

21 *hap* fortune
22 *overthwart* contrary
23 *Eke* also
24 *Swage* reef in
254 6 *chere* expression, favour   *reve* deprive
11 *frowardly* contrarily
12 *ruthe* suffering
16 *eke* also   *care* sorrow, anxiety

He seeketh to foresee the peril of thy fall.
He findeth out thy faultes and warnes thee of them all.
Thee, not thy luck he loves, what ever be thy case,
He is thy faithfull frend and thee he doth embrace.
    If churlish cheare of chance have thrown thee into
        thrall,
And that thy nede aske ayde for to releve thy fall:
In him thou secret trust assured art to have,
And succour not to seke, before that thou can crave.
    Thus is thy frende to thee the comfort of thy paine,
The stayer of thy state, the doubler of thy gaine.   30
In wealth and wo thy frend, an other self to thee,
Such man to man a God, the proverb sayth to be.
    As welth will bring thee frendes in louring wo to prove,
So wo shall yeld thee frendes in laughing wealth to love.
With wisedome chuse thy frend, with vertue him retaine:
Let vertue be the ground, so shall it not be vaine.

255. *The lover lamenteth other to have the frutes of his service.*

Some men would think of right to have,
For their true meaning some reward,
But while that I do cry and crave:
I see that other be preferd,
I gape for that I am debard.
I fare as doth the hound at hatch:
The worse I spede, the lenger I watch.
    My wastefull will is tried by trust:
My fond fansie is mine abuse.
For that I would refraine my lust: 10
For mine availe I cannot chuse,
A will, and yet no power to use.
A will, no will by reason just,

30 *stayer* supporter
33 *louring* threatening/frowning
255 5 *for that* because

Sins my will is at others lust.
   They eate the hony, I hold the hyve.
I sow the sede, they reape the corne.
I waste, they winne, I draw they drive.
Theirs is the thanke, mine is the scorne.
I seke, they spede, in waste my winde is worne.
I gape, they get, and gredely I snatch:
Till wurse I spede, the lenger I watch.
   I fast, they fede: they drink, I thurst.
They laugh, I wayle: they joy, I mourne.
They gayne, I lose: I have the wurst.
They whole, I sicke: they cold, I burne.
They leape, I lye: they slepe, I tosse and turne.
I would, they may: I crave, they have at will.
That helpeth them, lo, cruelty doth me kill.

256. *Of the sutteltie of crafty lovers.*

Such waiward waies have some when folly stirres their
    braines
To fain & plain full oft of love, when lest they fele his
    paines.
And for to shew a griefe such craft have they in store,
That they can halt and lay a salve wheras they fele
    no sore.
As hound unto the foote, or dog unto the bow,
So are they made to vent her out, whom bent to love
    they know.
That if I should discribe one hundred of their driftes,
Two hundred wits beside mine owne I should put to
    their shiftes
No woodman better knowes how for to lodge his dere,

14 *Sins* since
256 2 *lest* least
  4 *halt and lay a salve* limp and wear a bandage
  6 *vent* flush

Nor shipman on the sea that more hath skill to guide
    the stere. 10
Nor beaten dogge to herd can warer chose his game.
Nor scholeman to his fansie can a scholer better frame.
Then one of these which have old Ovids arte in ure,
Can seke the wayes unto their minde a woman to
    allure.
As round about a hyve the Bees do swarme alway,
So round about the house they prease wherin they seke
    their pray.
And whom they so besege, it is a wonderous thing,
What crafty engins to assault these wily warriers bring.
The eye as scout and watch to stirre both to and fro,
Doth serve to stale her here & there where she doth
    come and go. 20
The tong doth pleade for right as herauld of the hart:
And both the handes as oratours do serve to point
    their part.
So shewes the countenance then with these fowre to
    agree,
As though in witnes with the rest, it would hers
    sworne be.
But if she then mistrust it would turne blacke to white,
For that the woorrier lokes most smoth when he wold
    fainest bite.
Then wit as counsellour a helpe for this to finde:
Straight makes the hand as secretair forthwith to write
    his minde.
And so the letters straight embassadours are made,
To treate in haste for to procure her to a better trade. 30
Wherin if she do thinke all this is but a shewe,

11 Nor can an experienced dog more carefully choose his target in herding
13 *ure* practice
20 *stale* decoy
26 *woorrier* hostile dog   *when he wold fainest bite* when he would most
    like to bite
28 *Straight* immediately

Or but a subtile masking cloke to hide a crafty shrewe:
Then come they to the larme, then shew they in the fielde,
Then muster they in colours strange, that waies to make
    her yeld
Then shoote they batry of, then compasse they her in,
At tilt and turney oft they strive this selly soule to win.
Then sound they on their lutes, then strain they forth
    their song,
Then romble they with instrumentes to lay her quite
    a long.
Then borde they her with giftes, then do they woo
    and watch,
Then night and day they labour hard this simple hold
40   to catch,
As pathes within a wood, or turnes with in a mase:
So then they shew of wiles & craftes they can a
    thousand wayes.

257. Of the vanitie of mans lyfe.

Vaine is the fleting welth,
Whereon the world stayes:
Sithe stalking time by privy stelth,
Encrocheth on our dayes.
    And elde which creepeth fast,
To taynte us with her wounde:
Will turne eche blysse unto a blast,

33 *larme* mustering trumpet call
35 *of* off   *compasse* encircle
36 *selly* naive
38 *lay her quite a long* come alongside her (nautical)
42 *can* know
257 2 *stayes* depends
  3 *Sithe* since
  5 *elde* old age

Which lasteth but a stounde.
　Of youth the lusty floure,
Which whylome stoode in price: 10
Shall vanish quite within an houre,
As fire consumes the ice.
　Where is become that wight,
For whose sake Troy towne:
Withstode the grekes till ten yeres fight,
Had rasde their walles adowne.
　Did not the wormes consume,
Her caryon to the dust?
Did dreadfull death forbeare his fume
For beauty, pride, or lust?   20

258. The lover not regarded in earnest sute, being become wiser, refuseth her profred love.

Do way your phisike I faint no more,
The salve you sent it comes to late:
You wist well all my grief before,
And what I suffred for your sake.
Hole is my hart I plaine no more,
A new the cure did undertake:
Wherfore do way you come to late.
　For whiles you knew I was your own,
So long in vaine you made me gape,
And though my fayth it were well knowne,   10
Yet small regard thou toke therat,

8 *stounde* moment
10 *whylome* formerly
13 *wight* person
258　3 *wist* knew
　6 *A new* i.e. a new lover
　7 *do way* be off with you

But now the blast is overblowne.
Of vaine phisicke a salve you shape,
Wherfore do way you come to late.
    How long or this have I bene faine,
To gape for mercy at your gate,
Untill the time I spyde it plaine,
That pitie and you fell at debate.
For my redresse then was I faine:
Your service cleane for to forsake,
Wherfore do way you come to late.
    For when I brent in endlesse fire,
Who ruled then but cruell hate?
So that unneth I durst desire
One looke, my fervent heate to slake.
Therfore another doth me hyre,
And all the profer that you make,
Is made in vayne and comes to late.
    For when I asked recompence,
With cost you nought to graunt God wat:
Then said disdaine to great expence,
It were for you to graunt me that.
Therfore doway your rere pretence,
That you would binde that derst you brake,
For lo your salve comes all to late.

13 *salve* remedy
15 *or* before   *faine* eager
20 *cleane* completely
22 *brent* burned
24 *unneth* hardly
28 *to* too
30 Which wouldn't have cost you anything to grant, God knows
33 *rere* retrospective

259. The complaint of a woman ravished, and also mortally wounded.

A cruell Tiger all with teeth bebled,
A bloody tirantes hand in eche degre,
A lecher that by wretched lust was led,
(Alas) deflowred my virginitee.
And not contented with this villanie,
Nor with thoutragious terrour of the dede,
With bloody thirst of greater crueltie:
Fearing his haynous gilt should be bewrayed,
By crying death and vengeance openly,
His violent hand forthwith alas he layed   10
Upon my guiltles sely childe and me,
And like the wretch whom no horrour dismayde,
Drownde in the sinke of depe iniquitie:
Misusing me the mother for a time,
Hath slaine us both for cloking of his crime.

260. The lover being made thrall by love, perceiveth how great a losse is libertye.

Ah libertie now have I learnd to know,
By lacking thee what Jewell I possest,
When I received first from Cupids bow
The deadly wound that festreth in my brest.
    So farre (alas) forth strayed were mine eyes,
That I ne might refraine them backe, for lo:
They in a moment all earthly thinges despise,

259 1 *bebled* blooded
     6 *thoutragious* the outrageous
     8 *bewrayed* revealed
    11 *sely* innocent
    15 *for cloking of* in order to cloak

In heavenly sight now are they fixed so.
    What then for me but still with mazed sight,
10 To wonder at that excellence divine:
Where love (my freedome having in despight)
Hath made me thrall through errour of mine eyen,
For other guerdon hope I not to have,
My foltring toonge so basheth ought to crave.

261. *The divers and contrarie passions of the lover.*

Holding my peace alas how loud I crye,
Pressed with hope and dread even both at ones,
Strayned with death, and yet I cannot dye.
Burning in flame, quaking for cold that grones,
Unto my hope withouten winges I flye.
Pressed with dispayre, that breaketh all my bones.
Walking as if I were, and yet am not.
Fayning with mirth, most inwardly with mones.
Hard by my helpe, unto my health not nye.
10 Mids of the calme my ship on rocke it rones.
I serve unbound, fast fettred yet I lye.
In stede of milke that fede on marble stones,
My most will is that I do espye:
That workes my joyes and sorowes both at ones.
In contrairs standeth all my losse and gaine:
And lo the giltlesse causeth all my paine.

260 13 *guerdon* reward
  14 *basheth ought to crave* is ashamed to ask for anything
261 *divers* various
  2 *ones* once
  3 *Strayned* afflicted
  10 *rones* runs aground
  13 What I most want is what I see
  16 *the* thee

262. *The testament of the hawthorne.*

I sely Haw whose hope is past,
In faithfull true and fixed minde:
To her whom that I served last,
Have all my joyefulnes resignde,
Because I know assuredly,
My dying day aprocheth nye.

   Dispaired hart the carefull nest,
Of all the sighes I kept in store:
Convey my carefull corps to rest,
That leaves his joy for evermore.   10
And when the day of hope is past,
Geve up thy sprite and sigh the last.

   But or that we depart in twaine,
Tell her I loved with all my might:
That though the corps in clay remaine,
Consumed to asshes pale and white.
And though the vitall powres do ceasse,
The sprite shall love her natrelesse.

   And pray my lives lady dere,
During this litle time and space,   20
That I have to abiden here,
Not to withdraw her wonted grace,
In recompensing of the paine,
That I shall have to part in twaine.

   And that at least she will withsave,
To graunt my just and last request:
When that she shall behold his grave,
That lyeth of lyfe here dispossest,

262 1 *sely* naive
   7 *carefull* full of sorrow, anxiety
  12 *sprite* life-force, soul
  13 *or that* before
  18 *natrelesse* transcending mere natural desires, but possibly a misprint
for 'natheless' (i.e. nonetheless)
  25 *withsave* condescend

In record that I once was hers,
To bathe the frosen stone with teares.
　　The service tree here do I make,
For mine executour and my frende:
That living did not me forsake,
Nor will I trust unto my ende,
To see my body well conveyde,
In ground where that it shalbe layde.
　　Tombed underneth a goodly Oke,
With Ivy grene that fast is bound:
There this my grave I have bespoke,
For there my ladies name do sound:
Beset even as my testament tels:
With oken leaves and nothing els.
　　Graven wheron shalbe exprest,
Here lyeth the body in this place,
Of him that living never cest
To serve the fayrest that ever was,
The corps is here, the hart he gave
To her for whom he lieth in grave.
　　And also set about my hersse,
Two lampes to burne and not to queint,
Which shalbe token, and rehersse
That my good will was never spent.
When that my corps was layd alow,
My spirit did sweare to serve no mo.
　　And if you want of ringing bels,
When that my corps goth into grave:
Repete her name and nothing els,
To whom that I was bonden slave.
When that my life it shall unframe,
My sprite shall joy to heare her name.
　　With dolefull note and piteous sound,

---

31 *service tree* the *Pyrus domestica*, a tree bearing small pear-shaped fruit
50 *queint* snuff out
54 *mo* more

Wherwith my hart did cleave in twaine:
With such a song lay me in ground,
My sprite let it with her remayne,
That had the body to commend:
Till death therof did make an end.
    And even with my last bequest,
When I shall from this life depart:
I geve to her I loved best,
My just my true and faithfull hart,   70
Signed with the hand as cold as stone:
Of him that living was her owne.
    And if he here might live agayne,
As Phenix made by death anew:
Of this she may assure her plaine,
That he will still be just and trew.
Thus farewell she on live my owne.
And send her joy when I am gone.

263. The lover in dispeire lamenteth his case.

Adieu desert, how art thou spent?
Ah dropping teares how do ye washe?
Ah scalding sighes, how be ye spent?
To pricke them forth that will not hast,
Ah payned hart thou gapst for grace,
Even there where pitie hath no place.
    As easy it is the stony rocke,
From place to place for to remove,
As by thy plaint for to provoke:
A frosen hart from hate to love,   10
What should I say such is thy lot,
To fawne on them that force the not.

77 *on live* while living
263 9 *plaint*: poetic complaint, expressing injustice or sorrow
  12 *force the not* do not care for thee

Thus maist thou safely say and sweare,
That rigour raighneth and ruth doth faile,
In thanklesse thoughts thy thoughts do wear
Thy truth, thy faith, may nought availe,
For thy good will why should thou so,
Still graft where grace it will not grow.
    Alas pore hart thus hast thou spent,
Thy flowryng time, thy pleasant yeres.
With sighing voyce wepe and lament:
For of thy hope no frute apperes,
Thy true meanyng is paide with scorne,
That ever soweth and repeth no corne.
    And where thou sekes a quiet port,
Thou dost but weigh agaynst the winde,
For where thou gladdest woldst resort,
There is no place for thee assinde.
Thy desteny hath set it so
That thy true hart should cause thy wo.

264. Of his maistresse. m. B.

In Bayes I boast whose braunch I beare,
    Such joy therin I finde:
That to the death I shall it weare,
    To ease my carefull minde.
In heat, in cold, both night and day,
    Her vertue may be sene:
When other frutes and flowers decay,
    The bay yet growes full grene.
Her berries fede the birdes full oft,
    Her leves swete water make:
Her bowes be set in every loft,
    For their swete savours sake.

14 *ruth* pity
26 *weigh* set up one's sail
264 4 *carefull* full of cares or miseries

The birdes do shrowd them from the cold,
    In her we dayly see:
And men make arbers as they wold,
    Under the pleasant tree.
It doth me good when I repayre,
    There as these bayes do grow:
Where oft I walke to take the ayre,
    It doth delight me so.   20
But loe I stand as I were dome,
    Her beauty for to blase:
Wherwith my sprites be overcome,
    So long theron I gase.
At last I turne unto my walk,
    In passing to and fro:
And to my self I smile and talk,
    And then away I go.
Why smilest thou say lokers on,
    What pleasure hast thou found?   30
With that I am as cold as stone,
    And ready for to swound.
Fie fie for shame sayth fansy than,
    Pluck up thy faynted hart:
And speke thou boldly like a man,
    Shrinke not for little smart.
Wherat I blushe and change my chere,
    My senses waxe so weake:
O god think I what make I here,
    That never a word may speake.   40
I dare not sigh lest I be heard,
    My lokes I slyly cast:
And still I stand as one were scarde,
    Untill my stormes be past.
Then happy hap doth me revive,

21 *as I were dome* as if I were mute
22 *blase* blazon, delineate
23 *sprites* vital powers
37 *chere* expression, mood
45 *hap* fortune

The blood comes to my face:
A merier man is not alive,
    Then I am in that case.
Thus after sorow seke I rest,
    When fled is fansies fit.
And though I be a homely gest,
    Before the bayes I sit,
Where I do watch till leaves do fall,
    When winde the tree doth shake:
Then though my branch be very small,
    My leafe away I take.
And then I go and clap my hands,
    My hart doth leape for joy.
These bayes do ease me from my bands,
    That long did me annoy:
For when I do behold the same,
    Which makes so faire a show:
I finde therin my maistresse name,
    And se her vertues grow.

265. *The lover complaineth his harty love not requited.*

When Phebus had the serpent slaine,
He claymed Cupides boe:
Which strife did turne him to great paine,
The story well doth prove.
For Cupide made him fele much woe,
In sekyng Dephnes love.
    This Cupide hath a shaft of kinde,
Which wounded many a wight:
Whose golden hed had power to binde,
Ech hart in Venus bandes.

---

51 *homely gest* unprepossessing person
265 7 *of kinde* with a certain natural power
    8 *wight* person

This arrow did on Phebus light,
Which came from Cupides handes.
 An other shaft was wrought in spite,
Which headed was with lead:
Whose nature quenched swete delight,
That lovers most embrace.
In Dephnes brest this cruell head,
Had found a dwellyng place.
 But Phebus fonde of his desire,
Sought after Dephnes so: 20
He burnt with heat, she felt no fire,
Full fast she fled him fro.
He gate but hate for his good will,
The gods assigned so.
 My case with Phebus may compare,
His hap and mine are one,
I cry to her that knowes no care,
Yet seke I to her most:
When I approche then is she gone,
Thus is my labour lost.   30
 Now blame not me but blame the shaft,
That hath the golden head,
And blame those gods that with their craft
Such arrowes forge by kinde.
And blame the cold and heavy lead,
That doth my ladies minde.

266. A praise of .m. M.

In court as I behelde, the beauty of eche dame,
Of right my thought from all the rest should .M. steale
  the same,

22 *him fro* from him
26 *hap* fortune
36 *doth* influences
266 2 *same* probably a misprint for 'fame'

But, er I ment to judge: I vewed with such advise.
As retchlesse dome should not invade: the boundes of
    my devise.
And, whiles I gased long: such heat did brede within,
As Priamus towne felt not more flame, when did the
    bale begin.
By reasons rule ne yet by wit perceve I could,
That .M. face of earth yfound: enjoy such beauty should.
And fansy doubted that from heaven had Venus come,
To norish rage in Britaynes harts, while corage yet doth
10   blome,
Her native hue so strove, with colour of the rose,
That Paris would have Helene left, and .M. beauty chose.
A wight farre passyng all, and is more faire to seme,
Then lusty May the lodg of love: that clothes the earth
    in grene.
So angell like she shines: she semeth no mortall wight,
But one whom nature in her forge, did frame her self
    to spight.
Of beauty princesse chiefe: so makelesse doth she rest,
Whose eye would glad an heavy wight: and pryson
    payne in brest,
I waxe astonied to see: the feator of her shape,
And wondred that a mortal hart: such heavenly
20   beames could scape
Her limmes so answeryng were: the mould of her faire face,
Of Venus stocke she semde to spring, the rote of beauties
    grace.
Her presens doth pretende: such honour and estate,

---

3 Before I put my mind to making a judgement, I looked very carefully
4 So that ill-considered judgement should not transgress the limits of my
ingenuity
6 *bale* doom
8 *.M.* here may be a mistake for 'any'
13 *to seme* in appearance
17 *makelesse* matchless
19 *feator* elegance
23 *pretende* give the impression of

That simple men might gesse her birthe: if folly
    bred debate.
Her lokes in hartes of flint: would such affectes imprese,
As rage of flame not Nilus stremes: in Nestors
    yeres encrease.
Within the subtill seat, of her bright eyen doth dwell,
Blinde Cupide with the pricke of paine: that princes
    fredom sell.
A Paradice it is: her beauty to behold,
Where natures stuffe so full is found, that natures ware
    is sold.   30

267. An old lover to a yong gentilwoman.

Ye are to yong to bryng me in,
And I to old to gape for flies:
I have to long a lover bene,
If such yong babes should bleare mine eyes,
But trill the ball before my face,
I am content to make you play:
I will not se, I hide my face,
And turne my backe and ronne away.
   But if you folowe on so fast,
And crosse the waies where I should go,   10
Ye may waxe weary at the last,
And then at length your self orethrow.
I meane where you and all your flocke,
Devise to pen men in the pound:
I know a key can picke your locke,
And make you runne your selves on ground.
   Some birdes can eate the strawie corne,
And flee the lime that fowlers set,

267 2 *flies* butterflies
  5 *trill* roll
 10 *go* walk
 18 *lime* string covered with birdlime as a trap

And some are ferde of every thorne,
20   And so therby they scape the net.
But some do light and never loke,
And seeth not who doth stand in waite,
As fish that swalow up the hoke,
And is begiled through the baite.
　　But men can loke before they leape,
And be at price for every ware,
And penyworthes cast to bye good cheape,
And in ech thyng hath eye and care.
But he that bluntly runnes on hed,
30   And seeth not what the race shal be:
Is like to bring a foole to bed,
And thus ye get no more of me.

268. The lover forsaketh his
unkinde love.

Farewell thou frosen hart and eares of hardned stele,
Thou lackest yeres to understand the grefe that I did fele,
The gods revenge my wrong, with equall plage on thee,
When plesure shal prick forth thy youth, to learn
　　　　what love shalbe.
Perchance thou provest now, to scale blinde Cupides
　　　　holde,
And matchest where thou maist repent, when al thy
　　　　cards are told
But blush not thou therfore, thy betters have done so,
Who thought they had retaind a dove, when they but
　　　　caught a cro
And some do lenger time, with lofty lokes we see,
That lights at length as low or wors then doth the
10   　　betell bee.

27 *good cheape* bargains
28 *care* probably a misprint for 'eare'
268 3 *plage* plague, suffering
5 Perhaps you'll try at some stage to climb blind Cupid's stronghold

Yet let thy hope be good, such hap may fall from hye:
That thou maist be if fortune serve, a princesse er thou dye.
If chance prefer thee so, alas poore sely man,
Where shall I scape thy cruell handes, or seke for succour
    than?
God shild such greedy wolves, should lap in giltlesse
    bloode,
And send short hornes to hurtful heads, that rage like
    lyons woode.
I seldome se the day, but malice wanteth might,
And hatefull harts have never hap, to wreke their
    wrath aright.
The madman is unmete, a naked sworde to gide,
And more unfit are they to clime, that are orecome
    with pride.   20
I touch not thee herein, thou art a fawcon sure,
That can both soer and stoupe sometime, as men cast
    up the lure.
The pecock hath no place, in thee when thou shalt list,
For some no soner make a signe, but thou percevest
    the fist.
They have that I do want, and that doth thee begilde,
The lack that thou dost se in me, doth make thee
    loke so wilde.
My luryng is not good, it liketh not thine eare,
My call it is not half so swete, as would to god it were.
Well wanton yet beware, thou do no tiryng take,
At every hand that would thee fede, or to thee
    frendship make,   30
This councell take of him that ought thee once his love,

11 *hap* fortune
13 *sely* innocent
16 *lyons woode* mad, enraged lions
19 *unmete* unfit
22 *soer and stoupe* soar and dive
23 *list* please
25 *begilde* beguile
29 *tiryng* dressing
31 *ought* owed

Who hopes to mete thee after this among the saintes
    above.
But here within this world, if he may shonne the place,
He rather asketh present death, then to beholde thy face.

269. *The lover preferreth his lady*
above all other.

Resigne you dames whom tikelyng brute delight,
The golden praise that flatteries tromp doth sown
And vassels be to her that claims by right,
The title just that first dame beauty found.
Whose dainty eyes such sugred baits do hide,
As poyson harts where glims of love do glide.
    Come eke and see how heaven and nature wrought,
Within her face where framed is such joy:
As Priams sonnes in vaine the seas had sought,
If halfe such light had had abode in Troy.
For as the golden sunne doth darke ech starre,
So doth her hue the fayrest dames as farre.
    Ech heavenly gift, ech grace that nature could,
By art or wit my lady lo retaynes:
A sacred head, so heapt with heares of gold,
As Phebus beames for beauty farre it stayns,
A sucred tong, where eke such swetenesse snowes,
That well it semes a fountain where it flowes.
    Two laughyng eyes so linked with pleasyng lokes,
As wold entice a tygers hart to serve:
The bayt is swete but eager be the hookes,

10

20

269 1 *whom tikelyng brute delight* whom chattering rumour delights
   2 *tromp* trumpet
   6 *glims* gleams or glimpses
   7 *eke* also
  13 *could* knows
  15 *heares* hairs
  16 *stayns* surpasses
  17 *eke* also

For Dyane sekes her honour to preserve.
Thus Arundell sits, throned still with fame,
Whom enmies trompe can not attaynt with shame.
    My dased head so daunted is with heapes,
Of giftes divine that harber in her brest:
Her heavenly shape, that lo my verses leaps
And touch but that wherin she clowds the rest.
For if I should her graces all recite,
Both time should want, and I should wonders write.   30
    Her chere so swete, so christall is her eyes,
Her mouth so small, her lips so lively red:
Her hand so fine, her wordes so swete and wise,
That Pallas semes to sojourne in her hed.
Her vertues great, her forme as farre excedes,
As sunne the shade that mortall creatures leades.
    Would God that wretched age would spare to race,
Her lively hew that as her graces rare:
Be goddesse like, even so her goddesse face,
Might never change but still continue faire   40
That eke in after time ech wight may see,
How vertue can with beauty beare degree.

270. *The lover lamenteth that he would forget love, and can not.*

Alas when shall I joy,
When shall my wofull hart,
Cast forth the folish toy
That breadeth all my smart.
A thousand times and mo,

28 *clowds* overshadows
30 *time should want* there wouldn't be enough time
31 *chere* expression
37 *race* raze, erase
42 *beare degree* walk hand in hand
270 5 *mo* more

I have attempted sore:
To rid this restlesse wo,
Which raigneth more and more.
    But when remembrance past,
Hath laid dead coales together:
Old love renewes his blast,
That cause my joyes to wither.
Then sodaynely a spark,
Startes out of my desire:
And lepes into my hart,
Settyng the coles a fire.
    Then reason runnes about,
To seke forgetfull water:
To quench and clene put out,
The cause of all this matter.
And saith dead flesh must nedes,
Be cut out of the core,
For rotten withered wedes,
Can heale no grevous sore.
    But then even sodaynely,
The fervent heat doth slake:
And cold then straineth me,
That makes my bodies shake.
Alas who can endure,
To suffer all this paine,
Sins her that should me cure,
Most cruell death hath slaine.
    Well well, I say no more,
Let dead care for the dead,
Yet wo is me therfore,
I must attempt to lead,
One other kinde of life,
Then hitherto I have:
Or els this paine and strife,
Will bring me to my grave.

31 *Sins* since

SONGES WRITTEN BY N. G
[NICHOLAS GRIMALD 1519/20–c. 1562]

271. Of the ix. Muses.

Imps of king Jove, and quene Remembrance lo,
The sisters nyne, the poets pleasant feres.
Calliope doth stately stile bestow,
And worthy praises paintes of princely peres.
Clio in solem songes reneweth all day,
With present yeres conjoyning age bypast.
Delitefull talke loves Comicall Thaley:
In fresh grene youth, who doth like laurell last.
With voyces Tragicall sowndes Melpomen,
And, as with cheins, thallured eare she bindes.   10
Her stringes when Terpsichor doth touche,
        even then
She toucheth hartes, and raigneth in mens
        mindes,
Fine Erato, whose looke a lively chere
Presents, in dauncing keepes a comely grace.
With semely gesture doth Polymnie stere:
Whose wordes holle routes of rankes doo rule
        in place,
Uranie, her globes to view all bent,
The ninefold heaven observes with fixed face.
The blastes Eutrepe tunes of instrument,
With solace sweet hence heavie dumps to chase.   20

271 1 *Imps* offspring
     2 *feres* companions
     4 *peres* nobles
    10 *thallured* the allured
    13 *chere* expression
    16 *holle routes of rankes* whole companies of people/soldiers
    17 *bent* directed

Lord Phebus in the mids (whose heavenly sprite
These ladies doth enspire) embraceth all.
The graces in the Muses weed, delite
To lead them forth, that men in maze they fall.

272. *Musonius the Philosophers saying.*

In working well, if travell you sustain:
Into the winde shall lightly passe the paine:
But of the dede the glory shall remain,
And cause your name with worthy wights to raign.
In working wrong, if pleasure you attaine:
The pleasure soon shall vade, and voyde, as vaine:
But of the deed, throughout the life, the shame
Endures, defacing you with fowl defame:
And still tormentes the minde, both night and day:
Scant length of time the spot can wash away.
Flee then ylswading pleasures baits untrew:
And noble vertues fair renown purseew.

273. *Description of Vertue.*

What one art thou, thus in torn weed yclad?
Vertue, in price whom auncient sages had.
Why, poorely rayd? For fading goodes past care.

21 *mids* midst   *sprite* spirit
23 *weed* dress
24 *maze* amazement
272 1 *travell* labour
    4 *wights* people
    6 *vade* pass away   *voyde* depart
    8 *defacing you with fowl defame* disfiguring you with foul disgrace
   11 *ylswading* ill-persuading
273 1 *weed* clothes
    2 *price* high regard
    3 *rayd* dressed

Why doublefaced? I marke ech fortunes fare.
This bridle, what? Mindes rages to restrain.
Tooles why beare you? I love to take great pain.
Why, winges? I teache above the starres to flye.
Why tread you death? I onely cannot dye.

274. *Praise of measurekeping.*

The auncient time commended, not for nought,
The mean: what better thing can ther be sought?
In meane, is vertue placed: on either side,
Both right, and left, amisse a man shall slide.
Icar, with sire hadst thou the mid way flown,
Icarian beck by name had no man known.
If middle path kept had proud Phaeton,
No burning brand this earth had fallne upon.
Ne cruel powr, ne none to soft can raign:
That kepes a mean, the same shall still remain.   10
Thee, Julie, once did toomuch mercy spill:
Thee, Nero stern, rigor extreem did kill.
How could August so many yeres well passe?
Nor overmeek, nor overferse he was.
Worship not Jove with curious fansies vain,
Nor him despise: hold right atween these twain.
No wastefull wight, no greedy goom is prayzd.
Stands largesse just, in egall balance payzd.
So Catoes meal, surmountes Antonius chere,
And better fame his sober fare hath here.   20
To slender building, bad: as bad, to grosse:

274 2 *mean* moderation, middle way
    6 *beck* stream
    17 *wight* person   *goom* man
    18 *in egall balance payzd* in equal balance weighed
    19 *chere* hospitality
    21 *To . . . to* too . . . too

One, an eyesore, the tother falls to losse.
As medcines help, in measure: so (God wot)
By overmuch, the sick their bane have got.
Unmeet mee seems to utter this, mo wayes:
Measure forbids unmeasurable prayse.

275. Mans life after Possidonius, or Crates.

What path list you to tread? what trade will you
        assay?
The courts of plea, by braul, & bate, drive gentle peace
        away.
In house, for wife, and childe, there is but cark and
        care:
With travail, and with toyl ynough, in feelds we use
        to fare.
Upon the seas lieth dreed: the rich in foraine land,
Doo fear the losse: and there, the poore, like misers
        poorely stand.
Strife, with a wife, without, your thrift full hard
        to see:
Yong brats, a trouble: none at all, a maym it seems
        to bee:
Youth, fond, age hath no hert, and pincheth all to nye.
Choose then the leefer of these twoo, no life, or soon
10   to dye.

22 *tother* the other
23 *measure* moderation   *wot* knows
24 *bane* destruction, death
25 *Unmeet* unsuitable   *mo* more
275 1 *list* wish
    2 *bate* contention, discord
    3 *cark* trouble   *care* sorrow, anxiety
    4 *travail* labour
    7 *thrift* prosperity
   10 *leefer* more preferable

276. Metrodorus minde to the
contrarie.

What race of life ronne you? what trade will you assay?
In courts, is glory got, and wit encreased day by day.
At home, wee take our ease, and beak our selves in rest:
The feeldes our nature doo refresh with pleasures of the best.
On seas, is gayn to get: the straunger, hee shall bee
Estemed: having much: if not, none knoweth his lack,
        but hee.
A wife will trim thy house: no wyfe? then art thou free.
Brood is a lovely thing: without, thy life is loose to thee.
Yong bloods be strong: old sires in double honour dwell.
Doway that choyse, no life, or soon to dye: for all is well.   10

277. Of frendship.

Of all the heavenly giftes, that mortall men commend,
What trusty treasure in the world can countervail a frend?
Our helth is soon decayd: goodes, casuall, light, and vain:
Broke have we sene the force of powre, and honour suffer
        stain.
In bodies lust, man doth resemble but base brute:
True vertue gets, and keeps a frend, good guide of our pursute:
Whose harty zeale with ours accords, in every case:
No terme of time, no space of place, no storme can it deface.
When fickle fortune failes, this knot endureth still:
Thy kin out of their kinde may swarve, when frends owe
        the good will.   10
What sweter solace shall befall, than one to finde,

276 3 *beak* bask
     7 *trim* adorn
     8 *loose* free
277 2 *countervail* be equivalent to
     10 *out of their kinde* away from their bond of kinship
     swarve turn away   *the* thee

Upon whose brest thou mayst repose the secretes of thy minde?
He wayleth at thy wo, his teares with thine be shed:
With thee doth he all joyes enjoy: so leef a life is led.
Behold thy frend, and of thy self the patern see:
One soull, a wonder shall it seem, in bodies twain to bee.
In absence, present, rich in want, in sicknesse sound,
Yea after death alive, mayst thou by thy sure frend be found.
Eche house, eche towne, eche realm by stedfast love doth
     stand:
20 Where fowl debate breeds bitter bale, in eche devided land.
O frendship, flowr of flowrs: O lively sprite of life,
O sacred bond of blisfull peace, the stalworth staunch of strife:
Scipio with Lelius didst thou conjoyn in care,
At home, in warrs, for weal and wo, with egall faith to fare.
Gesippus eke with Tite, Damon with Pythias,
And with Menetus sonne Achill, by thee combined was.
Euryalus, and Nisus gave Virgil cause to sing:
Of Pylades doo many rimes, and of Orestes ring.
Down Theseus went to hell, Pirith, his frend to finde:
30 O that the wives, in these our daies, wer to their mates so kinde.
Cicero, the frendly man, to Atticus, his frend,
Of frendship wrote: such couples lo doth lot but seldome lend.
Recount thy race, now ronne: how few shalt thou there see,
Of whom to say: This same is he, that never fayled mee.
So rare a jewell then must nedes be holden dere:
And as thou wilt esteem thy self, so take thy chosen fere.
The tirant, in dispaire, no lacke of gold bewayls.
But, Out I am undoon (saith he) for all my frendship fails.
Wherfore sins nothing is more kindely for our kinde:
Next wisdome thus that teacheth us, love we the frendful
40   minde.

14 *leef* happy
20 *fowl* foul   *bale* suffering
21 *sprite* spirit
25 *eke* also
32 *lot* destiny, fortune
36 *fere* companion
39 *sins* since   *kindely* natural

278. The death of Zoroas, an Egyptian Astronomer, in the first fight, that Alexander had with the Persians.

Now clattering armes, now ragyng broyls of warre,
Gan passe the noyes of dredfull trompets clang:
Shrowded with shafts, the heven: with clowd of darts,
Covered the ayre: against full fatted bulls,
As forceth kindled yre the Lyons keen:
Whose greedy gutts the gnawyng honger pricks:
So Macedoins against the Persians fare.
Now corpses hide the purpurde soyl with blood:
Large slaughter, on ech side: but Perses more
Moyst feelds be bledd: their harts, and nombers bate.   10
Fainted while they geve back, and fall to flight:
The lightening Macedon, by swoords, by gleavs,
By bands and trowps, of fotemen with his garde,
Speeds to Darie: but him, his nearest kyn,
Oxate preserves, with horsemen on a plump
Before his carr: that none the charge could geve.
Here grunts, here grones, echwhere strong youth is spent:
Shakyng her bloody hands, Bellone, among
The Perses, soweth all kynde of cruel death.
With throte ycutt, he roores: he lieth along,   20
His entrails with a lance through girded quite:
Him smites the club, him wounds farstrikyng bow,
And him the sling, and him the shinyng swoord:
Hee dieth, he is all dead, he pants, he rests.
Right overstood, in snowwhite armour brave,
The Memphite Zoroas, a cunning clarke:

278 1 *broyls* turmoils
   10 *be bledd* sprinkled with blood   *bate* diminish
   12 *gleavs* lances, spears
   15 *on a plump* in a group
   21 *girded* struck
   26 *cunning clarke* knowledgeable scholar

To whom the heaven lay open, as his boke:
And in celestiall bodies he could tell
The movyng, metyng, light, aspect, eclips,
30   And influence, and constellacions all:
What earthly chances would betide: what yere
Of plenty, storde, what signe forwarned derth:
How winter gendreth snow, what temperature
In the primetide doth season well the soyl:
Why somer burns, why autumne hath ripe grapes:
Whether the circle, quadrate may become:
Whether our tunes heavens harmony can yelde:
Of four begins, among them selves how great
Proporcion is: what sway the erryng lightes
40   Doth send in course gayn that first movyng heaven:
What grees, one from another distant be:
What starre doth let the hurtfull fire to rage,
Or him more milde what opposition makes:
What fire doth qualify Mavorses fire:
What house ech one doth seke: what planet raignes
Within this hemisphere, or that, small things
I speake, whole heaven he closeth in his brest.
This sage then, in the starres had spied: the fates
Threatned him death, without delay: and sithe
50   He saw, he could not fatall order change:
Forward he preast, in battayle that he might
Mete with the ruler of the Macedoins:
Of his right hand desirous to be slayne,
The boldest beurn, and worthiest in the felde:
And, as a wight now weary of his life,
And sekyng death: in first front of his rage,

38 *begins* basic levels
39 *erryng* wandering
41 *grees* degrees
44 *qualify* mitigate   *Mavorses* warlike
49 *sithe* since
54 *beurn* warrior
55 *wight* man

Comes desperatly to Alexanders face:
    At him, with darts, one after other throwes:
With reckles wordes, and clamour him provokes:
And saith, Nectanabs bastard, shamefull stain   60
Of mothers bed: why losest thou thy strokes,
Cowards among? Turne thee to me, in case
Manhod there be so much left in thy hart:
Come fight with me: that on my helmet weare
Appolloes laurell, both for learnings laude,
And eke for martiall praise: that, in my shield,
The sevenfold sophie of Minerve contein:
A match, more meet, sir king, than any here.
The noble prince amoved, takes ruthe upon
The wilfull wight: and with soft wordes, ayen,   70
O monstrous man (quod he) what so thou art,
I pray the, lyve: ne do not, with thy death,
This lodge of lore, the Muses mansion marr.
That treasure house this hand shall never spoyl:
My sword shall never bruse that skilfull braine,
Long gatherd heapes of science sone to spyll.
O, how faire frutes may you to mortall men
From wisdomes garden geve? How many may
By you the wiser and the better prove?
What error, what mad moode, what phrensy thee   80
Perswades to be downe sent to depe Averne:
Where no arts florish, nor no knowledge vails?
For all these sawes, when thus the soverain sayd,
Alighted Zoroas: with sword unsheathed,
The careles king there smot, above the greve,

62 *in case* if
65 *laude* praise
66 *eke* also
67 *sophie* wisdom
68 *meet* fitting
69 *ruthe* pity
73 *lore* learning
82 *vails* helps, is beneficial
85 *greve* leg-armour

At thopenyng of his quishes: wounded him
So that the blood down reyled on the ground.
The Macedon perceivyng hurt, gan gnash:
But yet his minde he bent, in any wise,
Him to forbear: set spurs unto his stede,
And turnde away: lest anger of his smart
Should cause revenger hand deale balefull blowes.
But of the Macedonian chieftains knights
One Meleager, could not beare this sight:
But ran upon the said Egyptian reuk:
And cut him in both knees: he fell to ground:
Wherwith a whole rout came of souldiers stern,
And all in pieces hewed the silly seg.
But happily the soule fled to the starres:
Where under him, he hath full sight of all,
Wherat he gased here, with reaching looke.
The Persians wailde such sapience to forgo:
The very fone, the Macedonians wisht.
He would have lived: king Alexander self
Demde him a man, unmete to dye at all:
Who won like praise, for conquest of his yre,
As for stout men in field that day subdued:
Who princes taught, how to discerne a man,
That in his hed so rare a jewell beares.
But over all, those same Camenes, those same
Devine Camenes, whose honour he procurde,
As tender parent doth his daughters weal:
Lamented: and for thankes all that they can,
Do cherish him deceast, and set him free,
From dark oblivion of devouring death.

86 *thopenyng* the opening   *quishes* thigh-armour
95 *reuk* rook, crow (disparaging term for person)
97 *rout* group
98 *silly seg* helpless man
103 *fone* enemies
105 *unmete* unfit
112 *weal* well-being

279. *Marcus Tullius Ciceroes*
death.

Therfore, when restlesse rage of winde, and wave
Hee saw: By fates, alas calld for (quod hee)
Is haplesse Cicero: sayl on, shape course
To the next shore, and bring me to my death.
Perdy these thanks, reskued from civill swoord,
Wilt thou my countrey paye? I see mine end:
So powers divine, so bid the gods above,
In citie saved that Consul Marcus shend.
Speakyng no more, but drawyng from deep hart
Great grones, even at the name of Rome rehearst: 10
His eies and chekes, with showrs of teares, he washt.
And (though a rout in dayly daungers worne)
With forced face, the shipmen held their teares:
And, strivyng long the seas rough floods to passe,
In angry windes, and stormy showres made way:
And at the last, safe ancred in the rode.
Came heavy Cicero a land: with pain,
His fainted lims the aged sire doth draw:
And, round about their master stood his band:
Nor greatly with their owne hard hap dismayd,   20
Nor plighted fayth, prove in sharp time to break:
Some swordes prepare: some their dere lord assist:
In littour layd, they lead him unkouth wayes:
If so deceave Antonius cruell gleaves
They might, and threats of folowyng routs escape.
Thus lo, that Tullie, went, that Tullius,
Of royall robe, and sacred senate prince:

279 3 *haplesse* unfortunate
   5 *Perdy* certainly
   8 *shend* is destroyed
  12 *rout* company
  16 *rode* shipping-lane
  20 *hap* fortune
  23 *unkouth* unknown
  24 *gleaves* spears

When he a far the men approch espieth,
And of his fone the ensignes doth aknow:
30 And, with drawn swoord, Popilius threatning death:
Whose life, and holl estate, in hazard once,
Hee had preservde: when Room as yet to free
Herd him, and at his thundring voyce amazde.
Herennius eek, more eyger than the rest,
Present enflamde with furie, him purseews.
What might hee doo? Should hee use in defense
Disarmed hands? or pardon ask, for meed?
Should he with wordes attempt to turn the wrath
Of tharmed knight, whose safegard hee had wrought?
40 No, age, forbids, and fixt within depe brest
His countryes love, and falling Romes image.
The charret turn, sayth hee, let loose the rayns:
Roon to the undeserved death: mee, lo,
Hath Phebus fowl, as messenger forwarnd:
And Jove desires a neew heavensman to make.
Brutus, and Cassius soulls, live you in blisse:
In case yet all the fates gaynstrive us not,
Neither shall we perchaunce dye unrevenged.
Now have I lived, O Room, ynough for mee:
50 My passed life nought suffreth me to dout
Noysom oblivion of the lothesome death.
Slea mee: yet all the offspring to come shall know:
And this deceas shall bring eternall life.
Yea, and (onlesse I fayl, and all in vain
Room, I soomtime thy Augur chosen was)
Not evermore shall frendly fortune thee
Favour, Antonius: once the day shall coom:
When her deare wights, by cruell spight, thus slain,
Victorious Room shall at thy hands require.

29 *fone* enemies
37 *meed* reward
39 *tharmed* the armed
44 *fowl* bird
51 *Noysom* horrible
58 *wights* people

Me likes, therwhile, go see the hoped heaven.   60
Speech had he left: and therwith hee, good man,
His throte preparde, and held his hed unmoved.
His hasting to those fates the very knightes
Be lothe to see: and, rage rebated, when
They his bare neck beheld, and his hore heyres:
Scant could they hold the teares, that forth gan burst
And almost fell from bloody hands the swoords.
Onely the stern Herennius, with grym looke,
Dastards, why stand you still? he sayth: and straight,
Swaps of the hed, with his presumptuous yron.   70
Ne with that slaughter yet is he not fild:
Fowl shame on shame to heape, is his delite.
Wherefore the handes also doth hee of smyte,
Which durst Antonius life so liuely paynt.
Him, yeldyng strayned goste, from welkin hye.
With lothy chere, lord Phebus gan behold:
And in black clowd, they say, long hid his hed.
The latine Muses, and the Grayes, they wept:
And, for his fall, eternally shall weep.
And lo, hertpersing Pitho (straunge to tell)   80
Who had to him suffisde both sense, and words,
When so he spake: and drest, with nectar soote,
That flowyng toung: when his windpipe disclosde,
Fled with her fleeyng frend: and (out alas)
Hath left the earth, ne will no more return.
Popilius flyeth, therwhile: and, leaving there
The senslesse stock, a grizely sight doth bear
Unto Antonius boord, with mischief fed.

69 *straight* immediately
70 *Swaps* strikes
71 *fild* satisfied
73 *of smyte* cut off
75 *welkin* heavens
76 *chere* expression
78 *Grayes* Graiae, i.e. Greek
82 *soote* sweet
87 *stock* body, trunk
88 *boord* table

280. Of M. T. Cicero.

For Tullie, late, a tomb I gan prepare:
When Cynthie, thus, bad mee my labour spare:
Such maner things becoom the ded, quoth hee:
But Tullie lives, and styll alyve shall bee.

N. G.

Appendix: Poems from Q1 excluded from Q2 and later editions

SONGES WRITTEN BY NICOLAS GRIMALD.

A128. A truelove.

What sweet releef the showers to thirstie plants we see:
What dere delite, the blooms to beez: my truelove is
    to mee.
  As fresh, and lusty vere foule winter doth exceed:
As morning bright, with scarlet sky, doth passe the
    evenings weed:
  As melow peares above the crabs esteemed be:
So doth my love surmount them all, whom yet I hap to se.
  The oke shall olives bear: the lamb, the lion fray:
The owle shall match the nightingale, in tuning of her lay:
  Or I my love let slip out of mine entiere hert:
So deep reposed in my brest is she, for her desert.   10
  For many blessed giftes, O happy, happy land:
Where Mars, and Pallas strive to make their glory
    most to stand

A128 3 *lusty* cheerful, vigorous   *vere* springtime
  4 *weed* garment, especially a dark mourning garment
  5 *crabs* wild apples with sour taste
  7 *fray* frighten, scare away
  8 *lay* song
  10 *desert* deserving, merit

Yet, land, more is thy blisse: that, in this cruell age,
   A Venus ymp, thou hast brought forth, so stedfast,
     and so sage.
   Among the Muses nyne, a tenth yf Jove would make:
And to the Graces three, a fourth: her would Apollo
     take.
   Let some for honour hoont, and hourd the massy golde:
With her so I may live, and dye, my weal cannot be tolde.

A129. *The lover to his dear, of his exceding love.*

Phebe twise took her horns, twise layd them by:
I, all the while, on thee could set no yie.
Yet doo I live: if life you may it call,
Which onely holds my heavy hert, as thrall.
Certesse for death doo I ful often pray,
To rid my wo, and pull these pangs away.
So plains Prometh, his womb no time to faile:
And ayelife left, had leefer, he might quaile.
I erre, orels who this devise first found,
By that gripes name he cleped love unsound.
In all the town, what streat have I not seen?
In all the town, yet hath not Carie been.
Eyther thy sier restraines thy free outgate,
O woman, worthy of farre better state:
Or peeplepesterd London lykes thee nought,
But pleasant ayr, in quiet countrie sought.

10

---

  14 *A Venus ymp* a child of Venus
  17 *massy* solid, heavy
  18 *weal* happiness, prosperity, well-being
A129 7 *his womb no time to faile* his stomach/internal organs never fail
   8 And would rather that any life he had left might die
   9 *orels* or else
  10 *gripes* spasms of pain
  13 *outgate* exit, action of going out
  15 People-pestered London is not pleasing to you

Perchaunce, in olds our love thou doest repeat,
And in sure place woldst every thing retreat.
Forth shall I go, ne will I stay for none,
Untyll I may somwhere finde thee alone.   20
Therwhile, keep you of hands, and neck the heew:
Let not your cheeks becoom or black, or bleew,
Go with welcoverd hed: for you incase
Apollo spied, burn wold he on your face.
Daphne, in grove, clad with bark of baytree:
Ay mee, if such a tale should ryse of thee.
Calisto found, in woods, Joves force to fell:
I pray you, let him not like you so well.
Eigh, how much dreed? Here lurks of theevs a haunt:
Whoso thou beest, preyseeker prowd, avaunt.   30
Acteon may teach thee Dictynnaes ire:
Of trouth, this goddesse hath as fiers a fire.
What doo I speak? O chief part of my minde,
Unto your eares these woords no way doo finde.
Wold god, when you read this, observe I might
Your voyce, and of your countinaunce have sight,
Then, for our love, good hope were not to seek:
I mought say with myself, she will be meek.
Doutlesse I coom, what ever town you keep,
Or where you woon, in woods, or mountanes steep: 40
I coom, and if all pear not in my face,
Myself will messenger be of my case.
If to my prayer all deaf, you dare saye, no:
Streight of my death agilted shall you go.
Yet in mid death, this same shall ease my hart:
That Carie, thou wert cause of all the smart.

17 *in olds* for old times' sake(?)   *repeat* think about
22 *or black, or bleew* either black or blue
27 *to fell* too fierce
30 *avaunt* go away
39 *keep* remain in
40 *woon* stay, live
41 *pear* appear
44 *Streight* immediately   *agilted* guilty

A130. *The lover asketh pardon*
of his dere, for
fleeyng from
her.

Lovers men warn the corps beloved to flee,
From the blinde fire in case they wold live free.
Ay mee, how oft have I fled thee, my Day?
I flee, but love bides in my brest alway.
Lo yet agayn, I graunt, I gan remove:
But both I could, and can say still, I love.
If woods I seek, cooms to my thought Adone:
And well the woods do know my heavy mone.
In gardens if I walk: Narcissus there
10   I spy, and Hyacints with weepyng chere:
If meads I tred, O what a fyre I feel?
In flames of love I burn from hed to heel.
Here I behold dame Ceres ymp in flight:
Here bee, methynk, black Plutoes steeds in sight.
Stronds if I look upon, the Nymphs I mynde:
And, in mid sea, oft fervent powrs I fynde.
The hyer that I clyme, in mountanes wylde,
The nearer mee approcheth Venus chylde.
Towns yf I haunt: in short, shall I all say?
20   There soondry fourms I view, none to my pay.
Her favour now I note, and now her yies:
Her hed, amisse: her foot, her cheeks, her guyse.
In fyne, where mater wants, defautes I fayn:

A130 1 *corps beloved* the beloved's (live) body
       2 *in case* if
       5 *I gan remove* I left
      10 *chere* expression
      15 *Stronds* strands, shores   *mynde* bring to mind
      20 *pay* liking
      21 *favour* appearance
      22 *guyse* manner
      23 In short ('In fyne') I pretend ('fayn') there are defects ('defautes')
          where that fact ('mater') is lacking

Whom other, fayr: I deem, she hath soom stayn.
What boots it then to flee, sythe in nightyde,
And daytyme to, my Day is at my side?
A shade therfore mayst thou be calld, by ryght:
But shadowes, derk, thou, Day, art ever bright.
Nay rather, worldly name is not for thee:
Sithe thou at once canst in twoo places bee.   30
Forgive me, goddesse, and becoom my sheeld:
Even Venus to Anchise herself dyd yeeld.
Lo, I confesse my flight: bee good therfore:
Jove, oftentimes, hath pardond mee for more.
Next day, my Day, to you I coom my way:
And, yf you suffer mee, due payns wyll pay.

A131. N. Vincent to G. Black-
wood, agaynst wedding.

Sythe, Blackwood, you have mynde to wed a wife:
I pray you, tell, wherefore you like that life.
What? that henceforth you may live more in blisse?
I am beguylde, but you take mark amisse.
Either your fere shall be defourmd: (and can
You blisful be, with flower of frying pan?
Orels, of face indifferent: (they say,
Face but indifferent will soone decay.)
Or faire: who, then, for many men semes fine:
Ne can you say, she is all holly mine.   10
And be she chaste (if noman chaunce to sew)
A sort of brats she bringes, and troubles new:

25 *boots* remedies   *sythe* since   *nightyde* night-time
36 *suffer* allow
A131 1 *Sythe* since
     4 *beguylde, but* mistaken, unless
     5 *fere* companion
     7 *Orels* or else
    11 *if noman chaunce to sew* if no man should happen to ask her
    12 *sort* group, pack

Or frutelesse will so passe long yeres with thee,
That scant one day shall voyd of brawlyng bee.
Hereto heap up undaunted hed, stif hart,
And all the rest: eche spouse can tell a part.
Leave then, this way, to hope for happy life:
Rather be your bed sole, and free from strife.
Of blessed state if any path be here:

20   It lurketh not, where women wonne so nere.

A132. G. Blackwood to .N. Vincent, with weddyng.

Sythe, Vincent, I have minde to wed a wife:
You bid me tell, wherfore I like that life.
Foule will I not, faire I desire: content,
If faire me fayle, with one indifferent.
Fair, you alledge, a thousand will applie:
But, nere so oft requirde, she will denie.
Meane beautie doth soone fade: therof playn hee,
Who nothing loves in woman, but her blee.
Frute if she bring, of frute is joyfull sight:

10   If none, what then? our burden is but light.
The rest, you ming, certesse, we graunt, be great:
Stif hert, undaunted hed cause soom to freat.
But, in all thinges, inborne displeasures be:
Yea pleasure we, full of displeasure, se.
And marvail you, I looke for good estate,
Hereafter if a woman be my mate?

20 *wonne* live
A132 *with* in favour of
  1 *Sythe* since
  5 *applie* proposition
  6 *nere so oft requirde* however often asked
  7 *playn hee* may he complain
  8 *blee* appearance
  11 *ming* mention   *certesse* certainly
  12 *freat* fret, distress oneself
  16 *I looke for good estate* I expect a good life/condition/state

Oh straight is vertues path, if sooth men say:
And likewise, that I seek, straight is the way.

[*A133–4 are Q2 271–2*]

A135. Marcus Catoes comparison of mans
life with yron.

Who wold beleeve mans life like yron to bee,
But proof had been, great Cato, made by thee?
For if, long time, one put this yron in ure,
Folowing ech day his woork, with bysye cure:
With dayly use, hee may the metall wear,
And bothe the strength, and hardnesse eke impaire.
Again, in case his yron hee cast aside,
And carelesse long let it untoucht abide:
Sythe, cankerd rust invades the mettall sore,
And her fowl teeth there fastneth more and more.   10
So man, incase his corps hee tyre, and faint
With labor long: his strength it shall attaint.
But if in sluggard slothe the same dothe lye:
That manly wight will fall away, and dye:
That bodies strength, that force of wit remoove:
Hee shall, for man, a weaklyng woman proove.
Wherfore, my childe, holde twene these twaine the waye:
Nother with to much toyl thy lyms decaye,
In idle ease not give to vices place:
In bothe who measure keeps, hee hath good grace.   20

A135 3 *ure* use
      4 *bysye cure* diligent application
      6 *eke* also
      9 *Sythe* then
     10 *fowl* foul
     11 *corps* body
     12 *attaint* infect
     13 *But if* unless
     14 *wight* person

A136. *Cleobulus the Lydians riddle.*

One is my sire: my soons, twise six they bee:
Of daughters ech of them begets, you see,
Thrise ten: wherof one sort be fayr of face,
The oother doth unseemly black disgrace.
Nor this holl rout is thrall unto deathdaye,
Nor worn with wastful time, but live alwaye:
And yet the same alwaies (straunge case) do dye.
The sire, the daughters, and the soons distry.
Incase you can so hard a knot unknit:
You shall I count an Edipus in wit.

10

A137. *Concerning Virgils Eneids.*

By heavens hye gift, incase revived were
Lysip, Apelles, and Homer the great:
The moste renowmd, and ech of them sance pere,
In gravyng, paintyng, and the Poets feat:
Yet could they not, for all their vein divine,
In marble, table, paper more, or lesse,
With cheezil, pencil, or with poyntel fyne,
So grave, so paynt, or so by style expresse
(Though they beheld of every age, and land
The fayrest books, in every toung contrived,

10

A136   1 *sire* father
     5 *holl* whole
     8 *distry* destroy
     9 *Incase* if
A137   1 *incase* if
     3 *sance pere* without peer
     4 *gravyng* engraving, sculpting
     6 *table* tablet
     7 *cheezil* chisel   *poyntel* stylus/pencil
     8 *style* stylus

To frame a fourm, and to direct their hand)
Of noble prince the lively shape descrived:
As, in the famous woork, that Eneids hight,
The naamkouth Virgil hath set forth in sight.

A138. Of mirth.

A heavy hart, with wo encreaseth every smart:
A mirthfull minde in time of need, defendeth sorowes dart.
The sprite of quicnesse seems, by drery sadnesse slayn:
By mirth, a man to lively plight, revived is agayn.
Dolour dryeth up the bones: the sad shall sone be sick:
Mirth can preserve the kyndly helth, mirth makes the body
      quick.
Depe dumps do nought, but dull, not meet for man but beast:
A mery hart sage Salomon countes his continuall feast.
Sad soll, before thy time, brings thee unto deaths dore:
That fond condicions have bereft, late daye can not restore.   10
As, when the covered heaven, showes forth a lowryng face,
Fayr Titan, with his leam of light, returns a goodly grace:
So, when our burdened brest is whelmd with clowdy thought,
A pleasant calm throughout the corps, by chereful hart is
      brought
Enjoye we then our joyes, and in the lorde rejoyce:
Faith makyng fast eternall joye, of joyes while wee have choyce.

  11 *To frame a fourm* to create a shape
  12 *descrived* represented
  13 *hight* is called
  14 *naamkouth* known by name, famous
A138 3 *sprite* animated spirit
  4 *plight* health
  6 *kyndly* natural   *quick* lively, alive
  7 *meet* suitable
  10 *fond* sickly
  11 *lowryng* scowling
  12 *leam* gleam
  14 *corps* (living) body

A139. To L. J.S.

Charis the fourth, Pieris the tenth, the second Cypris, Jane,
One to assemblies thre adjoynd: whom Phebus fere, Diane,
Among the Nymphs Oreades, might wel vouchsafe to place:
But you as great a goddesse serve, the quenes most noble
    grace:
Allhayle, and while, like Terpsichor, much melody you make:
Which if the field, as doth the court, enjoyd, the trees wold
    shake:
While latine you, and french frequent: while English tales
    you tel:
Italian whiles, and Spanish you do hear, and know full well:
Amid such peares, and solemne sightes, in case convenient
    tyme
10 You can (good Lady) spare, to read a rurall poets ryme:
Take here his simple sawes, in briefe: wherin no need
      to move
Your Ladishyp, but thus lo speakes thabundance of his love.
The worthy feates that now so much set forth your noble
    name,
So have in ure, they still encreast, may more encrease your
    fame.
For though divine your doings be, yet thews with yeres may
    grow:
And if you stay, streight now adayes fresh wits will overgo.

A139 2 *One to assemblies thre adjoynd* added one to the group of three
    2 *fere* companion, peer
    7 *frequent* are familiar with
    8 *whiles* sometimes
    9 *peares* peers *in case* if
   11 *sawes* utterances
   12 *thabundance* the abundance
   13 *feates* actions
   14 *in ure* in use
   15 *thews* customs
   16 *overgo* go unheeded

Wherfore the glory got maintayne, maintayne the honour
    great.
So shal the world my doom approve, and set you in
    that seat,
Where Graces, Muses, and Joves ymp, the joyful Venus,
    raigne:
So shall the bacheler blessed bee, can such a Nymph
    obtaine.   20

A140. To maistres D. A.

What cause, what reason moveth me: what fansy fils my
    brains
That you I minde of virgins al, whom Britan soile sustains
Bothe when to lady Mnemosynes dere daughters I resort,
And eke when I the season slow deceave, with glad
    disport?
What force, what powcr have you so great, what charms
    have you late found,
To pluck, to draw, to ravish hartes, & stirre out of ther
    stownd?
To you, I trow, Joves daughter hath the lovely gyrdle lent,
That Cestos hight: wherin there bee all maner graces blent,
Allurementes of conceits, of wordes the pleasurable taste:
That same, I gesse, hath she given you, and girt about your
    waste   10
Beset with sute of precious pearl, as bright as sunny day.
But what? I am beguilde, and gone (I wene) out of the way.
These causes lo do not so much present your image prest,

18 *doom* judgement
19 *ymp* daughter
A140 2 *minde* remember
  6 *stownd* position
  7 *trow* believe
  8 *hight* is called   *blent* mixed
10 *waste* waist
12 *wene* believe

That will I, nill I, night and day, you lodge within this brest:
Those gifts of your right worthy minde, those golden gifts
    of mind
Of my fast fixed fansiefourm first mooving cause I finde:
Love of the one, and threefold powr: faith sacred, sound,
    sincere:
A modest maydens mood: an hert, from clowd of envy clere:
Wit, fed with Pallas food divine: will, led with lovely lore:
20 Memorie, conteining lessons great of ladies five, and fowr:
Woords, sweeter, than the sugar sweet, with heavenly nectar
    drest:
Nothing but coomly can they carp, and wonders well
    exprest.
Such damsels did the auncient world, for Poets penns, suffise:
Which, now a dayes, welnye as rare, as Poets fyne, aryse.
Wherfore, by gracious gifts of god, you more than thrise
    yblest:
And I welblest myself suppose: whom chastefull love imprest,
In frendships lace, with such a lasse, doth knit, and fast
    combine:
Which lace no threatning fortune shall, no length of tyme
    untwine:
And I that daye, with gem snowwhite, will mark, & eke
    depaynt
With pricely pen: which, Awdley, first gan mee with you
30   acquaint.

A141. Of m. D. A.

Deserts of Nymphs, that auncient Poets showe,
Ar not so kouth, as hers: whose present face,
More, than my Muse, may cause the world to knowe

14 *will I, nill I* whether I wish it or not, willingly or unwillingly
16 *fansiefourm* fancied shape
22 *carp* speak/sing
A141 1 *Deserts* woody dwellings
    2 *kouth* well-known

A nature nobly given: of woorthy race:
So trayned up, as honour did bestowe.
Cyllene, in sugerd speech, gave her a grace.
Excell in song Apollo made his dere.
No fingerfeat Minerve hid from her sight.
Exprest in look, she hath so soverain chere,
    As Cyprian once breathed on the Spartan bright.   10
Wit, wisdom, will, woord, woork, and all, I ween,
Dare nomans pen presume to paint outright.
Lo luyster and light: which if old tyme had seen,
Entroned, shyne she should, with goddesse Fame.
Yeeld, Envie, these due prayses to this dame.

A142. A neew yeres gift, to the l. M. S.

Now flaming Phebus, passing through his heavenly
    region hye,
The uttrest Ethiopian folk with fervent beames doth frye:
And with the soon, the yere also his secret race doth
    roon:
And Janus, with his double face, hath it again begoon:
O thou, that art the hed of all, whom mooneths, and
    yeres obey:
At whose commaunde bee bothe the sterres, and surges
    of the sea:
By powr divine, now prosper us this yere with good
    successe:
This well to lead, and many mo, us with thy favour
    blesse.
Graunt, with sound soll in body sound that here we
    dayly go:

8 *fingerfeat* manual skill, handicraft
9 *soverain chere* regal expression
11 *ween* think
A142 3 *soon* sun
  8 *mo* more

10   And, after, in that countrey lyve, whence bannisht is all wo:
     Where hoonger, thirst, and sory age, and sicknesse may
          not mell:
     No sense perceivs, no hert bethinks the joyes, that there
          do dwel.

A143. *An other to .l. M. S.*

     So happy bee the course of your long life:
     So roon the yere intoo his circle ryfe:
     That nothyng hynder your welmeanyng minde:
     Sharp wit may you, remembrans redy fynde,
     Perfect intelligence, all help at hand:
     Styll stayd your thought in frutefull studies stand.
     Hed framed thus may thother parts well frame,
     Divine demeanour wyn a noble name:
     By payzed doom with leasure, and good heed:
10   By upright dole, and much avayling deed:
     By hert unthirld, by undiscoomfite chere,
     And brest discharged quite of coward fere:
     By sobermood, and orders coomly rate:
     In weal, and wo, by holdyng one estate.
     And to that beauties grace, kynde hath you lent,
     Of bodies helth a perfite plight bee blent.
     Dame fortunes gifts may so stand you in sted,
     That well, and wealfully your lyfe be led.
     And hee, who gives these graces not in vayn,
20   Direct your deeds, his honour to maintain.

     11 *mell* meddle, occupy themselves
   A143 2 *ryfe* large, bountiful
     7 *thother* the other
     9 *payzed* weighed   *doom* judgement
     10 *dole* charity
     11 *unthirld* unenslaved   *chere* expression
     13 *orders coomly rate* attractive pace of orderliness
     15 *kynde* nature
     16 *plight* combination   *blent* mixed
     18 *wealfully* prosperously

A144. To .l K. S.

To you, madame, I wish, bothe now, and eke from yere
    to yere,
Strength with Debore, with Judith faith, with Maudlen
    zeal, Anns chere
With blessed Mary modest moode: like Sibill, life full long:
A mynde with sacred sprite enspired, wit fresh, and body
    strong:
And, when of your forepointed fate you have outroon the
    race:
Emong all these, in Joves hye raygn of blisses full, a place.

A145. To .l. E. S.

As this first daye of Janus youthe restores unto the yere:
So bee your minde in coorage good revived, and herty chere.
And as dame Tellus labreth now her frutes conceived to
    breed:
Rightso of your most forward wit may great avail proceed.
So lucky bee the yere, the mooneths, the weeks, the dayes,
    the howrs
That them, with long recours, you may enjoy in blisfull
    bowrs.

A146. To .m. D. A.

Gorgeous attire, by art made trym, and clene,
Cheyn, bracelet, perl, or gem of Indian river,
To you I nil, ne can (good Damascene)

A144 4 *sprite* spirit
  5 *forepointed* preordained
A145 2 *chere* expression
  4 *avail* advantage
A146 3 *nil, ne* will not, nor

This time of Janus Calends, here deliver.
But, what? My hert: which, though long sins certain
Your own it was, aye present at your hest:
Yet here itself doth it resigne agayn,
Within these noombers closde. Where, think you best
This to repose? There, I suppose, where free
10   Minerve you place. For it hath you embraste,
As thHeliconian Nymphs: with whom, even hee,
That burn for soom, Apollo liveth chaste.
Presents in case by raarnesse you esteem:
O Lord, how great a gift shall this then seem?

A147. To .m. S. H.

To you this present yere full fayre, and fortunable fall,
Returning now to his prime part: and, good luck therwithall,
May it proceed: and end, and oft return, to glad your hert:
O Susan, whom among my frendes I count, by your desert.
Joy may your heavenly sprite: endure fresh wit, in that
        fyne brayn:
Your knowledge of good things encreas: your body, safe
        remain:
A body, of such shape, as showeth a worthy wight by
        kynde:
A closet, fit for to contein the vertues of that minde.
What shall I yet moreover add? God graunt, with
        pleasaunt mate
10   A pleasaunt life you lead. Well may that man rejoyse
        his fate.

4 *Calends* first day of the month
5 *sins* since
6 *aye* always   *hest* bidding
8 *noombers* metrical lines of poetry
A147 4 *desert* deserving, merit
5 *sprite* spirit
7 *wight* person   *kynde* nature

A148. To his familiar frend.

No image carved with coonnyng hand, no cloth of
     purple dye,
No precious weight of metall bright, no silver plate gyve I:
Such gear allures not hevenly herts: such gifts no grace
     they bring:
I lo, that know your minde, will send none such, what
     then? nothing.

[A149–52 are Q2 273–6]

A153. Of lawes.

When princes lawes, with reverend right, do keep the
     commons under
As meek as lambes, thei do their charge, & scatter not
     asunder.
But if they raise their heades aloft, and lawe her brydle slake:
Then, like a tyger fell, they fare, and lust for law they take.
Where water dothe prevail, and fire, no mercy they expresse:
But yet the rage of that rude rout is much more mercilesse.

[A154 is Q2 277]

A155. The Garden.

The issue of great Jove, draw nere you, Muses nine:
Help us to praise the blisfull plott of garden ground so fine.
The garden gives good food, and ayd for leaches cure:

A148 1 *coonnyng* skilful, expert
A153 3 *slake* slacken
    4 *fell* terrible *lust* appetite
    6 *rude rout* rough rabble
A155 3 *leaches* physicians

The garden, full of great delite, his master doth allure.
Sweet sallet herbs bee here, and herbs of every kinde:
The ruddy grapes, the seemly frutes bee here at hand
    to finde.
Here pleasans wanteth not, to make a man full fayn:
Here marveilous the mixture is of solace, and of gain.
To water sondry seeds, the forow by the waye
A ronning river, trilling downe with liquor, can convay.
Beholde, with lively heew, fayr flowrs that shyne so bright:
With riches, like the orient gems, they paynt the molde in
    sight.
Beez, humming with soft sound, (their murmur is so small)
Of blooms and blossoms suck the topps, on dewed leaves
    they fall
The creping vine holds down her own bewedded elms:
And, wandering out with branches thick, reeds folded
    overwhelms.
Trees spred their coverts wyde, with shadows fresh and
    gaye:
Full well their branched bowz defend the fervent sonne
    awaye.
Birds chatter, and some chirp, and some sweet tunes doo
    yeeld:
All mirthfull, with their songs so blithe, they make both
    ayre, & feeld.
The garden, it allures, it feeds, it glads the sprite:
From heavy harts all doolfull dumps the garden chaseth
    quite.
Stength it restores to lims, drawes, and fulfils the sight:
With chere revives the senses all, and maketh labour light.
O, what delites to us the garden ground dothe bring?
Seed, leaf, flowr, frute, herb, bee, and tree, & more, then
    I may sing.

10

20

5 *sallet* salad
7 *wanteth not* is not lacking   *fayn* glad
12 *molde* earth
15 *bewedded elms* the elms the vine is wedded to, i.e. twined around
21 *sprite* spirit

A156. An epitaph of sir James
Wilford knight.

The worthy Wilfords body, which alyve,
Made both the Scot, and Frenchman sore adrad:
A body, shapte of stomake stout to strive
With forein foes: a corps, that coorage had
So full of force, the like nowhere was ryfe:
With hert, as free, as ere had gentle knight:
Now here in grave (thus chaungeth ay, this lyfe)
Rests, with unrest to many a wofull wight.
Of largesse great, of manhod, of forecast
Can ech good English souldiour bear record.   10
Speak Laundersey, tell Muttrel marvails past:
Crye Musselborough: prayse Haddington thy lord,
From thee that held both Scots, and frekes of Fraunce:
Farewel, may England say, hard is my chaunce.

A157. An other, of the same
knightes death.

For Wilford wept first men, then ayr also,
For Wilford felt the wayters wayfull wo.
The men so wept: that bookes, abrode which bee,
Of moornyng meeters full a man may see.
So wayld the ayr: that, clowds consumde, remaynd
No dropes, but drouth the parched erth sustaynd.

A156 2 *adrad* full of dread
    4 *corps* (living) body
    5 *force* power   *ryfe* common
    6 *ere* ever
    7 *ay* always
    8 *to* too   *wight* person
    9 *forecast* prudence
   13 *frekes* men, warriors
   14 *chaunce* fortune

So greeted floods: that, where ther rode before
A ship, a car may go safe on the shore.
Left were nomo, but heaven, and erth, to make,
Throughout the world, this greef his rigor take.
But sins the heaven this Wilfords goste dothe keep,
And earth, his corps: saye mee, why shold they weep?

A158. An Epitaph of the ladye
Margaret Lee.
1555.

Man, by a woman lern, this life what we may call:
Blod, frendship, beauty, youth, attire, welth, worship,
        helth & al
Take not for thine: nor yet thy self as thine beknow.
For having these, with full great prayse, this lady did
        but show
Her self unto the world: and in prime yeres (bee ware)
Sleeps doolfull sister, who is wont for no respect
        to spare,
Alas, withdreew her hence: or rather softly led:
For with good will I dare well saye, her waye to him
        shee sped:
Who claymed, that he bought: and took that erst hee
        gave:
More meet than any worldly wight, such heavenly gems
        to have.
Now wold shee not return, in earth a queen to dwell.
As shee hath doon to you, good frend, bid lady Lee,
        farewell.

A157 7 *greeted* wept
    8 *car* carriage, chariot, cart
    9 *nomo* no more
    11 *sins* since
A158 9 *erst* previously
    10 *meet* suitable, fitting *wight* person

A159. *Upon the tomb of A. W.*

Myrrour of matrones, flowr of spouslike love,
Of fayr brood frutefull norsse, poor peoples stay,
Neybours delite, true hert to him above,
In yeelding worlds encreas took her decaye:
Who printed lives yet in our hertes alway:
Whose closet of good thews, layd here a space,
Shall shortly with the soull in heaven have place.

A160. *Upon the deceas of W. Ch.*

Now, blythe Thaley, thy feastfull layes lay by:
And to resound these doolfull tunes apply.
Cause of great greef the tyrant death imports:
Whose ugsoom idoll to my brayns resorts.
A gracefull ymp, a flowr of youth, away
Hath she bereft (alas) before his daye.
Chambers, this lyfe to leave, and thy dear mates,
So soon doo thee constrayn envyous fates?
Oh, with that wit, those maners, that good hert,
Woorthy to lyve olde Nestors yeres thou wert,   10
You wanted outward yies: and yet aryght
In stories, Poets, oratours had sight.
Whatso you herd, by lively voyce, exprest,
Was soon reposde within that mindefull brest.
To mee more pleasant Plautus never was,
Than those conceits, that from your mouth did passe.
Our studiemates great hope did hold alway,

A159 2 *stay* support
   6 *thews* habits, qualities
A160 1 *layes* songs
   3 *imports* brings in
   5 *ymp* child
   6 *bereft* taken away
   11 *wanted* lacked   *yies* eyes

You wold be our schooles ornament, one day.
Your parents then, that thus have you forgone,
Your brethren eke must make theyr heavy mone:
Your lovyng feres cannot their teares restrayn:
But I, before them all, have cause to playn:
Who in pure love was so conjoynd with thee,
An other Grimald didst thou seem to bee.
Ha lord, how oft wisht you, with all your hart,
That us no chaunce a sonder might depart?
Happy were I, if this your prayer tooke place:
Ay mee, that it dothe cruell death deface.
Ah lord, how oft your sweet woords I repeat,
And in my mynde your woonted lyfe retreat?
O Chambers, O thy Grimalds mate moste dere:
Why hath fell fate tane thee, and left him here?
But wherto these complaintes in vain make wee?
Such woords in wyndes to waste, what mooveth mee?
Thou holdst the haven of helth, with blisfull Jove:
Through many waves, and seas, yet must I rove.
Not woorthy I, so soon with thee to go:
Mee styll my fates reteyn, bewrapt in wo.
Live, our companion once, now lyve for aye:
Heavens joyes enjoy, whyle wee dye day by daye.
You, that of faith so sure signes here exprest,
Do triumph now, nodout, among the blest:
Have changed sea for porte, darknesse for light,
An inn for home, exile for countrey right,

20 *eke* also
21 *feres* companions
22 *playn* complain, make a complaint
26 *chaunce* fortune *a sonder* asunder
30 *woonted* accustomed
32 *fell* terrible *tane* taken
39 *for aye* forever
42 *nodout* no doubt

Travail for rest, straunge way for citie glad,
Battail for peas, free raign for bondage bad.
These wretched erthly stounds who can compare
To heavenly seats, and those delites moste rare?
We frayl, you firm: we with great trouble tost,
You bathe in blisse, that never shall bee lost.   50
Wherfore, Thaley, reneew thy feastfull layes:
Her doolfull tunes my chered Muse now stayes.

A161. Of .N. Ch.

Why, Nicolas, why doest thou make such haste
After thy brother? Why goest thou so? To taste
Of changed lyfe with hym the better state?
Better? yea best of all, that thought can rate.
Or, did the dreed of wretched world drive thee
Leste thou this afterfall should hap to see:
Mavortian moods, Saturnian furies fell,
Of tragicall turmoyls the haynous hell?
O, whose good thews in brief cannot be told,
The hartiest mate, that ever trod the mold: 10
If our farewell, that here live in distresse,
Avayl, farewell: the rest teares do suppresse.

45 *Travail* labour
46 *peas* peace
47 *stounds* places
52 *stayes* supports
A161 7 *Mavortian* warlike   *fell* terrible
  9 *thews* qualities
  10 *mold* earth
  12 *Avayl* is of any use

A162. A funerall song, upon the deceas of Annes his moother.

Yea, and a good cause why thus should I playn.
For what is hee, can quietly sustayn
So great a grief, with mouth as styll, as stone?
My love, my lyfe, of joye my jeewell is gone.
This harty zeale if any wight disproove,
As womans work, whom feeble minde doth moove:
Hee neither knowes the mighty natures laws,
Nor touching elders deeds hath seen old saws.
Martius, to vanquish Rome, was set on fire:
But vanquisht fell, at moothers boon, his ire.
Into Hesperian land Sertorius fled,
Of parent aye cheef care had in his hed.
Dear weight on shoulders Sicil brethren bore,
While Etnaes gyant spouted flames full sore.
Not more of Tyndars ymps hath Sparta spoke,
Than Arge of charged necks with parents yoke.
Nor onely them thus dyd foretyme entreat:
Then, was the noorsse also in honour great.
Caiet the Phrygian from amid fireflame
Rescued, who gave to Latine stronds the name.
Acca, in dubble sense Lupa ycleaped,
To Romane Calendars a feast hath heaped.
His Capra Jove among the sterres hath pight:
In welkin clere yet lo she shineth bryght.

A162 1 *playn* mourn, make a complaint
       5 *wight* person *disproove* calls into question
      10 *boon* request, entreaty
      12 *aye* always
      15 *ymps* children *spoke* been famed for
      18 *noorsse* nurse
      21 *ycleaped* called
      23 *pight* set up
      24 *welkin* sky

Hyades as gratefully Lyai did place,
Whom, in primetide, supports the Bulls fayr face.
And should not I expresse my inward wo,
When you, most lovyng dam, so soon hence go?
I, in your frutefull woomb conceyved, born was,
Whyle wanderyng moon ten moonths did overpasse.   30
Mee, brought to light, your tender arms sustaynd:
And, with my lips, your milky paps I straynd.
You mee embraced, in bosom soft you mee
Cherished, as I your onely chylde had bee.
Of yssue fayr with noombers were you blest:
Yet I, the bestbeloved of all the rest.
Good luck, certayn forereadyng moothers have,
And you of mee a speciall judgement gave.
Then, when firm pase I fixed on the ground:
When toung gan cease to break the lispyng sound: 40
You mee streightway did too the Muses send,
Ne suffered long a loyteryng lyfe to spend,
What gayn the wooll, what gayn the wed had braught,
It was his meed, that me there dayly taught.
When with Minerve I had acquaintance woon:
And Phebus seemd to love mee, as his soon:
Browns hold I bad, at parents hest, farewell:
And gladly there in schools I gan to dwell:
Where Granta gives the ladies nyne such place,
That they rejoyse to see theyr blisfull case.   50
With joyes at hert, in this pernasse I bode,
Whyle, through his signes, five tymes great Titan glode:
And twyse as long, by that fayr foord, whereas

26 *primetide* springtime
28 *dam* mother
35 *yssue* children
39 *pase* pace, steps
41 *too* to
43 *wed* presumably a misprint for 'web'
44 *meed* reward
46 *soon* son
47 *hest* bidding

Swanfeeder Temms no furder course can passe.
O, what desire had you, therwhile, of mee?
Mid doutfull dreeds, what joyes were wont to bee?
Now linnen clothes, wrought with those fyngers fyne,
Now other thynges of yours dyd you make myne:
Tyll your last thredes gan Clotho to untwyne,
And of your dayes the date extreem assygne.
Hearyng the chaunce, your neybours made much mone:
A dearworth dame, they thought theyr coomfort gone.
Kinswoomen wept: your charge, the maydens wept:
Your daughters wept, whom you so well had kept.
But my good syre gave, with soft woords, releef:
And clokes, with outward chere, his inward greef:
Leste, by his care, your sicknes should augment,
And on his case your thoughtfull hert be bent.
You, not forgetting yet a moothers mood,
When at the dore dartthirling death there stood,
Did saye: Adeew, dear spouse, my race is roon:
Wher so he bee, I have left you a soon,
And Nicolas you naamd, and naamd agayn:
With other speech, aspiring heavenly raign:
When into ayre your sprite departed fled,
And left the corps a cold in lukewarm bed.
Ah, could you thus, deare mother, leave us all?
Now, should you live: that yet, before your fall,
My songs you might have soong, have heard my voyce,
And in commodities of your own rejoyce.
My sisters yet unwedded who shall guide?
With whose good lessons shall they bee applyed?
Have, mother, monumentes of our sore smart:

54 *Temms* Thames
56 *doutfull dreeds* apprehensive fears
60 *extreem* last
61 *the chaunce* your fate
66 *chere* expression
67 *care* anxiety, grief
70 *dartthirling* dart-piercing
75 *sprite* spirit
80 *commodities* interests

No costly tomb, areard with curious art:
Nor Mausolean masse, hoong in the ayre:
Nor loftie steeples, that will once appayre:
But waylful verse, and doolfull song accept.
By verse, the names of auncient peres be kept:
By verse, lives Hercules: by verse, Achil:
Hector, Ene, by verse, be famous still.   90
Such former yeres, such death hath chaunced thee:
Closde, with good end, good life is woont to bee.
But now, my sacred parent, fare you well:
God shall cause us agayn togither dwell,
What time this universall globe shall hear
Of the last troomp the rynging voyce: great fear
To soom, to such as you a heavenly chear.
Til then, reposde rest you in gentle sleep:
While hee, whom to you are bequeathd, you keep.

A163. Upon the death of the lord Mautravers, out of doctor Haddons latine.

The noble Henry, he, that was the lord Mautravers named:
Heyr to the house of thArundels, so long a time now famed:
Who from Fitzalens doth recount discent of worthy race,
Fitzalens, earls of hye estate, men of a goodly grace:
Whom his renowmed father had seen florish, and excell,
In arms, in arts, in witt, in skill, in speaking wonders well:
Whose yeres, to timely vertue had, and manly gravenesse
        caught:
With soden ruine is downfalln, and into ashes braught:
While glory his coragious hert enflames to travail great:
And, in his youthly brest ther raigns an overfervent heat.   10
The perelesse princesse, Mary quene, her message to present,

86 *appayre* decay
88 *peres* heroes
A163 9 *travail* labour

This Britan lord, as one moste meet, to Cesars broother sent.
On coursing steeds hee rids the waye: in ship hee fleeteth fast:
To royall Cesars court he comes, the payns, and perils past:
His charge enjoynd perfourmeth hee, attaind exceeding
      prayse:
His name, and fame so fully spred, it dures for afterdayes.
But lo, a fervent feever doth, amid his triumphs, fall:
And, with hertgripyng greef, consumes his tender lyms
      and all.
O rufull youth, thy helth toofar forgot, and toomuch heed
To countrie, and too parent yeven: why makest thou such
20   speed?
O, staye your self: your country so to serve dothe right
      require,
That often serve you may: and then, at length, succeed
      your sire.
But thee perchaunce it likes, thy life the price of praise
      to paye:
Nor deth doest dreed, where honor shines, as bright,
      as sonny day.
Certesse no greater glory could, than this, to thee betide:
Though Jove, six hundred yeres, had made thy fatall
      thread abide
Of journeys, and of travails huge the cause thy country was:
Thy funerall to honour, forth great Cesars court gan passe.
And thus, O thus (good lord) this ymp, of heven most
      worthy wight
30   His happy life with blisfull death concluded hath aright:
When, in fourt yere quene Maries raign proceeded: & what
      day,

    13 *coursing steeds* galloping horses   *rids* rides
    15 *His charge enjoynd* the instructions given to him
    16 *dures* endures
    19 *rufull* pitiable   *heed* careful attention
    20 *too* to   *yeven* given
    21 *staye* stop, slow down
    25 *Certesse* certainly
    29 *ymp* young man   *wight* person

Was last of Julie moneth, the same his last took him awaye.
From yeres twise ten if you in count wil but one yere abate:
The very age then shall you finde of lord Mautravers fate.
Likewise, was Titus Cesar hence withdrawn, in his prime
    yeres:
Likewise, the yong prince Edward went: and divers other
    peres.
Father, forbear thy wofull tears, cease, England, too lament:
Fates favour none, the enmie death to all alike is bent.
The onely mean, that now remains, with eloquence full fine,
Hath Shelley used, in setting forth this barons name divine.   40
Your Haddon eke, who erst in your life time, bore you
    good hart,
Presenteth you this monument, of woonted zeal some part.
And now farewell: of English youth most chosen gem,
    farewell:
A worthyer wight, save Edward, did in England never dwell.

A164. *Upon the sayd lord*
Mautravers death.

Mee thought, of late when lord Mautravers dyed,
Our common weal, thus, by her self shee cryed:
Oft have I wept for mine, so layd a sleep,
Yet never had I juster cause to weep.

[*A165–7 are Q2 278–80*]

36 *peres* nobles
37 *too* to
39 *mean* means
A164 2 *common weal* commonwealth, nation

Notes

ABBREVIATIONS

Manuscripts

AH	Arundel Harington MS
B	Blage MS (Trinity College Dublin MS D. 27, vols. 2–3)
D	Devonshire (BL MS Add. 17492)
E	Egerton MS (BL MS Egerton 2711)
H	Hill MS (BL MS Add. 36529)
H78	BL MS Harley 78
V	*The Court of Venus* (1537–64), fragments of three separate volumes of poetry. V1 was published 1537–9, the extant leaves are in the Bodleian; V2 was probably published 1547–9; the surviving leaves are in the Miriam Lutcher Stark collection of the University of Texas library, and V3, probably published 1561–4, now in the Folger Shakespeare Library. All published in *The Court of Venus*, ed. Russell A. Fraser (Durham, NC: Duke University Press, 1955)
Q1–Q10:	See Note on the Text.

Books Cited

Harrier	Richard Harrier, *The Canon of Sir Thomas Wyatt's Poetry* (Cambridge, Mass.: Harvard University Press, 1975)
Hughey	Ruth Hughey (ed.), *The Arundel Harington Manuscript of Tudor Poetry*, 2 vols. (Columbus, Ohio: Ohio State University Press, 1960)
Jones	Henry Howard, Earl of Surrey, *Poems*, ed. Emrys Jones (Oxford: Clarendon Press, 1964)

Marquis   *Richard Tottel's* Songes and Sonettes: *The Elizabethan Version*, ed. Paul A. Marquis, ACMRS (Tempe, Ariz., 2007)

Merrill   L. R. Merrill, *The Life and Poems of Nicholas Grimald* (New Haven: Yale University Press, 1925)

Muir 1947   Kenneth Muir, 'Unpublished Poems in the Devonshire Manuscript', *Proceedings of the Leeds Philosophical Society*, 6 (1947), pp. 253–82

Muir 1961   Kenneth Muir, *Sir Thomas Wyatt and his Circle: Unpublished Poems edited from the Blage Manuscript* (Liverpool: Liverpool University Press, 1961)

Muir and Thomson   *The Collected Poems of Sir Thomas Wyatt*, ed. Kenneth Muir and Patricia Thomson (Liverpool: Liverpool University Press, 1969)

NA   Henry Harington (ed.), *Nugæ Antiquae: being a miscellaneous collection of original papers in prose and verse. Written in the reigns of Henry VIII, Edward VI, Mary, Elizabeth, James I, &c by Sir John Harington*, 2 vols. (London, 1769–75)

Nott   *The Works of Henry Howard Earl of Surrey and of Sir Thomas Wyatt*, ed. G. F. Nott, 2 vols. (London, 1815–16); Surrey is vol. 1.

Padelford   F. M. Padelford (ed.), *The Poems of Henry Howard, Earl of Surrey* (Seattle: University of Washington Press, 1920)

Puttenham   George Puttenham, *The Art of English Poesy: A Critical Edition*, ed. Frank Whigham and Wayne A. Rebhorn (Ithaca, NY: Cornell University Press, 2007)

Rebholz   Sir Thomas Wyatt, *The Complete Poems*, ed. R. A. Rebholz, revised edn. (Harmondsworth: Penguin, 1997)

Rollins   *Tottel's Miscellany*, ed. Hyder Edward Rollins, 2 vols., revised edn. (Cambridge, Mass.: Harvard University Press, 1965)

Sessions   W. A. Sessions, *Henry Howard, the Poet Earl of Surrey: A Life* (Oxford: Clarendon Press, 1999)

Thomson   Patricia Thomson, *Sir Thomas Wyatt and his Background* (London: Routledge & Kegan Paul, 1964)

Tilley   Morris Palmer Tilley, *A Dictionary of the Proverbs in England in the Sixteenth and Seventeenth Centuries: A Collection of the Proverbs found in English Literature* and the Dictionaries of the Period (Ann Arbor: University of Michigan Press, 1950)

Other Reference Works

ODNB   *Oxford Dictionary of National Biography*
OED   *Oxford English Dictionary*

Editions of Other Authors Used

All references to Latin and ancient Greek authors are to the Loeb editions. Unless otherwise stated, all references to the Bible are to the Authorized/King James Version. Chaucer and Shakespeare are quoted from the Riverside editions. Translations from Latin and Italian are our own.

At the beginning of each note, we indicate the position of the poem concerned in Q1, the first printing of the *Miscellany*, or indicate its absence from Q1; if there is no note to that effect (as with poems 1–26), the poem is to be found in the same position in Q1 as in Q2. The numbering of the Q1 poems is that of Rollins's edition; that also applies to the numbering of poems in the Appendix, which are to be found only in Q1.

We have silently expanded contractions and modernized 'u/v' and 'i/j' in quotations from manuscripts in these Notes.

SURREY

1

A poem in terza rima; note how Surrey returns at the poem's end to the rhyme with which he began. A love complaint. There is a copy of the poem in H, whose most significant variants are noted below. AH (74) has a version of the poem's last six lines, its main variants being given below. The poem is also witnessed in BL, MS Hargrave 205.

1–6   cf. Chaucer's *Troilus and Criseyde*, V. 8–14:

> The gold-tressed Phebus heighe on-lofte
> Thries hadde alle with his bemes cleene
> The snowes molte, and Zepherus as ofte

> Ibrought ayeyn the tendre leves grene,
> Syn that the sone of Ecuba the queene
> Bigan to love hire first for whom his sorwe
> Was al, that she departe sholde a-morwe.

1   That is, two springs have passed.

4   Q1 reads 'new' for 'ones', whereas H reads 'now'.

9–10   Cf. Petrarch, *Rime*, 202. 1–2: 'D' un bel chiaro polito et vivo ghiaccio / move la fiamma che m' incende et strugge' [From lovely, clear, shining, living ice the flame which sets me alight and melts me comes].

10   H reads 'my inflame' for 'mine in flame'.

12   Q8 omits 'yeres'.

13   H reads 'to' for 'hath'.

14   H reads 'somtyme' for 'in time'.

15   H reads 'Yet' for 'In'.

17   Q6 reads 'frye' for 'trie', but later editions correct this.

18   Derives from Petrarch, *Rime*, 224. 12 ('s' arder da lunge et agghiacciar da presso'). Wyatt also translated this sonnet as poem 102 below, giving the line as 'If burning farre of, and if frysing nere'. See also lines 41–2 in Surrey's 'Such waiward waies' (poem 4).

21–30   May have a faint echo of Petrarch, *Rime*, 22. 1–6. Surrey's strongest echo is in line 30, where his diction imitates the Italian idiom of Petrarch's line 2. Line 16, as Jones points out, also uses a similar Italianate idiom.

23   H reads 'Him' for 'It'.

26   H reads 'To' for 'And'.

27   H reads 'represt' for 'opprest'.

28   H reads 'yet' for 'it'.

32–4   There may be an echo of Petrarch, *Rime*, 35. 1–4.

33   H reads 'in' for 'by' and 'should pere' for 'appere'.

34   H reads 'with' for 'in'.

35–7   cf. Petrarch, *Rime*, 175, 1–4.

36   A common image found in Petrarch (e.g. *Rime*, 59. 4–5) but also in medieval English love poetry (cf. Chaucer, *The Canterbury Tales*, I. 1815–18).

41–4   The metaphors of guiding stars and the lover as floundering
ship are not only Petrarchan (for the former, see e.g. *Rime*,
73. 46–51 and the latter *Rime*, 189); they are popular
images in medieval and later Renaissance English verse.
Criseyde is Troilus's 'lode-sterre' (Chaucer, *Troilus and Cri-
seyde*, V. 232 and 1392).qra

44   H reads 'atgaas' for 'agazed'.

47–9   Cf. Petrarch, *Rime*, 209. 9–11:

> Et qual cervo ferito di saetta
> col ferro avelenato dentr' al fianco
> fugge et più duolsi quanto più s' affreta.

[And like a deer struck by an arrow, with the venomed barb
in its side, flees and suffers more pain the more it hurries].

51   AH reads 'good will' for 'my tene'; H reads 'will' for 'tene',
and this seems necessary for the terza rima, though perhaps
'ill' would make more sense.

2

This fourteen-line poem has the unusual scheme ABABABABABABAA,
and thus resembles a roundel as much as a sonnet, although it lacks
the roundel's repeated lines. Sessions argues that it is '[w]ritten in
the older English rhyming scheme of *equivocatio* derived from the
medieval Latin rhyming treatises' (Sessions, p. 83). A complaint, not
necessarily on the subject of love. It is adapted from Petrarch, *Rime*,
310. As with the adaptation of Chaucer in poem 1, Surrey has notice-
ably muted mythological reference and replaced it with his feeling for
nature (which is not as amorous as it is for Petrarch). In not identify-
ing his sorrow as Petrarch does (referring to the death of Laura),
Surrey also gives it a wider resonance even as he makes the poem less
insistent on it. For further discussion of the poem, see Alastair Fowler,
Conceitful Thought: The Interpretation of English Renaissance Poems
(Edinburgh: Edinburgh University Press, 1975), and Michael Haldane
'"The Soote Season": Surrey and the Amatory Elegy', *English Studies*,
87 (2006), pp. 402–14.

1   The word 'soote' is a clear allusion to Chaucer's opening to
The Canterbury Tales, 'Whan that Aprill with his shoures
soote', and may be a conscious archaism.

5   This probably echoes the popular anonymous medieval
           lyrics 'Somer is come and winter gon' and 'Somer is
           y-comen in' (see Thomas Duncan (ed.), *Medieval English
           Lyrics 1200–1400* (London: Penguin, 1995), poems 106
           and 110).

9   Q8 reads 'flings' for 'slings'.

3

Eight quatrains rhyming ABAB. A repudiation of love. There is a copy
of the poem in H, whose most significant variants are noted below.
This poem is one of the 'five short lyrics of small merit' which Jones
chose to exclude from his edition, but there is no doubt that it is
Surrey's.

2   For the love-god Cupid's whip, see Malcolm Bull, *The Mirror
           of the Gods: Classical Mythology in Renaissance Art* (Lon-
           don: Allen Lane, 2005), pp. 189–90.

6   H reads 'By ill gydyng, had let my waye' – 'let' here mean-
           ing impeded.

8   H reads 'lost me manye a noble' for 'made me lose a better'.

11   H reads 'Their' for 'The'.

12   H reads 'fervent rage of hidden' for 'persant heat of secrete'.
           Q8 reads 'present' for 'persant'.

15   H reads 'the brewt therof my frewt' for 'Her beauty hath
           the frutes'.

16   H reads 'bloomes' for 'buds'.

22   H reads 'flaming' for 'glowyng'.

28   H reads 'sparkled' for 'specled'. Given that Cupid's colour
           is probably red, it is hard to say whether H or the *Miscel-
           lany* is to be preferred here.

4

In poulter's measure. A love complaint. A number of sources have
been proposed: Padelford notes several by Petrarch, including *Trionfo
d'Amore*, III. 151–90, IV. 139–53, and Nott argues for the second
canto of Ariosto's *Orlando Furioso*. There is a copy of the poem in
AH (77), in H and in B; their most significant variants are noted below
(the spelling used is that of AH, if they differ). This poem is much

imitated by the 'Uncertain Authors' below: see poems 138, 140 (though that may be Surrey's), 256 and 265.

3   Q1 reads 'is' for 'in', probably rightly.

5–6   Conventional images. See Ovid's *Metamorphoses*, I. 466–71, and compare with poem 265 below, lines 1–6.

5   Q1 reads 'makes the one' and AH and B read 'hartes' for 'thone'.

10   Both AH and B read 'the darke deepe well' for 'a depe dark hel' as does H, with a different spelling.

14   AH, H and B read 'spilt' for 'lost'.

15   AH and H read 'Lo,', and B 'Law' for 'So'; all read 'theise rules' for 'this meanes'.

17   AH, H and B read 'convert' for 'content' and 'will' for 'self'.

19   AH and H read 'dissemblid' and B reads 'dyssymyled' for 'dissembling'.

24   Spenser uses the image of a blacksmith's forge for Care, in Book IV, canto v of *The Faerie Queene*.

30   Q8 reads 'of his' for 'all in'.

31   AH, H and B read 'face' for 'grace'.

39   AH, H and B more comprehensibly – if less strikingly – read 'withouten' for 'with others'.

40   Beating a dog in front of a lion as a means of teaching the lion to behave is proverbial (Tilley D443; this instance is the first given). The idea is most clearly expressed in Edward Topsell's *The Historie of Foure-Footed Beastes* (1607): 'the best way to tame lyons is to bring vp with them a little dogge, and oftentimes to beate the same dogge in their presence, by which discipline, the lion is made more tractable to the will of his keeper' (Rollins).

42   AH, H and B read 'to' for all three instances of 'I'.

43   AH, H and B read 'yolden' for 'yelding'.

44   AH, H and B read 'mashe' for 'meash'.

45   AH, H and B read 'whiche seeldome tasted swete / to seasoned heapes of gall'.

46   AH reads 'glyntt' for 'glimse'. H has 'glyns'.

5

In poulter's measure. A love complaint. Jones points out significant echoes of the opening to Chaucer's *Troilus and Criseyde*. Though it does not contain a version of this poem, AH does have an apparent companion piece to it, beginning 'When wynter with his shivering blastes' (272).

10   'space', in this beautiful line, is temporal at least as much as it is spatial.

20   Birds were supposed to choose their mates on Valentine's Day; see Chaucer's *Parliament of Fowls*, lines 309–10.

25   'resolve' may be an error for 'revolve'.

30–46   The speaker's rebellion, and delusive consolation may well have theological resonances as much as amorous ones.

34   Q1 reads 'Unwillingly' for 'Unwittingly'.

6

An English sonnet, translated from Petrarch, *Rime*, 140 (as is poem 42, by Wyatt, below):

> Amor, che nel penser mio vive et regna
> e 'l suo seggio maggior nel mio cor tene,
> talor armato ne la fronte vene;
> ivi si loca et ivi pon sua insegna.
>
> Quella ch' amare et sofferir ne 'nsegna
> e vol che 'l gran desio, l'accesa spene
> ragion, vergogna, et reverenza affrene,
> di nostro ardir fra se stessa si sdegna.
>
> Onde Amor paventoso fugge al core,
> lasciando ogni sua impresa, et piange et trema;
> ivi s' asconde et non appar più fore.
>
> Che poss' io far, temendo il mio signore,
> se non star seco infin a l'ora estrema?
> ché bel fin fa chi ben amando more.

[Love, which lives and reigns within my thought, and holds his principal seat in my heart, from time to time appears with his armour in my forehead; there he camps and puts forth his banner. She who teaches love and suffering, and who wants great desire and kindled hope to be reined in by reason, shame and reverence, puts herself in disdain at our ardour. On which account Love flees frightened to the heart, leaving all his avouched cause, and weeps and trembles; there he hides and won't appear outside any more. What can I do, as my lord is afraid, except stay with him to the last? What a good end it is to die loving well].

A love complaint. There is another copy of the poem in H, whose main variants are noted below. If the poem is read historically, it might well seem like a rebuke to Henry VIII accompanied by honourable professions of loyalty.

1	H reads 'doth raine and live within' for 'liveth, and raigneth in'
2	H reads 'And' for 'That'.
5	H reads 'But she that tawght me love' for 'She, that me taught to love'.
7	H reads 'looke' for 'cloke'.
9	Q8 reads 'covered' for 'coward'.
10	H reads 'where he doth lurke and playne' for 'wheras he lurkes and plaines'.
14	H reads 'Swete is the death that taketh end by love'.

7

An English sonnet. Nott notes that the two springs at Cyprus may be suggested by the two fountains in Boiardo's *Orlando Innamorato*, I. iii, and Ariosto's *Orlando Furioso*, I. 78. A love complaint. There is another copy of the poem in H, whose main variants are noted below. In most cases, later editions return to the readings of Q1 rather than Q2's considerable (and quite thoughtful) revisions.

2	Q1 reads the metrically preferable 'whoso' for 'who', also omitting the word 'is'.
3	Q8 reads 'chawed' for 'thawed'.
4	Q4 and later editions read 'fixed' for 'fired'; the word is 'secret' in H.
5–7	Q1 has 'hate' for Q2's 'hart' in line 5 (as does Q8); this is associated with changes in the rhyming line 7, which in Q1 and Q8 appears as 'That in the hart that harborde freedome late'. Q8 also reads 'This' for 'With' and 'so' for 'ar' in line 6.

9   H reads 'One, eke' for 'An other'; Q1 and Q8 read 'so colde in' for 'well of'.

14   Q1 and Q8 read 'My service thus is growen' for 'Wherby my service growes'.

8

An English sonnet. An encomium of a specific lady. Despite the fact that 'Geraldine' and Surrey became in legend a great poetic couple on a par with Petrarch and Laura, this is the only poem by Surrey which was certainly written in honour of 'Geraldine' (Elizabeth Fitzgerald). There is a copy of the poem in H, whose main variants are noted below. Sessions points out that the poem erases the Fitzgeralds' 'bloody family history' in Ireland, and that it was an 'advertising strategy' designed to market Elizabeth for marriage (Sessions, pp. 194–5).

2   The Fitzgeralds were descended from the Geraldi family from Florence (Rollins). 'Her' is perhaps the older form of 'their'.

4   Q1 reads 'did geve' for 'furst gave'.

6   Elizabeth Fitzgerald's mother, Lady Elizabeth Grey, was of royal blood in that her grandmother was Elizabeth Woodville, wife of Edward IV and descendant of Edward I.

7   Q1 reads 'she doth' for 'did she'.

8   Q1 omits 'a' and reads 'where she tasteth costly' for 'who tasteth ghostly', as does Q8. Probably a reference is intended to the deceased Duke of Richmond, Surrey's boyhood friend, and Henry VIII's illegitimate son. Q2 has added an element of pathos in reminding us of Richmond's early death, and pointing forward to the Windsor elegy (poem 15 below).

9   It is likely that Surrey saw the 9-year-old Elizabeth Fitzgerald in 1537 when she was in attendance on Princess Mary at Hunsdon (which had been Surrey's childhood home before his father ceded it to the King), and at Hampton Court.

12   This is because Surrey was imprisoned at Windsor in July 1537, for assaulting a courtier in the royal grounds at the court in London (see poems 11 and 15).

13   H omits the first 'Her'.

9

A sonnet with the scheme ABABABABABABABCC, probably not by Surrey. A repudiation of love. It appears in AH (298), signed 'L. Vawse', and Rollins tentatively supports the attribution to Lord Vaux. The poem, as Rollins argues, was perhaps suggested by Seneca's *Hippolytus*, 761–74. Puttenham presents an imitation of the poem as his own composition. It is given as an example of 'some verses made all of bisyllables and others all of trisyllables, and others of polysyllables equally increasing and of divers quantities and sundry situations, as in this of our own, made to daunt the insolence of a beautiful woman.

> *Brittle beauty, blossom daily fading,*
> *Morn, noon, and eve in age and eke in eld*
> *Dangerous, disdainful, pleasantly persuading,*
> *Easy to grip, but cumbrous to wield,*
> *For slender bottom, hard and heavy lading,*
> *Gay for a while, but little while durable,*
> *Suspicious, uncertain, irrevocable,*
> *O, since thou art by trial not to trust,*
> *Wisdom it is, and it is also just,*
> *To sound the stem before the tree be felled,*
> *That is, since death will drive us all to dust,*
> *To leave thy love ere that we be compelled.*

In which ye have your first verse all of bisyllables and of the foot *trocheus*; the second all of monosyllables and all of the foot *iambus*; the third all of trisyllables and all of the foot *dactylus*; your fourth of one bisyllable and two monosyllables interlarded; the fifth of one monosyllable and two bisyllables interlaced; and the rest of other sorts and situations, some by degrees increasing, some diminishing' (pp. 208–9). Paul Hammond argues that this poem, along with Puttenham's imitation, 'was in Shakespeare's mind – possibly even that the text was open on the table – when he composed Sonnet 129, and that Sonnet 129 might be regarded as a rejoinder to it' (Paul Hammond 'Sources for Shakespeare's Sonnets 87 and 129 in *Tottel's Miscellany* and Puttenham's *The Arte of English Poesie*', *Notes and Queries*, 50 (2003), p. 407).

1–4   Cf. Petrarch, *Rime*, 350. 1–2: 'Questo nostro caduco et fragil bene, / ch' è vento et ombra et à nome beltate' [This brittle, fragile good of ours, which is made of wind and shadow and has the name beauty].

2	AH reads 'shorter' for 'short'.
7	AH reads 'Slipperer' for 'Slipper' and 'than' for 'as'.
8	AH reads 'obtayne' for 'attain' and 'never' (replacing a crossed-out 'and not') for 'not'.
9	AH reads 'Well' for 'Jewel'.
10	AH omits this line.
11	AH reads 'men' for 'may I'.
12	AH omits this line.
13	AH reads 'the fruite' for 'frute'.

10

A sonnet with the scheme ABABABABABABCC, based on Petrarch's *Rime*, 164, which is in turn inspired by Virgil's *Aeneid*, IV. 522–9, lines translated by Surrey thus:

> It was then night; the sounde and quiet slepe
> Had through the earth the weried bodyes caught;
> The woodes, the ragyng seas were falne to rest;
> When that the starres had halfe their course declined;
> The feldes whist; beastes and fowles of divers hue,
> And what so that in the brode lakes remainde
> Or yet among the bushy thickes of bryar
> Laide down to slepe by silence of the night,
> Gan swage their cares, mindlesse of travels past.
> Not so the spirite of this Phenician [Dido] . . . (lines 702–11)

A love complaint. Note that Surrey's structure, as in his poem 41 below, does not follow Petrarch, and the sense is divided into three parts: lines 1–5, 6–10 and 11–14, Surrey characteristically giving more space to nature than his sources do.

| 3 | 'ayre' probably means wind, as Surrey is rendering Petrarch's 'vento'. |
| 9 | Q8 reads 'doleful case' for 'doutfull ease'. |

11

An English sonnet. A complaint, not necessarily about love. There is a copy of the poem in H, its most important variants being noted below.

The poem is inspired by Surrey's imprisonment at Windsor in 1532 for striking a courtier – see also poem 15 below.

3	H reads 'Ech' for 'Yet'; Q1 reads 'The pleasant plot' for 'Yet pleasant plots'.
6	H reads 'discovered. Than did to' for 'discover: and to my'.
7	Poem 15 further elaborates past pleasures at Windsor; here 'hatelesse shorte debate' refers to spirited competition, whether verbal or martial, between young men. Q8 reads 'hartlesse' for 'hatelesse'.
9–10	Cf. poem 19, line 29.
9	H reads 'myne' for 'the'.
11	H reads 'And' for 'In'.
12	Cf. poem 34, line 13.
13	H reads 'to' for 'which'.
14	H reads 'have bent' for 'halfbent', giving an entirely different attitude to the poem's conclusion: where H is self-excoriating and suicidal, the *Miscellany*'s version is only half-despairing.

12

An English sonnet translated from Petrarch, *Rime*, 145, a much-translated poem. A promise of fidelity. There are substantial differences between this version of the text and the one found in H, so we give the full version of the poem here:

> Set we wheras the sonne dothe perche the grene,
> Or whear his beames may not dissolve the ise,
> In temprat heat, wheare he is felt and sene;
> With prowde people, in presence sad and wyse;
> Set me in base, or yet in highe degree;
> In the long night, or in the shortyst day;
> In clere weather, or whear mysts thickest be;
> In lofte yowthe, or when my heares be grey;
> Set me in earthe, in heaven, or yet in hell;
> In hill, in dale, or in the fowming floode;
> Thrawle, or at large, alive whersoo I dwell;
> Sike, or in healthe; in yll fame, or in good;
> Yours will I be, and with that onely thought
> Comfort my self when that my hape is nowght.

The poem was also copied into BL MS Egerton 2230, an early seventeenth-century MS. Puttenham quotes the poem, attributing it to Wyatt, and comments, 'All which might have been said in these two verses: "*Set me wheresoever ye will, / I am and will be yours still*"' (p. 308). Sessions argues that '[a] great deal of the text appears . . . to be a reinscription of the exchange of wedding vows' that Surrey made in 1532 (Sessions, p. 201).

13

An English sonnet translated from Petrarch, *Rime*, 11. A love complaint. There is a copy of the poem in H, its most important variants being noted below; as with poem 12, the key difference between H and the *Miscellany* is the latter being in the third person rather than addressing the lady in the second person.

1	H reads 'youe, Madam' for 'my Ladie'.
2	H reads 'Your' for 'Her'.
3	H reads 'ye' for 'she' and 'of my desire so greate' for 'my griefe was growen so great'.
4	H reads 'chaced cleane' for 'driveth'.
5	H reads 'Whiles' for 'That' and 'did' for 'do'.
6	H reads 'That so unware' for 'The which unwares'.
7	H reads 'Pytie I saw within your hart dyd rest'.
8	Q1 and Q8 read 'Yet, sins' for 'Sins that'; H reads 'But since ye knew I did youe' for 'Sins that she knew I did her'.
9	Q1 and Q8 read 'tresses' for 'tresse'; H reads 'Your' for 'Her' and 'was' for 'is'.
10	Q1 reads 'that hid' for 'to hide', whereas Q8 reads 'that had'; H reads 'Your' for 'Her' and 'were hid' for 'to hide'.
11	H reads 'All that withdrawne that I did crave so sore'.
12	Both H and Q1 have 'cornet' not 'corner'. While this may seem obviously correct in the context, 'corner' could mean battlement (*OED*, 'corner', *n*2), and may perhaps imply that her headdress is a battlement against his eyes. Q1 and Q8 read 'me alacke' and H reads 'me, a lacke!' for 'my alacke'.
13	Q1 and Q8 read 'a' for 'of'.
14	H reads 'Of your faire eies whereby the light is lost'.

14

An English sonnet. Jones and Rollins both see analogues in Petrarch, *Rime*, 159, but it would be going too far to consider that poem a direct source. A love complaint. The mention of a golden gift, and of 'domes' may suggest that the poem obliquely alludes to the Judgement of Paris, in which the Trojan prince had to choose between the merits of Venus, Juno and Minerva, choosing the first.

9   'Garret' is unique to Q2. Other texts of the *Miscellany* give
            'Ladie'. Since 'Garret' is a common rendering of Fitzgerald,
            this may be an attempt to adjust the poem to fit the popular
            Geraldine myth.

15

Quatrains rhyming ABAB with a couplet at the end of the poem. Both an elegy and a complaint. Probably written whilst Surrey was banished from Court to Windsor Castle for striking a fellow courtier (possibly Edward Seymour); the 'Windsor Elegy' contrasts present 'imprisonment' with his youthful friendship with Henry Fitzroy, Duke of Richmond, the illegitimate son of Henry VIII and husband of Surrey's sister. Splendid evocation of friendship as it may be, the poem also surely reminds King Henry of past ties, perhaps also rebuking the proud and even tigerish king for banishing a nobleman for the sake of a conflict with an upstart. There is another copy of the poem in H, its most important variants being noted below. The poem is discussed at length in Candace Lines, 'The Erotic Politics of Grief in Surrey's "So Crewell Prison"', *Studies in English Literature*, 46 (2006), pp. 1–26.

2   That is, Henry Fitzroy.

8   From Chaucer, *Troilus and Criseyde*, III. 1363.

9   Chaucer uses 'bright of hewe' to describe women in *Troilus
            and Criseyde*, III. 303 and V. 1772. H reads 'sales' for
            'seates'.

13   Q8 reads 'plaine' for 'palme'.

21   For exploration of this difficult line, see Amanda Holton
            and Tom MacFaul, '"Ruth" in Surrey's Windsor Elegy',
            Notes and Queries, 56 (2009), pp. 29–33.

23   H reads 'trayled by' for 'trained with'.

27   H reads 'soft' for 'oft'.

33   H reads 'voyd walles' for 'wide vales'.

41	H reads 'my face' for 'the face'.
45	Cf. Wyatt's poem 67, line 1, to which the line may allude.
46	The Duke of Richmond died in 1536, aged 17.
49	Q8 reads 'Eche Stone' for 'Eccho'.

16

Six-line stanzas, rhyming ABABCC – what later came to be known as the Venus and Adonis stanza, after Shakespeare's famous poem in that form; here the lines alternate between tetrameters and trimeters. A promise of fidelity. Sessions describes the poem as an 'extended *frottola*', and discusses it subtly and at length (Sessions, p. 178). The first letters of each stanza spell out 'WIATT'; this may imply a tribute to the older poet (cf. poem 169 below). The poem was much favoured by Puttenham, who mentions it three times: its first line is given as an example of 'verses made of monosyllables and bisyllables interlaced' (p. 208), and of a caesura that 'falls just in the middle'; lines 1–4 are also described as 'passing sweet and harmonical' (p. 216).

3–5	Cf. Petrarch, *Rime*, 17. 1–2: 'Piovonmi amare lagrime dal viso / con un vento angoscioso di sospiri' [bitter tears rain down my face, with an anguished wind of sighs].
8	'Troye' is probably to be pronounced as two syllables for the sake of the metre.
11	The Greek fleet to Troy was becalmed at the island of Aulis until Agamemnon propitiated the goddess Artemis (Diana) by sacrificing his daughter Iphigeneia.
15	Q8 reads 'from' for 'full'.
17	Q8 reads 'overcome' for 'overron'.
29–30	Q8 transposes 'care' and 'fare'.

17

In stanzas rhyming ABABCCC (i.e. Venus and Adonis stanzas with an extra final rhyme). Lines are octosyllabic with the exception of the B-lines which have six syllables, and the final C-line in each stanza, which has ten. Based in part on the sixth epistle of the poet Serafino de' Cimirelli (1466–1500). This epistle is itself derived from Ovid's *Heroides*, 2. A female complaint. This poem also appears in *NA* under

the heading 'By John Harington, 1543, for a Ladie moche in Love',
and in D and H78; in D the poem is in the hand of Surrey's sister, the
Duchess of Richmond. BL MS Add. 30513 contains a musical setting
for the poem. The poem, like 19 below, was probably written by Sur-
rey in the voice of his own wife during his 1546 military service in
Boulogne.

12–13   Cf. Petrarch, *Rime*, 189. 7–8: 'la vela rompe un vento
           umido eterno / di sospir, di speranze et di desio' [a wet, end-
           less wind breaks the sail – made up of sighs, hopes and
           desires].

25–7   Cf. Serafino, *Epistles*, 6. 37–40:

> Ah quante volte quando el ciel se imbruna
>   À meza nocte uscio del freddo lecto
>   À sentir le hore, à remirar la luna?
>   Facta son marinar per questo effecto.

[Oh, as often as the sky darkens in the middle of the night
on my cold bed so that I feel the time pass and contemplate
the moon – so I am made a mariner in this way].

33   Cf. Serafino, *Epistles*, 6. 79–80:

> E se affondato è alcun dal tempo rio
>   Che 'l sappia, dico: ohimè, questo è summerso
>   E uno altro mar de lacrime faccio io.

[And plunged in another evil time, I say what I know: alas,
this is submerged in another sea of tears I have made].

18

In poulter's measure. A *pastourelle* (pastoral narrative). It is striking
that the lover in this poem actually dies; it is more usual for death to
be threatened than enacted (Rollins). Nott considers that Spenser
made heavy use of this poem in his *Daphnaïda*.

1   Boreas is the North Wind.

1–2   Commenting on these lines, Puttenham says: 'I would fain
           learn of some good maker, whether the Earl spake this in
           figure of *periphrasis* or not. For mine own opinion, I think
           that if he meant to describe the winter season, he would not
           have disclosed it so broadly as to say "winter" at the first
           word, for that had been against the rules of art and without

any good judgement, which in so learned and excellent a personage we ought not to suspect. We say therefore that for "winter" it is no *periphrasis* but language at large. We say, for all that, having regard to the second verse that followeth, it is a *periphrasis*, seeming that thereby he intended to show in what part of the winter his loves gave him anguish – that is, in the time which we call the fall of the leaf, which begins in the month of October and stands very well with the figure to be uttered in that sort, notwithstanding winter be named before, for winter hath many parts, such namely as do not shake off the leaf nor unclothe the trees as here is mentioned. Thus may ye judge as I do, that this noble earl wrote excellently well and to purpose' (p. 279).

23   Q8 reads 'forbyd' for 'fordid'.

41   cf. Chaucer's *Book of the Duchess*, lines 445–7:

> I was war of a man in blak,
> That sat and had yturned his bak
> To an ook, an huge tree.

48   Cf. Petrarch, *Rime* 57. 7–9: 'et corcherassi il sol là oltre, ond' esce / d'un medesimo fonte Eufrate e Tigre // prima ch' i' trovi in ciò pace né triegua' [And the sun will lie down beyond the common source of the Euphrates and the Tigris before I find peace or respite here].

52   Priam's loss of his many sons was a conventional image of misery – cf. poem 15, line 4.

78   As Chaucer's *Troilus and Criseyde* recounts, the Trojan prince suffered for love of the unfaithful Criseyde.

80   Blue is conventionally the colour of faithfulness. Q8 reads 'so' for 'as'.

19

In poulter's measure. Like poem 17, this was presumably written for the Countess of Surrey by her husband while he was in France in 1545–6. There are a number of variants from AH (85), the most notable of which are given below. It is there signed 'ffinis Preston'.

9   AH reads 'lord and love' for 'love and lorde'.

11   AH reads 'That' for 'Whom', inserts 'for' before 'tembrace', and omits 'with well'.

13	AH reads 'Theare god hym well preserve/ and safelye me hym send'.
15–16	AH omits these lines.
18	AH reads 'and stand' for 'I lye'.
20	AH reads 'that my sweete lorde in dawnger greate/ alas doth often lye'.
22	Surrey's first son, Thomas, was born in March 1536. AH reads 'with T. his lytle sonne' for 'with his faire little sonne'.
34	AH reads 'some hydden wheare to steale the gryfe/ of my unquyet mynd'.
36	AH reads 'there is' for 'I finde' and 'some' for 'good'.
37	AH reads 'feele the' for 'think, by'.
39	AH reads 'that we two' for 'we'.
41	AH reads 'convart' for 'conjure'.
42	AH reads 'me' after 'lord' and Q8 inserts 'dooe' after 'Lord', evidently to fix the metre.

20

In tetrameter Venus and Adonis stanzas. Rollins believed this poem is an imitation of Heywood's poem 168 below, but the influence is more likely to be the other way around. An encomium of a lady. Puttenham quotes the poem's first six lines as an example of '*Hyperbole*, or the Overreacher; otherwise called the Loud Liar', commenting: 'if we fall a-praising, especially of our mistress's virtue, beauty or other good parts, we be allowed now and then to overreach a little by way of comparison' (p. 277).

8	Odysseus' wife Penelope was a traditional exemplum of marital constancy.
15–18	This conceit is a common one, also found in Surrey's poem 35 below (line 34), as well as in the work of others, e.g. poems 142, line 32 and 168, line 13.

21

In trimeter quatrains with alternating rhyme. A love complaint. The speaker's reference to himself as 'a man of war' (line 7) may indicate that the poem was written after August 1542 when Surrey undertook his first military service in Scotland (Rollins). It is possible that the chess imagery may be related to Chaucer's *Book of the Duchess*, lines 617–86. Jones omits the poem as being 'of small merit'.

22

In poulter's measure. A poem of friendship/advice.

16   Q8 reads 'yeldst' for 'held'.

23

Trimeter stanzas rhymed ABABCDCD. A repudiation of love.

36   Q8 reads 'to' for 'so'.

37   The word 'tought' was probably pronounced 'toft' in the early sixteenth century, thus rhyming with 'aloft'.

24

Tetrameter quatrains with alternating rhyme. A love complaint. This poem bears a strong resemblance to one which may be by Wyatt, 'Lyke as the wynde with raging blaste'. It is an open question whether one poem influenced the other, or whether they simply have a common source. Surrey's poem also appears in H, which contains a number of extra lines as follows:

After line 8:

> Like as the flee that seethe the flame
> And thinkes to plaie her in the fier,
> That fownd her woe, and sowght her game,
> Whose grief did growe by her desire.

After line 12:

> Wherein is hid the crewell bytt
> Whose sharpe repulse none can resist,
> And eake the spoore that straynith eche wytt
> To roon the race against his list.

After line 24:

> And as the spyder drawes her lyne,
> With labour lost I frame my sewt;
> The fault is hers, the losse ys myne.
> Of yll sown seed such ys the frewte.

There are several other interesting variants in H which suggest less of an emphasis on the personal. These include 'this' for 'my' (line 10), 'these' for 'her' (line 11) and 'his unrest' for 'mine unrest' in line 24.

5–8   Cf. Petrarch, *Rime*, 48. 1–4:

> Se mai foco per foco non si spense
> né fiume fu giamai secco per pioggia,
> ma sempre l'un per l' altro simil poggia
> et spesso l'un contrario l' altro accense ...

[If fire is not put out by fire nor river made dry by rain, but always one is made greater by another like it, and sometimes the opposite inflames]. Note Surrey's curious adaptation of the sentiment.

25

Six stanzas, each of eight six-syllable lines, rhymed ABABCDCD. A promise of fidelity. Jones omits the poem as being 'of small merit'. Q8 inserts 'such' before 'suspected' in the title.

30   An annotation on the Bodleian's copy of Q9 reads 'the sowe or hogge or rather fox' (Rollins).

41   Q8 omits 'it', making 'fire' into two syllables.

44   Q8 reads 'constancye of' for 'constance of the'.

45–6   Cf. Petrarch, *Rime*, 30. 9–10: 'quando avrò queto il cor, asciutti gli occhi, / vedrem ghiacciare il foco, arder la neve' [when I shall have a quiet heart and dry eyes, we will see fire freeze and snow burn].

26

In poulter's measure. A condemnation of women.

1   The 'careless cloke' is conventional for lovers, and such dishabille would continue to be the mark of one in love in Elizabethan drama; but also cf. Wyatt's poem 135, line 5.

2–3   Love here is personified as Cupid, with his bow.

27

[Q1: 243, in the Uncertain Authors section, as 'Of the dissembling lover']. Both Padelford and Jones include a longer version of the poem in their editions of Surrey, but Tottel's attribution implies that it is very probably not by him (see Sessions, p. 197 n., for an argument that it is Surrey's). Like the poem it answers, it is in poulter's measure. A defence of women. The full version of the poem is in AH (72), giving the following extra lines at the end:

> Muche lyke untruth to this/ the storye doth declare
> Wheare th' elders layd to Susans chardge/ meete matter to compare
> They did her both accuse/ and eke condempne her to
> and yet no reason right nor truthe/ did lead them so to do
> And she thus judg'd to dye/ toward her death went forthe
> Fraughted with faith a pacient pase/ taking her wrong in worthe
> But he that dothe defend/ all those that in hym trust
> Did Raise a Childe for her defence/ to shyeld her from th' unjust
> And Danyell chosen was/ then of this wrong to weete
> How, in what place and eke with whome/ she did this Cryme comytt
> He caws'd the Elders part/ the one from th' others sight
> and did examyne one by one/ and chardged bothe say right
> Und'ra a Mulberye trye/ it was fyrst sayd the one
> The next nam'de a Pomegranate trye/ whereby the truth was knowne
> Than Susan was dischardg'd/ and they condempen'd to dye
> as right requeares and they deserve/ that fram'de so fowll a lye
> And he that her preserv'd/ and lett them of their lust
> Hath me defendyd hetherto/ and will do still I trust

The removal of this commonly cited biblical tale (Daniel 13, but relegated to the Apocrypha in the Great Bible, Geneva Bible, Bishops' Bible and subsequent Protestant Bibles) does away with a redemptive ending for the poem, leaving us to think of those, like Surrey perhaps, who are unjustly condemned to death. Removing the story may, however, simply be a signal of Protestant sensibilities on the part of the editor or of the scribe who transmitted the poem. The slight changes in lines 6–8 make those who take the reins of justice, like Surrey's enemy Seymour, seem more grasping of power. There was no Daniel to save Surrey – his monarch being the less than merciful Henry VIII (whom it was increasingly acceptable to attack in Mary's reign – see Eamon Duffy, *Fires of Faith: Catholic England under Mary Tudor* (New Haven: Yale University Press, 2009)). Those who force a fire where they can raise no smoke may be those who trump up charges against the likes of Surrey, but he was not burned; twenty-eight Protestants, however, were burned in the month of the *Miscellany*'s publication. Other substantive variants in AH are noted below.

6   AH reads 'styckes not' for 'seke for'.

7   AH reads 'Whose skill and Conninge tryed' for 'Whose practise if were proved'.

8   AH reads 'they wolde sone shau yow shold sone see' for 'Assuredly beleve it well'.

11   Q8 reads 'they' for 'the'.

14   AH reads 'right' for 'full'.

16   AH reads 'in' for 'With'

17   AH reads 'mett' for 'joynde'.

19   Q8 reads 'falsly' for 'safely'.

28

[Q1: 262] Tetrameter Venus and Adonis stanzas. A promise of fidelity. It incorporates many standard Petrarchan motifs, but has its own elegant defiance, highly characteristic of Surrey. Sessions argues that '[t]his *frottola* transforms Petrarchan clichés amid a changing landscape of winter, summer, and sea. It ends in an epigram of total fidelity' (Sessions, p. 209).

7   Boreas was the classical god of the North Wind. The line probably refers to Surrey's attendance on his father's abortive invasion of Scotland in 1542 (see Jessie Childs, *Henry VIII's Last Victim: The Life and Times of Henry Howard, Earl of Surrey* (London: Jonathan Cape, 2006), p. 188). They did burn down a monastery, but the spite to which Surrey refers here is probably Henry's, the Scottish king's, or that of fortune, preventing him from gaining a glorious victory like his grandfather's at Flodden – anyone's, in short, but Surrey's.

29

[Q1: 264] Jones chooses not to print the poem in his edition, but it is certainly Surrey's. In poulter's measure; a transparent beast fable with hints of the dream vision. There are a number of variants from AH (78), the most important of which are listed in the notes. Q4's title reads 'to a Lady', which obviously makes more sense. Drayton, in *England's Heroical Epistles* (1597) identifies the addressee as Lady Anne Stanhope, who later married Edward Seymour (see notes to poem 169 below). The lion was the emblem of the Howard family. The poem constitutes a sharp attack on courtly *arrivistes* through one of their women. The references to his grandfather's defeat of a king seems quite minatory to modern kings, particularly when Surrey identifies himself with the regal lion. It is perhaps his most dangerously rebellious poem; it is certainly his angriest.

9	The Seymour family seat was Wulfhall in Wiltshire.
10	This line is quoted by Puttenham as an example of 'verses made of monosyllables and bisyllables interlaced' (p. 208).
11	AH reads 'fearce' for 'coy'.
22	AH reads 'seeke oute' for 'finde'.
30	Surrey's grandfather, Thomas Howard, defeated the 'crowned king' James IV of Scotland at Flodden Field in 1513.
35	AH reads 'dothe know' for 'have heard'.
36–7	The poet's uncle, another Thomas Howard, was sent to the Tower of London in 1536 for a secret betrothal to Lady Margaret Douglas, Henry VIII's niece. He died in gaol in 1537 (Sessions, p. 118).
37	AH reads 'both strong' for 'strong'.
40	AH reads 'secke his death' for 'lese his life'.
41	AH reads 'lyfe/ to' for 'lives do'.
47	AH reads 'my kynd' for 'our kindes'.
49	AH reads 'fedd' for 'fled'.
56	AH reads 'a Currant fawne' for 'of currant sort'.
67	AH reads 'happ' for 'lucke'.
69	AH reads 'to low' for 'and bow'.
72	AH reads 'of symple sheepe/ go slake your wrath' for 'go slake your thirst on simple shepe'.

30

[Q1: 265] In poulter's measure. A love complaint/promise of fidelity. The *Miscellany* is the most authoritative copy-text for this poem, which was evidently popular: much-adapted versions, set to music, appear in *The Melville Book of Roundels* (1612), and John Forbes, *Cantus, Songs and Fancies* (1666), song 1. There are other copies of the poem in Bodleian MS Ashmole 176, Yale MS Osborn and BL Stowe. For a discussion of the poem's circulation in seventeenth-century Scotland, see A. S. G. Edwards, 'Manuscripts of the Verse of

Henry Howard, Earl of Surrey', *Huntington Library Quarterly*, 67 (2004), pp. 288–9.

5–8	The source may be Petrarch, *Rime*, 22. 1–6; cf. poem 1, lines 21–30 and notes.
8	Cf. Shakespeare, 2 *Henry IV*, III. i. 19.
13	Cf. Ecclesiastes 1: 9.
21–2	Quoted by Puttenham as an example of '*Omiosis*, or Resemblance' (p. 326).
37	Q8 reads 'rueth' for 'riveth'.
44	Q8 reads 'trie' for 'tie'.
46	Neptune is the Roman god of the sea.
47–8	Also quoted by Puttenham as an example of '*Omiosis*, or Resemblance' (p. 326).
49	cf. the refrain of Wyatt's poem 111, which is surely the source.
57	Q8 reads 'dedly' for 'feble'.
59–60	Cf. Chaucer's *Troilus and Criseyde*, IV. 319–22, and *The Canterbury Tales*, I. 2768–70.

31

[Q1: 27] A poem in tetrameters, with alternating rhyme. A version of Martial, *Epigrams*, X. 47:

> Vitam quae faciant beatiorem,
> iucundissime Martialis, haec sunt:
> res non parta labore, sed relicta;
> non ingratus ager, focus perennis;
> lis numquam, toga rara, mens quieta;
> vires ingenuae, salubre corpus;
> prudens simplicitas, pares amici;
> convictus facilis, sine arte mensa;
> nox non ebria, sed soluta curis;
> non tristis torus et tamen pudicus;
> somnus qui faciat breves tenebras:
> quod sis esse velis nihilque malis;
> summum nec metuas diem nec optes.

[Most joyful Martial, the things that make for a happy life are these: inherited wealth, not worked for; land that isn't unproductive, a fire all year round; no lawsuits, rarely needing to wear a toga, a quiet mind; a well-bred strength, a healthy body, wise simplicity, equal friends; easy company, an artless dinner-table; nights not drunken but free from cares; a marriage-bed not solemn but modest; sleep which makes the darkness short: wish to be what you are, and nothing more; don't fear the end, and don't hope for it].

The poem is also found in six MSS, three of which (including H) can be linked to the Haringtons: we record the major variants from H, but for a full discussion see A. S. G. Edwards, 'Surrey's Martial Epigram: Text and Transmission', in Peter Beal and A. S. G. Edwards (eds.), *Scribes and Transmission in English Manuscripts 1400–1700*, English Manuscript Studies, 12 (London: British Library, 2005), pp. 74–82.

1   H reads 'for to' for 'that do'. MS Cotton Titus A. 24 reads 'My frende' for 'Martial'.

3   Inherited riches (Martial's 'res . . . relicta') were commonly considered superior to earnings.

5   It is a common notion in the sixteenth century, deriving mostly from Cicero, that only social equals (Martial's 'pares amici') could be true friends (Tom MacFaul, *Male Friendship in Shakespeare and his Contemporaries* (Cambridge: Cambridge University Press, 2007)).

8   Living in one place rather than moving about was commonly considered the mark of a settled aristocracy, in contrast to the flitting of parvenus.

12   H reads 'Where wyne may beare no soverany'.

13   Martial refers to 'non tristis torus' – a marriage-bed that isn't sad/solemn/prudish. Surrey clearly considers sadness in marriage to be caused by debate on a wife's part (for which, of course, a man could not be held responsible).

16   H reads 'Neyther wisshe death, nor' for 'Ne wish for death, ne'.

32

[Q1: 28] In pentameters, with alternating rhyme. A version of Horace, *Odes*, II. 10, also translated as poems 163 and 253:

> Rectius vives, Licini, neque altum
> semper urgendo neque, dum procellas
> cautus horrescis, nimium premendo
>   litus iniquum.

auream quisquis mediocritatem
diligit, tutus caret obsoleti
sordibus tecti, caret invidenda
     sobrius aula.

saepius ventis agitatur ingens
pinus et celsae graviore casu
decidunt turres feriuntque summos
     fulgura montis.

sperat infestis, metuit secundis
alteram sortem bene praeparatum
pectus. informes hiemes reducit
     Iuppiter; idem

summovet. non, si male nunc, et olim
sic erit: quondam cithara tacentem
suscitat Musam neque semper arcum
     tendit Apollo.

rebus angustis animosus atque
fortis appare: sapienter idem
contrahes vento nimium secundo
     turgido vela.

[You will live better, Licinius, by neither always rushing out into the deep nor too closely pressing to the rocky shore in fear of storms. Whoever loves the golden mean is safe in avoiding a dirty house and sober in avoiding a palace that will bring envy. The tall pine is more often shaken by winds; the lofty towers have a greater fall; lightning strikes high mountains. The heart prepared for good or ill is hopeful in adversity and fears what is to come when fortunes are better. Jupiter brings back the ugly winters, but he also takes them away. If things are bad now, they won't always be. Apollo sometimes rouses the silent Muse with his lyre, and doesn't always stretch his bow. In straitened circumstances seem spirited and strong; yet wisely reef your sails when they are swollen with too favourable a wind].

A moral ode on the golden mean. The *Miscellany* is the most authoritative copy-text for this poem, which is also in H78. Q8 reads 'manne' for 'meane' in the title.

1   Thomas may be Wyatt the elder or younger, but may just as probably be Surrey's son or brother.

8   Surrey translates Horace's palace/hall inciting envy as a palace inciting disdain, though he may mean roughly the same thing.

13   Q8 reads 'Heapeth amendes in swete' for 'Hopeth amendes:
            in swete'.

15   Q8 reads 'No will' for 'Now il'.

15–17   Phoebus was the Roman god of plague and of the sun (rep-
            resented by his bow), and of poetry (represented by his
            harp); the lines may be paraphrased: 'At some stage Phoe-
            bus will cease frowning with his bow that brings heat and
            plague and will turn to singing along with his harp.'

20   The final two sentiments, 'hast is wast, profe doth finde',
            are not in Horace, and represent Surrey's laconic conclu-
            sions on the matter.

                                      33

[Q1: 29] An English sonnet. H has a few variants, the most important
being given below. The poem is also found in E. An encomium. Sir
Thomas Wyatt's translation of the penitential psalms was published
posthumously in 1549; Surrey's sonnet was written as a commenda-
tory poem for this volume, but was not published there. Versions of
the Psalms were an increasingly important mark of Protestant sympa-
thies. The concealment of Wyatt's name here and in the next three
poems may seem merely part of a larger tendency to avoid names in
the *Miscellany*, but it also reflects the fact that Wyatt's name was a
dangerous one: his son had led a Protestant rebellion against the Mar-
ian regime in 1554 and was executed for his pains. Putting this poem
first in the group of poems about Wyatt establishes a pious character
for the poems' subject before lamenting his death.

1–2   Refers to Alexander the Great, who defeated the Persian
            King Darius at the Battle of Issus in 333 BC. The word
            'chased' here may pun on chaste, suggesting a purification,
            a concept picked up at line 7.

3   According to Plutarch, Alexander took the works of Homer
            with him on his military expeditions. This was a favourite
            anecdote with sixteenth-century poets: see Philip Sidney,
            Defence of Poesy: 'Alexander left his schoolmaster, living
            Aristotle, behind him, but took dead Homer with him'
            (*The Major Works*, ed. Katherine Duncan-Jones (Oxford:
            Oxford University Press, 1989), pp. 237–8).

4   The literary works of heathens, though much admired, are
            to be treated as feigned in comparison to the supposed
            truth of the Bible.

5   Puttenham comments as follows: 'The Earl of Surrey upon
         the death of Sir Thomas Wyatt made among other this
         verse pentameter and of ten syllables:

> *What holy grave (alas), what sepulcher. . . .*

         But if I had had the making of him, he should have been of
         eleven syllables and kept his measure of five still, and would
         so have run more pleasantly a great deal. For as he is now,
         though he be even, he seems odd and defective for not well
         observing the natural accent of every word, and this would
         have been soon helped by inserting one monosyllable in the
         middle of the verse, and drawing another syllable in the
         beginning into a dactyl, this word *holy* being a good pyr-
         richius and very well serving the turn, thus:

> *Whāt hŏlў grāve, âlās, whât fīt sêpŭlchêr.*

         Which verse, if ye peruse throughout, ye shall find him after the
         first dactyl all trochaic and not iambic, nor of any other foot of
         two times. But perchance if ye would seem yet more curious, in
         place of these four trochees, ye might induce other feet of three
         times, as to make the three syllables next following the dactyl
         the foot amphimacer, the last word *sepulcher* the foot *amphib-
         rachus*, leaving the other middle word for an iamb, thus:

> *Whāt hŏlў grāve, âlās, whât fīt sêpŭlchêr'* (pp. 210–11).

         The latter version of the scansion does not in fact seem to dif-
         fer; and Puttenham is not helped in all this tangle by misquoting
         the line in the first place (H only varies from Tottel in punctu-
         ation here); but we give this as an example of the kind of
         preoccupations and revisions prompted by Surrey's metrics.

8–12   King David was supposed the author of the Psalms; the group
         of psalms known as the penitential psalms were considered
         the king's penance for sending Uriah, husband of Bathsheba,
         to his death in battle; the story is recounted in 2 Samuel 11.

13–14   The poem's conclusion makes quite explicit the barb
         against sinful monarchs like Henry VIII that is probably
         intended by the very act of translating the penitential
         psalms (see Greg Walker, *Writing under Tyranny: English
         Literature and the Henrician Reformation* (Oxford: Oxford
         University Press, 2005)).

14   H reads 'Mowght' for 'Ought'.

34

[Q1: 30] An English sonnet. An elegy. H has some variants, given in the notes. Sir Thomas Wyatt died in 1542, prompting a number of poetic laments, including several by Surrey.

1–4	Implies that some of those lamenting Wyatt's death were his enemies in life, but also cf. Wyatt's poem 51, lines 7–9.
2	H reads 'that livelye hedd' for 'thy livelyhed'. Misquoted by Puttenham as an example of the use of dactyls (p. 211), as is line 4.
2–3	Particular enemies of Wyatt were Edmund Bonner and Simon Heynes, who caused his imprisonment in 1540 (Rollins).
3	H reads 'sowne' for 'swolne'.
4	Cf. Wyatt's poem 50, which may have inspired Surrey here; Plutarch tells the story that Julius Caesar cried crocodile tears when his enemy Pompey's head was brought to him.
7	The end of life is happy because life is conventionally a vale of tears.
9	Surrey insists on his intimacy with Wyatt, which seems to have been real.
13	Cf. poem 11, line 12.
14	The story of Pyramus and Thisbe, most familiar to us from *A Midsummer Night's Dream*, is told in Ovid, *Metamorphoses*, IV. 55–166. Pyramus does not, in Ovid's version, weep on his beloved Thisbe's breast: he finds her bloody cloak, which has been chewed by a lion, and kills himself, spurting streams of blood onto the mulberry tree, giving it its colour; Thisbe, in fact, is still alive, but soon kills herself in turn when she finds Pyramus' body.

35

[Q1: 31] In pentameter quatrains, with alternating rhyme, ending with a couplet. Also in H78. Though the poem may be regarded as an elegy like 34 above, its first line indicates that it is more formally an epitaph – i.e. a poem to be (or imagined to be) engraved on a tomb. The poem was the first of Surrey's to be published, in a pamphlet with two other 'epitaphs', probably in 1542; that printed version has no significant variants other than giving W.'s name as 'Wyat'.

1   Q4 is the only edition to spell Wyat[t]'s name in full; how-
           ever, Q5 and following editions misread this and print
           'What'. So much for literary fame; though it may be that
           the later editions are attempting to turn the poem into a
           riddle. As Sessions points out, the line plays on 'the old
           Roman burial formula the Renaissance had renewed: "Hic
           mortuus requiescit semel / Qui vivus requievit nunquam"
           ("Here rests the ever dead / Who living never rested")' (Ses-
           sions, p. 253).

13   Q6 reads 'tyme' for 'rime'.

14   Geoffrey Chaucer (c. 1343–1400) was regarded as England's
           premier poet, his reputation burnished by William Thynne's
           editions of 1532 and 1542; Surrey is therefore making a very
           large claim for Wyatt's significance as a writer.

15   The idea that Wyatt's poetry is unperfected for lack of time
           may be an attempt to qualify the extravagance of the previ-
           ous line's claim, and reflects a sense that Wyatt's work was
           rough in its metre (see Introduction), requiring the kind of
           finishing job that the *Miscellany*'s editor does; it also leads
           on to the subject of the other activities that prevented
           Wyatt polishing his work.

17   On Wyatt's diplomatic services, see Introduction.

35   The word 'witness' is an English equivalent of the Greek
           'martyr', thus imbuing Wyatt's death with considerable reli-
           gious significance.

                                   36

[Q1: 263, with the title 'A praise of sir Thomas wyate thelder for his
excellent learning'] An English sonnet. As much an encomium as an
elegy. H has some variants, the most significant of which are noted
below.

   Jones comments: 'In this third tribute to Wyatt Surrey attempts an
involved syntactical scheme in the manner of Petrarch. The result is
unfortunate; the sonnet is a tangle, although good phrases occur.' The
general sense is clear enough if the details are at times obscure (caused,
no doubt, by different kinds of textual corruption in H and in the *Mis-
cellany*), and can be paraphrased thus: 'In pagan times, though people
didn't know for certain where to go, they still went to the temples of
Jove and the like in order to provide themselves with incentives for

good action (and warnings against bad); in the Christian age, then, it's only reasonable for some to bewail Wyatt, whose example leads us to virtue; and his enemies still choke with envy on his cinders.'

1 H reads 'scyence' for 'knowledge', 'not so' for 'not'.

2 Crete was traditionally the birthplace of Jupiter/Jove. Surrey seems to be expressing scepticism about this. H reads 'where they' for 'were that'.

3 H reads 'reverte' for 'convert'.

4 H reads 'Wan' for 'Wend'.

5 H reads 'in no' for 'no voide'.

8 That is, to inflame us to follow virtue's footsteps in our following lives. Q8 reads 'her' for 'our'.

9 The Christian age is taken to be the era of truth – cf. poem 33, line 4.

12 H reads 'deserve they monnis blame' for 'we led to vertues traine'.

14 H reads 'doo the' (i.e. thee) for 'they do'.

37

[Q1: 32] An English sonnet. A moral *exemplum*. H has a few insignificant variants. Sardanapalus was the mythical last king of Assyria, and a byword for debauchery: in the version of his story Surrey seems to be following, he burned down his own palace, killing himself and his wives. Surrey adds the motive of military defeat and martial disgrace, perhaps because such a motive had a personal resonance for him (see Introduction).

38

[Q1: 33] In poulter's measure. A very loose imitation of Horace, *Satires*, I. 1. AH (76) has one minor variant, noted below, and there is a version of the first twelve lines in BL MS Cotton Titus A. 24; there is a revised version, as 'A pleasant sweet song', in *Brittons Bowre of Delights* (1591), which breaks the lines in half to make the poem a song.

16 AH reads 'Jawes' for 'chewes'.

20 Lines of true belief are biblical verses.

39

[Q1: 34] Pentameter rhyming ABABABACDCDCDCDEE; one might call it an English sonnet with a hypertrophied third quatrain, and possibly a missing seventh line. A complaint. H has no significant variants. The title is a version of Psalm 119: 71. The poem was probably written during Surrey's imprisonment in the Tower of London before his execution (as his son Henry Howard, Earl of Northampton asserted in his *Dutiful Defence of the Royal Regimen of Women* (*c.* 1559)); if so, it was Surrey's last work.

6   Surrey's revenge is his ability to endure his imprisonment patiently (doing away with his sufferings, which were all in the anticipation of trouble), not in the punishment itself.

9   Cf. Virgil, *Aeneid*, I. 203–4: 'revocate animos maestumque timorem / mittite' [recall your spirits and banish sad fear].

12   Cf. Shakespeare, Sonnet 62, line 9.

15–17   The blood so often shed for Britain's sake is presumably the blood of the Howard family in Surrey himself; the identity of the cowardly wretch spilling it is obscure, but presumably the line refers to one of the poet's enemies.

40

[Q1: 35] Pentameter Venus and Adonis stanza. An epigram. There are no extant MS versions. The positioning after poem 39 may imply that the poem was also written in Surrey's last imprisonment, and it draws a clearer moral lesson than its printed precursor. The allusion to a poem of Wyatt's written in prison would support this possibility.

1   Probably addressed to Thomas Radcliffe, Earl of Sussex (1526/7–83), who participated with Surrey in the French war of 1544.

5   Probably refers to Ecclesiasticus 27: 21, thought at the time to have been written by Solomon.

6   Mainly referring to poem 126, line 8, but Wyatt also says something similar at poem 105, line 14.

41

[Q1: 36] A sonnet with the scheme ABABABABACACCC. A complaint. There are no extant MS versions. The poem may well have been written to Surrey's wife.

10   The guide is probably faith.

12   Surrey was governor of Boulogne from September 1545 to
            March 1546.

WYATT

Where similar variant readings for poems 42–137 are found in E and
AH, E's spelling is given unless otherwise indicated.

42

[Q1: 37] A sonnet in the form ABBAABBACDCCDD. Like poem 6,
it is a translation of Petrarch, *Rime*, 140. A love complaint. The poem
also appears in E (4) and AH (99), with minor variations. The E text
is annotated by Grimald. Harrier notes that Tottel, though not AH,
maintains most of Grimald's medial and terminal punctuation,
although exactly the same marks are not used. In more general terms
he notes that AH responded to Grimald's spellings but not his punctu-
ation (p. 111).

1   For 'I', E has 'doeth'. By this change Tottel's editor has changed
            the meaning of the verb from 'live' to 'give shelter to'.

4   E and AH read 'spreding' for 'displaying'.

5   E has 'lerneth' where the *Miscellany* and AH have 'learns';
            interestingly, Grimald's hand corrects E to 'lerns', presum-
            ably the basis for the AH and *Miscellany* readings.

6   AH also reads 'willes', making the verb parallel with
            'learns' as in Petrarch, where the lady teaches and wishes. E
            reads 'will', making the verb parallel with 'love' and 'suffer'
            as an action performed by the lover. Grimald, however,
            emended E to 'wills', which was presumably the source of
            the AH and *Miscellany* readings.

9   E and AH have 'Wherewithall unto' where the *Miscellany*,
            reiterating the subject of the verb, has 'Wherwith love to'.

43

[Q1: 38] A sonnet with the scheme ABBAABBACDDCEE. Its source
is Petrarch, *Rime*, 82. A love complaint. The poem also appears in AH
(101) and E (9) with minor variations, noted below. Grimald has anno-
tated E. Hughey notes: 'On comparing *AH* we find that it never agrees

with the readings peculiar to *TM*, and that it differs from *E* only in line
1 by a transference of "yet," a change which lessens the emphatic use
of the word.' She also notes that AH adopts Grimald's spelling correc-
tions in lines 1, 8–10, 13 and 14, but not his punctuation.

1   The phrase 'your love' perhaps means 'my love for you'.
           Word-order and metre are very fluid in this line; in AH it
           appears as 'Was I never of your love yet greevid', and in E,
           'Was I never yet of your love greved'; 'greevid' and 'agreved'
           are metrically rather than semantically distinct.

6–11   The punctuation is tricky, as line 8 can be interpreted as
           belonging to the lines either preceding or following it. Here
           it is punctuated to belong with lines 9–11, with the mean-
           ing 'If a heart of amorous faith and will raised from the
           unhappy bones by great sighs can content your mind then
           may it please you to do relief to that heart'. The scribes
           who copied the poem in AH and E do not include any
           punctuation, but Grimald's hand has added punctuation to
           E, inserting a colon at the end of line 6, a comma after
           'cause' in line 7, a colon after 'bonys' in line 8, and a full
           stop at the end of line 8. This groups line 8 with lines 6–7,
           with the sense 'Nor will I have your name fixed fast on my
           tombstone [identifying you] as the cruel cause [of my
           death], [the person] who hastened my spirit away early
           from the unhappy bones, moved by great sighs'. The first
           edition of the *Miscellany* places full stops at the end of lines
           7 and 8, which reflects the difficulty but does not propose
           a solution.

7   E and AH read 'the' for 'my'.

10   E reads 'may content you' for 'Content your minde'; the
           Miscellany's editor contrasts the speaker's heart and the
           lady's mind.

13   E and AH read 'disdain' for 'wrath'; Grimald's hand adds a
           colon after the word in E, a punctuation mark which is
           transferred to the *Miscellany*.

44

[Q1: 39] A sonnet with the scheme ABBAABBACDDCEE. A love
complaint and repudiation of love. The poem appears in E (16), in
two versions in AH (98 and 108), D and B, with minor variations, the

most notable in D. Hughey notes that the first line of AH 98 may be derived from D.

1–4   At play here are the associations of file with polish, sharpness and defilement, suggesting the brilliance, danger and defilement of courtliness; this would become a favourite trope of Spenser's: e.g. *Colin Clouts Come Home Againe*, line 701.

1   E reads 'There Was never ffile half so well filed'.

7   D reads 'My little perceiving' for 'Of my last yeres'; 'last' is also found in AH 98, but it appears as 'lost' in E and AH 108; and also in other editions of the *Miscellany*. Hughey writes: 'The first edition of *TM* has one variant from *AH*: line 7, laste] lost; but in the second and succeeding editions the line agrees with *AH*. Since "laste" is a poor reading, suggesting a printer's mistake, it is reasonable to believe that No. 98 may have been copied from the printed version.'

8   AH 98, like the *Miscellany*, reads 'misguided'; D reads 'guiled', and both E and AH 108 read 'guyded'.

10   Q8 omits 'is'.

13–14   D reads '& gylys Reward is small trust for euer, / gyle begyld shuld be blamyd neuer'.

45

[Q1: 40] A sonnet with the scheme ABBAABBACDDCEE. A love complaint. The poem is loosely based on Petrarch, *Rime*, 258. Wyatt's first lines are similar to Petrarch's, but the images of the sun, thunder and lightning from line 5 onwards are original to Wyatt. Muir and Thomson argue that Wyatt also draws on Vellutello's commentary on Petrarch. The poem appears in E (47), AH (118) and D, the most important variants being noted below.

1–2   Cf. Dante, *La Vita Nuova*, XIX. 68–71. The idea of eyes inflicting pain is a common and long-standing one; cf. *Troilus and Criseyde*, I. 304–7.

3   AH and E read 'prest' for 'perst'.

10   AH and E read 'erryng' for 'crying'.

14   AH, E and D read 'nay' for 'noyse'.

46

[Q1: 41] A sonnet with the scheme ABBABBAACDDCEE, the anomaly in the second quatrain caused by Tottel's shift of the line which appears here as line 8, but in other versions as line 5. The source of the poem is Petrarch, *Rime*, 169. A love complaint. The poem appears in E (56), AH (121) and D.

2	The phrase 'by well assured mone' is difficult; Muir and Thomson cite Otto Hietsch's suggestion that 'assured' should read 'assurded', a word meaning 'break out' or 'burst forth', otherwise attested only once, in Skelton's 'Garlande or Chapelet of Laurell', line 302.
7	Q1 reads 'lockyng' for 'lacking', the latter being the form of E, AH and D.
8	AH and E read 'She fleith as fast' for 'So fleeth she'. Q8 reads 'Go' for 'So'.
9	The scribal copy of the poem in E reads 'that scornefull' for 'disdainfull', but Wyatt's hand has revised it to 'disdaynfull' in the only emendation to this poem in his hand. D reads 'skornfull'.
10	AH and E read 'pitie' for 'ruth'.
12	AH and E read 'and therewithall bolded I seke the way how'.
13	E reads 'to utter the smert that I suffre within'.

47

[Q1: 42] A sonnet with the scheme ABBAACCADEEDFF, the irregularity of the octave caused by changes in rhyme-words made by Tottel's editor. Its source may be Marcello Filosseno's strambotto beginning 'Pareami in questa mocte esser contento'; this is reproduced in Muir and Thomson. As Rebholz points out, however, dream poems are found in Petrarch. A love complaint/dream vision. The poem is found in E (81) and AH (122) with minor variants. This is a difficult poem about an erotic dream, and it seems Tottel emended it to try to make the sense clearer (see details below). Lines 1–4 describe the lover's dream; 5–8 appear to refer to the lover's state when awakened, and 9–13 contrast the two states and mourn the loss of the dream and the return to the torment of desire and lack.

4	Line omitted in Q8.
5	The tone appears to be highly sarcastic here; the dream

does not bring his lady to him (whether in the form of a dream or in reality is unclear), because after much consideration, it has decided that it would be far too 'daungerous' for her to be in his arms. For similar irony, cf. poem 57, line 18.

6–7   Both of the rhyme-words are different here from their counterparts in E and AH, which have 'mew' (i.e. cage) for 'seas' and 'to renew' for 'tencrease'. The version of the poem in the *Miscellany* may be meant to develop the idea suggested by 'tempest' (line 8), envisaging the speaker as being at sea and grateful for the sake of her safety that his lady is not with him.

8   AH and E read 'succour to enbrace' for 'delight timbrace'.

12   AH and E read 'retorning' for 'But thus returne'.

48

[Q1: 43] A sonnet with the scheme ABBAABBABCBCBB. A love complaint. Also found in E (98) and AH (123) with minor, mainly metrical, variants and the omission of line 6 from AH. The poem echoes Chaucer at several points. Turberville produced a greatly extended version of this poem, entitled 'The Lover hoping in May to have had redresse of his woes . . . bewailes his cruell hap' (*Epitaphes* (1567), pp. 195–8).

2   Cf. Chaucer, 'The Complaint unto Pity', line 39.

3   Cf. Chaucer, *The Canterbury Tales*, I. 1042.

4   Cf. Chaucer, *Troilus and Criseyde*, II. 111–12.

6   E reads 'the happs most vnhappy' for 'my mishappes unhappy'. May did seem to be an unlucky month for Wyatt himself; in May 1534 he was imprisoned for fighting in the streets, and in May 1536 he was imprisoned again as a result of a quarrel with the Duke of Suffolk. In the same month Anne Boleyn was executed. It may also have been in May, in 1527, when he returned from Italy, that he discovered the King's interest in Anne Boleyn.

8   Cf. Chaucer, *Troilus and Criseyde*, I. 518.

9   'Stephan' (unclear in E, but probably 'Sephame'; 'Sephances' in AH) is presumably someone who cast horoscopes. An Edward Sephame cast a horoscope for Edward VI (Muir and Thomson).

12   AH and E read 'liff' for 'wittes'.

49

[Q1: 44] A sonnet with the scheme ABBAABBACDCDEE. It was probably suggested by Petrarch, *Rime*, 224. The poems are not very similar; most strikingly, where Wyatt writes of the replacement of one lady by another, there is only one lady in Petrarch's poem. A love complaint. Wyatt's poem also appears in E (103) and AH (124). Turberville produced a version of this poem (*Epitaphes*, pp. 68–9).

1–4, 6   Puttenham quotes these lines, with some mistakes, as an example of '*Hirmos*, or the Long Loose', commenting 'all the whole sence of the ditty is suspended till ye come to the last three words, "then do I love againe," which finisheth the song with a full and perfect sense' (pp. 260–61). Petrarch's poem is a much more extended version of the figure, with 'the whole sense of the ditty' suspended until line 13.

5   'To hast to slake my passe lesse or more' in E and AH.

6   AH and E read 'by' for 'Be'.

8–9   Brunet is probably Anne Boleyn (see E. K. Chambers, *Sir Thomas Wyatt and Some Collected Studies* (London: Sidgwick & Jackson, 1933), p. 139, for evidence). Candidates for the identity of Phillis include Mary, Duchess of Richmond, Surrey's sister, and Elizabeth Darrell, Wyatt's mistress (see Chambers for discussion). The scribal copy of the poem in E records line 8 as 'her that ded set our country in a rore', but this is altered in Wyatt's hand to 'brunet that set my welth in suche a rore', which Rebholz argues 'may have been an attempt to obscure the identification', and Thomson argues that the change was made 'as though to cover up Anne's tracks' (Thomson). The line appears in AH in the revised form.

11–14   Rebholz argues that the theological metaphor here contains a distinctively Protestant take on grace; Phillis's 'help' is given regardless of the worthlessness of the one who receives it.

50

[Q1: 45] A sonnet with the scheme ABBAABBACDDCEE. Its source is Petrarch, *Rime*, 102, which it follows closely in content and structure. A complaint, not necessarily about love. The poem also appears in E (3), D and *NA*. The emendations Grimald made to the punctuation in E have generally persisted into the *Miscellany*, although exactly the same marks are not used. A different translation of the same Petrarch sonnet is found in H (reproduced by Rollins).

1–4	'the traitour of Egipt' is the Egyptian King Ptolemy, who had Pompey killed on his arrival in Egypt. According to Plutarch, Julius Caesar wept when Pompey's head was sent to him.
5	D reads 'ded flitt' for 'him out shit'; cf. Spenser, *Colin Clouts Come Home Againe*, line 709.
6–8	These lines are substantively different in D: 'from him and to Rome ded her whele relent / ded laugh among thim whom tearis had besprent / her cruell dispight inwardelye to shitt'.
13	Both the *Miscellany* and D contain the phrase 'I have none other way', but the original scribal copy of the poem in E reads 'I have not her way'. Grimald's hand has crossed out 'not her' and written 'nother' above it, and the *Miscellany* retains the spirit of this with 'none other'. Harrier comments: 'Wyatt is relating the political psychology of this sonnet to his amorous experiences, but Tottel apparently found the association unacceptable, as did those hands that produced the highly corrupted version in D.'

51

[Q1: 46] A sonnet with the scheme ABBAABBACDDCEE. No source is known. A promise of fidelity. Appears in E (10), D and AH (102).

2–3	Cf. the proverbs 'A wise man ought not to be ashamed to change his purpose' and 'A wise man changes his mind, a fool never will' (Tilley M431 and M420).
3	AH has 'purpose', as here, but E has 'propose'.
13	AH reads 'now' for 'nor', unlike the *Miscellany* and E.

52

[Q1: 47] A sonnet with the scheme ABBAABBACDDCEE. Its source is Petrarch, *Rime*, 19. A love complaint. The poem appears in E (24) and AH (109); Harrier notes that in substance AH is a perfect copy of E. A different translation of the same Petrarch sonnet occurs in H, f.

45^v (reproduced by Rollins); Puttenham describes the poem as 'very well Englished' (p. 327) – he then gives his own version.

1–2   Rebholz suggests this may be a proverbial reference to the eagle, as Tilley E3 'Only the eagle can gaze at the sun'.

1   Q8 reads 'no' for 'so'.

53

[Q1: 48] A sonnet with the scheme ABBAABBACDDCEE. Its source is Petrarch, *Rime*, 49. A love complaint. The poem appears in E (25) and AH (110). Tottel's editor has made emendations to the ends of lines 6 and 7 which mean they potentially form a separate rhyme group independent of the B-rhymes in the first half of the octave; see note to 6–7 below. Hughey comments: 'Evidently the compiler of *AH* did not understand the sense in lines 3 and 14 and so altered the lines in such a way as to destroy the point. In both lines, however, *TM* conveys the sense of *E*.' The poem is imitated by Turberville, *Epitaphes*, pp. 181–2.

3   AH reads 'right well' for 'to yl'; E reads 'right ill'.

6–7   The word 'afraied' appears in E as 'aferd', while line 7 appears there as 'alway moost cold & if thou speke towerd'. A later hand has corrected 'towerd' to 'kowerd'. AH also has 'a feard' for 'afraied', but line 7 reads 'alwaye moste colde and if thow speake a worde'.

8   In E the line reads 'it is as in dreme vnperfaict & lame'.

14   AH reads 'Love' for 'loke'.

54

[Q1: 49] A sonnet with the scheme ABBAABBACDDCEE. Its source is Petrarch, *Rime*, 134:

> Pace non trovo et non ò da far guerra,
> e temo et spero, et ardo et son un ghiaccio,
> et volo sopra 'l cielo et giaccio in terra,
> et nulla stringo et tutto 'l mondo abbraccio.
>
> Tal m' à in pregion che non m' apre né serra,
> né per suo mi riten né scioglie il laccio,
> et non m' ancide Amore et non mi sferra,
> né mi vuol vivo né mi trae d' impaccio.

Veggio senza occhi, et non ò lingua et grido,
et bramo di perir et cheggio aita,
et ò in odio me stesso et amo altrui.

Pascomi di dolor, piagendo rido,
egualmente mi spiace morte et vita.
In questo stato son, Donna, per vui.

[I find no peace and don't look to make war; I fear and hope, I burn and am ice, I fly above the sky and lie on the ground; I hold on to nothing and embrace the whole world. Such a person as neither opens nor locks has me in prison, and neither keeps me for his own or loosens my bonds; Love neither kills me nor unchains me, neither wants me to live nor releases me from the knot. I see without eyes, I have no tongue but cry out; I long to die and ask for help; I hold myself hateful and love another. I feed on pain, weeping I laugh; life and death are equally despicable to me. I am in this state, Lady, because of you].

Petrarch's sonnet is also the source of 261 below. The paradoxes described are highly characteristic of both Petrarch and Wyatt. A love complaint. The poem appears in E (26), D, H and NA.

1–2	Puttenham slightly misquotes these lines as an example of monosyllabic iambic verse (p. 208).
3	Where the *Miscellany* has 'flye aloft', E reads 'fley above the wynde', and D 'flye aboute the heaven'.
4	The word 'season' is probably a mistake for 'seize on', which makes more sense here, but 'seson' is also the form found in E. Petrarch has 'abbraccio', meaning 'embrace'.
10	E reads 'desire' for 'wish'.
11	H reads 'I have' for 'I hate'.
13	E reads 'likewise' for 'Lo, thus'. D and H agree with the *Miscellany* in reading 'death and life', but E has 'lyff and deth'. Since this is an easier reading and disrupts the rhyme-scheme, it is probably a mistake in E. H has 'pleaseth' for 'displeaseth'.
14	H reads 'my gryeff' for 'this strife'.

55

[Q1: 50] A sonnet with the scheme ABBAABBACDDCEE; the A and B rhymes are close to each other, sharing the same consonant.

The source is Petrarch, *Rime*, 189. A love complaint. The poem
appears in E (28) and AH (112). As Hughey comments: 'The *AH* ver-
sion is clearly copied from *E*, with the changes in lines 6 and 8 made
later.'

3   AH and E read 'myn ennemy' for 'my fo'.

4   That is, love ('my lord').

5   E reads 'owre', i.e. 'oar' for the *Miscellany*'s and AH's
           'houre'. Muir and Thomson cite E. M. W. Tillyard's para-
           phrase 'Every oar is a thought ready to think that death is a
           small matter in this extremity'. E's reading is supported by
           the fact that 'oar' translates 'remo' in line 5 of the source.

6   In AH, the word 'light' is crossed through and replaced
           with 'lif'. E reads 'light'.

8   E reads 'sight*es*' for 'sighes', though that may be a variant
           spelling for the same word; AH has 'sightes' crossed out
           and replaced with 'sighes' above.

56

[Q1: 51] A sonnet with the scheme ABBAABBACDDCEE. Its source
is Petrarch, *Rime*, 173. A love complaint. The poem appears in E (29)
and AH (113). Hughey comments that AH was clearly taken from E
despite the differences in lines 1, 3 and 6. She notes that in line 10, 'the
AH copyist has followed the senseless "though" of *E*, which should
have been written "thought." The *TM* reviser has attempted to bring
meaning to the line. The *AH* copyist misunderstood "Auysing," i.e.,
gazing at, in line 1 of *E*, and curiously has made less smooth the metre
of line 3. It is interesting to notice that *TM* agrees with *E* against *AH*,
although *TM* has many other variants from *E*.'

1   E also begins 'Auysing', but AH has 'Advysing'.

2   By 'he' Love is meant, who is living in the lady's eyes, but
           makes the lover's eyes wet. According to Rebholz, the idea
           of Cupid living in eyes is derived from Anacreon. Q8 reads
           'wasteth' for 'washeth'.

10   In E and AH, this reads 'in frossen though [an error for
           'thought'] nowe and nowe it stondeth in flame'.

11   E and AH have 'misery and welth' for 'wo and wealth'.

57

[Q1: 52] A ballade in rhyme royal stanzas. A love complaint. It appears in E (37) and D. There is no specific source, although some details may be derived from Ovid, *Amores*, I. 5. Muir and Thomson comment on the 'numerous disastrous improvements' made by Tottel's editor in this poem.

10   Q8 reads the ambiguous 'thine' for 'thynne'.

17   E reads 'straunge' for 'bitter'.

19   The word 'newfanglenesse' is favoured by Chaucer when describing love of novelty; see e.g. *Anelida and Arcite*, line 141.

20   E reads 'so kyndely' for 'unkindly so', giving a sarcastic edge. The word 'kind' refers to thoughtfulness and consideration, but the sense of natural/unnatural behaviour is also in play. D reads 'so gentillye'.

21   In E, the line reads 'I would fain knowe what she hath deserued'.

58

[Q1: 53] Tetrameter; in quatrains with alternating rhymes. This is a translation of a madrigal by Dragonetto Bonifacio, first printed *c.* 1535. Muir and Thomson reproduce the source. A promise of fidelity. The poem appears in E (34) and B. A poem answering this one (starting 'Of few wourdes sir you seme to be') appears in E and B, and is reproduced by Harrier and by Muir and Thomson. It is probably not by Wyatt, although in B, as Harrier notes, the original poem (beginning 'Mestris what nedis' in B) and the answer are copied in the same hand. Q8 reads 'The' for 'To a' in the title.

7   E reads 'any pitie' for 'pity or ruth'.

9   Line omitted in Q8.

59

[Q1: 54] One stanza of ottava rima. The source is a strambotto by Serafino; it is reproduced by Muir and Thomson. An apology to a lady. It appears in E (44) and AH (103); in E the poem was revised twice by Wyatt and twice by other hands. Hughey comments, '*AH* incorporates all revisions in *E* and is clearly copied directly from it.

TM appears to be printed from a copy made from the *E* MS., for some of Wyatt's corrections are included and that of the second corrector in line 2, but *TM* shows additional editorial revision. The texts of the three versions of this little poem offer us a rare and instructive lesson in sixteenth-century textual criticism, for it is not often that we have such an admirable opportunity to check versions with a manuscript showing both authorial and editorial revision.'

1	In E 'stealing' appears as 'robbing', but is altered by Wyatt to 'stelyng', which is how it appears in AH.
4	Tottel's editor is responsible for the double negative; in E the line is 'that by no meanes it may be amended' and in AH 'that by no meanes the matter maybe mendid'.
5	In E this line originally reads 'then to revenge you then and sure ye shall not mysse', but Wyatt revises it to 'then revenge you and the next way is this', which is how it appears in AH.
6	This is a much-remoulded line: it originally appears in E as 'to have my liff with an othr ended', but Wyatt corrects it to 'an othr kysse shall have my liffe endid'; what is probably a different hand has added 'through' and another word which may be 'amysse' between 'liffe' and 'endid'. In AH it appears as 'an other kisse shall haue my lief throughe endid'.
7–8	According to Rebholz, it was a neo-Platonic belief that souls came up to the mouth to be united with another soul through a kiss; it was also thought that devils could suck out the soul through the mouth; cf. Marlowe, *Doctor Faustus*, V. i. 94 (A Text).

60

[Q1: 55] In ottava rima. A celebration of success in love. The poem is also found in E (46), D, H and *NA*. The figure of stepping on a snake was a common one, found e.g. in *Aeneid*, II. 378–81. As Rollins notes, when translating that passage, Surrey draws on this poem of Wyatt. Harrier comments that the E text of this poem 'is one of the most interesting for studying Wyatt's relation to his copyist'.

4	The *Miscellany* follows E substantively in 'As jealous despite did', but D has 'As I Alous dyspyte Dyd', and H 'as did gelosy'.

61

[Q1: 56] In ottava rima. Its source is a strambotto by Serafino, which is reproduced by Muir and Thomson. An epigram on love. It also appears in E (48) and AH (126). Turberville produced an extended version of the poem in *Epitaphes*, pp. 179–80, with the title 'To a Gentlewoman from whome he tooke a Ring'.

1   E has 'threning' for 'threatning', which Rebholz deduces is formed from the noun 'threne' (dirge), yielding the sense 'lamenting'; 'threning' may simply be a mistake, however. AH has 'threatning', like the *Miscellany*.

5   Interestingly, 'finde' reads 'meit' in E and AH, a less satisfactory rhyme.

7   AH and E read 'she toke from me an hert' for 'She reft my hart'.

62

[Q1: 57] A rhyme royal stanza, but the B and C rhymes are the same. A poem on friendship. The poem is also found in E (49) and AH (119). Harrier remarks that the punctuation marks in E recall the practices of Grimald. In AH, the poem runs directly on to the poem which follows it with no break; this second poem appears in the *Miscellany* as 118.

2   Proverbial; Tilley B17, 'To claw one by the back'. The original text in E has 'by the back', as in Tottel, but 'the' has been corrected to 'thy', which is what appears in AH.

4   E and AH have 'though they' for 'Though thee'; both of these readings, which have the same gist, make more sense than 'Thought he', which appears in the first edition of the *Miscellany*, and is apparently a misprint.

5   Proverbial; see Tilley V68 'To nourish a viper (snake) in one's bosom' and cf. Chaucer, *The Canterbury Tales*, III. 1992–5.

63

[Q1: 58] A ballade in rhyme royal stanzas; tetrameter. A love complaint? The poem also appears in E (21) and B. The title here is potentially misleading, as the poem is not necessarily about love.

5   E reads 'The wyndy wordes the Ies quaynt game'.

10   The word 'hase' is probably a shortened form of 'hazard', as
        Rebholz suggests, in spite of the fact that Wyatt does not use
        the word 'hazard' elsewhere. Nott argues that 'hase' is
        unlikely to mean 'has' (as Muir and Thomson suggest)
        because Wyatt does not use 'I has' elsewhere. Rebholz
        rejects Nott's own suggested emendation to 'halse' (embrace)
        on the grounds that it does not rhyme with 'mase'.

                                   64

[Q1: 59] A ballade in rhyme royal stanzas; pentameter. Its source may
be a strambotto by Serafino (reproduced by Muir and Thomson). A
love complaint. It also appears in E (22) and D.

7   Q8 omits 'it'.

12   E reads 'to suffre' for 'I endure'.

14   D reads 'moving in the' for 'complaynyng in their'.

16   Q8 inserts 'els' after 'Or'.

18   For 'thus framed', E has 'this Ioyned', D has 'so clokid';
        D reads 'tygres' for 'stony'.

19   D reads 'so cruell' for 'cloked'.

20-21   Rebholz suggests: 'Wyatt probably intends an ironic theo-
        logical metaphor in the opposition of "grace" and "rewarded".
        The lover addresses the lady as the God who denies the sinner
        grace and treats him according to his merit – in this case,
        "rewarding" him with death. But the lover – despite the pos-
        ture of humility implicit in his definition of death as a
        "reward" for his merit – does not really think it an appropri-
        ate response to his conduct; and he thinks that, at the least, he
        should be granted grace. He is therefore judging this "God"
        as defective by both Catholic and Lutheran standards.'

                                   65

[Q1: 60] A ballade of tetrameter rhyme royal stanzas. A repudiation
of love? It also appears in E (23). The poem itself offers no evidence
that it is about love, despite the title it has been given here.

3-4   May recall Horace's *Odes*, III. 29, as Nott suggests.

5   Q8 omits 'the'.

20   E reads 'lapped' for 'wrapt', with a similar meaning.

66

[Q1: 61] In tetrameter in monorhymed quatrains. There are also internal rhymes binding couplets, e.g. lines 13–16 'paine'/'sustaine' and 'song'/'among'. Tottel's editor seems not to have noticed this, or else he thought it unimportant, as changes are made without regard to it; see note on line 4 below. A repudiation of love? The poem also appears in E (11). The poem need not be about love in spite of the title it has been given here.

1   E reads 'rayn' (reign) for 'hart'.

3   E reads 'yet shall surete' for 'and wofully'.

4   E reads 'conduyt my thoght of Ioyes nede'; this sustains the
           internal rhyme, with 'thoght' rhyming with 'bought' in line
           3. The edit in the *Miscellany* disrupts the internal rhyme-
           scheme.

13–14   An instruction to his heart to rejoice that it can experience
           both a part of joy (at no longer being enslaved) and a part
           of pain (as a result of being without the pleasure, and of
           fearing recapture).

67

[Q1: 62] A ballade in rhyme royal stanzas. A love complaint. The source may be Petrarch, *Rime*, 234, but the resemblance is not very close. The poem appears in D. In E, reproduced by Harrier, there is a condensed eight-line version copied by Grimald underneath 'Who so list to hounte' (E 7):

> Too hiz bedde.
>
> O restfull place: reneewer of my smart:
> O laboorz salue: encreasing my sorowe:
> O bodyez eaze: o troobler of my hart:
> Peazer of mynde: of myne unquyet fo:
> Refuge of payene: remembrer of my wo:
> Of care coomefort: where I dispayer my part:
> The place of slepe: wherin, I doo but wake:
> Bysprent with tearez, my bedde, I thee forsake[.]

Turberville produced an expanded version of this poem, 'The Lover to his carefull bed, declaring his restlesse state' (*Epitaphes*, pp. 62–4).

1–7   Puttenham gives these lines, with some mistakes, as an
           example of '*Hirmos*, or the Long Loose', commenting

'Ye see here how ye can gather no perfection of sense in all this ditty till ye come to the last verse' (p. 260).

19   In D, the line is 'Yet that I gave I cannot call agayn'.

68

[Q1: 63] In ottava rima. There are analogues to this poem, detailed in Rollins and Muir and Thomson, but none of them is necessarily a source, and the likening of love to a river was conventional in Italian. An epigram on love. The poem is found in E (101) in Wyatt's holograph, and in B.

6   Q8 reads 'course' for 'sourse'.

7–8   Cf. Chaucer, *Parliament of Fowls*, line 140, 'Th'eschewing is only the remedye'. The original lines in E are 'his rayne rage then botythe no deny / the first estew is only remedy', edited by Wyatt to 'his rayne is rage resistans vaylyth none / the first estew is remedy alone'. Rebholz suggests Wyatt made this revision to improve the rhyme.

69

[Q1: 64] In rhyme royal stanzas. The source of the poem is a *canzone* by Petrarch, *Rime*, 360, but the form is entirely different. Muir and Thomson make the interesting suggestion that Wyatt's use of rhyme royal here 'may have been suggested by Chaucer's use of it in poems . . . based on Italian sources'. Rebholz includes detailed consideration of source- and target-texts in his notes. A love complaint. The poem appears in E (8) and AH (144), but E lacks lines 1–21 because pages are missing from the MS, and AH lacks line 80 onwards, also because of missing pages. Grimald intervened extensively in the E text, particularly in its punctuation, and some of these emendations survive into the *Miscellany*, but in many cases the *Miscellany*'s readings reflect readings in AH and are unaffected by Grimald's emendations. Some examples are given below, but for a complete list, see Harrier. AH and the *Miscellany* are closely related in this poem, while the relationships with E are more distant.

1–2   'Mine old dere enmy' is Love, and 'that Quene' is Reason.

1   Puttenham quotes this line, giving the phrase 'dear enemy' as an example of a dactyl (p. 211).

8   Muir and Thomson state that '[a]ccording to Vellutello's note on the original, while the right foot is reason, the left is sense or appetite'.

24   E reads 'swetenes' for 'semblance'. The idea of the world turning as a ball is proverbial; see Tilley W901, 'The world is round (turns as a ball)'.

26   E reads 'ataced' for 'araced', which is the reading of AH as well as the *Miscellany*.

29   E reads 'He hath made me regarde god muche lesse then I ought'. AH is closer to the *Miscellany*, but its punctuation is clearer: 'God made he me regard, lesse than I oughte'.

45   AH has 'through bitter passions', as here, but E has 'strait pressions'; this use of 'pressions' is the first recorded in *OED* – and the last until 1641. The *Miscellany* and AH favour a less exotic piece of vocabulary.

54   'Gods': 'goodenes' in E, emended to 'Godds' by Grimald. This emendation persists into AH. E has 'shake', emended to 'slake' by Grimald, as it appears in the *Miscellany* and in AH.

55   AH has 'note they this', as here; it appears in E as 'not this', with a different meaning.

60–63 In E, these lines read:

> by decept and by force over my sprites
> he is rueler and syns there never bell strikes
> where I ame that I here not my playntes to renew
> and he himself he knoweth that that I say is true

AH has:

> by guyle and force, over my thralled sprites
> He is Ruler/ syns whiche bell never strykes
> That I heare not, as sownding to renewe
> My playntes/ hym self, he knowes, that I say true[.]

71–2   In E, Grimald made several alterations to this line which persist into the *Miscellany*. In line 71, he re-spells E's 'reprouff' as 'reproofe'. Line 72 reads in E: 'thus he began here lady thothr part', which Grimald emends to: 'thus he began: Heare, Lady, thoother part:'. In AH, some of these emendations survive: 'This he began/ Heare Ladye, thother parte'.

76   Q8 reads 'felleth' for 'selleth'.

79   Q1 differed from the MS by ending this line with 'gain', which disrupts the rhyme scheme of the stanza into AAAB-BCC; but it was changed back for Q2.

85   'Atride': Agamemnon, son of Atreus; leader of the Greek army in the Trojan War.

86   Hannibal was leader of the Carthaginians fighting against Rome in the Second Punic War.

87   Achilles, the star of the Greek army in the Trojan War, and the focus of Homer's *Iliad*.

88   Scipio Africanus conquered Spain and led the Romans to victory in the Second Punic War, defeating Hannibal in Africa (hence Africanus); as Thomson points out, Scipio is not directly mentioned in Petrarch's *Rime* 360, but is mentioned in Vellutello's commentary on that poem (Thomson, p. 193).

89–90   E has 'vertue' instead of 'honour' in line 89, and 'hono' instead of 'actes' in line 90; Q1 reads 'honor' for 'actes' in line 89 and 'lift them up' for 'bring them' in line 90.

94   E reads 'the mone was never' for 'sunne yet never was'.

108   E reads 'sweter then for to inIoye eny othr in all'.

109   A challenge to a tranche of proverbs like Tilley T494, 'Such as the tree is such the fruit'; S209, 'He that sows good seed shall reap good corn'; 'Good fruit of a good tree', F777, etc.

111–12 'To nourish a viper in one's bosom' is proverbial; see Tilley V68. E has 'unger my wyng', emended by Grimald to 'under my wyng:'.

124   Cf. Tilley B424.

125   E reads 'pleasur' for 'ease'.

126   E reads 'remayn' for 'his gain'.

129–30 In E, 'if he would to higher / Then mortal thinges' reads 'if he would farther / by mortall thinges', suggesting in a Platonic manner that one must reach the heavens by contemplation of earthly things.

138   E reads 'me' for 'once'.

139   E reads 'streight' for 'ayen'.

140   The lover may have been deprived of the lady by death, because her value ('price') is too high for him, or because God, the one of 'more worth than thou', has won her by his greater power and goodness, rewarding her with 'price'. Alternatively, the 'price' may refer to the amount paid for

the lady by a very wealthy man, or indeed signify the wealthy man himself. It has been suggested that Henry VIII is 'Price' and has taken Anne Boleyn the lady (see Herbert Howarth, 'Wyatt, Spenser and the Canzone', *Italica*, 41 (1964), pp. 80–81). In E, the line appears as 'not I quoth he but price that is well worth', which does not fit the rhyme-scheme.

145   Cf. Surrey's *Aeneid*, II. 1: 'They whisted all'. E reads 'after thissaid' for 'at the whisted'.

147   Cf. the deferred resolution in Chaucer's *Parliament of Fowls*, lines 648–65. The formel is allowed to put off for a year her decision about which lover to take, despite Nature's advice, 'If I were Reason, thanne wolde I / Conseyle yow the royal tercel take' (lines 632–3).

70

[Q1: 65] Trimeter; in eight-line stanzas rhymed ABABACAC (presented in the *Miscellany* and in E as four-line stanzas). A love complaint. Also found in E (52), D, *NA* and V3. A marginal annotation in a later edition of the *Miscellany* reads '& it semeth hir name was Souch, or Chaunce' (Rollins). The placement of the word in parentheses throughout the poem suggests the editor considered it to be a proper noun (parentheses were the equivalent of quotation marks in the sixteenth century); in E neither parentheses nor initial capitals are used, and the word appears simply as 'such'. 'Souche' may refer to Mary Souche who was a maid of honour of Jane Seymour.

17–20   Proverbial (Tilley M180).

29   'Souche' was inserted into E later; 'It is impossible to tell whether this insertion came before or after T gave the word topical value as a play on a mistress' name' (Harrier, p. 144).

71

[Q1: 66] In tetrameter quatrains with alternating rhyme. The opening may have been suggested by a poem by Giusto de' Conti (printed 1531); this is reproduced by Muir and Thomson. A love complaint. The poem also appears in E (53) and AH (135). In E it has corrections by Wyatt and by the scribe, and Wyatt's hand has added the tag 'podra esser che no es' to the end of the poem. Several scribal emendations to

E bring the text closer to Tottel's (see notes to lines 29, 34, 37, 39, 41 below); it is unclear whether these influenced Tottel's editor, or whether they were transferred from the *Miscellany* to E at a later point.

8	A proverbial idea; cf. Tilley T301, 'In time of prosperity friends will be plenty, in time of adversity not one among twenty'.
10	Proverbial; see Tilley W831, 'Words and feathers the wind carries away'.
12	E reads 'all' for 'still'.
13	Q8 reads 'how' for 'now'.
14	Wyatt's hand adds 'rue' to the line in E.
24	As the line states, 'Like will to like' is proverbial; see Tilley L286.
29	E reads 'your owne' for 'her, of'. A scribe's hand corrects 'your owne cruelnes' to 'hir of cruelnes', as found in the *Miscellany*. AH has 'And you withe [*blank*] of crewelnes'.
34	In E, a scribe's hand corrects 'where your' to 'where is your', as found in the *Miscellany* and AH.
37	In E, a scribe's hand corrects 'But forbicause' to 'But synce somuche', as found in the *Miscellany* and AH.
38, 40	Where the *Miscellany* repeats the word 'wretched', E and AH have 'very' at line 40 (perhaps a mistake for or a spelling of 'wery').
39	In E, a scribe's hand corrects 'trouth shall' to 'trouth naught shall', similar to the readings of the *Miscellany* and AH.

72

[Q1: 67] Ottava rima. Analogues/possible sources include a dizaine by Maurice Scève (reproduced by Muir and Thomson). An epigram on love. The poem also appears in E (54), AH (127) and D. In E, Wyatt annotated the poem on two separate occasions.

7	In E, the scribal copy of the poem has 'with her owne wepon did make her fynger blede', which Wyatt's hand emends to 'made her owne wepon do her fynger blede', as found in the *Miscellany* and AH.

73

[Q1: 68] Ottava rima. On the same theme and with the same analogues as poem 72. An epigram on love. The poem also appears in E (42), AH (125) and D. In E, Wyatt's hand appears in two different inks, indicating he had examined the text at least twice.

1   'What man hath heard': 'who hath herd of' in E and AH. The change was presumably made in the interests of metrical regularity. In the scribal copy in E, 'crueltye' is Wyatt's emendation of 'tyranny'.

74

[Q1: 69] A sonnet with the curious scheme AABBAAABAAABBA, its strangeness related to the fact that Wyatt actually wrote the poem as a rondeau; it was the editor of the *Miscellany* who edited it into a sonnet-form (cf. poems 75, 107). Its source is Petrarch, *Rime*, 121, although Muir and Thomson suggest that the content may have reached Wyatt via a French rondeau translation of the Petrarch. The likeness between the poems is most marked at their beginnings and ends. A love complaint. The poem also appears in E (1) and D, as a rondeau in both instances. In E it has been extensively edited by Grimald, although he sticks with the rondeau form. The *Miscellany* is not affected by his doubling of vowels except in the case of 'the/thee', but his capitalization of the first letter in each line is reflected in Tottel. Grimald has edited for metre here. Here is the E version:

> Behold love thy power how she dispiseth
>   my great payne how litle she regardeth
>   the holy oth wherof she taketh no cure
>   broken she hath and yet she bideth sure
>   right at her ease & litle she dredeth
>   Wepened thou art and she vnarmed sitteth
>   to the disdaynfull her liff she ledeth
>   to me spitefull withoute cause or mesur
>   Behold love
>
> I ame in hold if pitie the meveth
>   goo bend thy bowe that stony hertes breketh
>   and with some stroke revenge the displeasur
>   of thee & him that sorrowe doeth endur
>   and as his lorde/ the lowly entreath
>   Behold love

1   The punctuation in this line follows Grimald's emendations
         of E.

2   D reads 'greef' for 'pain'.

3   Grimald emended 'taketh' to 'takes' in E.

4   The punctuation in this line follows Grimald's emendations
         of E.

75

[Q1: 70] A sonnet with the curious scheme AABBAAABBAABBA.
As with poems 74 and 107, this is a result of the *Miscellany*'s editor
rewriting what was originally a rondeau into sonnet-form. A love
complaint. The poem also appears in E (2), with considerable emend-
ation by Grimald, some of which persists into the *Miscellany*, and
some of which is ignored. See below for some examples. The spirit of
Grimald's heavy punctuation is maintained, but different marks are
often used in the *Miscellany*. The version in E is as follows:

> What vaileth trouth or by it to take payn
>   to stryve by stedfastnes for to be tayne
>   to be iuste & true & fle from dowblenes
>   sythens all alike where rueleth craftness
>   rewarded is boeth fals & plain
>   sonest he spedeth that moost can fain
>   true meanyng hert is had in disdayn
>   against deceipt & dowblenes
>   What vaileth trouth
>
>   Deceved is he by crafty trayn
>   that meaneth no gile and doeth remayn
>   within the trapp withoute redresse
>   but for to love lo suche a maisteres
>   whose crueltie nothing can refrayn
>   What vaileth trouth

2   In E a scribal hand emends 'to be tayne' to 'to attayne';
         Grimald inserts 'ob-' before 'tayne'. Tottel does not reflect
         Grimald's emendation.

4   In E a scribal hand (probably not Grimald's) emends 'syth-
         ens' to 'Sins,' similar to the reading of the *Miscellany*.

6   Grimald emends E's 'sonest he spedeth' to 'soonest hee
         speedes', similar to the reading of the *Miscellany*.

76

[Q1: 71] Ottava rima. An epigram on love. The poem also appears in E (59), AH (128), D and H78 (lines 1–4). The poem is often thought to be about the visit of Henry VIII and Anne Boleyn to Francis I at Calais in October 1532. See Rollins and Nott; Nott speculates that Wyatt was in Anne Boleyn's train.

4   AH and E read 'against my' for 'with willing'.

8   AH and E read 'all to torne' for 'onely torne'. The MS version of this line makes much better sense, as it contrasts the present experience of being caught in metaphorical briars with the past experience of being savagely torn by them. Tottel's version suggests that the past experience was more minor (*only* torn) than the present suffering, which does not fit with the rest of the poem. To be in the briars is a proverbial expression for being in danger (Tilley B672 and B673); here being '[m]eashed in the breers' suggests a forced and dangerous intimacy with someone no longer loved.

77

[Q1: 72] Ottava rima. The source is a strambotto by Serafino, reproduced by Muir and Thomson. An epigram. It has been associated with Wyatt's imprisonments by several critics; Nott considers it to be about his incarceration of 1541, and A. K. Foxwell (cited by Rollins) thinks it refers to the imprisonment of 1534. The poem is also found in E (60), D, H and *NA*.

1   Cf. the proverb 'He that falls today may be up again tomorrow' (Tilley F38). The original scribal version of the poem in E reads 'I ame not ded all though I had a fall'; Wyatt's hand emends this to 'He is not ded that somtyme hath a fall'. D and H both maintain 'I am'.

2   Proverbial; see Tilley C442, 'After black clouds clear weather'.

3–6   Quoted by Puttenham as an instance of '*Etiologia*, or the Reason-Renderer, or the Tell-Cause' whose role is 'first pointing then confirming by similitudes' (pp. 313–14).

5–6   Cf. Tilley S344, 'As broken a ship has come to land'.

7–8   Cf. Tilley W404, 'Willows are weak yet they bind other wood'.

78

[Q1: 73] Ottava rima. The source is a strambotto by Serafino, repro-
duced by Muir and Thomson. An epigram on love. The poem is also
found in E (61) and AH (129); it shows revisions by Wyatt in E, which
are incorporated by both AH and the *Miscellany*. Hughey comments,
'Exceptionally *AH* shows considerable variation from *E*, differing in
lines 2, 3, and 8 in ways that indicate an editorial hand, but these dif-
ferences do not accord with *TM*.' Turberville produced an expanded
version of this poem, in a piece beginning 'Lyke as the gunne'
(*Epitaphes*, p. 74).

1   The poem begins 'Like as the canon' in E, subsequently
        edited by Wyatt first to 'Like as the bombard', and then to
        'the furyous gonne'. Puttenham quotes this line as an
        instance of the use of one dactylic foot in a line – 'The furi-'
        being the supposed dactyl (p. 211).

3   The exact meanings of 'flame' and 'fire' are difficult here,
        as Rebholz discusses; he suggests that 'the burning gun-
        powder cannot eject that which is to be fired'. AH has
        'same' for 'flame', which simplifies the matter considerably
        (AH reads 'and it the same can not parte from the fyre').

6   E begins the line with 'which daily', emended in Wyatt's
        hand to 'whose flame', as it appears in AH and the *Miscel-
        lany*.

7   E begins the line with 'whose flame to open', emended in
        Wyatt's hand to 'wyche to let owt', as it appears in AH and
        the *Miscellany*.

8   'inward': particularly difficult to read in E; it may be either
        'inwhard' or 'now hard'. AH has 'so that of force'.

79

[Q1: 74] Stanza with the rhyme-scheme, ABABABABABCC, which
resembles an elongated ottava rima stanza. An apology to a lady. The
poem also appears in B. The twelve-line length is required by the fact
that the poem originally formed an acrostic, with the first letter of
each line spelling 'Anne Stanhope'. The editor of the *Miscellany* seems
not to have noticed this; he makes changes in lines 2–4 which destroy
the acrostic. The acrostic on a lady's name was common in English
verse. Anne Stanhope was married to Sir Michael Stanhope, a favour-
ite of Henry VIII.

1	Quoted by Puttenham as an instance of *Etiologia* (p. 314); cf. note on poem 77.
2	'Noone can hit proue, yet ye beleue hit treue' in B.
3	B reads 'Nor' for 'For'.
4	B reads 'Intendid I to be false or untrewe'. B's re-spelling of E's 'Entended' spoils the acrostic. The changes made by Tottel's editor were presumably on the grounds of metre.
6	B reads 'thyng' for 'word'.
12	B reads 'frynds' for 'frend'. The *Miscellany* refers to causing the lover pain, while B implies that the lady's poor judgement will pain her circle of friends. The *Miscellany*'s reading is more consistent with the rest of the poem.

80

[Q1: 75] A sonnet with the scheme ABBA[A]BBACDCDEE, lacking a line. A repudiation of love. It also appears in D, with some notable variants, including the *Miscellany*'s smoothing-out of the use of pronouns to avoid the shift after line 8 from 'she' to the direct address 'you'.

1	For 'to skorne', D has 'toke scorn', with a rather different meaning: D can be paraphrased 'My lady scorned to retain my service, in which I thought she was cruel', versus the *Miscellany*'s 'You were cruel to scorn my love and retain my service'.
2	D reads 'she' for 'you'.
3	There is a line missing after this line. It appears in D as 'To followe her wich causith all my payne'.
7	D reads 'her' for 'your'.
10	D reads 'the' (i.e. thee) for 'you'.

81

[Q1: 76] Monk's Tale stanza (rhyming ABABBCBC; the stanza is so named from Chaucer's use of it in 'The Monk's Tale'). No specific source is known for this poem, and neither is the poem found elsewhere. A promise of fidelity. There is an annotation on a copy of a later edition of the *Miscellany* objecting to the poem's title: 'or rather, A Lady embracinge a gentlemans loue' (Rollins).

2   If the speaker is indeed a woman (see above), the line might
            be paraphrased 'To take away the freedom of noble minds'.

4   Q8 reads 'fautllesse' for 'faultes'.

8   Q8 reads 'retain' for 'train'.

82

[Q1: 77] Trimeter quatrains with alternating rhymes, printed as eight-line stanzas. The poem may have been suggested by Petrarch, *Rime*, 153, although Wyatt translated it much more closely in poem 107. A love complaint. This poem also appears in B.

2   Q8 reads 'cares' for 'eares'.

4   B has 'Dothe' for the *Miscellany*'s 'Doe'. The *Miscellany*'s
            verb takes the ears of the lady as the subject, but there is no
            singular noun available as a subject for B's 'Dothe'; pre-
            sumably the lady herself is implied.

11   B reads 'And wythe tygers ful Longe'.

11–12   Cf. Virgil, *Aeneid*, IV. 366–7: 'perfide, sed duris genuit te
            cautibus horrens / Caucasus, Hyrcanaeque admorunt ubera
            tigres' [traitor, rugged Caucasus on his horrid rocks begot
            you, and Hyrcanian tigers suckled you].

13   Q8 reads 'not' for 'that'.

17–22   The ability of water to pierce stone is proverbial. See Tilley
            D618, 'Constant dropping will wear the stone'. Nott sug-
            gested that Wyatt may have derived the image from
            Serafino, and Muir and Thomson think it is from Petrarch,
            Rime, 265. 9–14.

18   B reads 'of' for 'or'.

22   B reads 'at Lengthe' for 'at last'.

24   B reads 'Cawse hir' for 'Winne'.

27   B reads 'it' for 'ye'; in the *Miscellany*, the speaker hopes his
            'plaintes' will be fruitful; in B he hopes his 'sute' will be.

32   B reads 'my' for 'a'.

83

[Q1: 78] Monk's Tale stanza, in trimeter. One might call this an extended epigram on love. The poem also appears in B; Rebholz considers that the *Miscellany*'s text is better than B, and is probably a copy of a text Wyatt had revised, but Harrier generally prefers B to Tottel because of Tottel's well-established habit of metrical intervention, which is noticeable here.

6 B reads 'Yet' for 'It'.

9–10 Perhaps related to the proverb 'Fire cannot be hidden in flax' (Tilley F255).

13–14 B reads 'Ye can not Love so gide / That yt not issue wynn'.

22 B reads 'Your selfe from Loue to quitt'. In the *Miscellany*, 'quit' means to acquit oneself, but in B it means to extricate oneself.

25 B reads 'Cawses' for 'Your sighes'.

26 B reads 'wrap' for 'wry'.

27 B reads 'neuer the nar' for 'neare the narre'.

32 B reads 'The cawse of all your payne'.

38 B reads 'dyssemblynge' for 'such frowning'.

84

[Q1: 79] In tetrameter quatrains with alternating rhyme. A love complaint. The poem also appears in BL MS Add. 18752 and V3, with some variation including a refrain at the end of each stanza which in all cases but the last consists of the first three words of the following stanza. The last reads 'Thus leve me not' in BL and 'Disdayne me not' in V3.

2 BL reads 'payne' for 'leave'.

4 'I meane nothing but honesty' (V3); 'meane nothing but faythfully' (BL).

6 BL reads 'unkynd' for 'unjust'.

7–8 In BL these lines read 'My hart is yours vntyll I dy / And that yn short space ye shall yt fynd'. Rebholz discusses the meaning of the word 'fantasy' on p. 426.

85

[Q1: 80] Rhyme royal stanzas; tetrameter. A love complaint. The poem does not appear in any of the MSS.

6–9 According to Rollins, who quotes the passage, Emil Koeppel thinks a strambotto by Serafino is the source of these lines.

7   Q8 reads 'swelling' for 'swelting'.

8–9 Proverbial; see Tilley G125, 'He that gives quickly (in a trice) gives twice'; cf. Chaucer's *Legend of Good Women*, G, 441–2.

19   Q8 reads 'hande' for 'band'.

24   A difficult line. Perhaps 'Like the dying of a fire, which diminishes'.

86

[Q1: 81] Quatrains with alternating rhyme and alternating tetrameter and trimeter lines. Quatrains grouped into eight-line stanzas. The poem does not appear in any of the MSS. The title is misleading; there is no particular reason to consider this a love-poem rather than a poem on any of the vicissitudes of Fortune.

1   'every': 'ever' in Q1.

33–6 These are difficult lines. Rebholz hazards: 'yet I would that it – that is, saving my requests from peril – might appear advisable to Fortune, who is still my chief object of regard, although what I have deserved and received from her in the past was too valuable to enable me to claim that I merit the reward I am asking from her now.' But perhaps 'Though' is an error for 'Those' or 'That', yielding the much clearer meaning 'I very much wish it might be clear to her, my chief object of regard, that my deserts have been too high to deserve such a reward'.

87

[Q1: 83] In stanzas rhyming ABABB. Also found in E (96), where the poem seems to take the form of a dialogue, if rather a one-sided one, with two unrhymed lines from a second speaker, perhaps the lady. Alternatively, the poem may be a rather stormy interior monologue, with the questions in the unrhymed lines merely rhetorical. As Harrier notes, in E the poem was copied by the same hand but on two separate occasions, with lines 12/13–22 added later. In consequence, three lines from the third stanza (now reduced to the two unrhymed lines) were lost. The orphaned lines, reproduced below, are omitted from Tottel's text. Rebholz points out of E that the lady seems to have given a rather contradictory answer, both appalling, blameless, friendly, and designed to spare pain. Tottel's editor has attempted to suggest the answer was simpler if harsher, however; see the notes on lines 16 and 17 below.

6–7   As Thomson points out, it is unusual for Wyatt to acknow-
        ledge he has no grounds for grievance, but the essence of
        his philosophy of love is that 'Love is a bargain, a bond
        conferring rights and demanding obligations' (Thomson,
        p. 145).

10   In E, two extra lines appear after line 10: 'Another/ why
        shall lyberty be bond / ffre hart may not be bond but by
        desert'. Their absence from the *Miscellany* is smoothed
        over by the emendation in line 11.

11   E reads 'Nor' for 'Yet'.

16   E reads 'frendly' for 'bitter'.

17   In E, the line is 'that seithe your frende in saving of his
        payne'.

88

[Q1: 84] A sonnet with the unusual scheme ABABABABABABCC. This scheme is not used by Wyatt elsewhere, although Surrey uses it in poems 9 and 10. It resembles an extended ottava rima stanza. A love complaint. The *Miscellany* is the only early witness of the poem; it does not appear in any of the MSS.

4   Proverbial (Tilley L316, 'The lion spares the supplicant');
        cf. poem 29, lines 50 and 58.

5   Q8 reads 'by' for 'thy'.

6   Cf. Fulke Greville, *Caelica* (1633), 60. 3.

89

[Q1: 85] Ottava rima. It has been suggested the poem's source is a dizaine by Mellin de Saint-Gelais (reproduced in Rollins), but it is more likely an analogue, perhaps derived from a common Italian source. A love complaint. The poem appears in E (64).

1   A slightly garbled version of this line is quoted by Putten-
        ham as an instance of a dactylic foot – 'Th' enemy' (p. 211).

90

[Q1: 86] Tetrameter quatrains with alternating rhymes. A celebration of success in love. The poem is also found in E (65), in two forms in D, and *NA*. Rebholz suggests that in E, this poem may be an extended pun; the speaker wishes for his dear heart, which may mean either his lady, or his own heart, i.e. his release from love and the return of his heart. The *Miscellany* does not allow for this ambiguity, however, as the variant in line 5 indicates.

5   E reads 'dere' for 'ladies'.

10, 12   The transposition of these lines' rhyme-words caused diffi-
            culty in later editions; Q8 reads 'nay' in both cases.

17   Q8 reads 'mye' for 'may'.

27   E reads 'sufferaunce' for 'soveraigne'. The line initially
            closed 'I have my redres' in E, but a scribe deleted 'my'.

28   Cf. Luke 10: 7.

91

[Q1: 87] Stanzas in the form AABAB, where the last line is a refrain. A love complaint. The poem also appears in E (66), D, B, V2 (lacking lines 26–30 and 33–40), V3 (omitting 26–30) and *NA*. In *The Court of Venus*, this poem is the subject of a moralizing parody (complete with music), with the title 'A Song of the lute in the prayse of God, and disprayse of Idolatrie'. Rollins reproduces extracts. The lute was the instrument which most commonly accompanied songs in the six-teenth century.

9   There is some variation in the verbs in this line; where the
            Miscellany has 'sigh? or singe', and E the same with spell-
            ing variants, D reverses the verbs, B has 'synge or walle',
            and V has variants on 'syng wepe'.

16   All versions of V read 'splen' for 'spoile' and 'shot' for
            'gotte'.

17   V3 reads 'got' for 'shot'.

24   V has forms of 'ungently' instead of 'Unquit'; V2 reads
            'payne' for 'plain'.

26   E reads 'Perchaunce they lay wethered and old'.

92

[Q1: 88] Ottava rima. An epigram on love. The poem is also found in
E (68), D, B and H78. Wyatt's hand makes some interesting spelling
emendations in E.

1–4   A very common comparison in the sixteenth century and
           subsequently. Rollins provides details of similar instances,
           including one from the poet Thomas Howell, 'But venomde
           Spyders poyson take, where Bee doth honey finde'.

1   For 'feate', B reads 'fayre', and H78 'fatt'. D has 'swete'
           crossed out and replaced with 'fete'.

93

[Q1: 89] Quatrains with alternating rhyme. A love complaint. The
poem is also found in D.

5–6   Cf. Chaucer, *The Canterbury Tales*, I. 1096–7.

8   Cf. Chaucer, *Troilus and Criseyde*, IV. 235, for the phrase
           'pale and wan'.

10   i.e. the Phoenix.

24   Q8 reads 'fende' for 'lead'.

94

[Q1: 90] Ottava rima. The source is a strambotto by Serafino, repro-
duced by Rollins and by Muir and Thomson. The poem is also found
in D.

1   D reads 'sight' for 'loke'.

3   D reads 'saue' for 'helpe'.

6–8   In D, these lines read 'For if I dye then maiste thou lyve
           no more, / Sins ton bye tother dothe lyve and fede thy herte,
           / I with thye sight, thou also with my smerte'.

95

[Q1: 91] Trimeter. Eight-line stanzas in the form ABABACAC. The
source is Petrarch, *Rime*, 206; the disapproving stars and the reference
to Rachel and Leah at the end of the poem are distinctive local bor-
rowings. An apology to a lady. Wyatt chooses a less complex form
than Petrarch, but both poems are structurally dominated by

repetitions of 'if'; Thomson argues that it is 'a brilliant rendering of Petrarch in point of tone and style' (Thomson, p. 187). The poem is also found in D and B.

1–18	Quoted by Puttenham as an example of '*Ecphonesis*, or the Outcry' (p. 298), 'this figure by way of imprecation and obtestation'.
7	Rebholz suggests this may echo the proverb 'Where the knot is loose the string slips' (Tilley K169); cf. poem 97, line 8.
13–14	cf. Chaucer, *Troilus and Criseyde*, V. 1061–2; Criseyde laments that her shameful betrayal of Troilus shall be rung out throughout the world.
18–20	Cf. Petrarch, *Rime*, 206, 5.
45–6	Cf. Petrarch's lines 55–7. For the story of Leah and Rachel, see Genesis 29: 13–30. Jacob loved Rachel, whose father Laban agreed that if Jacob worked for him for seven years, he could marry her. But Rachel's sister Leah was secretly substituted for Rachel on the wedding night, and Jacob had to work a further seven years to win Rachel as well. It seems from this reference that the speaker of the poem has been accused of disloyalty to his lady. Muir and Thomson suggest Rachel and Leah may be puns on rakehell and liar; 'Lea' is spelt 'Lya' in B.

96

[Q1: 92] Ottava rima. A complaint. Also found in H and *NA*. 'The poem was probably written after the execution in July, 1540, of Thomas Cromwell, Earl of Essex, and before Wyatt was imprisoned in 1541. It expresses truthfully Wyatt's precarious situation' (Rollins).

1	H reads 'Luckes' for 'Lux'. The *Miscellany*'s spelling of the bird's name emphasizes the possibility of a pun on 'lux' (Latin for light), while the MS stresses the play on 'luck'.
3	H reads 'might ye befall' for 'mought you fal'.

97

[Q1: 93] Ottava rima. An epigram on love. Also found in B, H and *NA*.

2	B reads 'cumley' for 'lovely'. 'Lovely' suggests a more sensuous and animated beauty than the comparatively glacial 'faire'.

3   'Of lively loke . . . repel': 'With gladsome cheare . . . expell'
             in H.

4   H reads 'sober lookes' for 'right good grace'.

7   In H, 'these perchance I might be tride' reads 'thus might
             chaunce I might be tyde'. H's reading fits better with the
             rope and knot image in the following line.

8   Cf. poem 95, line 7 and note.

98

[Q1: 94] A sonnet with the scheme ABBAABBACDDCEE. Its source
is Petrarch, *Rime*, 57. The resemblance to the source is close; for the
most striking difference see note to line 7. A love complaint. The
poem is also found in closely related versions in E (30) and AH (114).

3   E and AH have 'that leve it or wayt it doeth me like pain';
             'That loue or wait it, alike doth me payne' in Q1.

5–8   Similar catalogues of impossible events occur in a range of
             Latin sources; the main source here is perhaps Ovid, *Meta-
             morphoses*, I. 293–310. Muir and Thomson compare the
             figure with Chaucer's use of it in a love-context in *Troilus
             and Criseyde*, III. 1495–8.

7   Wyatt replaces the Tigris and Euphrates of Petrarch (lines
             7–8) with the Thames.

13   'One drop of swete': 'Any thing swete' in Q1, as in AH.
             They follow E's 'any thing swete'.

99

[Q1: 95] A sonnet with the scheme ABBAABBAEFEFGG. Its source
is Petrarch, *Rime*, 124, and the resemblance is close. A love complaint.
The poem also appears in E (31) and AH (115). Rollins comments,
'Both Miss Foxwell and Nott stigmatize this as one of Wyatt's poorest
compositions. They are unable to forgive his putting four *that's* into
line [2] [three in the *Miscellany*] . . . and Nott is especially disturbed
by the licentious rhymes'.

2   Q8 omits one 'that'.

4   The word 'them' corresponds to Petrarch's 'quei che son su
             l'altra riva' ('those who are on the other shore', line 4), in
             other words, those who have died.

5	Q8 reads 'is' for 'his'.
8	E originally had 'lyveth & rest', but a scribal change of '&' to 'in' seems to have influenced the line in the *Miscellany* and in AH.
12–13	The speaker's 'trust', or confidence, is made of glass, not steel. In the source, the speaker's 'speranza' (hope) is made of glass, not diamond.

100

[Q1: 96] A sonnet with the scheme ABBAABBACDDCEE. Its source is Petrarch, *Rime*, 21, and the poems are closely related except for the last line (see note below). A love complaint. The poem also appears in E (32) and AH (116).

2	In E, the line reads 'with those your Iyes for to get peace and truyse'; AH is similar. Q8 reads 'from' for 'som'.
6	AH reads 'weite' for 'weake'.
9	AH and E read 'I then' for 'you'.
14	As Nott comments, this line is taken from the last line of a different poem by Petrarch, namely *Rime*, 224: 'vostro, Donna, 'l peccato et mio fia 'l danno' [yours will be the blame, Lady, mine the loss]. *Rime* 224 is also the source of poem 102.

101

[Q1: 97] A sonnet with the scheme ABBAABBACDDCEE. Its source is printed as sonetto 3 in Sannazaro's *Rime*, part III, reproduced by Rollins and by Muir and Thomson, although the latter note the authorship of the source is uncertain. A love complaint. Wyatt's poem is also found in E (33) and AH (117).

1–4	Puttenham quotes these lines (with a couple of slight mistakes), giving the following comments: 'The Greeks and Latins used verses in the odd syllable of two sorts, which they called catalectic and acatalectic, that is, odd under and odd over the just measure of their verse. And we in our vulgar find many of the like, and especially in the rhymes of Sir Thomas Wyatt, strained perchance out of their original, made first by Francis Petrarch [quotes the lines]. Where in

your first, second and fourth verse, ye may find a syllable superfluous, and though in the first ye will seem to help it, by drawing these three syllables *ĭmmĕsŭ* into a dactyl, in the rest it cannot be so excused, wherefore we must think he did it of purpose, by the odd syllable to give greater grace to his meter' (p. 214).

10   'in': E's and AH's reading, 'from', makes more sense here.

11   AH and E read 'cattell' for 'Wilde beastes', and 'and in me love' for 'fierce love in me'.

13   E reads 'that restles' for 'singing'.

102

[Q1: 98] A sonnet with the scheme ABBAABBACDDCEE. Its source is Petrarch, *Rime*, 224, and the resemblance is close. A different translation of the same poem appears in H. A love complaint. Wyatt's poem also appears in E (12) and AH (105). As Nott points out, this poem is imitated by Turberville, *Epitaphes*, pp. 68–9, and Samuel Daniel's *Delia*, 15.

1   Puttenham quotes this as an instance of a dactylic foot, in the word 'amorous' (p. 211). E reads 'Yf amours faith an hert vnfayned'; 'amours' may be a noun, though Tottel's editor transforms it into the adjective 'amorous', which is also how it appears in AH.

5   AH and E read 'depaynted' for 'distained'. The editor of the *Miscellany* is perhaps trying to perfect the rhyme.

6   As Rollins notes, 'my sparkelyng voice' is replaced in later editions of the *Miscellany* by 'my speaking voice', which first appears in Q5. He prefers this reading, though 'sparkelyng' mirrors both of the MSS readings. The word can mean scattering, which Muir and Thomson compare with Petrarch's 'voci interrotte', or broken tones.

10   E reads 'sighting' for 'sighing', but this is only a spelling variant (see *OED*, 'sighting', vbl. n.[1]).

12   Q8 reads 'burned' for 'burning'.

13   AH has 'or' for 'Are'. E is very difficult to read at this point because of deletions and over-writings, but it probably has 'ar'.

103

[Q1: 99] A sonnet with the scheme ABBAABBACDDCEE. A repudiation of love. It is also found in E (13), AH (106) and D. The AH copy is closely related to E, but D differs notably from them.

1	Puttenham quotes this as an instance of 'a verse wholly trockaic' (p. 216).
3	For 'Senec, and Plato call' D reads 'to sore a profe hathe called'; the *Miscellany*'s version closely resembles E. Seneca (*c.* 4 BC–AD 65) was a writer and orator, known for his moral essays, among other things. The Greek philosopher Plato (427–347 BC) was the founder of philosophical idealism. Q8 reads 'love' for 'lore'.
7	E and AH have 'hath taught me to sett in tryfels no store'; that word-order is clearer.
10	Q8 reads 'time' for 'me'.
14	AH and E read 'lusteth' for 'list'. This line refers to the proverb 'Who trusts to rotten boughs may fall' (Tilley B557).

104

[Q1: 100] A sonnet with the scheme ABBAABBACDDCEE. Its source is two consecutive strambotti by Serafino, reproduced in Rollins and in Muir and Thomson. A repudiation of love. The poem also appears in E (14) with half of the last line missing, AH (107), and in two incomplete versions in D, the first lacking lines 10–11, and the second line 11. Hughey comments, '*AH* is, as frequently, closer to *E* than are the other texts. Through a fault of the editor or the copyist line 7 in *AH* disturbs the sense. If *E* is to be taken as the authoritative text, we must recognize that *D1* and *D2* are not as reliable as *AH*.' Thomson gives this poem along with the source as an example of how Serafino's cynical, bargaining attitude to love is more congenial to Wyatt than Petrarch's sense of love's duties (Thomson, p. 220).

5	D1 reads 'slave' for 'servant'.
6	E and AH read 'but not to be payed vnder this fasshion'.
8	D2 has 'restraine' for 'refrain'.
9	D1 has 'thy' for 'my'.
11	AH has 'no sens' for 'But, sins'.

13–14   These lines have been copied independently, e.g. in Bod-
           leian Rawlinson 108, f. 7 (Rollins). It is a translation of the
           last line of Serafino's second poem, but is also proverbial in
           Italian and English; see Tilley S87, 'He sows the sand' and
           S184, 'to plow the sea'.

105

[Q1: 101] Two sonnets, both with the scheme ABBACDDCEFFEGG.
Wyatt does not use this scheme elsewhere. Despite the title it carries in
the *Miscellany*, there is no particular reason to think this a love-poem,
and it may refer directly to Wyatt's experience in prison in 1541. Reb-
holz, in supporting this, makes the interesting point that the image of
the scar which cannot be erased (line 14) is also found in poem 126,
another poem about being in prison; he also notes that Wyatt used the
same image when defending himself against the charges which resulted
in his being imprisoned in 1541. This poem also appears in AH (310)
in a very similar form.

3   Q8 reads 'he doth feare' for 'it doth fare'.

5   Q8 reads 'shatered' for 'watred'.

6   As Nott suggests, 'force' may mean 'secret spring' or may
           be an error for 'source'.

8   Q8 reads 'in the' for 'is in'.

10   Q8 reads 'sore' for 'force'.

12   Q8 reads 'me' for 'no'.

14   Cf. poems 40, line 6, 115, line 10, 126, line 8, and see head-
           note above. The idea of the enduring scar is proverbial; see
           Tilley W929, 'Though the wound be healed yet the scar
           remains'.

21   AH reads 'tasting' for 'trifling'.

23   For 'save on the second day', Rebholz conjectures 'except
           every other day'.

25   'she': i.e. '[m]y fever' (line 24).

106

[Q1: 102] A sonnet with the scheme ABBAABBACDCDEE. A com-
plaint/elegy. This is not necessarily the lament of a lover, despite the
title assigned to it here. It may be about the loss of a friend. Its source

is Petrarch, *Rime*, 269, which uses the loss of the pillar, or 'colonna' (column), to allude to the death of Cardinal Giovanni Colonna, who died in 1348. The poem also appears in AH (96). It may constitute a lament for Thomas Cromwell, Wyatt's patron, who was executed in 1540. However, there are potential difficulties with this interpretation; see Rebholz for a discussion. Another translation of Petrarch's poem into English appears in H; the end of this poem is closer to Petrarch's than Wyatt's is.

8   AH reads 'Dearlye' for 'Dayly'.

10–11   AH has 'wofull' in both lines 10 and 11; the *Miscellany* has more variety with 'wofull' in line 10 and 'carefull' in line 11.

14   AH reads 'cause' for 'ease'.

107

[Q1: 103] A sonnet with the curious scheme AABBAAABBAABBA. As with poems 74 and 75, this is a result of the *Miscellany*'s editor rewriting what was originally a rondeau into sonnet form. See Amanda Holton, 'An Obscured Tradition: The Sonnet and its Fourteen-Line Predecessors', *Review of English Studies*, 62 (2011), for a discussion of the poem's form. Its source is probably Petrarch, *Rime*, 153, but the resemblance is close only in the first four lines. It is possible that Wyatt was working with a French rondeau derived from the Petrarch sonnet (see Muir and Thomson). A love complaint. The poem also appears in E (20) and D. In E it reads:

> Goo burnyng sighes Unto the frosen hert
> goo breke the Ise with pite paynfull dert
> myght never perse and if mortall prayer
> in hevyn may be herd at lest I desir
> that deth or mercy be ende of my smert
> Take with the payn wherof I have my pert
> and eke the flame from which I cannot stert
> and leve me then in rest I you require
> Goo burning sighes
> I must goo worke I se by craft & art
> for trueth & faith in her is laide apert
> Alas I cannot therefor assaill her
> with pitefull plaint & scalding fyer
> that oute of my brest doeth straynably stert
> Goo burning sighes[.]

2   'with pities': 'which pities' in Q1; 'with pite' corrected by a
           scribal hand to 'whiche pites' in E; 'with piteus' in D.

108

[Q1: 104] In poulter's measure. The source of the poem is Petrarch,
Rime, 37. Lines 1–14 correspond to the first stanza of the Petrarch
poem, lines 15–28 to the second stanza, lines 29–42 to the third stanza,
lines 43–54 to the fourth stanza, lines 55–68 to the fifth stanza, lines
69–80 to the sixth stanza, lines 81–94 to the seventh stanza, and lines
95–100 loosely to the eighth stanza. Wyatt may have chosen poulter's
measure as a means of reflecting the varying line lengths of the source
(Muir and Thomson), or, as Rebholz suggests, 'because its movement
seemed to him, as to poets later in the century, particularly appropriate
to the mood of "complaint"'. A love complaint. The poem also appears
in E (104), AH (139) and D; in E it is in Wyatt's own hand and there are
many revisions, also in his hand. See Harrier for a discussion of the rela-
tionship between witnesses and a full record of the variants; he
comments: 'one of the most interesting group of variants is the last in
line 74, where A[H] and T[ottel] adopt the deleted reading "erst" while
D is consistent in supplying the revision "suche". This suggests that the
editors of the A and T copy had access to E. The fact that T preserves
the word "spere" (l. 40), where A revises to "sphaere," indicates inde-
pendent checking and editing on the part of T. Since D nowhere gives a
deleted or earlier reading of E, it is likely that the copyist was following
a fair copy of the revised text' (p. 229). In E, the heading 'In Spayne' has
been added above this poem (cf. poem 131); which may indicate that it
was written between April 1537 and June 1539 when Wyatt was
ambassador to Spain. Q8 reads 'lover' for 'love' in the title.

1–4   The image of life as a thread is a common one, ultimately
           derived from the classical representation of the Fates as
           three spinners, Clotho, who held the distaff, Lachesis, who
           wound the thread, and Atropos, who cut it off.

7   For 'sored minde' (also the reading in AH), E reads 'wof-
           ull', emended to 'sory'.

8   E reads 'spryte' for 'wight'.

12   For 'wrap' E reads 'wrape' with the 'w' subsequently
           deleted. The *Miscellany*'s substitution here seems to have
           been chosen to fit in with the word 'cover' at the end of the
           line. But 'rape' and 'cover' (meaning 'protect') also fit
           together in a military metaphor, as Rebholz notes: 'Time

may become an ally, forcibly remove the enemy "woe" from the lover, and thereafter defend and protect him'.

18   AH and E read 'hyds' for 'hies'.

36   'I neuer saw the thing that myght my faytfull hert delyght' in E and AH.

39   AH and E read 'shining' for 'shene'.

42   Q8 reads 'hate' for 'bate'.

49   'transplendant': here and in AH; 'transparant' in E.

52   'feares': 'fiers' in E and 'fearce' in AH. The *Miscellany*'s editor seemingly took the word as a noun instead of an adjective, which disrupts the structural parallel with the next phrase. Q8 reads 'teares' for 'feares'.

61   Q8 reads 'do' for 'to'.

72   Q8 reads 'to' (i.e. too) for 'so'.

81   D reads 'morn' for 'mone'.

82–3   'that firmly do embrace / Me from my self': Nott suggests this is from Horace, *Odes*, IV. 13.

83   D reads 'streme' for 'sterne'.

86   D reads 'Charged' for 'rage'.

87   'ragged': 'craggyd' in E, 'Craggie' in AH, both being more conventional words to describe hills. Q8 reads the ambiguous 'raged'.

88   The *Miscellany* follows Wyatt's revisions; the original text in E reads 'my faintyng hope my brytill lyff willing despaire fulfilles'.

92   The phrase 'ere that I dye' is Tottel's addition.

97   AH and E read 'dred' for 'grief'; 'serve': 'sterve' in E but not AH.

98   Familiar from Catullus, 2, where the poet envies his beloved's pet sparrow.

99   The *Miscellany* follows Wyatt's revisions; the original text in E reads 'Then say I come for here I may not tary'.

109

[Q1: 105] Quatrains rhymed ABBA. A love complaint. This poem occurs only in the *Miscellany*.

110

[Q1: 106] Venus and Adonis stanzas with tetrameter lines. Its source may be a sonnet by Antonio Tebaldeo (see Muir and Thomson for a discussion). A love complaint. The poem does not occur in any of the MSS, but it does occur later with the title 'He repenteth his folly' in the first edition of *The Paradise of Dainty Devices* (1576) with some lines omitted and three lines added.

7   Q8 reads 'mone' for 'move'.

16   Q8 reads 'thy' for 'thee'.

111

[Q1: 107] Venus and Adonis stanzas with tetrameter lines. The last line of each stanza is a refrain, and the penultimate line a partial refrain with one particular line being repeated in the first, third and fifth stanzas, and a different line repeated in the others. This, together with three other Wyatt poems, may form a group which was inspired by Serafino, *Canzona de la Patientia* (see Rebholz, p. 388). A promise of fidelity. The poem appears only in the *Miscellany*.

6   This refrain may be derived from a phrase in Seneca's *De Moribus (Of Customs)*, 'Dolor patientia vincitur' (Rollins).

8   Q8 reads 'cruelly' for 'cruelty'.

112

[Q1: 108] Trimeter quatrains with alternating rhymes. A complaint, but there is no reason to think this a love-poem, despite the title it has been given in the *Miscellany*. The poem is not found outside the *Miscellany*. It may refer to false accusations made of Wyatt after Cromwell's execution (Rollins) or indeed to any of the periods when Wyatt was under threat from his enemies.

3–4   Refers to a proverb; see Tilley T333, 'Time reveals (discloses) all things'.

9–12   Proverbial; see Tilley S99, 'To be served with the same sauce'.

113

[Q1: 109] Ottava rima. A dialogue. The poem is found only in the *Miscellany*.

7   Q8 inserts 'my' after 'rew'.

32   This line is probably a narratorial comment rather than
               part of the dialogue.

114

[Q1: 110] Ottava rima. An epigram on love. The poem also appears
in E (106) in Wyatt's hand and with his revisions. The *Miscellany*'s
version is very close to Wyatt's emended version; indeed, Harrier com-
ments, 'Considering the amount of editing *T*[ottel] gives to poem 105
from the same leaf, the fidelity is surprising.'

1   Cupid was traditionally blind.

7   Q8 reads 'dredly' for 'dedly'.

8   I serve and suffer woe with those who can see (as opposed
               to Cupid).

115

[Q1: 111] In stanzas rhyming AAAB. The A-lines are pentameter and
the B-lines trimeter. A love complaint. The poem also occurs in E
(107) both written and revised in Wyatt's hand. The first stanza seems
to have been added to the copy later. Muir and Thomson discuss the
composition process in detail; Rebholz adds the suggestion that the
first stanza was added later.

1–4   Before revision, E read 'What rage is this? what furour of
               excesse? / what powre what poyson doth my mynd opresse?
               / with in the bons to rancle doth not cesse / the poysond
               plesantnesse swete'. The revised lines are close to those in
               the *Miscellany*.

5   For 'myne eyes', E has 'my chekes', emended to 'my iyes'; E
               reads 'swell' for 'flow'.

9   'In depe wide wound': E originally read 'The strok doth
               streche' before being corrected to 'In to wid wound' and
               then 'In diepe wid wound'.

10   E reads 'curid' for 'cureles'. Both words are trying to cap-
               ture the idea of a wound which has healed, but left an
               ineradicable scar, but E stresses the former and the *Miscel-
               lany* the latter. For the image, cf. poems 105 and 126.

11   Q8 reads 'the' for 'thy'.

14   For 'plaint', E has 'wowe', replaced first by 'deth', and then
            by 'plaint'.

17–20   E shows extensive revision here.

116

[Q1: 112] Ottava rima. A love complaint. The poem appears in two
very different versions in E (76) and D. In E it appears in Wyatt's hand
with his emendations. The *Miscellany*'s version is much closer to E,
and because differences in D are not related to earlier drafts of lines
present in E, it is unlikely that D is a copy of an earlier version of the
poem. The poem tells how the speaker who once desired a lady now
hates her, whereas the lady who used to despise him now desires him.
Tottel's editor, however, seems to have considered 'leadst' ('ledst' in
E), line 4, as present tense, consequently altering the verb in line 3 to
a present tense ('sekest') as well. This rather garbles the sense.

1   D reads 'Cruell desire' for 'Desire (alas)'.

2   D reads 'thy silf so chaungid for shame' for 'So sore altered
            thy self'.

3   After emendation, E reads 'some tyme I sowght that
            dryvys'. D reads 'that I have sought dothe chase'.

5   D reads 'right' for 'reason'.

8   D reads 'dred' for 'hate'.

117

[Q1: 113] Venus and Adonis stanzas with tetrameter lines. The second
half of the penultimate line and the entire final line form a refrain in each
stanza. A love complaint. The poem appears only in the *Miscellany*.

3   Q8 reads 'thee free' for 'the fee'.

4   Cf. Tilley M337.

6   Cf. Tilley S691.

118

[Q1: 266] Rhyme royal with tetrameter lines. An epigram/riddle on
love for a specific lady. The poem also appears in E (50) and AH
(120), and in E a scribe has written 'Anna' above it. (Harrier, p. 140
suggests that this may not have been there when AH was copied from

E, given that the scribe presented this poem as a continuation of the previous one). The poem may be about Anne Boleyn (Thomson, p. 22). In Q1, the poem appears in the second tranche of Wyatt poems which closes the edition.

1–2   'Anna' is a palindrome.

3   'Anna': 'aunswer' in E and AH, where the answer to the riddle is submerged. Rebholz suggests 'aunswer' may pun on 'Anne, sir'.

5   E reads 'rewardeth' for 'medeth'; in AH the line appears in an abbreviated form as 'A Love withe disdayne'.

7   E and AH reads 'helth' for salve'.

119

[Q1: 267] Ottava rima. An epigram. The source of the poem is a strambotto by Serafino, reproduced by Muir and Thomson and by Rollins. The poem also appears in E (77) in Wyatt's hand, D, H, H78, Cambridge University, MS FF.5.14 and NA. In Q1, the poem appears in the second tranche of Wyatt poems which closes the edition.

1–2   Proverbial; cf. Tilley R179, 'Every rose grows from prick-les'. The *Miscellany*'s misprint of 'thrones' may accidentally suggest the venomous nature of royal power.

3–4   Refers to proverb Tilley P457 'One poison expels another'.

5–6   Rebholz suggests that fire may heal by cauterizing.

5   Reads 'ffyre that purgithe allthing that is vnclene' in E.

8   Proverbial; cf. Tilley W188, 'No weal without woe'.

120

[Q1: 268] Monorhymed. A riddle. It also appears in Bodleian MS Rawlinson Poetical 172 and AH (97). The AH version is virtually identical with the one in the *Miscellany*, except that the word 'whiche' in line 2 has been crossed out. Variants in Rawlinson (recorded in Hughey) are very minor. In A, it appears in the second tranche of Wyatt poems which closes the edition. According to Rollins, there is a marginal annotation in Q10: 'I think it is a Kysse'. Alternatively the gift may be the lady's virginity, or simply her sexual participation.

121

[Q1: 269] Rhyming couplets. An epigram. The poem appears only in the *Miscellany*, and in Q1 it is in the second tranche of Wyatt poems which closes the edition. This is a tricky poem; Rebholz notes that this is 'because of the difficulty of identifying the possessors of the "will", "power", and "need"'. He proposes the following paraphrase: 'State your request to another and succeed in getting what you ask if either the other person's willingness to assist you or your own power can be of any help. Where your power is lacking, the other's willingness to help must [usually] be secured by bribing him with your money. For the other person's need for money will make your suit successful even when his will is not so generously inclined as it should be by nature. And your offer of money will cause you to discover that your foes are your friends. For a mere suit or request will obtain anything from a good man, and the offer of gold as a bribe will obtain anything from a bad man.'

1   Proverbial; see Tilley S719 ('Speak and speed, ask and have').

5   Refers to proverb 'What will not (cannot) money (gold) do?'; see Tilley M1102.

122

[Q1: 270] A ballade in rhyme royal. The source is Boethius' *De Consolatione Philosophiae*: the first stanza is from III. m. 5, the second from III. m. 6, and the third from III. m. 3. A moral ode. In view of lexical likenesses documented below, Chaucer's *Boece* was probably the version used. The *Miscellany* is the sole early witness; the poem does not appear in any of the MSS. In Q1, the poem appears in the second tranche of Wyatt poems which closes the edition. The poem may well be a criticism of Henry VIII, a reading that seems to be accentuated by the *Miscellany*'s title. The first stanza of the poem, ascribed to Surrey, is quoted in *England's Parnassus* (1600).

1–7   There are several lexical parallels with *Boece*, III. m. 5 here: 'mighty' (1) corresponds with 'myghti' (1); 'cruel' (2) with 'cruel' (2); 'foule' (3) with 'foule' (3); 'stretche' (4) with 'strecche' (4); 'desire' (6) with 'desires' (9); 'power' (6) with 'power' (11).

5   'Thylee' is perhaps 'Thulē', a land north of Britain, 'supposed by Polybius to be the most northerly region of the world; the type of the extreme limit of travel, discovery, and rule' (Rebholz).

10–14   Lexical parallels with *Boece* are sparser in the second stanza, but compare 'starre' (10) with 'sterres' (III. m. 6. 6); 'geves the Moone her hornes' (11) with 'he yaf to the moone hir hornes' (4–5); 'heaven' (10) with 'hevene' (6), and 'vice' (14) with 'vices' (14); 'vice', however, is not unlike the Latin 'vitiis' (9).

18–19   There are two lexical parallels with *Boece* here; 'precious' and '[y]charged' correspond with 'precyous' and 'charged' (III. m. 3. 104–5)

20   The phrase 'busy biting' perhaps means 'anxious acquisitiveness'. It echoes *Boece*, III. m. 3. 7, 'bytynge bysynesse'.

21   Perhaps 'Your death will not profit your wretched life', or 'Your wretched life will not benefit your death'. Rebholz suggests deleting the comma at the end of line 20 and following Chaucer's syntax; this would give the sense 'anxiety about money will never leave him while alive, nor benefit him when he is dead'.

123

[Q1: 271] Rhyme royal, with the last line of each stanza acting as a refrain. A moral ode. The poem is also found in Corpus Christi College, Cambridge, MS Parker 168. In Q1, it appears in the second tranche of Wyatt poems which closes the edition.

4   Q8 reads 'the' for 'to'.

15–16   'By leynght off liefe yet shulde I suffer, / Adwayting time and fortunes chaunce' in Parker; Rebholz comments that Tottel's editor 'recognized the awkwardness of changing attitudes, without transition, within the stanza'.

22   Q8 reads 'lengthens' for 'lengths'.

23   The word 'best', found in the *Miscellany* and Parker, is usually emended to 'lest' by editors to make sense of the reference to the proverb 'Of two ills choose the least' (Tilley E207).

124

[Q1: 114] Ottava rima. The source is probably one of two brief Latin epigrams by Ausonius (*Epigrams*, 22, 23), themselves derived from Plato. Rollins quotes Plato, and a translation by Coleridge: 'Jack finding gold left a rope on the ground: / Bill missing his gold used the rope which he found.' The *Miscellany* is the earliest witness to the poem; it does not appear in the MSS.

5   'where he preparde this dede': i.e. where he was preparing
            to hang himself.

125

[Q1: 115] Ottava rima. The source of the first six lines of the poem is
a Latin riddle which forms part of an allegorical dialogue by Pandulfo
Collinutio, who ruled Siena in the early sixteenth century. The riddle
is reproduced by Nott and subsequently Rollins. The poem appears in
E (109) in an italic script; Harrier considers it is in Wyatt's hand, but
Jason Powell ('Thomas Wyatt's Poetry in Embassy: Egerton 2711 and
the Production of Literary Manuscripts Abroad', *Huntingdon Library
Quarterly*, 67 (2004), pp. 261–82) concurs with Rebholz in consider-
ing it is not. It may have been copied into E from the *Miscellany*; see
Rebholz for a summary of the debate. It also appears in H78. The rid-
dling quality of the poem is rather spoiled by the title which has been
affixed to it in the *Miscellany*.

1   Vulcan was the gods' blacksmith, and Minerva the goddess
            of wisdom.

2   Nature is the gun's mother because it is made of naturally
            occurring materials which Craft shapes.

3   The source specifies that the three foods of the gun are salt-
            petre, sulphur and charcoal, the ingredients of gunpowder
            (Nott).

4   H78 reads 'slawghter' for 'Anger'

7   H78 reads 'have' for 'Know'.

126

[Q1: 116] Ottava rima. A complaint. The poem was probably written
between 17 January and 21 March 1541, when Wyatt was in prison
for the last time. It also appears in H78, with minor variants. For
information about Sir Francis Brian, see headnote to poem 136.

2   That is, the clinking of fetters craves the accompaniment of
            sighs and whatever sounds are associated with 'teares'.

4   Wyatt maintained he was innocent of the charges of trea-
            son which were brought against him (see Introduction).

7–8   The idea of the enduring scar is proverbial; see Tilley W929.
            Cf. poems 105, line 14 (and headnote) and 115, line 10.

127

[Q1: 117] Venus and Adonis stanza with tetrameter lines. An epigram. The *Miscellany* is the only early witness of this poem; it does not appear in any of the MSS.

3   The idea of words being cheap is proverbial; see Tilley
            W804, W805 and W808.

4   Proverbial; see Tilley W833.

128

[Q1: 118] The rhyme-scheme here is ABABCBCCCC; in AH the scheme is different (see below). The source of the poem is Seneca, *Thyestes*, 391–403:

> Stet quicumque volet potens
> aulae culmine lubrico:
> me dulcis saturet quies.
> obscuro positus loco
> leni perfruar otio,
> nullis nota Quiritibus
> aetas per tacitum fluat.
> sic cum transierint mei
> nullo cum strepitu dies,
> plebeius moriar senex.
> illi mors gravis incubat
> qui, notus nimis omnibus,
> ignotus moritur sibi.

[Whoever wants to may stand in power on the slippery top of a palace: let sweet peace be enough for me. Placed in an obscure place, let me flourish in soft leisure, unknown to the Quirites, and let my time flow by in silence. So, when my days have passed without uproar, let me die as an old plebeian. Death weighs heavy on one who, too well known to all, dies unknown to himself].

A moral ode on fortune. The poem is also found in AH (311), in such a different form that it probably represents a different stage of composition:

> Stond who so list upon the Slipper toppe
> of courtes estates/ and lett me heare reioyce
> and use me quyet without lett or stoppe
> unknowe in courte, that hath suche brackishe ioyes

> in hidden place, so lett my dayes forthe passe
> that when my yeares be done withouten noyse
> I may dye aged after the common trace
> ffrom hym death greep the right hard by the croppe
> that is moche knowen of other/ and of him self alas
> Doth dye unknowen/ dazed with dreadfull face

For other poems on the mean estate, see 134, 140, 160, 169.

8   Q8 reads 'yarely' (i.e. quickly) for 'hardly'.

129

[Q1: 119] Rhyme royal. The *Miscellany* is the only early witness to the poem; it is not found in the MSS.

3   Q8 reads 'is' for 'in'.

130

[Q1: 120] Ottava rima. The source for the opening lines is Petrarch, *Rime*, 103. 1–2: 'Poi che 'l camin m' è chiuso di mercede, / per desperata via son dilungato' [Since the road of mercy is closed to me, [I have come] along a despairing track]. (The first four lines of this Petrarch poem are also translated in H, in Wyatt's hand, quoted in Rollins.) A complaint. Wyatt's poem is also found in E (83) in Wyatt's hand. The poem may express a failure to seize either a personal or a political opportunity. It is most likely to refer to the fact that Wyatt's embassy to the Imperial Court in Spain, designed to prevent the Catholic powers of Europe allying against Reformed England, began with high hopes of success but ended in 'despair' (Thomson, p. 61).

1–2   Hannibal is the man from Carthage. Despite his victories against Rome in the Second Punic War, he did not attempt to take Rome itself.

8   This suggests the poem was written in 1537 when Wyatt was ambassador to Charles V. 'Mountzon' refers to Monzòn, near Barbastro in Spain.

131

[Q1: 121] Ottava rima. An epigram. The poem is also found in E (105), where the title 'in Spayn' has been added (cf. note to poem 108), suggesting that it was written when Wyatt was in Spain between

1537 and 1539. As Rollins notes, the poem presumably celebrates
Wyatt's return to England from Spain in April 1539.

1   'The sands of the Spanish river Tagus were famous for
        looking like grains of gold already refined' (Rebholz). Rollins
        suggests that this refers to Boethius, III. m. 10, possibly in
        Chaucer's translation.

3   The Thames, symbol of London's merchant wealth, flows
        eastwards, whereas the Tagus flows westwards.

5   According to legend, the Trojan Brutus, great-grandson of
        Aeneas, founded London.

6   E reads 'doth lend' for 'that leanes'. The river is crescent-
        shaped.

8   'O . . . Jove . . . windes': 'Of . . . love . . . winges' in E. Tot-
        tel's editor seemingly misread E's 'love' as 'Iove'.

132

[Q1: 122] Rhyme royal. An epigram. The poem also appears in B and D.

6–7   Proverbial; see Tilley T595, 'Try your friend before you
        trust'.

133

[Q1: 123] Ottava rima. The source is an anonymous Italian stram-
botto, reproduced by Muir and Thomson. An epigram. Wyatt's poem
also appears in E (82). Josephus gives an account of how Mary,
daughter of Eleazer, killed, cooked and ate her son during the siege of
Jerusalem in AD 70 (see *The Jewish War*, VI. iii. 4).

3   E reads 'saythe thebrew moder' for 'The mother sayth'.

7   E has the more comprehensible reading 'for of on body' for
        'For one of body', as does Q8.

134

[Q1: 124] Terza rima. The Aesopian fable which underlies the poem
would have been available to Wyatt in a number of forms, including
Horace, *Satires* II. 6. 77–117, and perhaps Henryson's version of the
story (the second of his *Fables*). Wyatt's version differs from other
known versions in two major ways, however: usually the country

mouse's visit to the town mouse is a reciprocal visit, and the previous stay of the town mouse with the country mouse is described first. And in other versions the country mouse escapes from its predator and returns home. For a discussion of the relationship of the poem and its analogues and possible sources, see Rebholz and Muir and Thomson. A satire. Wyatt's poem is found in E (78), AH (142) and D (lines 1–18 only). Harrier notes that 'E and T[ottel] frequently agree against A[H], but never E and A[H] against T[ottel]. The A[H] texts of the satires are notably less accurate than the A[H] texts of the shorter poems.' Little is known of John Poins, although according to Rollins, he was from an Essex family which included Sir Francis Poyntz and Sir Anthony Poyntz, who were important diplomats. Although there is a portrait of John Poins by Holbein, according to Thomson, he was 'an inconspicuous courtier' (Thomson, p. 44), which may be the point of addressing to him a poem about the dangers of being conspicuous.

1–2	In E the verbs are in the past tense ('did sowe' and 'sang'), and line 2 differs in various ways, reading 'they sang sometyme a song of the feld mowse'. AH is closest to Tottel, with present tenses and the form 'fieldishe mowse'.
18	The mice are twin sisters in Henryson, but elsewhere they are not related (Rebholz).
27	In E, the city mouse is envisaged feasting on 'boyled bacon meet & roost'; cf. Horace (line 85), where the country mouse gives the town mouse bacon to eat.
37	For the probable misprint 'scarpes', E reads 'scrapeth' and AH 'scrapes'.
42	Cf. Henryson, 26 and 147, where the town mouse cries 'peip'.
46–7	Perhaps a verbal echo of Chaucer, *Troilus and Criseyde*, III. 1366–7.
50	For the phrase 'be fell a sory chance', cf. *Troilus and Criseyde*, II. 464 ('me is tid a sory chaunce').
53	For 'stemyng eyes', cf. Chaucer, *The Canterbury Tales*, I. 201–2.
55	Except for spelling variants, AH agrees with the *Miscellany*'s reading 'the unwise', but E has 'tho' in the place of this phrase.
57	Q8 omits 'had'.
66	To catch by the hip, meaning to have at a disadvantage, is proverbial; see Tilley H474.

68	Confusingly spelt and punctuated here. The meaning is 'who had forgotten the security and rest which her poverty was responsible for' ('power' = 'poor'), or 'her security and rest however poor they may have been'. Q8 reads 'poore' with no succeeding comma.
69	E reads 'semyng' for 'seking'; the latter appears in AH.
73	E has 'blynde' for AH's and the *Miscellany*'s 'blindes'.
77–9	Perhaps an imitation of Horace, *Odes*, II. 16 (Nott).
79	AH reads 'That can repulsse the care that follow shulde'.
84	Rebholz identifies the 'thing' (also in lines 90 and 98) as 'mental peace that comes with the Christian stoic virtue of detachment from false goods and evils and acceptance of one's lot'.
85–6	Proverbial; see Tilley G411, 'One cannot gather grapes of thorns or figs of thistles'.
87	Q8 reads 'For' for 'Nor'.
94	E has 'ever' for 'never'. AH has 'ffor' for 'From'.
97–8	Nott compares Persius, *Satires*, I. 7.
99	E reads 'sitting' for 'stickyng'.
100	E has 'Madde' for 'Made'; there is a common pun here which reflects that being 'made' (i.e. successful) or desiring to be so may make one mad: cf. *Twelfth Night*, III. iv. 52–3.
101–2	Usually thought be an instruction to fix the mind on the metaphysical possibilities of the future, and with an eye to that, to work hard either in learning or virtuous acts. But Rebholz suggests the alternative reading 'forget that the present is the only moment that counts and long for the future [i.e. have the attitude toward time that makes for the mad anxiety described in line 100] and plunge yourself more and more deeply into the pointless labours after false goods'.
105–12	Nott compares Persius, *Satires*, 3. 35–8.
108	In AH, the word 'Vertue' does not appear.

135

[Q1: 125] Terza rima. The source of the poem is Luigi Alamanni's tenth satire 'A Thommaso Sertini', first published in 1532–3, and reproduced by Muir and Thomson. For detailed discussions of the relationships between source and target texts, see notes in Rebholz and in Muir and Thomson. A satire. The poem also appears in E (75), where it lacks lines 1–52, D, where it lacks lines 28–30, AH (104), where it lacks lines 18–19 and 29–31, H, which strongly resembles AH; Cambridge University MS Ff. 5.14; and Corpus Christi College, Cambridge, MS Parker 168. See Harrier for a full record of the variants. Given line 100, it was probably written while Wyatt was exiled in Kent after being released from prison in 1536. For 'John Poins', see headnote of poem 134.

3   Nott suggests that 'where so they go' may refer to court progresses.

5   Cf. Horace, Horace, *Odes*, III. 29. 53–6:

> laudo manentem; si celeres quatit
> pinnas, resigno quae dedit et mea
> virtute me involvo probamque
> Pauperiem sine dote quaero.

[I praise her [Fortune] while she stays; if she shakes her swift wings, I resign what she has given, wrap myself in my virtue, and seek trusty Poverty though she has no dowry]. Cf. poem 26, line 1.

8–9   These lines indicate Wyatt's acceptance of the King's power over him, even though that power is not the primary reason given in the poem for his withdrawal from court (Thomson, 44).

18   See Tilley B436 for the proverb 'Black will take no other hue'. The colour black is being equated with the speaker's honesty; he cannot be turned into a liar any more than something black can be dyed another colour.

21   Q8 reads 'vile' for 'vice'.

23   Venus was the goddess of love, and Bacchus the god of wine.

30   Perhaps from Horace, *Ars Poetica,* 389–90 (Nott), but also proverbial; see Tilley W777, 'A word spoken cannot be called back'.

31   Q8 omits 'as'.

33   Q8 reads 'paine' for 'paint'.

36   AH has 'and do my self hurt wheare my self I offer'.

38   Cato was a supporter of the republican cause in Rome, and supporter of Pompey. He committed suicide after Pompey's death and Julius Caesar's victory at the battle of Thapsus in

46 BC, and thus escaped from Caesar. Alamanni had cited Caesar's assassin Brutus rather than Cato, but the former was too controversial a figure to be praised by Wyatt (Thomson, p. 258).

45–6   Syntax and punctuation make this tricky. 'Nor call the greatest of cowardly beasts, who cannot catch a mouse as a cat can, by the name of lion.'

48–9   Pan, a satyr who played on rustic pipes, challenged the god Apollo, famous for his music, to a competition. Pan lost. Alexander the Great (356–323 BC) was the greatest conqueror of antiquity.

50–51   The story of Sir Thopas, the first tale told by the pilgrim Chaucer in *The Canterbury Tales*, is notoriously poor and is interrupted on those grounds (VII. 919). *The Knight's Tale*, on the other hand, is much esteemed, and was praised by the other pilgrims ('In al the route nas ther yong ne oold / That he ne seyde it was a noble storie'; I. 3110–11).

56   There is probably a pun on John Pointz's name here.

57   AH (but not E) has 'to waye' not 'the way', transforming the noun into the verb 'to weigh'.

59   AH also has the last word in the line as a verb, but in E it is a noun, reading 'of devise'.

60–63   Rebholz comments: 'Wyatt alludes to the ethical doctrine, Aristotle's in origin, that the virtuous act is that which avoids both an excessive and a deficient response to the circumstances and can therefore be called "the mean" or middle position between "each extremity" or vice.'

61   Perhaps adopted from Horace, *Satires*, I. 3.41–2 (Nott).

67   'Favel' was a common medieval figuration for flattery and cunning, his name deriving from the Centaur in the French romance *Fauvel*.

69   Recalls the proverb 'An ounce of fortune is worth a pound of wit' (Tilley O85).

75   Q8 omits 'the'.

82   Q8 omits 'to'.

84   For 'lusty leas', cf. *Troilus and Criseyde*, II. 750–52. AH (but not E) has 'Lustie leases'.

86   Seemingly proverbial, although it does not appear to be recorded in Tilley; Rollins quotes several instances of use of

the phrase in the sixteenth and seventeenth centuries. Though Wyatt was not under house arrest during his banishment to Kent, he was restrained in the sense that his father had given his parole for him.

89   Although the detail of judging wine occurs in the source, it was particularly apt for Wyatt, who was given permission to import wine when he was at Calais in 1529.

94   AH originally read 'lettes not my wittes to dymme', but the last word was crossed out and replaced with 'deeme' in an apparent rejection of the metaphor of dimming wits.

97–8   AH and E read 'Christ' for 'truth' and 'at Rome' for 'of some'. Clearly the changes were made by the editor of the *Miscellany* in recognition of the changed face of English religious conditions; during Mary's reign it was evidently considered wise to remove this attack on Catholicism.

99   For 'practise', AH has 'plague'. The change has been made in the *Miscellany* for the same reasons as the changes in lines 97–8.

100   Kent is a county in the south-east of England which converted to Christianity later than most of the rest of the country, leading to the proverb 'In Kent or Christendom' (Tilley K16). This line turns the proverb on its head by linking the two rather than opposing them.

136

[Q1: 126] Terza rima with pentameter lines. Its source may be Horace, *Satires* II. 5; see Rebholz, Nott and Thomson for discussion of the relationship between the texts. A satire. The poem is also found in E (86) and AH (141). Hughey comments that it is 'evident that *AH* and *TM* both stem from *E*, but *TM* has fewer changes than does *AH*. Notice, for example, lines 4, 14, 45, 51, 60, 66, 68, and 72, where *TM* agrees with *E*, but *AH* is independent. On the other hand, in such significant lines as 22 and 47, and in others where the readings are not so striking, *AH* and *TM* agree and *E* is independent. Certainly, therefore, there is a direct relation between *AH* and *TM* as well as between *E* and the other two, but the editors of *AH* and *TM* exercised "discretion" in their copies. It is, of course, impossible to say whether the marked changes in lines 22 and 47 appeared first in *AH* or *TM*.' Sir Francis Brian was a diplomat, courtier and poet. 'Because of his intimacy with Henry VIII in the king's youth, he had a reputation for dissoluteness. He maintained Henry's favour by assisting him in his change of wives, and by his efforts as a diplomat' (Rebholz). In this poem he is presented as a model of virtue, but there was apparently a later falling-out; the following appeared in a letter Wyatt wrote to Cromwell in 1539: 'I thank your lordship for the giving order for my money that I lent Mr Brian. If the king's honour more than his credit had not been afore mine eyes, he should have piped in an ivy leaf for aught of me' (quoted and modernized by Rebholz). This dispute suggests this laudatory poem was written pre-1539.

Brian collected proverbs. Poem 126 is also addressed to him.

1–2	See Tilley S738, 'Spend as you get'.
3–4	See Tilley S885, 'A rolling stone gathers no moss'.
9–10	Brian wrote a poem 'in which he "counsels man the right" in a series of proverbial and didactic sayings' (Rollins).
20	For casting pearls before swine, see Matthew 7: 6. For 'pearles', E has 'perilles' and AH 'pearells'.
21	That is, the ass hears not music but just a noise. See Tilley A366, and cf. *Boece*, I. 4. 2–3, and *Troilus and Criseyde* I. 731–5 (Nott).
22–3	'So sackes of durt be filled vp in the cloyster / that servis for lesse then do thes fatted swyne' in E. The lines have been altered in the *Miscellany* in the light of there being a Catholic queen on the throne. AH resembles the *Miscellany* here, but it is unclear which text generated the emendation initially.
28–9	Cf. Horace, *Satires*, II. 5. 2–3.
32	Q8 omits 'so'.
33	Proverbial; see Tilley T569, 'Truth begets hatred'.
44	E reads 'dogge' for 'calfe'. The precise significance (and provenance) of the idea of lending a calf or dog a cheese is uncertain (but you would be unlikely to get your cheese back).
47	E has 'kittson' instead of 'the ladde'. It is uncertain exactly who Kitson was (Nott thinks it was Sir Thomas Kitson, Sheriff of London, and Rollins suggests Anthony Kitson the bookseller). In any case, both Tottel's editor and AH generalize the reference, perhaps to avoid giving offence to whoever Kitson was.

55	Nott suggests that treading on the spit would please because it would efface the evidence of illness and approaching death. He also compares Horace, *Satires*, II. 5. 106–9.

56–7   Cf. *Canterbury Tales*, I. 587–622.

68   AH omits 'sister'. This may refer to various factions' attempts to gain favour with Henry VIII by baiting him with their womenfolk; the Howards, who produced both Anne Boleyn and Catherine Howard, were particularly adept at this kind of manoeuvre.

72   Q8 reads 'trane' for 'turne'.

75–7   Pandarus orchestrated the affair between his niece or cousin Criseyde, and Troilus. He is certainly no 'fole of conscience' in Chaucer's version of the story even though he does not gain materially (III. 260–64, 400–406).

78   'Be next thy selfe': Rebholz compares Terence, *The Girl from Andros*, IV. i. 12.

91   Proverbial; see Tilley WIII, 'To pour water into a sieve'.

137

[Q1: 127] Poulter's measure. The poem's source is probably Johannes de Sacrobosco's *Tractus de Sphaera*, a common basic textbook on Ptolemaic astronomy in the late medieval and Renaissance period. The poem also appears in AH (140) and E (124); in the latter it is in Wyatt's hand and the poem is revised, also in his hand. There is a direct relationship between E and the *Miscellany* in this poem; as Harrier comments, 'Despite the influence of the *A*[H] text on *T*[ottel], certain variants show that the editor of *T*[ottel] had access to *E*. *T*[ottel] reflects *E* in lines 49, 65, and 69, where *A*[H] shows emendation.' There has been much conjecture about why the poem is unfinished, ranging from Wyatt's death to pressing diplomatic work. See Rebholz for a summary. Iopas was the musician who sang about the moon, sun, time, space and seasons at the feast Dido gave for Aeneas when he arrived in Carthage (*Aeneid*, I. 740–46).

1–2   See *Aeneid*, I. Aeneas and a group of other Trojans who escaped from the fall of Troy were washed up in Carthage, Dido's kingdom. This was orchestrated by Juno (see *Aeneid*, I. 4), who wished to prevent Aeneas from reaching Italy and founding Rome. 'Libik' is Carthaginian.

2–3   Q8 reads 'Amos' for 'Juno' and 'Itlas' for 'Atlas', suggest-
            ing the unfamiliarity of these classical names.

3–4   The syntax is tricky here. Iopas, with his curly hair and
            golden harp, sang in song what mighty Atlas had taught
            him.

4   Q8 reads 'holden' for 'golden'.

7   This probably refers to the nine spheres, kept in place by
            'more power', i.e. the greater power of God, but Rebholz
            suggests that alternatively it may mean the eight spheres,
            kept in place by the ninth, 'the first and moving heaven'.

8   The 'repugnant kindes' are the four elements, air, fire,
            water, and earth, of which only earth is fixed and immov-
            able. The first version of the line in E has 'the dyuerse'
            instead of 'Repugnant', but Wyatt's hand changes it to
            'repugnant'.

9   Q8 omits 'thinges'.

12   Before Wyatt revised the line in E, it read 'the stery skye
            vnder the wiche there movith othr sevyn'. The opposite
            emendation is made in line 41, where 'firmament' is dis-
            carded in favour of 'sterry skye'.

15–16   'restlesse sours': originally 'restles recours' in E, before
            Wyatt revised it to 'restles sours'; 'the first' ('this hevin' in
            pre-revision E), i.e. 'the first and moving heaven' moves
            with swift revolution and a restless rising movement. E ini-
            tially has 'sevin' instead of eight, but is revised.

17   The 'rolling case' is the container within which are the
            eighth spheres.

23–31   These lines in E were the subject of confusing revisions by
            Wyatt; see Rebholz for a discussion. In line 23, 'discribd by
            sterres not bryght' was added as a replacement for the
            phrase 'as Axell is this lyik'.

31   The 'erring seven' are the seven planets which move east-
            wards, but occasionally stray backwards (taking 'smaller
            bywayes', line 33) before taking up their original path
            again. E read 'wandryng' until emended to 'erryng'.

32   Q8 reads 'Go' for 'So'.

39–40   A tenth sphere is introduced here between 'the first and
            moving heaven' and 'the firmament' (lines 11–12).

41–5	'[T]he seventh heaven, which gathers up all those degrees with aged pace and performs the same, carries Saturn' (Rebholz).
41	'next to the starry sky': E's initial reading 'movethe under that' is subsequently altered to 'under the firmament', and then to 'next to the sterry skye'. See note on line 12.
45	AH has 'boute' not 'bowt'.
48	E read 'Iorney' until Wyatt revised the word to 'viage'.
51	E read 'movithe all this war' until altered to 'in iij hunderd days'.
54	The sun is the eye of the day.
55	i.e. Venus.
61	This last sphere ('sky') is the moon, last because closest to the earth, has travelled 'those waies'. E reads 'first' for 'fixt'.
69–70	'[T]he Sun has the smallest epicycle, [and of course] the sphere of the fixed stars, which we have called the eighth sphere, has only one movement of its own (the epicycles of ll. 67–8 being confined to planets)' (Rebholz). AH has 'straye still' for 'stray lest' in line 69.
75	Q8 reads 'wil' for 'well'.
76–7	The spheres of the seven planets revolve on a different axis to that of the first moving heaven, but the eighth sphere, the 'firmament' has been omitted.

Q8 adds the title 'S.' (i.e. Sir) to Wyatt's name here.

UNCERTAIN AUTHORS

138

[Q1: 168] In poulter's measure. Generically the poem is, as the title suggests, a complaint, but it is addressed not to the beloved specifically, but to ladies in general, who are asked to intervene on the speaker's behalf. The style marks the poem out clearly as a mediocre imitation of Surrey's poems in poulter's measure.

| 11–12 | Puttenham quotes these lines as an example of '*Etiologia*, or the Reason-Renderer, or the Tell-Cause' (p. 314). |
| 15 | The 'ye' refers to the ladies addressed at the poem's beginning, not to God. |

17–18   The idea of the love-god Cupid firing his love-inducing arrows from the lady's eyes is a commonplace one.

38   Q8 reads 'content' for 'consent'.

41–2   Cf. Donne's 'The Good-Morrow', lines 6–7.

47–50   These lines imply that the speaker has gone overseas in war, perhaps in one of Henry VIII's French wars. This may be true of the poet himself, or it may be that he is ventriloquizing Surrey.

64   Cf. poems 6, line 14 and 42, line 14.

66   The passive-aggressive threat to the lady's 'name' or reputation is typical of certain kinds of courtly love poetry; though she is promised a bad name for cruelty, there may be an implication that the speaker, who has been her accepted lover (lines 21–2) can harm her reputation in other ways. Addressing the whole poem to the other ladies may also hint at this possibility.

139

[Q1: 169] By John Harington of Stepney (1517–82). In poulter's measure. An elegy. Also in BL MS Cotton Titus A. 24, with a few insignificant variants. Sir Richard Devereux, father of the future Earl of Essex, Walter Devereux, and grandfather of Penelope Devereux (Philip Sidney's Stella) and Elizabeth I's favourite Robert Devereux, second Earl of Essex (executed for treason in 1601), died in 1547. His father was Walter Devereux, third Baron Ferrers of Chartley, created Viscount Hereford in 1550 (that he is not given this title here indicates that the poem's title is probably authorial). Sir Walter was a significant figure, after his son's death, in the Edwardian regime; he was allied to the Grey family, and was briefly imprisoned on Mary's accession, when he lost his offices; the poem as published may constitute as much a lament for a family's worldly success as for the death of a son.

2   Fruits may refer to offspring or to worldly achievement (see Tom MacFaul, *Poetry and Paternity in Renaissance England: Sidney, Spenser, Shakespeare, Donne and Jonson* (Cambridge: Cambridge University Press, 2010)).

5   To long upward may be to yearn for heaven, or for social advancement.

13   Probably refers to service in Henry VIII's French wars in 1544, to which Sir Richard may well have followed his

father Sir Walter (who certainly fought there); the family's services to Henry and to Edward VI were considerable.

14   'Brutes' refers to Britons, the supposed descendants of Brutus; see note to poem 131, line 5; it might refer more specifically to the Welsh, as most of the Devereux estates were in Wales and the Welsh Marches.

17   Marcus Porcius Cato the Censor was a classic exemplar of wisdom, particularly for urging the destruction of Carthage; his grandson Cato the Younger was in turn a classic exemplar of incorruptibility and doomed republican virtue.

18   The mythical Athenian hero Theseus' friendship for Pirithous was one of the major classic exemplars of the friendship ideal – see also poem 166, line 30, and note to poem 277, line 29.

140

[Q1: 170] Possibly by Surrey. In tetrameter quatrains with alternating rhyme. Poems on this theme are quite a distinct subgenre of moral verse: the 'mean' (i.e. lowly) estate is not to be confused with the 'mean' (i.e. middle estate) praised in poems on the golden mean, such as poems 32, 163 and 253; other poems on the virtues of poverty are 128, 134, 160 and 169. There are other copies of this poem in AH (17) and B, with some variants, the most important of which are noted below. In B it follows Surrey's poem 4. The signing of this poem 'with the same distinctive H' as the 'H.S.' with which the Surrey poem is signed led Muir to conclude 'There is no reason to doubt that Surrey wrote this poem too' (Kenneth Muir, 'Surrey Poems in the Blage Manuscript', *Notes and Queries*, NS 7 (1960), p. 368). Another version of the poem was printed in Breton's *The Arber of Amorous Devices* (1597).

The poem is a good example of its kind, and is alluded to in William Warner's *Albion's England* (1602), IV. 20.

1   To be racked is to suffer very specific tortures, such as might well be in the minds of a mid-sixteenth-century audience, at a time when many people were being tortured for heresy. That it is right that is being racked is significant: either a Roman Catholic under Edward or a Protestant under Mary might think themselves in the right, but still be being put on the rack and trampled. Alternatively, the reference might be to the less painful sufferings of Elizabeth

Tudor, whom some might consider the rightful monarch (a sentiment particularly appropriate to John Harington, who attended her in the Tower of London during her imprisonment there in 1554).

3   B reads 'by' for 'my'.

4   B reads 'my' for 'The'.

5   Q8 omits 'God for'.

6   AH reads 'richesse leese his due' for 'riches lose his shape'.

8   AH reads 'sue' for 'hap'.

15   AH reads 'to stryf is bent' for 'impacient'. B reads 'for most part is' for 'is most part'.

21–8   The apologetic and well-wishing tone of the last two stanzas imply that the poem was written to a specific patron.

24   AH reads 'rove' for 'row'.

26   B reads 'good' for 'well'.

28   AH reads 'stay' for 'ceasse'.

141

[Q1: 171] The poem was attributed to John Harington by his descendant Henry Harington in NA, where a shorter version of the poem is given the title 'Elegy wrote in the Tower by John Harington, confined with the Princess Elizabeth, 1554'; Rollins is sceptical about the attribution, but it may represent a family tradition. John Harington was imprisoned with Elizabeth that year, suspected of complicity in the younger Sir Thomas Wyatt's rebellion. It is possible that a good number of the early Uncertain Authors poems are by Harington. In pentameter Venus and Adonis stanzas. A poem on the vanity of life. It appears in AH (19) and Bodleian MS Ashmole 48; the most important variants are listed below. A version of the poem was also printed in *The Paradise of Dainty Devices*.

The poem is a fine example of its kind; similar poems were often written by those imprisoned in the Tower, the greatest being Sir Walter Ralegh's 'The Ocean to Scinthia'. This poem, unlike most other such poems, might be read as a call to patient preparation against the day of a Protestant restoration.

6   Cf. poem 138, line 64. AH and MS Ashmole 48 read 'short[n]yth' for 'endeth'.

7   MS Ashmole 48 reads 'and' for 'Yet'.

9   AH reads 'my god I thanck' for 'The Lord be praised'.

12   AH reads 'shall' for the second 'doth'.

13   MS Ashmole 48 reads 'sown [i.e. 'soon'] so swyftly' for
         'seme, so swift that'. AH reads 'swiftlye' for 'swift that'.

16   MS Ashmole 48 reads 'hytt' for 'mete'; this rhymes with
         that MS's spelling 'flytt' in line 14.

20   AH reads 'shonne' for 'drede'.

24   The dance of death was a common medieval motif, and
         remained popular in the Renaissance – see Michael Neill,
         *Issues of Death: Mortality and Identity in English Renais-
         sance Tragedy* (Oxford: Clarendon Press, 1997). AH reads
         'hymself doth only' for 'the Lord alone'.

26   MS Ashmole 48 omits 'doth'.

27   AH reads 'what greefes do grow what daungers dayly springe'.

28   AH reads 'safe' for 'sure'. MS Ashmole 48 reads 'tyme' for
         'daies'.

30   MS Ashmole 48 reads 'ys happyar' for 'were better'.

33   MS Ashmole 48 reads 'swet' for 'dere'.

34   MS Ashmole 48 reads 'ytt yeldyth all in Vayne' for 'that all
         it yeldes is vayn'.

35   AH and MS Ashmole 48 read 'was' for 'is'.

36   MS Ashmole 48 omits 'likewise'.

37–8   The reference may be to 2 Corinthians 5: 1.

39   Cf. Ephesians 6: 11, and Romans 2: 5.

40   MS Ashmole 48 reads 'we may' for 'they'.

142

[Q1: 172] In poulter's measure. An Ovidian narrative ending with
an apostrophe to the beloved. The source of the tale of Pygmalion is
Ovid, *Metamorphoses*, X. 243–97. The story of Pygmalion, with its
considerable erotic possibilities, remained popular with the Eliza-
bethans: see, for example, John Marston, *The Metamorphosis of
Pygmalion's Image* (1598). The motif of Nature's attitude to creating
too beautiful a person turns up in a lot of Elizabethan verse, such as
Sidney's *Astrophel and Stella*, 7, and Shakespeare's Sonnet 20. There
is another copy of this poem in AH (143), with some variants, the
most important of which are noted below.

18   AH reads 'toucht' for 'coucht'.

21   The AH variant 'envious' for 'curious' may seem to make
            less sense, but envy was a broader-ranging word in the six-
            teenth century, implying general malice or tendency to
            cause harm; 'curious' often implies 'careful' more than its
            modern meaning.

24   The reference to an idol has a certain resonance in the mid-
            sixteenth century, so soon after the stripping of Catholic
            idols from churches in the Edwardian period.

32   The phrase 'break the mould' is proverbial. (In modern
            usage it seems to have slipped into meaning 'do something
            new'; in its original usage it means that something is unique
            because the mould used to make it has been discarded.)

143

[Q1: 173] An English sonnet. Printed versions, with significant vari-
ants, in *The Melville Book of Roundels* and John Forbes, *Cantus,
Songs and Fancies* testify to the poem's enduring popularity, as do
imitations by John Hall in *The Courte of Vertue* (1565) and George
Turberville in *Epitaphes*. A love complaint. The poem may have influ-
enced Shakespeare – his use of 'Like to the lark' in Sonnet 29, line 11,
is very different but is perhaps an echo; line 8 may be echoed in Son-
net 58, and the tone of the sonnet is similar to many others of
Shakespeare. If this be but a vain belief, the poem still seems a candi-
date to be regarded as the best of the uncertain authors' poems.

1–2   Cf. *Troilus and Criseyde*, III. 1191–2.

144

[Q1: 174] Just possibly by Surrey. Three tetrameter Venus and Adonis
stanzas with the last line of each acting as a burden. An example of
rhetorical climax (the ladder figure). Sidney would use this figure to
begin *Astrophel and Stella*, 1. A poem on the vanity of life. There are
other copies of this poem in BL MS Sloane 159 and Bodleian MS
Rawlinson Poetical 85, with some insignificant variants, the last
ascribing the poem to Surrey (but perhaps only doing so as some read-
ers assumed his authorship of the whole *Miscellany*); the last two
stanzas also appear in BL MS Add. 26737.

10   Q4 and Q8 read 'merier' for 'mery'.

145

[Q1: 175] Henry Harington, in *NA*, ascribed a revised version of this poem to his ancestor John Harington; Rollins is probably right to dismiss this. Tetrameter Venus and Adonis stanzas. A love complaint. There is another copy of this poem in AH (15); the most significant variants are listed below. There is also another similar poem in AH (269).

1–7   AH version reads as follows:

> Unto my songe geve eare that wyll
> and deeme my doinges as you please
> for I shall tell yf you be still
> what trade I toke to lyve in ease
> and how those wayes that I wayd best
> in fyne did fayle to myne unrest
> The dayes were once and very late . . .

10–12   The syntax is complicated: 'in any payn' seems a belated adverbial qualification of 'toke no charge'; thus the lines mean 'I didn't care for anything to do with love, at least not so far as to take any pains over it'.

14–16   Lines 14 and 16 are transposed in AH.

17   Reads 'From all suche thinges my hart was free' in AH.

21   AH reads 'their woes I mockt' for 'Where fortune laught'.

25–36   Cupid's attempts to entrap man would become a commonplace of Elizabethan poetry.

26   AH reads 'fourthe' for 'still'.

33   AH reads 'saw' for 'how', which makes better sense.

36   AH reads 'cast' for 'threw'.

43   Q8 omits 'even in a maze'. AH reads 'that' for 'even'.

47   AH reads 'that' for 'ever'

50   AH reads 'kyndes' for 'sortes', therefore not alliterating.

51   AH reads 'heale' for 'salve'.

53   AH reads 'health' for 'life'.

55   AH reads 'Wherefore synce' for 'But seing now'.

56   AH reads 'fest' for 'bounde'.

60   AH reads 'lack powre to flye the' for 'be caught within his'. Q2 ends the poem with a comma – other editions do not.

146

[Q1: 176] Tetrameter Venus and Adonis stanzas. A moral personifica-
tion and complaint, though expressing doubts as to the validity of
personifying Fortune in particular.

10	Fortune was traditionally pictured presiding over a wheel, which symbolized her power to make or break individuals' success.
13	Q8 reads 'so' for 'as'.
24	Q8 reads 'toles' for 'joyes'.
27	Q4 and Q8 read 'life' for 'lief'.
31	Q1 reads 'cause' rather than 'causes', which is metrically if not semantically preferable.
32	Jesus Christ is traditionally the Prince of Peace: to quarrel against the cause(s) of things would be to quarrel against God, considered as the prime mover or ultimate cause of the whole universe. A traditional complaint against Fortune therefore has to be qualified, as God/Christ must lie behind Fortune; however, one may quarrel against Fame, which seems less in divine control.

147

[Q1: 177] Two pentameter rhyme royal stanzas. A moral complaint
or ode against rumour.

1	It is a commonplace to imagine tongues as the clappers inside bells: e.g. Lording Barry, *Ram Alley* (*c.* 1608, pub. 1611): 'Come yo' are lusty, you wenches are like bells, / You give no musick, till you feele the clapper'.
9	Q8 reads 'in' for 'to'.
10	Q4 and Q8 read 'enhaunce' for 'enchaunce'.

148

[Q1: 179] An English sonnet. An epigrammatic sustained conceit or
comparison filled with commonplace images of Hades.

3	Pluto was the classical god of the underworld, Hades.
5	Tantalus' punishment was to inhabit a pool beneath a tree whose fruits would recede from his grasp; his various sins

included stealing ambrosia and nectar from the gods, and trying to serve the gods his son Pelops for dinner.

9   Prometheus' punishment was to have his liver pecked out by an eagle every day (it grew back overnight); his sin was stealing fire from the gods and giving it to man.

11   Sisyphus' punishment was to roll a boulder uphill only for it to roll back down again; his sins included violations of hospitality, and incest.

12   Probably refers to Cerberus, the hound of hell; the plural may be necessary because he had three heads. Alternatively, the hounds of hell may refer metonymically to the various sufferings of those in Hades.

149

[Q1: 180] A poem in fourteener couplets. A dream vision. There is another copy of this poem in AH (265).

1   AH reads 'In dumppes but late wheare as I lay' for 'By fortune as I lay in bed'.

5   AH reads 'even theare' after 'sodcinly' and omits 'wofull'.

6   AH reads 'waves' for 'waies'.

8   AH reads 'how sone from wealth ofte graunted' for 'And that from wealth ygraunted'.

9   AH reads 'yet' for 'it'.

10   The cockatrice was a mythical medieval beast, a chimerical mixture of a cock and a dragon, though sometimes with snaky bits too; like the basilisk of classical mythology, it was able to turn people to stone by looking at them, but it could also poison by touch or bite.

13–14   Placed after line 16 in AH.

17   Q8 reads 'to lynger' for 'no lenger'.

20   MS omits 'flying' and reads 'trulye' after 'seen'.

21–2   Placed after line 30 in AH, which omits 'saw' and 'do' and reads 'lyeth' for 'falleth'.

25–6   Omitted in AH.

26   Q8 reads 'spot' for 'sport'.

29   Virtue is here personified as spinning the threads of life, an

activity more normally ascribed to the three Fates (cf. note to poem 108, and poem 151). AH reads 'wheare Atrapose did sytt' for 'eke vertue, how she sat'; given that Atropos was the fatal sister who normally cut the thread of life (Clotho did the spinning), that may seem the better reading.

30   AH has different lines after 30: first its version of the *Miscellany*'s lines 21–2, and then the following (which incorporate a version of the *Miscellany*'s lines 31–2):

I saw a lofte uppon the wheele/ Honour in highe estate
Whose wretched end most eyes behelde/ loe, heare his fynall fate
The happyste man theare I saw then/ who sought no greedy gayne
but with his calling was content/ delighting in the meane
I saw and heard the dolefull crye/ of people in the land
how wickednes the world gan wylde/ and had the upper hand
In place of Judgement theare I sawe/ with fearce and cruell moode
wheare wrong that blooddye beast was sett/ drincking the giltles bloode
and when all theise with many moe/ I saw moste perfectlye
in me my thought eache one had wrought/ A perfect propertie
Then sighing said I thus o lord/ at thye moste dreadfull dome
When Riche and poore bothe good and bad/ before thie seat shall come
Thow lyke a just and rightuous judge/ there shalt rewarde each wight
according as he heare hath wrought/ to darknes ells to light[.]

AH then omits the *Miscellany*'s lines 33–4, before concluding with essentially the same couplet as the *Miscellany*.

32   Q8 reads 'brought' for 'wrought'.

35   Q8 and AH read 'constraine' for 'constayne'.

36   Branches may refer to lines of thought, but the word also frequently suggests the horns of a cuckold – e.g. John Marston, *The Insatiate Countess* (c. 1607), I. i. 453 and II. iii. 106, and Edward Sharpham, *Cupid's Whirligig* (1607), p. 8.

150

[Q1: 181] In four-line stanzas, alternating tetrameters and trimeters, with alternating rhyme. A pastoral narrative with embedded complaint. One of the earliest examples of pastoral in English, and a fine example too. There are no known MS versions, but the poem was much copied and imitated; a version is in *England's Helicon* (1600), ascribed to Surrey (or his son). The names are interesting: Corin is a standard pastoral name, as is Phyllida, but Harpalus was a boyhood friend of Alexander the Great.

7   Twisting corn-ropes was a key skill for a pastoral heroine (as was making garlands, lines 14–15).

32   Q8 reads 'shent' for 'spent'.

68   A reads 'face' for 'makes', obviously in error.

151

[Q1: 182] In alexandrine (i.e. hexameter) Venus and Adonis stanzas. An elegy. Sir James Wilford (c. 1517–50) was a soldier and friend of the younger Sir Thomas Wyatt. He fought in France in 1544–5 and was provost-marshal of the Duke of Somerset's army invading Scotland in 1547. He was the leader of a 'masterly' (ODNB) defence of the town of Haddington against the Scots, but was later captured, and his imprisonment ruined his health. Other poems on his death are 158 and A156–7.

1   Refers to the Fates, or Parcae; see note to poem 108.

4–5   The main point here is that Wilford died just before he reached 35 years of age, thus having lived only half the biblical threescore and ten. However, there may also be a reference in the idea of tripping to the story of Nisus and Euryalus in Virgil, Aeneid, V. 327–38: when Nisus slips in the footrace he trips up another competitor so as to allow his friend Euryalus to win. There may therefore be a hint here that the poet is a friend of Wilford's who will go on to win the race on his dead friend's behalf.

6   The House of Fame probably refers to Chaucer's poem of that name.

152

[Q1: 183] Poulter's measure. A moral ode about the state of the world. BL MS Cotton Titus A. 24 has some variants, the most interesting of which are listed below.

5   MS reads 'clime' for 'get' and 'eche' for 'hie'.

15   MS reads 'hydste' for 'hordst'.

153

[Q1: 184] Poulter's measure. A poem of repentance, perhaps in imita-
tion of the penitential psalms. There is another copy of this poem in
AH (73); the most significant variants are listed below, as are some
variants from BL MS Sloane 1896, which gives the poem's title as 'The
repentant sinner in adversity prayeth unto god for mercy'. The poem
puts a distinctly Protestant emphasis on faith as the only means to
God's grace. The *Miscellany*'s title may imply that the poem's author
was imprisoned ('durance', *OED* 5), presumably under the Marian
regime.

1   AH reads 'thee' for 'the'.

2   The idea of the shell as a starting point perhaps alludes to
            Horace, *Ars Poetica*, 147, which refers to the shell ('ab
            ovo'), from which Helen was born as a possible starting
            point for a Troy narrative.

4   MS Sloane reads 'call' for 'grate'; the verb 'grate' may mean
            importune (*OED*, 'grate', v.1:4, deriving its meaning from
            scrape, via irritate), or it may be a northernism, meaning
            weep (*OED*, 'greet', v.2). For the phrasing here, cf. poems
            249, line 43, and 250, line 62.

7   AH reads 'race' for 'way'.

9   AH reads 'The pathe that I pursude/ hath brought' for 'The
            throng wherin I thrust, hath throwen'. Q4 and Q8 read
            'through' for 'throng'.

12   AH reads 'of' for 'and'.

18   Q8 reads 'with faith' for 'which sayth'.

19   AH reads 'you' for first 'it', which is closer to the biblical
            'Ask, and it shall be given you; seek, and ye shall find;
            knock, and it shall be opened unto you' (Matthew 7: 7, cf.
            Luke 11: 9). Q8 reads 'Knocked' for 'Knocke and'.

21   Refers to the parable of the Prodigal Son: see Luke 15.

25   Cf. Psalm 38: 22.

26   MS Sloane reads 'me for passed' for 'the for passed'.

28   Q1 and MS Sloane read 'lone' for 'love'. Given that AH
            reads 'love', it is hard to decide which is right.

31   Cf. Christ's 'Father, if thou be willing, remove this cup
            from me: nevertheless not my will, but thine, be done'
            (Luke 22: 42).

33–4   Puttenham quotes these lines as an example of '*Synonymia,
         or the Figure of Store*', commenting 'Here "faith", "hope,"
         and "trust" be words of one effect, allowed to us by this
         Figure of Store' (p. 300).

37   AH reads 'eke confesse' for 'knowledge eke'.

38   AH ends after this line due to a torn page.

154

[Q1: 185] Tetrameter quatrains with alternating rhymes. Partly based
on Petrarch, *Rime*, 23, which is a *canzone*, beginning 'Nel dolce tempo
de la prima etade' [In the sweet time of my first age]. The poem was
imitated in *The Paradise of Dainty Devices*. C. S. Lewis, who admired
this poem greatly, observes: 'The canzone is Petrarch at his most medi-
eval. The English poet has omitted the characteristically Petrarchan
transformations of the lover into a fountain, a stag, and a laurel. He
sees his original through the eyes of Chaucer and produces what is
almost exactly an abridged version of the mourner's narrative in the
Boke of the Duchesse. The result is a very gem of this transitional art,
the disarming tenderness of the Middle Ages in the sober quatrains of
the Drab Age' (*English Literature in the Sixteenth Century Excluding
Drama* (Oxford: Clarendon Press, 1954), p. 238). A love complaint, it
is the longest poem in the *Miscellany*.

18–19   See note to poem 146, line 10.

59   The love-god Cupid was traditionally depicted as a blind
         archer.

66   Q8 omits 'yet'.

214   Q8 reads 'her' for 'his'.

226   Q1 reads 'Mishappe I meane' for 'Cruell mishappe'.

256   Q8 reads 'in' for 'all'.

155

[Q1: 186] An English sonnet. A celebration of success in love. The
poem's punning on a name invites us to identify the poet's mistress,
but sadly the name White is far too common for us to do more than
speculate: Sir Thomas White, founder of St John's College, Oxford,
and a notable philanthropist, was, as Lord Mayor of London, a key
figure in the suppression of Sir Thomas Wyatt the younger's rebellion;
he prompted considerable animosity for this and for his efforts to ban

city amusements (though his posthumous reputation was excellent), and it is just possible that he is the target here. His first wife, Avicia, died in 1558, without issue. White was certainly the most eminent married man of that name in Marian England, but the poem is suggestive without identifying a subject.

6   This lovely line is enriched by the idea that the woman's complexion is 'orient' not only in the sense of being brilliant like eastern jewels, but in being associated with the dawn, which not only does away with night (line 4), but is traditionally rosy in colour (line 5).

7   Q1 reads the metrically preferable 'nere' for 'nerer'. Q8 omits 'bewty'.

9   Clearly implies that White, the husband of this woman, is being cuckolded by the poet. As such, the poem might be a precedent for Sidney's attacks on his beloved's husband by punning on his surname Rich, e.g. *Astrophel and Stella*, 24.

156

[Q1: 187] The first stanza is in rhyme royal, i.e. rhymes ABABBCC (pentameters); the second stanza is clearly intended to be rhyme royal too, but is missing a line after line 10 (see below). The poem is set up as a riddle (the answer being love); H78 gives the first stanza, with an answer. There is another copy of this poem in AH (313); the most significant variants are listed below.

5   AH omits 'which' (in general the scansion of the *Miscellany* is superior to that of AH).

6   AH reads 'thus may I say I' for 'Still thus to seke, and'.

7   AH reads 'new' for 'newest'.

8   AH reads 'In wilfull Riches I have found povertie'.

10   After this line AH reads 'Nothing but plentie caused my scarcenes'.

157

[Q1: 188] Tetrameter quatrains with alternating rhyme. A moral ode, which is a textbook example of Erasmian *copia* – many proverbial examples being given of the same idea (summed up in the title).

16   Q8 reads 'at' for 'all'.

19–20	Rollins explains: 'no lack of residents (no abundance of soldiers) can defend the castle successfully when Wit and Will and Diligence unite to assault it.'
22	Q8 reads 'live' for 'lye'.

158

[Q1: 189] Poulter's measure. Ekphrasis of a portrait as well as an elegy. On Sir James Wilford, see note to poem 151.

4	Q1 reads 'his love to traine' for 'to end his life'.

159

[Q1: 190] Poulter's measure (though without the indentations that are normal for that form in the *Miscellany*). A female complaint. The poem probably imitates Surrey's poems on the same subject; see poems 17 and 19.

5	Line omitted in Q8.

160

[Q1: 191] Tetrameter Venus and Adonis stanzas. A moral ode on the superiority of the low estate; see poem 140, and cf. poems 128, 134 and 169.

9	Q8 reads 'beloved' for 'loved'.
14	Q8 reads 'wayling' for 'welling'.
28	Titan refers to Hyperion, the original sun-god before the usurpation of the Olympians.
31	The legendary bird the Phoenix was supposed to be reborn from its own ashes; here it may be confused with emblems of the eagle, which proverbially climbed as high as the sun, thus confounding an image of rebirth with one of proud overreaching.
34	Q8 reads 'masketh' for 'masheth'.

161

[Q1: 192] Tetrameter Venus and Adonis stanzas. A promise of fidelity with considerable moral *copia*.

10   A 'gogen gift' is presumably a gudgeon (the fish), which was not only little regarded, but was a byword for what a dupe might accept; hence by extension a dupe could be described as a gudgeon (with various spellings).

13   Q4 and subsequent editions read 'gain' rather than 'grain', probably rightly.

17   Q8 reads 'hart' for 'part'.

36   Q8 reads 'loe' for 'so'.

42   The idea of love as the leader of a military expedition may echo Surrey's and Wyatt's poems, 6 and 42 above.

43   Q8 reads 'ensing' for 'ensigne'.

45   Q8 reads 'yfold' for 'I fold'.

162

[Q1: 193] Rhymes ABABABAB, the A-lines tetrameter and the B-lines trimeter. An epigram. In Q1 it is titled 'Of a new married student'. It was generally agreed that marriage distracted a young man from his studies; however, Lord Herbert of Cherbury, in the early seventeenth century, thought his marrying while a student was helpful: 'now having a due remedy for that Lasciviousnes to which youth is naturally inclined I followed my booke more Close then ever' (Edward Herbert (Lord Herbert of Cherbury), *The Life of Edward, First Lord Herbert of Cherbury: Written by Himself*, ed. J. M. Shuttleworth (London: Oxford University Press, 1976), p. 16). The epigram's key joke (the marriage knot making the young man 'undone') became something of a commonplace, and may lie behind the (possibly apocryphal) joke about John Donne's marriage, '*John Donne, Anne Donne, Un-done*' (see R. C. Bald, *John Donne: A Life* (Oxford: Clarendon Press, 1986), p. 139). 'Fast and loose' is an impossible fairground game in which one must try to skewer a belt as it unrolls – its appearance in the title is the first known usage of the phrase, but it does not seem to allude very directly to the game itself.

163

[Q1: 194] The poem's form could be considered octameter couplets (hence the lack of capitals beginning the even lines), or tetrameter quatrains rhyming AxAx; lines 25–8 are a quatrain rhyming ABAB. A version of Horace, *Odes*, II. 10, also imitated as poems 32 and 253.

5   Q8 reads 'crooked' for 'crocked'.

6   Q8 reads 'gest' for 'lest'.

164

[Q1: 195] Poulter's measure. A love complaint. Puttenham discusses
the first line as an example of '*Catachresis*, or the Figure of Abuse',
commenting: 'Whereas this word "lent" is properly of money or some
such other thing as men do commonly borrow for use, to be repaid
again, and being applied to love is utterly abused, and yet very com-
mendably spoken by virtue of this figure. For he that loveth and is not
beloved again hath no less wrong than he that lendeth and is never
repaid' (p. 265).

12   Q8 reads 'of' for 'to'.

165

[Q1: 196] Poulter's measure. A translation of Lucretius, *De Rerum
Natura* (*On the Nature of the Universe*), II. 1–22:

> Suave, mari magno turbantibus aequora ventis,
> e terra magnum alterius spectare laborem;
> non quia vexari quemquamst iucunda voluptas,
> sed quibus ipse malis careas quia cernere suave est.
> suave etiam belli certamina magna tueri
> per campos instructa tua sine parte pericli.
> sed nihil dulcius est bene quam munita tenere
> edita doctrina sapientum templa serena,
> despicere unde queas alios passimque videre
> errare atque viam palantis quaerere vitae,
> certare ingenio, contendere nobilitate,
> noctes atque dies niti praestante labore
> ad summas emergere opes rerumque potiri.
> o miseras hominum mentes, o pectora caeca!
> qualibus in tenebris vitae quantisque periclis
> degitur hoc aevi quodcumquest! nonne videre
> nihil aliud sibi naturam latrare, nisi utqui
> corpore seiunctus dolor absit, mente fruatur
> iucundo sensu cura semota metuque?
> ergo corpoream ad naturam pauca videmus
> esse opus omnino, quae demant cumque dolorem,
> delicias quoque uti multas substernere possint.

[It is pleasant, when the winds trouble the waters on the great sea, to watch another man's great trouble from the shore; not because anyone in trouble is a joyful pleasure, but because it is pleasant to see what evils you are free from. It is also pleasant to see the great struggles of war laid out over the plains without participating in the dangers yourself. But nothing is sweeter than to possess serene temples well stocked with wise teachings, from which you may look down on and despise others all wandering about seeking the paths of life, struggling in their wits, competing over status, striving night and day with excessive labour to climb the pinnacle of wealth and for power over the world. O miserable minds of men, O blind hearts! In what shades of life and in how many dangers your portion of life is spent! Surely you see that nature barks for nothing but this – that pain be taken away from the body, and that the mind flourish in delight, away from worries and fear? Therefore we see that few things are necessary for bodily nature, except that which takes away pain, and that which can spread many delights for our use].

The *Miscellany*'s final couplet is not in the original, and its moral *sententia* makes the translation into a poem on the value of the mean or low estate.

166

[Q1: 197] In fourteener couplets. The poem is a loose translation of Horace, *Odes*, IV. 7. There is another copy of the poem in BL MS Cotton Titus A. 24, with a few variants, the most significant of which are noted below.

1	MS reads 'ougly' for 'griesly'.
2	MS reads 'tender' for 'lusty' – cf. poem 1, line 1.
9	Zephyrus was the classical god of the west wind, proverbially gentle.
16	MS reads the metrically preferable 'left us' for 'had made so'.
17–20	This section replaces lines in Horace discussing the fact that Aeneas and two later Roman kings are dust.
18	MS reads the metrically preferable 'abide' for 'continue'.
19	Q8 reads 'lost have' for 'have lost'.
22	MS reads 'What' for 'No'.
24	Minos was one of the three judges of the classical underworld; this is a textbook instance of confounding classical and Christian mythology, Horace's Minos functioning as a

typological equivalent for Christ at the Day of Judgement, invoked in the previous line. MS reads 'gyves of the' for 'doth pronounce'; the *Miscellany*'s version is clearer.

25   Q8 reads 'them' for 'the'.

26   Q1 reads 'surged' for 'sugred', obviously in error.

28   Cf. Virgil, *Aeneid*, VI. 126–9:

> facilis descensus Averno:
> noctes atque dies patet atri ianua Ditis;
> sed revocare gradum superasque evadere ad auras,
> hoc opus, hic labor est.

[The descent to Avernus (the underworld) is easy: the doors of dark Dis stand open day and night; but to recall one's step and escape to the air above, that is the difficulty, that's the real work].

29   In classical myth, Hippolytus, son of Theseus, was dedicated to hunting, chastity and the goddess of these vocations Artemis/Diana; he rejected the advances of his stepmother Phaedra, who accused him of raping her; Theseus therefore arranged for a sea-monster to scare his son's horses into killing him. His patron goddess could not save him, though she does appear at the beginning and end of Euripides' play, *Hippolytus*. MS reads 'helpe from thense the' for 'thence deliver'.

30   Theseus went down to Hades on an unsuccessful rescue mission when his friend Pirithous died.

167

[Q1: 198] Tetrameter quatrains with alternating rhyme. A love complaint.

4   Q8 omits 'her'.

15   Q8 reads 'my' for 'me'.

168

[Q1: 199] Possibly by John Heywood (1496/7–*c*. 1578). Quatrains with alternating rhyme; lines with A-rhymes are tetrameter and those with B-rhymes trimeter. As Rollins notes, a version of the poem in BL MS Harley 1703, made around 1572 (which attributes it to Heywood), states that the poem is in praise of Mary Tudor (perhaps during the period when she was declared illegitimate – *c.* 1534); there are many variants, only the most significant of which are noted below.

10   The naked boy is Cupid, the love-god, but the reference also reminds us of the little dolls of themselves (or *pupillae*) lovers can see in one another's eyes.

12   In MS, lines 29–32 are placed here, followed by these extra lines:

> Among her youthfull yeares,
>   shee triumps over age,
> And yeat shee still appeares,
>   Boath wyttye, grave, and sage.

Q8 reads 'lambe' for 'lampe'.

18   Only one Phoenix was supposed to exist at a time, the next one being born from its predecessor's ashes; it was therefore a common symbol for the perpetuity of the monarchy. It became one of Elizabeth I's favourite symbols. cf. Fulke Greville, *Caelica* 61.

21–2   Diana was goddess of chastity; Odysseus' wife Penelope was a favourite example of marital fidelity and patience.

21   Q8 inserts 'a' after 'is'.

25–9   Not in MS.

31   Q8 reads 'ruddier' for 'redier'.

33   Bacchus was the god of wine; women in particular were supposed to misbehave at his orgies.

36   One of the most frequent misogynist charges against women in the Renaissance period was their supposed tendency to 'gad' about, rather than staying quietly at home.

44   After this line, the following are to be found in the MS:

> Great sute to vyce, maye some Allure,
>   that thinkes to make no fawlte,
> Wee see a forte hadde neede be sure,
>   which manye doth assaulte,
>
> They seeke an endlesse waye,
>   that thinkes to wynne her love,
> As well they maye assaye,
>   the stoney rocke to move.

> For shee is none of those,
>> that settes not bye evill fame,
> She will not lyghtly lose,
>> her truth and honest name,

45–52   MS reverses the order of these two stanzas.

47   MS reads 'floure' for 'Jelifloure'. In *The Winter's Tale*, Perdita says that gillyflowers are called 'Nature's bastards' (IV. iv. 83); it would therefore be insensitive to bring these flowers up as a model if the poem were praising Mary Tudor, whose father had repudiated her. Redeployed without reference to Mary in the *Miscellany*, however, and the flower can be taken as a model of bright beauty.

55   Q8 omits 'ever'.

56   After this line, the following are to be found in the MS:

> This worthye ladye to bewraye
>> a kinges doughter was shee,
> Of whom John Heywood lyste to saye,
>> In such worthye degree,

> And Marye was her name weete yee,
>> with these graces Indude,
> At eightene yeares, so flourisht shee,
>> so doth his meane conclude.

The removal of the identification of Mary (if the MS is not an imitation based on the *Miscellany*) implies a refusal to praise the current Queen, who would surely not have been offended by the publication of such an elegant poem in her praise.

169

[Q1: 200] In two alexandrine rhyme royal stanzas. The most significant formal aspect of the poem, however, is that it is an acrostic (which is incomplete in Q1), spelling out the name 'EDWARD SOMERSET' with the first letters of each line and the last letter of the last. A poem on the mean/low estate; cf. poems 128, 134, 140 and 160. There is another copy of this poem in AH (293), with some variants, the most important of which are noted below. Editions of the *Miscellany* after Q2 do not provide the spaces that mark out the acrostic.

Edward Seymour, Duke of Somerset, was Henry VIII's brother-in-law, and was, as Lord Protector in the first years of Edward VI's reign, responsible for the movement to a radically Protestant national Church. He fell from power in 1549, and was executed in 1552. The poem is clearly about his fall from power, but was probably not written by him.

3   AH reads 'state' for 'fate'.

10   AH reads 'fynde' for 'fele'.

11   The legendary motif of Scylla and Charybdis – sea-monsters guarding either side of a strait – was commonly moralized to represent the difficulty of sailing the ship of state.

14   Q1 is missing the capitalization of the final T. The line may allude to Horace, *Odes*, II. 10. 5–8, an ode imitated as poems 32, 163 and 253 in the *Miscellany*.

170

[Q1: 201] In poulter's measure (though without the indentations that are normal for that form in the *Miscellany*). A pastoral. Printed as Surrey's in *England's Helicon*, but almost certainly not his. Thestylis, in both Theocritus' *Idylls* and Virgil's *Eclogues*, is a woman's name, but following the *Miscellany* English pastoral writers would use it for a man – metrically, it seems to be two syllables here and in the next poem. The 'desert' of the title is not used in the modern sense, but in the sense of a wilderness, an uncultivated and unvisited place.

3   Q8 reads 'in' for 'is'.

17   Croesus, last King of Lydia, the classic example of great wealth, supposedly threw himself on a pyre when he was defeated by the Persian King Cyrus.

28   Refers to the Fates; see note to poem 108, lines 1–4.

171

[Q1: 234] In poulter's measure, like the poem it answers. Moved here from its position in Q1 for obvious reasons. The voice of the poem is uncertain: it may be the woman herself speaking – though using a modestly distancing third person – or it may be a friend of Thestylis.

7   In the E version of poem 57 above the word 'strange' is used to describe the lady's forsaking of the lover: the word probably suggests coldness or snubbing.

11   In Homer's *Iliad*, Briseis is the captured woman whom

Achilles gets as a prize and whom he loves as a wife; Agamemnon's appropriation of her leads to Achilles' withdrawal from battle; she is returned to Achilles after the feud ends.

22   The reference to Etrascus is obscure: the annotator in the Bodleian's copy of Q10 thinks it means Odysseus (who might be called Ithacus from his home island); this at least indicates that it caused some confusion in the sixteenth century. It is just possible that the reference is to the sixth-century Latin poet Maximianus, who was sometimes given the cognomen Etruscus, and who wrote elegies reflecting on love in old age.

172

[Q1: 202] Pentameters, with the rhyme scheme ABAABCBBCBDD. A love complaint. Poems with animals as intermediaries are quite common: Catullus 2 is the most famous precedent (though there the animal, a sparrow, belongs to the beloved, not the poet).

5   Q1 reads 'play' for Q2's superior 'pray'.

12   The positioning of the word 'giltles', though mainly attached to the speaker and his dog, allows it to be attached to the woman too: this fits with this sweetly comic poem's refusal to be too harsh on the woman.

173

[Q1: 203] Another rhyming innovation, though less interesting than the previous: an odd number of alternating pentameter AB rhymes capped with a couplet. A love epigram. Poems accompanying the sending of a ring are also common, the most notable precedent being Ovid, *Amores*, II. 15; cf. poem 199 below.

4   A posy (poesy, or short poem) was often engraved inside a ring. It is doubtful, however, that all of the next five lines could be so engraved.

174

[Q1: 204] Poulter's measure. The poet seems, in some obscure way, to be defending himself from accusations of plagiarism (the 'crime' of line 25). Q8 reads 'estate' for 'state' in the title.

14   Q8 reads 'guided' for 'gide' and 'freted' for 'fettred'.

175

[Q1: 205] Possibly by Thomas Churchyard (see Introduction). In fourteener couplets. An elegy leading up to an epitaph. There is another copy of the poem in BL MS Add. 23971, titled 'An Epitaph upon the dethe of Mr Thomas Awdeleye' and signed 'C.'; the most important variants are noted below. Thomas, Baron Audley (1487/8–1544) was Lord Chancellor from 1532 until just before his death; he was Henry VIII's most consistent manager of Parliament, and played a key role in securing the divorce from Katherine of Aragon. Despite the fact that he was not a soldier at any stage, the editors of the *Miscellany* may have taken the poem to be about him, given that he is much the most famous individual of that name in the period. However, the poet is almost certainly writing about Thomas Audley (dates uncertain), a soldier and gentleman of the privy chamber to Henry VIII, as the passages present in the MS but excluded from the *Miscellany* clearly indicate. Given these omissions, whether they are deliberate or accidental, the sixteenth-century reader might easily mistake the identity of the poem's subject.

8   After this line, MS adds the following:

> Kynge Henry the viiith sent hym to Guynes
>   as provest marshall there,
> whose famous deedes in lytle tyme
>   dyd floryshe everye where,
> A tutour to thignorant,
>   A fathere to them all,
> He tought them howe to lede there men
>   as chyefe and principall,
> The worthiest men that yngland brede
>   thes manye hundred yeres,
> dyd thinke no skorne to lerne of hym
>   as nowe right well apperes.
> From Guynes the kinge to bullen toke
>   This noble mars sonne,
> and placed hym in tholde man
>   whan he the Tonne had wone
> his knowledge gate such credytt styll
>   The kinge tolove him thane
> One of his privye chamber has
>   he made this worthye mane

> and so he was unto his sonne
>   who sent this his lode starr,
> to skotteland as a Counseller,
>   in tyme of cruell warre,

Audley was made lieutenant of the Old Man at Boulogne in
1546, and was sent by the Edwardian regime to Scotland in
1548.

9   MS reads 'Jurneye' for 'tornay', probably referring to Aud-
        ley's being sent to Scotland.

10   After this line, MS adds the following:

> And fyrst of all his trueth was tryede
>   his faythe was throwzelye knowen
> whan Wyat did foresake the fylde
>   & at lenghe his men overthrowen
> what can be named that vertuous ys
>   but he hereof hade parte,
> In everye poyente to Souldyers all
>   a mastere of the Arte

It is instructive that this reference to helping put down the
rebellion of the younger Thomas Wyatt is missing from the
Miscellany.

11   MS reads 'free' for 'fierce'.

14   After this line, MS adds the following:

> Thoughe fame helde upe his name a lofte
>   yt fortune kepte hym lowe
> and worthye welthe dyd hym forsake
>   as his poure end dyd showe
> Some men wolde hys dedes deserved
>   great recompense to have
> but what lefte he behynd but fame
>   when he wente to hys grave
> Althoughe his meryttes clamed rewarde
>   His fortune was so yll
> when othere men there suetes obtayned
>   he was forgotten stylle

However poor the soldier Audley was when he died, Chan-
cellor Audley was massively wealthy (though he had
considerable expenses in showing off this wealth). It is

ironic that these lines and the others should be, as it were, forgotten by the *Miscellany*.

21 MS reads 'grave' for 'ground'.

22 MS reads 'in stone or' for 'ygrave in'.

23–4 These lines constitute the epitaph to be graven in a brass plate on his tomb.

24 MS reads 'fame on earthe' for 'name in earth'.

176

[Q1: 206] In poulter's measure (though without the indentations that are normal for that form in the *Miscellany*). A promise of fidelity, the poem is a good example of rhetorical climax; cf. poem 144. There is another version of this poem in AH (292), so different that it seems best to give the whole text rather than local variants:

> Eache thinge must have his tyme/ and tyme tryes out mens trowthe
> and trothe deserves a speciall trust/ on trust great frindship growth
> and frindship never fayles/ when faithfulnesse is fownde
> and faithfulnesse is full of frute/ and frutfull thinges are sownd
> The sownd is good in profe/ and profe is prynce of prayse
> and worthie prayse is suche a pearle/ as lightlye not decayes
> All this doth time bring forthe/ whiche tyme I must abyde
> How shulde I boldelye credyte crave/ till tyme my trothe have tryde
> And as a tyme I fownde to fall in fancyes frame
> So do I wishe a happie tyme/ at lardge to shewe the same
> Yf Fortune answere hope/ and hope maye have his hyre
> Then shall my hart possesse in peace/ the tyme that I desyre[.]

3–4 The confusion over these rhyme words continues in later editions of the *Miscellany*: Q8 reads 'found' in line 3, and 'sounde' in line 4, which seems the right way round, in terms of sense, as well as on the basis of the AH reading.

177

[Q1: 207] Quatrains with alternating rhyme, those lines with A-rhymes tetrameter, and those with B-rhymes trimeter. A lover's complaint and swansong. There is another copy of this poem in D, with significant variants noted below: in addition to these variants, every use of the word 'she' reads 'the' (i.e. they).

1	MS reads 'days' for 'yeres'.
2	MS reads 'pleasant eres' for 'joyfull dayes'.
3	MS reads 'dothe bot wast' for 'may not last'.
4	Q8 reads 'graut' for 'grave'. MS reads 'have won' for 'am one'.
5	MS reads 'al ys' for 'joyes are'.
7	MS reads 'Desyer' for 'Desirous'.
14	MS reads 'dethe' for 'life', the former giving a clearer contrast.
16	MS reads 'I se' for 'That is' and 'Fryndly' for 'deadly', giving a paradox that the *Miscellany* avoids. After this line, MS inserts the following:

> I se the know my hart
> and how I cannot Fain
> I se the se my smart
> and how I leff yn pane.

20	MS reads 'se' for 'sekes'.
23	MS reads 'by' for 'nye'.
32	After this line, MS inserts the following:

> the shal have ther rqwest
> and I must have my mend
> lo her my blody brest
> to ples the with unkynd[.]

178

[Q1: 208] In poulter's measure (though without the indentations that are normal for that form in the *Miscellany*). An ekphrasis of an imaginary painting.

1	Cf. Wyatt's poem 136, line 16.
10	Q8 reads 'never' for 'ever'.
12–14	Cf. Walter Ralegh, 'The Ocean to Scinthia', lines 69–87 and 123.
21–2	These lines constitute the speaker's epitaph.
23–6	These lines are an alternative ekphrasis, a description of his imaginary coat of arms. Such imagery appears frequently in the arms at tournaments in Sidney's *Arcadia*s, and had quite common currency at real Tudor tournaments.

179

[Q1: 209] Pentameters with the rhyme scheme ABABAACACDD, almost a forerunner of the Spenserian stanza. An elegy. The poem probably laments the death of Philip van Wilder (d. 1554), lutenist and chief musician to Henry VIII, who was made a gentleman of the privy chamber under Edward VI; his musical compositions generally circulated under the name Phillips.

6   For the classical Muses, see notes to poem 271.

180

[Q1: 210] Possibly by Thomas Churchyard. Quatrains with alternating rhyme; trimeter with the exception of the third line in each stanza, which is tetrameter. A love complaint.

5–8   Cf. poem 30, line 21; the whole poem has some similarities
            to this. Wounded deer will sometimes relieve their injuries
            by rubbing themselves on sphagnum moss.

23   Q8 reads the apparently nonsensical 'relling' for 'resting'.

181

[Q1: 211] By Lord Thomas Vaux (1509–56), an associate of Wyatt; it is often assumed (eg. *ODNB*) that he was a committed Catholic, largely on the basis of the recusancy of his son and grandson, but he did attend the coronation of Anne Boleyn (being made a Knight of the Garter for that purpose) as well as that of Mary Tudor. Tetrameter quatrains with alternating rhyme. A *pragmatographia*, i.e. a fictional description of a battle. There is another (partial) copy of this poem in BL MS Harley 6910; its most significant variants are noted below. Puttenham quotes lines 1–22, commenting: 'if such description be made to represent the handling of any business, with the circumstances belonging thereunto, as the manner of a battle, a feast, a marriage, a burial, or any other matter that lieth in feat and activity, we call it then the Counterfeit Action, *pragmatographia*. In this figure the Lord Nicholas [*sic*] Vaux, a noble gentleman, and much delighted in vulgar making, and a man otherwise of no great learning but having herein a marvelous facility, made a ditty representing the battle and assault of Cupid so excellently well as for the gallant and proper application of his fiction in every part, I cannot choose but set down

the greatest part of his ditty, for in truth it cannot be amended'
(p. 325).

8	MS reads 'awaye' for 'aray'.
10	On the heraldry here, cf. poem 178, lines 23–6.
11, 14	The heraldic tints silver and sable are the same as white and black.
16	MS reads 'them forth' for 'the fort'.
19	MS reads 'Expence' for 'For spence'.
36	Q8 reads 'dimps' (i.e. dimples?) for 'dims'.
37	Q8 reads 'now' for 'the'.
40	Q8 reads 'geaunt' for 'graunt'.
47	Q8 reads 'set' for 'fet'.

182

[Q1: 212] By Lord Thomas Vaux. Quatrains with alternating rhyme; trimeter with the exception of the third line in each quatrain, which is tetrameter. A repudiation of love. There are four extant MSS of the poem: Bodleian MS Ashmole 48 and BL MS Harley 1703, which both ascribe the poem to Vaux, BL MS Add. 38599, and BL MS Add. 26737; their most substantive variants are recorded below. A version of some stanzas of the poem is sung by the Gravedigger/1st Clown in *Hamlet*, V. i. 61–97:

> 'In youth when I did love, did love,
>   Methought it was very sweet,
> To contract – O – the time for – a – my behove,
>   O, methought there – a – was nothing – a – meet'.

Hamlet. Has this fellow no feeling of his business? 'a sings in grave-making.
Horatio. Custom hath made it in him a property of easiness.
Hamlet. 'Tis e'en so, the hand of little employment hath the daintier sense.
1st Clown. 'But age with his stealing steps
>   Hath clawed me in his clutch,
>   And hath shipped me into the land,
>   As if I had never been such.'
[*Throws up a shovelful of earth with a skull in it*]
Hamlet. That skull had a tongue in it, and could sing once.
. . .
Did these bones cost no more the breeding, but to play loggats with them? Mine ache to think on't.

> 1st Clown.   'A pickaxe and a spade, a spade,
>   For and a shrowding sheet:
>   O, a pit of clay for to be made
>   For such a guest is meet.'
> [*Throws up another skull*]

10   Q1 reads 'cowche' for 'crowch', all MSS read 'crutch'; that
            is clearly what is intended, despite Shakespeare's adapta-
            tion of the word to 'clutch'.

18, 20   MS Add. 38599 reads 'youthly wyldish toyes' for 'youthly
            idle rime' and 'in time these Ioies' for 'these toyes in time'.

20   Philip Sidney would regularly refer to his poems as 'toys';
            see e.g. *Astrophel and Stella*, 18.

23   Q8 reads 'lodge' for 'hedge'.

30   Q8 reads 'shreding' for 'shrowding'.

35   MS Ashmole 48 reads 'merye' for 'wofull'; MS Harley
            1703 and MS Add. 38599 read 'wearye'.

39   Cf. George Herbert, 'Affliction' (I), line 65.

45   Human skulls were commonly kept by scholars as a
            memento mori. The speaker may however be referring to
            his own bald head (baldness was often taken as a sign of
            venereal disease, so it may be apt punishment for his lustful
            youth).

56   All MSS read 'turne' for 'waste'. MS Ashmole 48 follows
            this line with 'Fynys, quod lord Vaws' (i.e. 'the end, says
            Lord Vaux').

183

[Q1: 213] Pentameters; innovative rhyme scheme ABBACCADD-
AEEA, concluding appropriately on the same rhyme word which
ended the first line. An elegy. The poem's subject is probably Lady
Anne Wentworth, who died giving birth to a stillborn child in 1554 at
Calais, where her husband Sir Thomas Wentworth was Lord Deputy;
he had been appointed to this post because, despite his Protestant
sympathies, he had supported the succession of Mary against the
claims of Lady Jane Grey. Less than six months after the *Miscellany*'s
publication, he would be disgraced when Calais, England's last toe-
hold on the Continent, fell to the French.

6   Anne Wentworth was her husband's cousin.

10   This odd sentiment seems to suggest that she might have
            had fame as a mother, but preferred not to sully herself
            with such worldly virtue, and so chose to die in childbirth.

                                    184

[Q1: 214] In Venus and Adonis stanzas, with tetrameter lines 1, 3, 5
and 6 and seven-syllable feminine-rhymed lines 2 and 4; cf. poem 192.
Puttenham discusses the poem, quoting lines 1–4 and 7–10 as a 'com-
mendable enough' example of 'meters in odd syllable' (p. 161). A love
complaint.

1   Puttenham also quotes this line as an example of '*Tau-
            tologia*, or the Figure of Self-Saying', commenting, 'such
            composition makes the meter run away smoother, and pas-
            seth from the lips with more facility by iteration of a letter
            than by alteration, which alteration of a letter requires an
            exchange of ministry and office in the lips, teeth, or palate,
            and so doth not the iteration' (p. 341).

10   Q8 reads 'swerving' for 'swering'.

11   Q1 reads 'oft' for 'of'.

14   Q8 reads 'my' for 'thy'.

16   Q8 reads 'never' for 'nothing'.

18   On the depredations of caterpillars, cf. Shakespeare's *Rich-
            ard II*, II. iii. 166 and III. iv. 47.

25   Q8 reads 'the' for 'thy'.

34   The tale of birds being deceived by the painter's art is nor-
            mally told of Zeuxis (Pliny the Elder, *Natural History*,
            XXXV. 65–6).

45–6   The reference is to Nauplius, who is described in Euripides'
            Helen (766–7, 1126–1131) as having wrecked the Greek
            fleet on its return from Troy by lighting false beacons at
            Cape Caphereus in Euboea, in vengeance for the death of
            his son Palamedes (wrongly executed for treason by Agam-
            emnon).

                                    185

[Q1: 215] Pentameters rhyming ABABABABCC. An epigrammatic
series of similes, demonstrating Erasmian *copia*; cf. poems 157 and
particularly 211. A love complaint/swansong.

2   Q8 reads 'better' for 'bereft'.

5   Q8 reads 'whan' for 'want'.

7   Chameleons were thought to live on air: cf. *Hamlet*, III. ii.
           93–4. Q2's misspelling indicates that the creatures were not
           familiar enough for the compositor to get this right, though
           other editions of the *Miscellany* do.

8   Phoebus is an alternative name for the sun-god Apollo.

9   Salamanders were thought to live on fire: cf. 1 *Henry IV*,
           III. iii. 46–8.

186

[Q1: 216] Tetrameter stanza rhyming ABABCCDD. An epigram, in
the form printed here; but a fuller version of the poem can be found in
AH (267), which reads as follows:

> No wight hym self happie can call
> Before the end whiche shewith all

> The Sheening season heare to some
> the glorye great eaven of dew right
> Renowmed fame throughe fortune wonne
> the glytt'ring goolde the eyes delight
> the censuall lyfe aye seemyng sweete
> the hart with joyfull dayes replete
> the thing theare to eache wight is thrall
> the happie end exceadith all

> The merrye meane who so can hytt
> that stable state aye standing sure
> the chaste wyfe by thie syde to sytt
> whose vertuse may thy love assure
> suche faithfull frendes as for to trust
> treasure, to serve, but none to rust
> theise guiftes moste rare they vanyshe shall
> the happye end exceedith all

> The hardie hartes that mars does sarve
> When blooddye battaills joyne in fight
> the fyrye strokes for to desarve
> the Lawrell greene even of due right
> the Coward knightes turning their backes
> the Victour, of his conquest crackes

> the Valyaunt to the Varlett thrall
> the Happie end exceadith all
>
> The Symple Soule that toylethe still
> by sweatt of browes to eate his bread
> of Venus Lawes hath he no skill
> ne Bacchus trobleth nought his head
> eache golden hall he doth detest
> his Thackyd howse hym lyketh best
> Yf Contentacon hym be fall
> His happie end exceadith all
>
> In Ceasers seate who lyst to sytt
> with Bodkins brought to shamefull end
> Catoes Cunning and his witt
> that with dispaire durst not contend
> Hercules honour, and yett be brentt
> Ryche as Cresus, in Orientt
> whome Syrus made to serve as thrall
> the happye end exceadith all
>
> Over thye head now dothe depend
> Hanging by Subtylle twyned threede
> Immortall fame whiche dothe assend
> upp to the Starrs who so can reede
> Tells contrarye, for aye suche shame
> As Crewell Nero had by name
> So that no wight happie I call
> before the end whiche shewith all
>> Finis

The title of the AH poem derives from the Latin tag 'Nemo felix ante obitum' ('call no man happy until he is dead'). For the general sentiment of the poem, see Herodotus, *Histories*, I. 32. In its compressed form in the *Miscellany* it becomes a poem of patience in conditions of adversity; it is perhaps significant that the first stanza does away with the idea of 'dew right' for such conditions.

3   Q8 reads 'though' for 'through'.

187

[Q1: 217] By Lord Thomas Vaux. Pentameter Venus and Adonis stanza. An invective epigram. There is another copy of the poem in AH (299); its most important variants are noted below.

1   AH reads 'delighting' for 'that delights'.

2   AH reads 'Tossinge' for 'totring'.

3   AH reads 'all' for 'swete'.

5   AH reads the much more meaningful 'envenomyd' for
            'environned'.

188

[Q1: 218] A sonnet with a Petrarchan octave (appropriately enough)
of the form ABBAABBACDDCEE. An encomium. The idea of
Petrarch being the perfect model for verse had become commonplace
by the mid-sixteenth century, so that the model could be surpassed by
the last decade of the century, when Sir Walter Ralegh insisted in com-
mendatory verses for *The Faerie Queene* that not only did Spenser
outdo Petrarch, but his subject, Queen Elizabeth, outdid Laura, the
subject of Petrarch's amatory verse.

14   The word 'paragon' here seems to be undergoing some slip-
            page, from its proper meaning of one who is the perfect
            example of something (cf. poem 175, line 18), to the
            extended meaning of a companion – partly due to the idea
            of Laura being the model for Petrarch's verse, but also
            partly due to the pressure of the word 'paramour'.

189

[Q1: 219] A sonnet rhyming ABBACAACDEEDFF. Lines are pen-
tameter, except for the last two which have eleven syllables including
feminine rhymes. Clearly an answer to the previous poem, and pos-
sibly by the same author. There is another copy of the poem in AH
(93), with no significant variants.

6   Q8 reads 'lime' for 'line'.

13   Momus is the classical god of satire, but most generally
            associated in the Renaissance with stupidity and pusillan-
            imous criticism. cf. Sidney, *Defence of Poesy*: 'if you have
            so earth-creeping a mind that it cannot lift itself up to look
            to the sky of poetry, or rather by a certain rustical disdain,
            will become such a mome as to be a Momus of poetry;
            then, though I will not wish unto you the ass's ears of
            Midas, nor to be driven by a poet's verses, as Bubonax was,
            to hang himself, nor to be rhymed to death, as is said to be

done in Ireland; yet thus much curse I send you, in the behalf of all poets, that while you live, you live in love, and never get favour for lacking skill of a sonnet; and when you die, your memory die from the earth for want of an epitaph'.

190

[Q1: 220] Pentameter ottava rima, missing a line after 29. Invective against women with heavy alliteration.

9   Q8 reads 'plaint' for 'plante'.

14   Q8 omits 'to'.

15   Q8 reads 'Swollen' for 'Solleyn' and 'stone' for 'stony'.

191

[Q1: 221] In poulter's measure (though without the indentations that are normal for that form in the *Miscellany*). A poem on the superiority of love to worldly success.

3–4   Cf. poem 128, line 1.

36   This comes close to idolatry, but is informed by the Neo-platonic doctrine of love as a means of access to the deity; cf. poem 196.

192

[Q1: 222] In Venus and Adonis stanzas, with tetrameter lines 1, 3, 5 and 6 and trimeter lines 2 and 4; cf. poem 184. A complaint in a female voice.

9   Q8 reads 'thus' for 'this'.

13–18   These lines are not printed in Q1.

31   The story of Dido's abandonment by her lover Aeneas (told in Virgil's *Aeneid*, IV) was a favourite example of female suffering in love; she committed suicide when he went off to continue his divinely appointed task of beginning the foundation of Rome.

41   Cf. poem 57, line 18.

42   Q8 reads 'at one' for 'alone'.

43–8   Puttenham discusses these lines as an example of '*Hyper-bole*, or the Overreacher, otherwise called the Loud Liar' (pp. 276–7), alongside Surrey's poem 20.

193

[Q1: 223] In tetrameter Venus and Adonis stanzas. A love complaint.

30   The metre of the line seems to require an elision of the 'a'.

194

[Q1: 224] In poulter's measure. A praise (or perhaps defence) of women, relying on the traditional and commonplace idea that all things are made for man's benefit.

36   The idea that women had, after the Fall, become men's punishment, is repeated by John Donne – see 'The First Anniversary', lines 99–107.

195

[Q1: 225] Tetrameter; stanzas rhyme ABABAA. A complaint. There is a substantially different version of the poem in Bodleian MS Ashmole 48, titled 'Tempore quo fodiebam' (i.e. roughly, 'I told you so'), whose stanzas, including one extra, run in a different order, with a refrain, as follows:

> Amyds my myrth and pleasantnesse,
> Such chaunce is chaunced sodainly,
> That in dispayre to have redresse,
> I finde my chiefest remedy.
> No newe kinde of unhappinesse,
> Wolde thus have left me comfortlesse.
>   so offten warnd
>
> In better case was never none
> And yet unwares thus am I trapt,
> My chiefe desyer dothe cause my mone,
> And to my woo and payn my welth is hapt,
> There is no man but I alone,
> That hath such cause sigh and grone.
>   so offten warnd

He is in welth that feleth no woe;
But I maye synge and thus reporte,
Farewell my joye and plesure to,
Thus maye I sing withought comforte;
For sorrowe hath caught me in her sner;
Alas! Why colde I not be ware,
          So often warnd?

Who wolde have thought that my request,
Should bryng me forthe such bytter frute:
For now is hapt that I fearedde least:
And all is com bye myne owne suyte
For when I thought me happiest
Then forthwyth came all myne unreste.
          so offten warnd

Thus am I taught for to beware
And trust no more such pleasant chance,
For happy happe hathe don this care,
And tourned my welthe to great grevance.
There is no man whom hap will here,
But weane she lyst welth is bare.
          so offten warnd

To my mishap alas I finde
That happy hap is daungerous:
And fortune worketh but her kynd,
To make the joyfull dolorus.
But all to lat it comes in minde,
To wayle the want whyght make me blynde.
          so offten warnd[.]

There is another copy of the poem in BL MS Add. 17492, with a few variants, the most important of which is adding 'thus am I warnd' at the end of the poem. This version, like the *Miscellany*'s, begins its stanzas with the letters T-A-W-I-T, which may be an imperfect acrostic on Wyatt's name; cf. headnote to poem 16 above. There is also a copy in B, whose major variants are the addition of the refrain 'So often warnyd' at the end of each stanza, and the transposition of the third and fourth stanzas. The poem was included in the Wyatt canon by Muir and Thomson, an inclusion continued by Rebholz, though neither editor believes that Wyatt wrote it.

28   B reads 'byrth' for 'mirth'.

196

[Q1: 226] Tetrameters rhyming ABABCCDD. A poem against love. As the title suggests, it warns against the kind of idolatry in love with which poem 191 ends. The poem relies on the fact that a mistress could be called a 'friend', resulting in confusion between the supposed reliability of male friendship and the perils of loving a woman. There is another copy of this poem in AH (18), with some variants, the most important of which are noted below.

5	AH reads 'my case more playne' for 'the circumstaunce'.
6	AH reads 'well skyld them selves did payne' for 'them selves that did avaunce'.
28	AH reads 'great' for 'fowle'.
32	AH reads 'as no man by hym self sett more'.
34	AH reads 'creapt in every part' for 'clene orecome my hart'.
35	AH reads 'frindly thought' for 'thought of her'.
48	AH reads 'hope' for 'hart'.
53	AH reads 'for my more' for 'the more to'.

197

[Q1: 227] Two pentameter Venus and Adonis stanzas. An elegy. There is another copy of this poem in BL MS Lansdowne 98, with a couple of insignificant variants. Sir Anthony Denny (1501–49) was a favourite of Henry VIII, and an enthusiastic promoter of the Reformation, acting as a Privy Councillor to Edward VI, who is probably the king imagined here contending with death for love of Denny.

198

[Q1: 228] Two pentameter Venus and Adonis stanzas. An epigram on love. The lover is compared to a horse – this motif probably derives from Petrarch, *Rime*, 147, and is later used by Sidney, *Astrophel and Stella*, 49.

199

[Q1: 229] Tetrameter ottava rima. An epigram to accompany a gift; cf. poem 173.

3	Q8 reads 'florishing' for 'flowring'.
7	Q8 reads 'my' for 'by'.

200

[Q1: 230] Pentameter ottava rima. An epigrammatic oath, promising fidelity.

201

[Q1: 231] Pentameter stanza rhyming ABAABBACC – an interesting forerunner of the Spenserian stanza (Bradner, cit. Rollins). Another epigram, this time responding to a gift.

1–3   In Greek legend the Trojan prince Paris gave the apple as a prize for beauty to Aphrodite (Venus) ahead of Hera (Juno) and Athene (Minerva) – in return for this he won the love of Helen, but incurred the anger of the losing goddesses against his city.

202

[Q1: 232] An English sonnet. A moral ode comprising a set of examples for one moral point – an instance of *copia*.

5–8   That is, the inexperienced man who never fought on unknown shores, and who has not therefore been taught to fear the sea-god Neptune, has sometimes had the skill to handle a wandering ship on untrustworthy waters which others would only have acquired by too long (and therefore perhaps fatal) experience.

8   Q8 reads 'sell' for 'fele'.

13   Q8 reads 'malice' for 'manly'.

203

[Q1: 233] A sonnet of the form ABBACDDCEFFEGG. A moral ode, praising a virtue.

204

[Q1: 235] Just possibly by John Harington (printed as such – and titled 'To Isabella Markham, 1549' – by *NA*, whose evidence Rollins describes as 'of little or no value'; Harington married Isabella in 1554). Trimeter Venus and Adonis stanzas. A love complaint.

9   Q8 reads 'thy' for 'they'.

205

[Q1: 236] Tetrameter quatrains with alternating rhyme. A love complaint.

206

[Q1: 237] Tetrameter Venus and Adonis stanzas. A legendary narrative allegorically applied to the speaker's state. On Troilus and Criseyde, see note to poem 18, line 78. The whole poem, particularly its last stanzas, seems ironic in its presumably deliberate forgetting of Criseyde's later infidelity.

4   Q8 reads 'here' for 'her'.

26   Q8 reads 'shrobbe' for 'throbbe'.

30   Cf. poem 30, lines 23–4. The conceit came to be the subject
           of some mockery; see J. C. [John Cumber], *The Two Merry
           Milkmaids* (1620) where two women discuss a love-sick
           man:

> *Julia.* What, doe you weepe Brother?
> *Dorigen.* Like a Watring-Pot; he wud make an excellent
>   Fountaine in the midst of a Garden. (B4^r)

39   Q8 reads 'were' for 'her'.

54   Q8 inserts 'was' after 'woman'.

207

[Q1: 238] By Geoffrey Chaucer. In rhyme royal. A moral ode praising the good (moderate) life; cf. poems 32, 163 and 253. The poem appears in many MSS and in early printed editions of Chaucer such as Thynne's of 1532; some of the more important variants are noted below. Two MSS title the poem 'B. [i.e. ballade] that Chaucier made on his death bedde'; in modern editions, it is titled 'Truth: Balade de Bon Conseyl'. The poem has an 'envoy' in one important MS – see *The Riverside Chaucer*.

2   The best MSS read 'unto thy thing' for 'to thee thy good'.

3   Q8 reads 'ficklnes' for 'ticklenes'.

4   Thynne reads 'Preace' for 'Praise', as do the MSS.

5   Thynne reads the clearly correct 'Savour' for 'Favour', as
           do the MSS.

6   Many MSS read 'Reule' for the first 'Rede'.

8   Many MSS read 'Tempest' for 'Paine'.

11   The MSS read 'an all' for 'a nall'.

13   The MSS read 'Daunte' for 'Deme' and 'dauntest' for 'demest'.

19   Many MSS read 'Know thy contree, look up, thank God
           of all'.

208

[Q1: 239] In poulter's measure. A love complaint.

7   The love-god Cupid's firebrands reappear in Sidney,
           Astrophel and Stella, 8; cf. also poem 214. Their source is
           probably the Greek poet Anacreon.

209

[Q1: 240] Tetrameter quatrains with alternating rhyme. A fine poem
of despair and guilt.

17–18   The love-goddess Venus is often portrayed with musical
           accompanists; she is generally too busy to be playing the
           instruments herself.

21   Q8 reads 'parkes' for 'sparckes'.

210

[Q1: 241] A Petrarchan sonnet. Rollins identified the source of the
poem as the first chorus of Seneca's *Phaedra*, 296–308:

> Thessali Phoebus pecoris magister
> egit armentum, positoque plectro
> impari tauros calamo vocavit.
> Induit formas quotiens minores
> ipse qui caelum nebulasque ducit!
> candidas ales modo movit alas,
> dulcior vocem moriente cygno;
> fronte nunc torva petulans iuvencus
> virginum strauit sua terga ludo,
> perque fraternos, nova regna, fluctus
> ungula lentos imitante remos
> pectore adverso domuit profundum,
> pro sua vector timidus rapina.

[Phoebus drove cattle as a master of a herd, setting aside his lyre he called the bulls with a bent pipe. Even he who leads the clouds and the sky put on lower forms many times! On one occasion he flapped white wings, with a voice more pleasant than the dying swan; on another, as a petulant bullock with a grim face he lowered his back in play for a virgin and, with his hooves as soft oars he pushed his chest through his brother's element – a new kingdom – and mastered the sea, concerned for the spoil he carried].

The poem expands considerably on the original, particularly in the section on Apollo. A moral ode. Note that the *volta* (or 'turning point') of the sonnet comes after line 7, balancing the Apollo and the Jupiter sections.

1–7	There are various versions of the sun-god Apollo becoming a shepherd in service to Admetus, King of Thessaly: in Euripides' *Alcestis*, his disguise was a punishment for killing a Cyclops; in Ovid's *Metamorphoses* (VI. 122), there is a brief mention of the myth, in which he takes on the disguise for love of Isse.
4	Q8 reads 'deade' for 'defide'.
6	Q8 reads 'od' for 'on'.
10–11	Jupiter king of the gods takes on a huge variety of disguises for love's sake in the *Metamorphoses*: his seduction of Leda as a swan is mentioned at VI. 109, and that of Europa as a bull is told at II. 858 ff.

211

[Q1: 244] Pentameters rhyming ABABBABABCC. As Rollins points out, this poem is very similar to poem 185 above. An epigrammatic oath of fidelity.

212

[Q1: 245] Pentameter couplets. A curse. There is another copy of this poem in AH (245), with some variants, the most important of which are noted below.

4	AH reads 'lyer' for 'R.'. The suppressed word is presumably a two-syllable surname.
12	AH reads 'over chardge' for 'charge so large'.
14	Q8 omits 'in'.

20   In early Roman legendary history Collatinus was the husband of Lucretia; he boasted of his wife's chastity, and Tarquin raped her; that crime brought about the end of the Tarquins as kings of Rome.

21–2   Refers to Dido: see note to poem 192, line 31.

23   Q1 reads 'R. so deepe can avoyde' for 'Rodopeian maide'. As AH reads the latter too, this is a sign that the compositors of Q2 went back to their MS (Q1's compositor having evidently been confused by an unfamiliar name). The Rhodopeian maid was Phyllis, who hanged herself when jilted.

26   AH reads 'Cadge' for 'brag'.

50   The story of Susannah and the elders is told in the apocryphal Daniel 13: when the heroine refuses the elders' advances, they accuse her of inchastity, but the just judge Daniel sees through their wicked scheme.

60   'us' refers to men in general.

213

[Q1: 246] In fourteener couplets. An allegorical competition between ladies; cf. poem 269. The name of the poem's subject, 'maistresse Ryce' is given in Q1 but suppressed in all subsequent editions; the name may just possibly be an equivalent of Rhys, an important but disgraced Welsh family. A number of allegorical figures speak in the poem.

5–6   We are to imagine this trial taking place at the court of Venus; the implication may be that the poem's subject is a lady in waiting at the court of Queen Mary.

26   The peacock, in addition to being a standard emblem of pride, was also the bird of Juno, queen of the gods.

41   The idea of the most modest court lady being called forth to win the prize may faintly echo Christ's point in Luke 4 that one should, at feasts, sit at as low a place as possible in order to be called to higher honours – an idea criticized as impractical for a courtier in Castiglione's *The Book of the Courtier* (trans. Thomas Hoby (London: Dent, 1928), p. 109).

43   For Lucretia, see note to poem 212, line 20. The idea doesn't really work: Lucretia's virtue was proved by her committing suicide after being raped; a Lucretia who was left alive would simply be a woman who had been raped,

not a model of special virtue – though of course what the poet means by his gauche phrase 'left alive' is that an ancient model has survived into the present day.

44   Q8 reads 'accepted' for 'excepted'.

49   Q8 reads 'maisters' for 'maistres', apparently masculinizing the object of the speaker's devotion.

214

[Q1: 247] Pentameters; two stanzas in the form ABABCCDCD plus one ABABCCDD. A defence of a woman; cf. poems 212 and 240 for other examples on the subject of slander. There is another copy of this poem in AH (95), with no important variants. Rollins comments on line 19: 'This cloudy poem seems to be addressed to a man, not a woman. One would like to believe that he was the Gray who contributed . . . to the miscellany, and who is referred to as G at [poem 239, line 1].' We are inclined to think the poem more likely to be addressed to a woman, on the basis of the emphasis on beauty, and on the basis of the conclusion. The complex attitude in this poem, in which beauty is a cause of external slander and disturbance, while concealing inner possession of virtue, looks forward to many of Shakespeare's more troubled depictions of the young man in the *Sonnets*.

9   Q3 and later editions read 'by' for 'thy'. As it stands, though, the line means 'Thus, Nature, your skill is deprived of virtue's light' – i.e. Nature in making G so beautiful has deprived him/her of the appearance of virtue.

11   The meaning of this immensely difficult line hinges on whether 'but' means 'unless' or has its more normal meaning, on whether 'the' means 'thee' or 'they', and on what 'entend' means. Roughly speaking, there are two broad interpretations available, attaching the line either to its predecessor or its successor: (*a*) outward show does not dull the wits of the wise, unless they look on you most intently; (*b*) outward show may dull the wits (not of the wise, of course) but of those who, however hard they look/stretch [*intend*] towards her, Minerva may not pierce their skulls.

12   Minerva was the classical goddess of wisdom.

14   Q8 reads 'the' for 'their'.

16–17   Syntactically obscure, but the meaning is not in doubt: 'your foe beauty, through the agency of your shape, doubles your trouble by hiding your wit and making your virtue appear empty'.

17   Q8 reads 'mede' for 'hide'.

19   Whether or not the suppressed name is 'Gray', it is clearly a monosyllable.

23   Q8 reads 'suttle' for 'setled'.

24   Silence and shame (i.e. modesty) here are other virtues, like steadfastness and patience above: they are characteristically feminine virtues; 'many' probably means 'many other virtues'.

26   'he' is any man who would marry this woman.

215

[Q1: 248] In pentameter quatrains with alternating rhyme. An elegy. Anne, Countess of Pembroke (c. 1514–52), was the younger sister of Henry VIII's last queen, Katherine Parr. Her husband, William Herbert, first Earl of Pembroke (1506/7–70), had been a prominent member of Edward VI's privy council and had supported (perhaps even proposed) the elevation of Lady Jane Grey to the throne; nonetheless, he remained in favour under Mary, playing an important role in the suppression of the younger Sir Thomas Wyatt's rebellion. Adam Nicolson describes Anne as bringing 'grace and courage' to the family and as 'a Protestant in the making' (*Earls of Paradise: England and the Idea of Perfection* (London: HarperPress, 2008), pp. 71, 56).

8   Q8 reads 'fo' for 'to'.

13–16   The punctuation does not help with the sense of these lines, which mean 'She was well fitted by her wit and learning to obey her husband's will, and he wished her to use the resources he gave her as a result of her love mainly as a support for all her friends – who supported her cause'. One might wonder if this last sentiment is an oblique reference to the Protestant cause.

19   .   Q8 reads 'sought' for 'though'.

20   Probably refers to the Countess's children: the heir Henry (1538–1601), who later married Philip Sidney's sister, and whose son William may well be the young man of Shakespeare's *Sonnets*; she also had another son, Edward, and a daughter, Anne.

216

[Q1: 249] Tetrameter quatrains with alternating rhyme. A moral ode demonstrating Erasmian *copia*.

217

[Q1: 250] Pentameter Venus and Adonis stanzas, though the first is faulty; the last stanza also uses its A rhyme as its couplet rhyme. A poem of moral advice.

3   'delight to heare' would fit the rhyme scheme. Q8 reads 'her' for 'heare'.

218

[Q1: 251] Poulter's measure. A condemnation of the world. About halfway through it becomes a poem on the value of the low estate. There are three MS versions (Bodleian MS Ashmole 48, BL MS Sloane 1896 and BL MS Add. 15225), the first ending with a prayer for Queen Mary and her consort Philip of Spain ('Thus here I mak an ende, wisshing for grace and helthe; / God save Philepe our kyng and Mary our quyne, and eke the commenwelthe'). The variants are otherwise too numerous and uninteresting to list – though, as Rollins points out (in giving them 'with no enthusiasm'), they do indicate how freely poems were often adapted. Probably the worst poem in the *Miscellany*.

55   Q8 reads 'I finde' for 'In fine'.

219

[Q1: 252] In tetrameter Venus and Adonis stanzas, with the couplet rhyme repeated to make a refrain. The couplet has nine syllables with feminine rhymes. A love complaint.

3   Q8 reads 'thought' for 'brought'.

220

[Q1: 259] Pentameters with a complex rhyme scheme; Rollins thinks the poem should be in three nine-line stanzas, but the sense divides better as it is after line 15, and line 17 rhymes with line 19, which would cut across the proposed stanzas. It is perhaps best to think of the poem as having a single complex rhyme scheme running: ABBAACCDDEFGEFGHIIHJJHHKKFF. This mixes couplets, closed quatrains and Petrarchan sonnet sestets. Similarly, the poem's genre is a mixture of narrative and love complaint.

1   The story of Procris and Cephalus is told in Ovid, *Metamorphoses*, VII. 694–862: the two were married and came to suspect each other's fidelity for various reasons; eventually, Procris went to spy on her husband as he was hunting a monster, and he inadvertently killed her. It is unusual to describe a woman in love as serving her beau, but this detail is presumably used in order to highlight the parallel with the speaker's situation.

2   Q8 reads 'har' for 'hart'.

10   Q8 reads 'so' for 'to'.

16–18   The lines may be paraphrased: 'so peculiar are the rights or rituals of Love that I have difficulty knowing whether to look into them, or turn a blind eye.'

16   Q8 reads 'rightes' for 'rites'.

25   Line omitted in Q8.

221

[Q1: 260] A pentameter tour de force of rhyme, the scheme running: ABABABBABABABBABAABBABAAACC. A blazon praising a woman.

1   For the Phoenix, see notes to poems 160, line 31, and 168, line 18. The colours it is given here emphasize an imperial aspect of the bird. The source for this line may be Petrarch, *Rime*, 323, a poem later translated by Spenser (via a version by Clement Marot) in *A Theatre for Worldlings* (1569).

22–3   The idea is that his mistress transcends the sun, which is taking her proper place in the heavens. The idea of usurpation is loaded at this time.

24   Q8 reads 'Her' for 'Here'.

222

[Not in Q1] Trimeter quatrains with alternating rhyme. A love complaint, with extended simile or conceit. There is another copy of this poem in AH (263), titled 'Of Purgatori'; its most important variants are noted below.

3   AH's title insists that the lover's state is being compared to Purgatory, whose existence Protestants denied. The poem as presented here clearly refers to Hell.

6   AH reads 'sckalding lead' for 'leade againe'.

8   AH reads 'from foote to head' for 'with deadly paine'.

10   Q8 reads 'cherin' for 'certaine'.

17–18   The idea that the absence of God is the worst punishment of the damned is a key idea in Dante's *Inferno*; it is repeated by Mephistopheles in Christopher Marlowe's *Doctor Faustus*, I. iii. 79–82 (A Text).

223

[Not in Q1] By Sir Anthony St Leger (?1496–1559), six-time Lord Deputy of Ireland, from which post he was finally removed in 1556. Pentameter rhyme royal. An elegy. There is another copy of the poem in H78, which identifies the poem's author; its most important variants are noted below.

1   H78 reads 'Thus lyvethe the deade' for 'Lo dead he lives'.

2   The punning emphasis on Wyatt's quickness surely imitates Surrey's poem 35.

4   H78 reads 'immortall fame' for 'lively name'.

6   The word 'here' may refer to the *Miscellany*, in whose pages Wyatt may be said to live. H78 reads 'is he thus' for 'lives he here'.

7   H78 reads 'no deathe cane that lyf from Wiattes' (with no comma) for 'Thus can no death from Wiate, life'.

224

[Not in Q1] Alexandrine couplet followed by trimeter quatrains with alternating rhyme. An epigram.

2   Q8 reads the preferable 'oft' for 'soft'.

225

[Not in Q1] Fourteener couplets. A female complaint. The poem is a version of Ovid, *Heroides*, 1. 1–12:

> Haec tua Penelope lento tibi mittit, Ulixe;
>   nil mihi rescribas attinet: ipse veni!
> Troia iacet certe, Danais invisa puellis;
>   vix Priamus tanti totaque Troia fuit.
> o utinam tum, cum Lacedaemona classe petebat,
>   obrutus insanis esset adulter aquis!
> non ego deserto iacuissem frigida lecto,
>   nec quererer tardos ire relicta dies;
> nec mihi quaerenti spatiosam fallere noctem
>   lasseret viduas pendula tela manus.
> Quando ego non timui graviora pericula veris?
>   res est solliciti plena timoris amor.

[Your Penelope sends you these words, tardy Ulysses; it won't be any good to me if you write back: come yourself! Troy – hateful to all Greek girls – is surely fallen; but Priam and the whole of Troy were hardly worth it. O would that the adulterer had been overwhelmed by raging waters when his ship was on its way to Sparta! Then I would not have lain cold in an empty bed, nor would I be abandoned to bewail the slow days; nor would I have to pass the long night with the weaving frame wearying my widowed hands. When have I not been afraid of dangers greater than the truth? Love is full of worrisome fears].

Penelope, wife of Odysseus (aka Ulysses) waited twenty years for her husband's return from Troy, putting off her many suitors in the meanwhile, and thus became a model of wifely fidelity and patience.

3–4   Troy is inimical to women in taking away their husbands, either through death or long absence; the women continue to suffer worse even than the dead king of Troy because, in Penelope's case at least, her husband has taken ten years to get home.

5   The lecher is Paris, whose abduction of Helen from Sparta (aka Lacedaemon) prompted the Trojan War.

6   Q8 reads 'sorowed' for 'forowed'.

10   The distaff is the traditional device of women, but has particular pertinence to Penelope as she put off her suitors by using a distaff to weave a funeral shroud for her husband, insisting that she would entertain no proposals until it was finished, but secretly unpicking it each night.

226

[Not in Q1] Fourteener couplets; the fact of the poem being fourteen lines prompted Rollins to think this and poem 227 to be attempts at sonnets, but the format is not fundamentally different from the twelve-line poem 225. A love complaint. A translation of Petrarch, *Rime*, 1, which is a sonnet.

5   'wavering words' translates Petrarch's 'vario stile' (varied style).

6   'toyes' may be a mistake for 'toyles'.

227

[Not in Q1] Fourteener couplets; see headnote to poem 226. A narrative of the beginning of love. A version of Petrarch, *Rime*, 3. There is another copy of this poem in AH (94), whose most important variant is noted below.

1   According to the Gospels, the sun went out for the last three hours of Christ's agony on the Cross.

2   Q8 reads '&' for 'amid'.

7   AH reads 'flight' for 'plight', the *Miscellany*'s version seeming better.

13   Petrarch addresses the lady rather than Cupid.

228

[Not in Q1] Tetrameter couplets. The second longest poem in the *Miscellany* (after poem 154), exploring different perspectives on love in a fundamentally optimistic manner. A fine, simple poem (if a little prolix), with something of Surrey's delight in nature.

42   Q8 omits one 'that'.

53   Q8 omits the second 'then'.

57   Cf. poems 1, line 24 and 30, line 9.

65   Q8 reads 'with' for 'for'.

114   Q8 omits 'all'.

133   The foe is probably Despair, as opposed to the friend Hope who appears at lines 195–6.

164   Q8 reads 'paine' for 'plain'.

193   It is possible that 'rold' here is the result of a broken letter 't', and that the word should be 'told', as it is in Q8.

207–10   Puttenham quotes these lines (with lines 213–14) as an example of '*Polysyndeton*, or the Couple Clause' (pp. 259–60).

269   Q8 omits 'so'.

229

[Not in Q1] Pentameter Venus and Adonis stanzas. An explicitly political poem against treason, but it is not quite clear which side it is on. A *pragmatographia* or description of battle. It would most obviously celebrate one of Queen Mary's key victories, the removal of Lady Jane Grey from the throne in 1553 or the suppression of the younger Wyatt's rebellion in 1554. On the other hand it may anticipate a victory for the Protestant cause. The story of the destruction of Troy mostly derives from Virgil, *Aeneid*, II, one of the books of the poem translated by Surrey. There is another copy of this poem in AH (297); its most important variants are noted below.

    Though this is the *Miscellany*'s most obviously political poem, it is also in some ways its most evasive. Certainly, it is most likely to be a pro-Marian poem, and therefore constitutes a serious challenge to the idea that the *Miscellany* is oppositional; on the other hand, if the poem could *only* be read as a celebration of the defeat of Lady Jane Grey or Wyatt it may be surprising (at least in the latter case) that an MS version was collected by the Harington family; in any case, one could be a supporter of Protestantism without being a supporter of the Northumberland *coup d'état*, which obviously aimed to displace Elizabeth as well as Mary.

6   AH reads 'did sett' for 'set', but the *Miscellany*'s version scans equally well if 'fire' is read with two syllables.

13   Sinon was a Greek who pretended that he had been abandoned by his countrymen and who tricked the Trojans into taking the horse into their city. He became a byword for deception.

18   According to a tradition different from that followed by Virgil, Aeneas and Antenor betrayed Troy to the Greeks.

21   The king of Troy, Priam, was killed by Neoptolemos (aka Pyrrhus). It is possible that there is a reference here to unfounded rumours that Edward VI was murdered (Jennifer Loach, George Bernard and Perry Williams (eds.),

Edward VI (New Haven: Yale University Press, 1999), p. 160), presumably by Catholics.

28–30   The reference here is mainly to the prophecies of Troy's destruction by Cassandra, who was fated to have her soothsaying ignored; there may also be a reference to Laocoön, whose warnings against the horse are set aside after he is killed by a giant serpent.

30   AH omits 'sad'.

36   'Troians' here could be pronounced as 'Trojans', but given that the poem has 'Troyans' at line 16, we have preserved undifferentiated spelling of the text.

41   AH reads the metrically superior 'eke of' for the second 'of'.

46   Q8 reads 'hande' for 'band'.

65   AH reads 'health' for 'welth'.

71–2   Lady Jane Grey was initially pardoned by her cousin Mary (whose fall she might be thought to have plotted), but was executed without trial in 1554, after her father's participation in the younger Wyatt's rebellion; those who had supported her, most notably her father-in-law the Duke of Northumberland, were more swiftly and decisively executed in 1553, as was the younger Wyatt the next year. Certainly all of these – and Elizabeth Tudor – were in the hands of those who had been rebelled against, but the Marian regime would not welcome being reminded of its stringency (particularly to the guiltless Jane) and it is possible that the future tense of God's speech here anticipates Protestants taking similar vengeance in the future.

77–8   The tale, from Exodus, of the people of Israel's captivity in Egypt was a favoured parallel for religious dissidents during the Reformation; it was rather more popular with Protestants. The use of the present tense here would certainly seem to suggest that the poem is pro-Marian; yet, as in Dryden's *Absalom and Achitophel* (particularly the final lines), it is possible to express a desirable state of affairs as if it has already occurred.

230

[Not in Q1] Pentameter ottava rima. An animal allegory of lost love; cf. poem 57.

231

[Not in Q1] Pentameter couplets. A justification of secret love with Ovidian parallel. For the story of Jupiter and Europa, see note to poem 210, lines 10–11.

3   Q8 reads 'An' for 'In'.

4   Q8 omits 'in'.

232

[Not in Q1] Just possibly by Surrey. Tetrameters alternating with trimeters, rhyming ABACBC. A complaint on the vicissitudes of love (but see note to line 28). There is another copy of the poem in H78, signed 'H.S.', possibly meaning Surrey; its most important variants are noted below. Some have seen a garbled acrostic on Wyatt's name in the first letters of each stanza: as it comes to IAWTT, this does not seem particularly convincing.

1–2   On Ulysses and Penelope, see note to poem 225.

2   H78 reads 'seeke' for 'finde'.

4   H78 reads 'say' for 'seke'.

5–6   On Troilus and Criseyde, see note to poem 18, line 78. The sense of the first stanza is 'I who spent twenty years like Odysseus seeking for a faithful Penelope find that my purpose was foolish as I'm in the situation of a Troilus, abandoned by one as faithless as Criseyde'.

7   H78 reads 'repent' for 'bewaile'.

9   H78 transposes 'wanton' and 'raging'.

11   H78 reads 'Cillas seas' for 'Scilla'. On Scylla and Charybdis, see note to poem 169, line 11.

13   H78 reads 'heaven' for 'haven'.

17   H78 reads 'his' for 'her'.

25–30   H78 omits this final stanza.

28   The idea that the speaker is sure to be saved may imply that he has found a new love, but may rather suggest that he has undergone a religious conversion, moving from earthly to heavenly love for his salvation.

233

[Not in Q1] In poulter's measure. A celebration of success in love and vow of fidelity.

6   On Paris and Helen, see note to poem 201, lines 1–3.

16   A theological idea here cuts into the amorous discourse: to be justified is to have the taint of Original Sin removed, which requires the agency of grace (see the next line).

23   It seems unlikely that the archaic past tense of 'shut' here has any obscene meaning; that cannot be said, however, when Spenser uses it in *Colin Clouts Come Home Againe*, line 709.

30   Q8 reads 'And' for 'A'.

34   Sidney would also use a mildly eroticized idea of springing joy at amorous success in *Astrophel and Stella*, 69.

234

[Not in Q1] By Sir John Cheke (1514–57). Tetrameter quatrains with alternating rhyme. A condemnation of the world. The title slightly misquotes 1 John 5: 19, which reads 'Et mundus totus in maligno positus est'. The King James Bible translates the whole verse thus: 'And we know that we are of God, and the whole world lieth in wickedness.' We may be expected to remember the first part of the verse when reading the poem, perhaps as a righteous Protestant minority in a wicked world. There is a copy of the poem (with the same title), which constitutes the whole of Bodleian MS Rawlinson Poet. 82, with a few insignificant variants. It is signed thus:

> Sir John Cheek.
> Who can persuade, where treson is above reson; and Might ruleth right; and it is had for lawful, whatsoever is lustful; and commotioners is better, then Commissioners; and common Wo is nam'd Common Welth.
>   Gabriel Harvey.

This is all probably in Harvey's hand; Harvey (1552/3–1631) was Edmund Spenser's tutor and friend. Cheke was first Regius Professor of Greek at Cambridge, and tutor to Edward VI, through which position he gained further important offices, rising to become Secretary of State. He was imprisoned in 1553 for having supported Lady Jane Grey's right to the throne, though subsequently released and allowed to leave the country. However, he was later arrested, brought back to

England and forced into a public declaration of Catholic adherence, which was a major propaganda coup for the Marian regime. There is also a copy in BL MS Add. 60577, dated 1549, whose main variants are noted below.

The poem is a fine example of its kind, and looks forward to the laconic *Weltschmerz* of Greville and Ralegh.

8   MS Add. 60577 reads 'who can yt save' for 'what man can save'.

10   MS Add. 60577 reads 'ys nothyng but payne' for 'is thought but vaine'.

11   The parentheses here represent speech marks.

18   MS Add. 60577 reads 'raynyth' for 'runth'.

28   MS Add. 60577 reads 'with the' for 'gainst'.

29   Q8 reads 'Will' for 'Wyly'.

33–6   Lines omitted in MS Add. 60577.

37   MS Add. 60577 reads 'dothe' for 'do love'.

40   MS Add. 60577 reads 'Lowe with the hye do pley cheke mate'.

41–4   Lines omitted in MS Add. 60577.

46   MS Add. 60577 reads 'Many thrystyth, few do uphold'.

48   MS Add. 60577 reads 'gon ys the staye' for 'The stay is gone'.

49   MS Add. 60577 reads the more sensible 'pratyth' for 'prayeth'.

50   MS Add. 60577 reads 'causyd' for 'faine'.

52   MS Add. 60577 reads 'scarse ons' for 'scant'. The line is then succeeded by the following stanza:

>   Tong is of guile an instrument
>   Trust may we not lest we shuld rewe
>   Hart to envy and hate ys bent
>   And dysceytfull love is ons untrue

56   MS Add. 60577 omits 'And' and reads 'owne' after 'his'.

57–64   MS Add. 60577 transposes these stanzas.

59   Q8 reads 'song' for 'sonk'.

61   MS Add. 60577 reads 'wyll' for 'wit'.

66   Cf. Matthew 23: 37: 'O Jerusalem, Jerusalem, thou that killest the prophets, and stonest them which are sent unto thee, how often would I have gathered thy children together,

even as a hen gathereth her chickens under her wings, and ye would not!'

68   MS Add. 60577 reads 'the father' for 'thee'.

235

[Not in Q1] English sonnet. A poem of moral counsel advising caution (which the poem seems to identify with wisdom).

2   Q8 omits 'alwaies the end'.

3   Cf. Gascoigne, *A Hundreth Sundrie Flowres*, 'The Devises of Sundrie Gentlemen', no. 60, line 49: 'Bought wytte is deare, and drest with sowre salt'.

236

[Not in Q1] Tetrameter couplets. A poem of moral counsel, advising keeping quiet. Though a weaker poem than the preceding two, it adds to their theme of advising patient dissident strategies in difficult times.

6   Q3 and later editions read the rather better 'bestow' for 'bestrow'.

15–16   This was – or became – a common proverb (e.g. Harvey, *The Trimming of Thomas Nashe* (1597), F4ᵛ). The ultimate sourse is Epictetus.

237

[Not in Q1] Alternating tetrameters and trimeters with alternating rhyme. A love complaint with extended conceit.

1   Coal that produces no flame and whose heat is increased by cold water is mentioned in Pliny the Elder, *Natural History*, II. 235.

26   Q8 reads 'women' for 'mowen'.

238

[Not in Q1] In fourteeners. Answering the conceit of the poem above, it ingeniously turns it around with some rather absurd detail. One might call this a forerunner of metaphysical wit.

8   Q8 reads 'therefore' for 'there fro'.

20   Q8 reads 'an' for 'on'.

239

[Q1: 255] By William Gray. Alternating tetrameters and trimeters with alternating rhyme. An epitaph (or auto-epitaph) condemning a woman. There is a copy of the poem in BL MS Lansdowne 98, identifying the author, but with no other significant variants. BL MS Sloane 1207 has a few insignificant variants to the printed text, but then continues thus:

> Yet now at the Last hathe gotten Rest
>   Amonge the Fathers olde,
> with clottes of yerthe apon his brest,
>   nott Felynge hott nor colde
>
> Not Ferynge ones the porgynge plase
>   Devysed by the pope,
> Butt in the marsy & the grace
>   of chryst that is my hoppe.
>
> As For the pardons and his mass
>   Whyche wher his cheffe chase,
> Lett chryston men nott on them pass,
>   the be butt the popes draff
>
> The holly oyle, hose consettes,
>   his mede shall be butt smale:
> beleve nott his sacrementes,
>   nor his sacrymentaule.
>
> As For the Rest of popesnes –
>   to longe now to Ressytt –
> Lett chryston men with qwytnes
>   this pass them over qwytt,
>
> And trust, – in that yow shall Fynd good,
>   yf sole helthe ye well wen, –
> yeven chrystes merettes, & his blud
>   that was shed ower solles to kepe From sen.
>
> For that is that that allwayes moste,
>   yf we well chryst attene,
> putt all yower conffydence and trust
>   All thenges elles ar butt vene.
>
> This is the ende of grat & smaule,
>   to torne as I am now:
> From yerthe we cam, to yerthe we shall,
>   no man knothe whan nor howe.

Yett was I once as now ar ye,
    yeven losty From my berthe;
shyche as I ame, syche shall ye be;
    all ye shall torne to yerthe.

Therffore leve hee accordingely,
    As holly wrytt doth tell,
And then shall god aswredly
    kepe yow From dethe & hell.

To leve as on should allway dye,
    Yt wer a blesed trade;
to change ower dethe For Lyfe so hey;
    no batter change is mayd.

For All the worldly thenges ar vene,
    in them ther is no trust;
ye se all stattes awhyle Remenethe,
    and then the torne to dust.

Yf Lust & Lykynge myght be bowght
    For syllver or For golde,
still to Indever yt wolde be sowght:
    what kynges wolde then be olde?

But all shall pass and Foulou me, –
    this is most sertin truthe, –
both hyghe & Lowe, & Ieche degre,
    the age and Ieke the youthe.

Yf yow be Found mett or un-mett
    Agynst the dredfull ower,
As ye be Found, so shall the swettar
    be served with the sower.

All this is sayd to mend ower harthis,
    that shall her or sey,
And then Acordinge to yower partis
    to Foulow dethe with me.

It will of course be noticed that the attack on popery is missing from the *Miscellany* as well as from the Lansdowne MS. We perhaps ought to be more than a little sceptical as to Gray's authorship of the poem; certainly we should not assume that he really wrote it on his death-bed; it is possible that a friend or friends ventriloquized Gray as a libel on his wife, or even that the whole situation is a fiction. William Gray seems to have been a favourite of Protector Somerset.

240

[Q1: 256] Alternating pentameters with tetrameters, with alternating rhyme. A defence of a libelled woman; cf. poems 212, 214. As with the poem to which it responds, there is a copy of the poem in BL MS Lansdowne 98, with a few insignificant variants. It is a much livelier piece than the poem that prompted it.

8   Q8 reads 'blisse' for 'blist'.

241

[Q1: 253] Pentameter rhyme royal. An epitaph or elegy. Henry Williams can be identified as the son of Sir John Williams, Baron Williams of Thame (c. 1500–59), Sheriff of Oxfordshire and Buckinghamshire, who in 1553 rallied his counties in favour of Mary's accession and who gave assistance against the younger Wyatt's rebellion. He also attended the Oxford executions of Latimer and Ridley in 1555 and of Cranmer in 1556. His relations with Elizabeth Tudor, whose confinement at Woodstock he supervised, were, however, very good, and he was promoted on her accession. His son Henry died in 1551.

1   Q8 reads 'cnde' for 'mede'.

5   It is possible that the author intended the more alliterative
           poetic commonplace 'salt sorrow' here.

12   Q8 reads 'to' for 'fo'.

13   Q8 reads 'her' for 'here'.

17   Q8 reads 'warmed' for 'unharmed'.

242

[Not in Q1] By Thomas Norton (c. 1531–84), who had been tutor to the Duke of Somerset's children, later became an eminent lawyer, and co-wrote *Gorbodoc* (c. 1559), the first important tragedy in English. Tetrameter quatrains with alternating rhyme. More obviously an epitaph than poem 241, it ventriloquizes the dead Williams. There is a copy of the poem in AH (300), whose most important variants are noted below, and in BL MS Cotton Titus A. 24, signed 'finis. norton'; it has a few variants in common with the other MS. *ODNB* asserts that Norton also wrote the preceding poem on Williams, saying it 'maintains that Williams ... will triumph over death by his recent conversion to Protestantism'.

3	AH reads 'they' for 'we'.
4	AH reads 'to' for 'and'.
7	Both MSS read 'resist' for 'withstand'.
9	Q8 reads 'light' for 'hight'; AH reads 'my' for 'me'.
19	AH reads 'of' for 'for'.

243

[Q1: 257] By Thomas Norton. An English sonnet in tetrameters. A condemnation of women. There is another copy of the poem, signed 'Norton', in BL MS Cotton Titus A. 24; its most important variants are noted below.

1	In legends of the Trojan War, including Homer's version, Nestor was the oldest member of the Greek army; he was therefore a byword for longevity (and often also either wisdom or wordiness).
2–3	For Ulysses/Odysseus and his famously faithful wife Penelope, see note to poem 225.
5	MS reads 'tim' (i.e. 'time') for 'age'. For the young prince Paris's seduction/abduction of the notoriously unfaithful Helen, see notes to poems 201, lines 1–3, and 225, line 5.
7	MS reads 'greate' for 'good'.
9–10	In Homer's *Odyssey*, the hero returns home and kills all his wife's suitors; the poet here seems to be blaming Penelope for this, but see the response in the next poem.
12	MS reads 'bothe' for 'Sith'.
13	MS reads 'Worke' for 'Bring'. The *Miscellany*'s version therefore tones down the accusation against Penelope at least.

244

[Q1: 258] By Thomas Norton, or an Inns of Court friend of his. The form here is innovative, tetrameters rhyming ABABBCDCDDABABEEE, which seems like a riff on the previous sonnet's form, its extra lines either serving to trump the poem it responds to, or alluding to supposed feminine loquacity (though the speaker is male, he is speaking for women). A defence of women. For the mythological allusions, see notes to previous poem.

4	The word 'now' probably refers not just to the present age, but to the Christian age in general, in which more women might be expected to be virtuous.
5	Q8 reads 'chaunce' for 'change'.
6–8	These lines seem to have two meanings: 'ladies as beautiful as Helen now behave differently' or 'ladies don't behave like that any more; the only Helens about are prostitutes, not ladies'.
9–10	That is, whether women behave badly or well depends on their root virtues, possibly implying that it has to do with their relative status, but also suggesting that their virtue is dependent on the behaviour of their menfolk.

245

[Q1: 254] In tetrameter Venus and Adonis stanzas. A condemnation of a woman. One might compare this poem and its answer to poem 26 and its answer.

19	Q8 reads 'such a' for 'such, as'.
28	Q8 reads 'want' for 'vaunt'.
30	The oath here (cf. poem 246, line 60) seems to swear on two birds (the cock being obviously male, and the magpie being a cant term for a prostitute); however, its origins are probably in a corruption of 'By god and the pie' – the latter being a fifteenth-century set of directions for church services.

246

[Not in Q1] In tetrameter Venus and Adonis stanzas. A defence of a woman. Note that the poem is exactly twice the length of that which it answers; as with poem 244, this may hint at supposed feminine loquacity.

6	Q8 omits 'heate'.
13	Q8 reads 'here' for 'her'.
17	Q8 reads 'lande' for 'laud'.
30	Q8 reads 'winde' for 'winne'.
56	Q8 omits 'not'.
57	Q8 reads 'oft' for 'ought'.

247

[Q1: 178] In poulter's measure. Moral *copia* on the idea of caution in love.

248

[Q1: 261] In poulter's measure. Commonplace *copia* in response to the above. In Q1 it is given the title 'An answere to a song before imprinted beginnyng. To walke on doutfull grounde'; as it is the last poem in Q1's 'Uncertain Authors' section the poem was evidently inserted as an afterthought, having been dug up too late to be properly attached to the poem it answers.

2   Q8 reads 'of' for 'oft'.

249

[Not in Q1] In fourteener couplets. A poem of amorous repentance.

11   Q8 reads 'Not' for 'That'.

13   Q8 reads 'the' for 'their'.

19   Q8 reads 'tuth' for 'ruth'.

23   Q8 reads 'of' for 'oft'.

31   The idea of amorous idolatry is pressed quite hard here – cf. poems 142, line 24, and 191, line 36.

32   Q8 reads 'plaint' for 'plant'.

37   The blind boy is Cupid, here set in opposition to God, who may offer a way out of the speaker's perplexity. Q8 reads 'faultrers' for 'fautles'.

39   The idea of spiritually efficacious penitence was mainly a Catholic doctrine, though Luther had been ambivalent about its sacramental status.

43   Cf. poems 153, line 4, and 250, line 62, for similar phrasing. The use of the rare words 'grates' and 'saltish' both here and in the next poem imply that they may be by the same author.

250

[Not in Q1] Tetrameter quatrains with alternating rhyme. A love complaint. As the syntax is unusually stretched across the quatrains, and as the punctuation obstructs this, we give below a paraphrase of the first thirty-two lines (after which the movement is clearer): 'I would have swapped the cruel arts that I've encountered from Cupid with those of Death – I deserved to suffer as little as innocents who have died as a result of death's roving about. If they had swapped their bows, death would have had less blame – in fact, death would be regarded as kind/ natural in giving those innocents reason to want to die; love, in turn, would bring lovers an end to their misery, or, when he intends to make someone fall in love, he'd kill him and thus spare future pain.'

18   Q8 reads 'leading' for 'lendyng'.

22   Q8 reads 'time' for 'life'.

48   Q8 reads 'quiete' for 'quite'.

53   Q8 reads 'Of' for 'Oft'.

60   Q8 reads 'overwaild' for 'overwayd'.

70   The word 'blent' here probably means blinded, but may also suggest mixed (i.e. doubt and trust).

251

[Not in Q1] Tetrameter quatrains with alternating rhyme. A condemnation of women.

3   On fortune's wheel, see note to poem 146, line 10. Q8 reads 'slight' for 'flight'.

252

[Not in Q1] Pentameters with an innovative rhyme scheme: AAAABABACACABABADADA (this may seem technically demanding, but it is helped by the refrain, and by the use of '-ess' rhymes). A love complaint.

13   Q8 omits 'it'.

253

[Not in Q1] Alexandrine triplets followed by a tetrameter tag line rhyming with that of the next stanza, thus grouping the stanzas into pairs. A poem on the golden mean. A version of Horace, *Odes*, II. 10, also imitated in poems 32 and 163.

4   Q8 omits 'the'.

6   Horace's poem makes it clear that 'coate' here means a
            poor man's cottage (*OED*, 'cote' n1).

9   Horace refers to the pine tree; the poet here has made an
            unfortunate expansion for the sake of the metre (the pine-
            apple plant is hardly a stout tree, but the English of the time
            would not have seen one).

10   The poet probably intended 'rising' rather than 'ruing', but
            his otiose expansion of Horace's 'turres ... summos' has
            led the compositor to invent a portmanteau word either
            meaning falling (cf. ruin) or pitiful.

254

[Not in Q1] Alexandrine couplets. A poem in praise of friendship. The
source for most of these ideas is Cicero's *De Amicitia (On Friendship)*.
There is another copy of the poem in BL MS Sloane 1896, with the
title 'A true freind is a rare Juell'; its most important variants are
noted below.

2   MS reads 'is worthy to aryse' for 'by worth is wont to rise'.

3   Q8 reads 'so is' for 'is so'.

16   Q8 reads 'of' for 'is'.

26   Q8 reads 'receive' for 'releve'.

27   MS reads 'fynde' for 'have'.

28   MS reads 'thou doe it mynde' for 'that thou can crave'.

30   Q8 reads 'my' for the first 'thy'.

31   The idea of the friend as another self derives from Cicero's
            De Amicitia.

32   The blasphemous idea of the friend as a god does not
            appear in Cicero; nor does it seem to be proverbial; but cf.
            Twelfth Night, III. iv. 365, where Antonio says of Sebastian
            (really Viola/Cesario) 'how vild an idol proves this god!'

33   Q8 reads 'loving' for 'louring'.

255

[Q1: 82] Tetrameter rhyme royal. A courtly complaint, which may be
as much about lack of preferment as it is about love (which is not

mentioned except in the title). This is a curious case of attribution: in Q1 it is given to Wyatt; moving it into the 'Uncertain Authors' section shows that the *Miscellany*'s compilers were taking care not to misattribute, and that suggests some knowledge that it was not written by him; there is a copy in B, which does contain many poems by Wyatt as well as several poems that might be his.

6–7   That is, I'm like a dog begging for food at a food counter: the less successful I am, the longer I have to wait.

8–14   These lines are rather obscure, but may be paraphrased thus: 'My trust only serves to prove that my desire is unavailing; my hopeful yearning redounds to my harm because I restrained my desires; I cannot choose my desires for my own good, and those that I have I can't put in action; such desires according to reason aren't desires at all, since their fruits are won by others/they are in others' control.'

256

[Q1: 242] In poulter's measure. An attack on courtly lovers (and perhaps on courtliness in general).

1   Cf. poem 4.

5   That is, like hounds assisting hunters on foot (presumably with spears), or like dogs assisting bowmen.

13   The reference is to Ovid's notorious handbook, the *Ars Amatoria* (*The Art of Love*).

20   Q8 reads 'state' for 'stale'.

35   Q8 reads 'them' for 'then'.

257

[Not in Q1] In quatrains with alternating rhyme; trimeter except for the third line in each stanza, which is tetrameter. A condemnation of the world. There is another copy of the poem in BL MS Sloane 1896, its most important variants being noted below.

2   MS reads 'wherupon' for 'Whereon'.

5   MS reads 'age' for 'elde'.

7   Q8 inserts 'true' after 'Will'.

10   MS reads 'sometymes' for 'whylome'.

13   That is, Helen.

18   MS reads 'body' for 'caryon'.

258

[Not in Q1] Formally innovative: seven-line tetrameter stanzas with a varied rhyme scheme, recurring frequently to two rhymes, and using a refrain; the overall pattern is thus:
ABACABC / DEDBDEB / FBFBFCB / GBGCGCB / HBHBHCB.
The poem is clearly a ballade, perhaps imitating Wyatt's manner; cf. poem 57 above. A repudiation of love. One of the better poems by uncertain authors, it deserves to be better known. Q8 reads 'his' for 'her' in the title.

25   Q8 reads 'slacke' for 'slake'.

30   Q8 reads 'Which' for 'With'.

34   Q8 reads 'erste' for 'derst'.

259

[Not in Q1] Pentameters rhyming ABABBACABCBCBDD, a formally innovative scheme – one might see this as a variation on a sonnet; cf. poem 244. A female complaint.

2   The phrase 'in eche degre' is probably mere filler or intensifier.

260

[Not in Q1] An English sonnet. A love complaint.

7   Alludes to the Neoplatonic idea of love as a means to escape worldly concerns.

8   Q8 reads 'sigh' for 'sight'.

261

[Not in Q1] Pentameter. Like Surrey's poem 2, it alternates two rhymes before concluding with a third rhyme in a couplet – except that line 7 is defective, probably due to mistranscription. It is either an imitation of Petrarch, *Rime*, 134, or of Wyatt's poem 54 (which is based on the Petrarch poem). A love complaint. Note the intensified images of torture (pressed, strained, burning, the fetters and stones of a prison, starvation – Petrarch only has a gaol and fetters), and the exoneration of the beloved at the end (not in Wyatt or Petrarch).

6   Refers to *peine forte et dure*, a punishment for refusal to plead in law courts, which involved being crushed to death with large rocks.

262

[Not in Q1] Tetrameter Venus and Adonis stanzas. A complaint by a tree. Rollins does not think the poem a genuine 'tree-testament', arguing that 'Haw' here means 'worthless man', but the speaker of the poem is friends with a tree (lines 31–2), and it seems more plausible that another tree would claim such friendship than that a man would; on the other hand, this tree does seem to be in love with a lady rather than another tree.

8   Q8 reads 'that' for 'I'.

18   Q8 reads 'nathelesse' for 'natrelesse'.

36   Q8 reads 'should be' for 'shalbe'.

45   Q8 reads 'lying' for 'living'.

73   Q8 omits 'here'.

74   For the Phoenix, see notes to poems 160, line 31, and 168, line 18.

263

[Not in Q1] Tetrameter Venus and Adonis stanzas. A love complaint.

2   Rhyme and reason both dictate that 'washe' should read 'waste'.

16–18   The language here neatly confounds the theological and the amorous: the speaker may have faith (simply as a matter of goodwill or fidelity to his lady), but this will do him no good unless he has grace (grace being the precondition of saving faith), in which divine and sexual favour are seemingly equated.

27   Q8 reads 'gladliest' for 'gladdest'.

264

[Not in Q1] Alternating tetrameters and trimeters with alternating rhyme. A praise of a specific lady. It seems likely that the poem has a real subject, probably a married woman called Bayes, but she has not been identified. If poem 262 concerns a tree loving a lady, here we encounter a man loving a tree; the story of Apollo and Daphne in poem 265 also involves the beloved becoming a tree. The bay tree (related to the laurel) provided the wreaths worn in Roman military triumphs.

22   Q8 reads 'He' for 'Her'.

34   Q8 reads 'fained' for 'faynted'.

42   Q8 reads 'sely' for 'slyly'.

59   Q8 reads 'hands' for 'bands'.

265

[Not in Q1] Alternating tetrameters and trimeters in six-line stanzas with the rhyme scheme ABACBC, though the fourth stanza rhymes ABABCB. A mythological analogue for the lover's state.

1–6   The story of the sun-god Phoebus Apollo killing the serpent
            Pytho, and that of his love for Daphne (who turned into a
            laurel tree) are recounted in Ovid, *Metamorphoses*, I. 441–
            567. The link between the stories, not clearly presented
            here, is that Apollo, exulting in his triumph over the snake,
            mocked Cupid's bowmanship, causing the love-god to
            prove his power over the adult god. The laurel provided the
            wreaths for master poets (cf. note to poem 264), and the
            analogy between the poet and Apollo may hint at a claim
            to laureate status.

5   Q8 reads 'himselfe' for 'him fele'.

7–16   For Cupid's two arrows, see poem 4, lines 5–6.

16   Q8 reads 'must' for 'most'.

266

[Not in Q1] In poulter's measure. A praise of a specific lady. Rollins partly approves Nott's conjecture that the poem is addressed to Mistress (Jane) Markham by her future husband John Harington of

Stepney. We find it hard to share Nott's and Rollins's evident admiration for the poem.

1   The term 'court' here of course refers to the royal court, but the poem goes on rather wittily to imply that the situation is also a law court, in which he sets himself up as a judge of ladies.

2   Whether or not the woman praised is Jane Markham, the suppressed name is certainly a surname of two syllables, with the stress on the first.

4   Q8 reads 'ritchelesse' for 'retchlesse'.

6   The analogy here with the burning of Troy suggests that the beloved is as beautiful as Helen; cf. poems 201, 225, 233, 243, 244, 257, and line 12 below.

14   Q8 reads 'may be' for 'May the'.

18   Q8 reads 'heaven' for 'heavy'.

26   The Nile was a byword for a large river; for Nestor, a byword for old age, see note to poem 243, line 1.

30   The sense of this last line is a little cloudy, but it probably means that her beauty is such a full stock of everything Nature makes that everything else Nature makes has to be sold at cut price.

267

[Not in Q1] Tetrameter quatrains with alternating rhyme (though printed here as eight-line stanzas). A repudiation of love. Misogynistic though it is, this is one of the most appealing of the uncertain authors' poems.

27   'penyworthes' is a two-syllable word, pronounced pen'uths.

31   This means either that he will go to bed as a fool himself, or that he will beget a fool.

32   Cf. Drayton, 'Since there's no help' (*Idea*, 61; 1609 version).

268

[Not in Q1] In poulter's measure. A repudiation of love. The poem's falconry metaphors may remind us of Wyatt's poem 57, with its treatment of former lovers as animals/birds; the poem's bitterness also recalls that of Wyatt, but it lacks his mitigating delicacy.

9   Q8 reads 'linger' for 'lenger'.

12   It is tempting to think this line refers to the careers of such
            women as Anne Boleyn and Catherine Howard, wives of
            Henry VIII whose dubious sexual reputation played a
            major part in bringing them to execution – and that it
            therefore wishes on the addressee a fate like theirs.

269

[Not in Q1] Pentameter Venus and Adonis stanzas. A poem in praise
of a specific lady above all other ladies; cf. poem 213. The Arundel to
which the poem refers at line 23 is surely some reference to the lady
herself, but whether it means her name or her home is not quite cer-
tain: she may be either Mary, daughter of the Earl of Arundel (who
would later marry Surrey's son Thomas Howard), or some member of
the Howard family (whose seat was Arundel Castle).

2   Q8 reads 'prise' for 'praise'.

9   The reference is to Paris (see note to poem 225, line 5), and
            therefore should read 'sonne'.

10   Cf. W. B. Yeats, 'The Gyres', line 7. Q8 omits one 'had'.

12   Q8 inserts 'in' after 'hue'.

15   Q8 reads 'heartes' for 'heares'.

16   The beams of the sun-god Phoebus Apollo are frequently
            described as being his hair.

17   Q8 reads 'surged' for 'sucred'.

22   Diana was goddess of chastity.

34   The reference is to Pallas Athena, goddess of wisdom, who
            was born from Jupiter/Zeus' head.

35–6   The poem here possibly refers to the Platonic notion of the
            superior reality of the world of ideas to the material world
            which supposedly reflects the ideas; the lines thus mean
            'Her virtues exceed her bodily form as much as the light of
            the sun exceeds the shadowy world of human life'.

270

[Not in Q1] Trimeter quatrains with alternating rhyme. A lament for
a dead lover.

34   The source is biblical – Matthew 8: 22: 'But Jesus said unto
            him, Follow me: and let the dead bury their dead'; Luke

9: 60: 'Jesus said unto him, Let the dead bury their dead: but go thou and preach the kingdom of God.'

37   The 'other kinde of life' is presumably religious.

GRIMALD

271

[Q1: 133] Pentameter quatrains with alternating rhyme. The poem is a version of the poem 'Nomina Musarum', a poem misattributed to the fourth-century AD Latin poet Ausonius:

> Clio gesta canens transactis tempora reddit.
> dulciloquis calamos Euterpe flatibus urguet.
> comica lascivo gaudet sermone Thalia.
> Melpomene tragico proclamat moesta boatu.
> Terpsichore affectus citharis movet, imperat, auget.
> plectra gerens Erato saltat pede carmine vultu.
> Urania motusque poli scrutatur et astra.
> carmina Calliope libris heroica mandat.
> signat cuncta manu loquiturque Polymnia gestu.
> mentis Apollineae vis has movet undique Musas:
> in medio residens complectitur omnia Phoebus.

[Clio, singing of famous deeds brings past times back to life. Euterpe fills the sweet-voiced flutes with her breath. Thalis rejoices in the lascivious speeches of comedy. Melpomene cries aloud with the gloomy sound of tragedy. Terpsichore moves, rules and increases the emotions with her lyre. Erato bearing the plectrum makes one dance from head to foot. Urania examines the movement of the poles and the stars. Calliope makes heroic songs appear in books. Polymnia signifies all things with her hand and speaks by gesture. The power of Apollo's mind enlivens all these Muses: Phoebus sitting in the midst encompasses all these things].

Grimald's poem is reprinted with variants in *England's Parnassus*, pp. 211–12, where it is attributed to Surrey, presumably on the basis that some Elizabethans thought the entire *Miscellany* was his work. The Muses, the daughters of Jupiter and Memory (Mnemosyne in Greek, Memoria in Latin), were the goddesses of music, literature and dance.

3   Calliope is the Muse of epic poetry.

5   Clio is the Muse of history.

7   'Thaley': Thalia, Muse of comedy and bucolic poetry.

9   'Melpomen': Melpomene, Muse of tragedy.

11   'Terpsichor': Terpsichore, Muse of dancing and associated
            song.

13   'Erato': Muse of the lyre and lyric poetry. *England's Par-
            nassus* calls her 'Fond' rather than 'Fine'.

15   'Polymnie': Polyhymnia, Muse of hymns to the gods.

15–16   *England's Parnassus* moves 'place' to the end of line 15,
            omitting 'in place' in line 16.

17   'Uranie': Urania, Muse of astronomy.

19   'Eutrepe': Euterpe, Muse of flute-playing and lyric poetry
            sung to the flute. Q8 reads 'blestes' for 'blastes'.

22–4   *England's Parnassus* omits everything after 'enspire'.

272

[Q1: 134] Pentameter; predominantly in rhyming couplets, but the
first six lines are monorhymed. An epigram. Musonius Rufus was a
Roman Stoic philosopher of the first century AD; there is an edition of
his sayings in Cora E. Lutz, 'Musonius Rufus: "The Roman Socrates"',
Yale Classical Studies, 10 (1947), pp. 3–147.

11   Q8 reads 'ill vading' for 'ylswading'.

273

[Q1: 149] Pentameter rhyming couplets. The poem's source is Beza's
epigram 'Descriptio Virtutis'. Theodore de Beze was a French theolo-
gian and one of the influential Genevese reformers. He is particularly
known for his edition of the Greek Testament (1565) and his biog-
raphy of Calvin. For discussion of Grimald's use of Beza, see H. H.
Hudson, 'Grimald's Translations from Beza', *Modern Language
Notes*, 39 (1924), pp. 388–94. An epigram; cf. poem 203. For the text
of Beza's poems, see Thomas Thomson, 'A Critical Edition of the
Poemata (1548) of Theodore de Beze' (D.Phil. thesis, University of
Oxford, 1983). The poem is printed in Kendall's *Flowers of Epi-
grammes* (1577) and *England's Parnassus*.

274

[Q1: 150] Pentameter rhyming couplets. Its source is Beza's Elegia II,
'In Mediocritatis laudem'. (For Beza, see headnote to poem 273.) A
moral ode.

5   'Icar': Icarus, son of Daedalus. Attempting to escape from
         imprisonment on Crete, Daedalus and Icarus made wings
         for themselves out of wax and feathers, but Icarus flew too
         near the sun, the wax melted, and he crashed into the sea.
         Presumably this is the 'Icarian beck' mentioned in line 6,
         but there may be a confusion with Phaethon, who did
         indeed fall into a river rather than the sea.

7   'Phaeton': Phaethon was son of Helios, the sun. Permitted
         to borrow his father's chariot, he could not control its
         horses, which bolted, risking the incineration of the earth.
         To prevent this, Jupiter struck Phaethon with a thunderbolt
         and he fell into the river Eridanus. See Ovid, *Metamor-
         phoses*, I. 747–II. 400.

9   Q8 reads 'so' for 'to'.

11   'Julie': Julius Caesar (100–44 BC), Roman general, polit-
         ician and ruler, known among many things for his mercy to
         his enemies. He pardoned Cassius and Brutus after the bat-
         tle of Pharsalia; they subsequently assassinated him.

12   Nero (AD 37–68) was a Roman emperor chiefly renowned
         for cruelty. He committed suicide to avoid execution.

13   'August': Augustus Caesar (63 BC–AD 14), the first Roman
         emperor, known for virtue, hard work and marital
         fidelity.

17   Q8 reads 'gut' for 'goom'.

19   Cato the Younger (95–46 BC) was a Stoic philosopher of
         extremely ascetic habits, and Mark Antony (*c.* 82–30 BC)
         was a politician and general famous for luxury and
         debauchery.

275

[Q1: 151] Poulter's measure. The poem is probably based on Eras-
mus's and/or George Buchanan's translations of a Greek poem,
possibly by Posidippus (alternatively by the comic poet Plato – not to
be confused with the philosopher). Another Latin version is found in
a Nuremberg volume of 1501 (see Rollins). However, it is possible
that Grimald translated straight from the Greek, which translates lit-
erally thus: 'What path of life should one pursue? In the market-place
there are struggles and business difficulties. At home there are anx-
ieties. There's too much work in the countryside, and there's peril at

sea. Abroad there's fear if you have wealth, and struggle if you have nothing. You have a wife? You won't be free of trouble. Not married? Life's more lonely. Children are a pain, but childless life is hobbled. Youth is witless, but old age is feeble. The choice then is between two things: to be unborn, or to die as soon as you're born.' Whichever version or versions Grimald used, translations of this material were common; Sir John Beaumont and Bacon were among those who produced versions of it; for this poem and the next, and their relationship to their sources, see Lawrence Manley, *Literature and Culture in Early Modern London* (Cambridge: Cambridge University Press, 1995), pp. 394–5. Other versions of the Greek epigrams translated here by Grimald are given as examples of '*Anthypophora*, or the Figure of Response' by Puttenham (pp. 289–91). Posidonius (*c.* 135–*c.* 50 BC) was an important philosopher, historian and scientist whose works have been almost entirely lost. He was head of the Stoic school at Rhodes, and was very influential in the development of Stoic philosophy. Cicero was his pupil, and Pompey came to his lectures when returning from Syria after the Mithridatic War. Crates (*c.* 365–285 BC) was a Cynic philosopher, a pupil of Diogenes.

4   Q8 omits 'with'.

9   Q8 reads 'founde' for 'fond'.

276

[Q1: 152] Poulter's measure. The ultimate source is a poem by the philosopher Metrodorus in the *Greek Anthology*, IX. 360: 'Pursue every path of life. In the market-place there are honours and prudent business dealings; at home there is rest; in the country there's the charm of Nature, in sea-travel there is profit; abroad, if you have wealth there is fame, but no one will know if you're poor. You have a wife? Your house will be the best. Not married? Life's easier. Children are lovely, but a childless life is free of care. Youth is vigorous, but old age is pious. Therefore the real choice is not between being unborn and being dead – for everything in life is splendid.' It is possible that Grimald worked directly from the Greek, but he would probably have known the Latin versions by Erasmus and George Buchanan, as in poem 275. Another Latin version is found in a Nuremberg volume of 1501 (see Rollins).

3   Q8 reads 'break' for 'beak'.

277

[Q1: 154] Poulter's measure. A poem in praise of friendship. The poem also appears in BL. MS. Sloane 1896, with some variations; its title there is 'A Commendacion of friendshippe'.

4   In MS, the following lines come next: 'The golden estate of emperors, / full sone doth weare away: / & other precious thinges doe fade, / freindshippe will never decay' (Rollins).

14   Q8 reads 'left' for 'leef'.

23–4 Scipio Aemilianus (Africanus Minor), c. 185–129 BC, was an important military and political figure at Rome and a lifelong friend of Laelius, who was consul at Rome in 140 BC. In Cicero's *De Amicitia* Laelius laments Scipio's death; Rollins quotes an extract from John Harington's 1550 translation of this lament: 'Truely of all the thynges whiche fortune or nature gave me, I haue nothyng to matche with Scipioes freendship.'

25   See Boccaccio, *Decameron*, X. 8 for the friendship of Gisippus and Titus Quintus Fulvius, but the most familiar source for Tudor readers would have been Sir Thomas Elyot's *The Boke Named the Governour* (1531), chapter XII, where Gisippus hands over his fiancée to his friend once he discovers that Titus has fallen in love with her too; Titus later saves Gisippus from false murder charges. Damon was a Pythagorean philosopher whose friendship with Pythias was famous; when Pythias was condemned to death, Damon stood surety for him while Pythias went home to arrange his affairs. When he returned to redeem Damon, both were freed in recognition of their loyalty.

26   This line follows line 28 in MS. The friendship of Achilles and Patroclus, son of Menoetius, is celebrated in the *Iliad*.

27   Nisus and Euryalus, followers of Aeneas, were proverbially devoted friends. See Virgil, *Aeneid*, IX. 176–82, and cf. poem 151.

28   Pylades and Orestes were close friends and brothers-in law (Pylades married Orestes' sister Electra); Pylades accompanied Orestes to the land of the Tauri, and to Mycenae, where Orestes took revenge on Aegisthus and Clytemnestra.

29   Pirithous, king of the Lapiths, was a close friend of Theseus, king of Athens. They went together to the underworld

to attempt to carry off Persephone. Q8 reads 'Pirch' for 'Pirith'.

31–2 Cicero's works *De Amicitia* and *De Senectute* (*On Old Age*) are dedicated to his intimate friend Atticus, and sixteen books of his letters to Atticus also survive.

32 Q8 omits 'lo' and 'lot'.

39 MS reads 'Joyfull' for 'kindely'.

278

[Q1: 165] Blank verse. The source is Book III of the medieval epic *Alexandreidos* by Philippus Galterus de Castellione, also known as Philippe Gautier de Chatillon, who wrote around 1170–80. There is an edition of 1541, close to the date Grimald was writing (it is too long to quote here – see Rollins). The last sixteen lines of Grimald's poem are not based on the source. A *pragmatographia* or description of battle. For Alexander, see note to poem 135, lines 48–9.

2 Q1 reads 'taratantars' for 'dredfull trompets'.

14–15 Oxate, or Oxathres, was the brother of Darius III, king of Persia (ruled 336–330 BC). He defended Darius against Alexander.

18 Bellona was the Roman goddess of war.

22 Q8 inserts 'the' after 'wounds'.

26 Zoroas was from Memphis.

39 The 'erryng lights' are the planets (so called because they wander the heavens; Greek *planao* = lead astray).

46 Q8 reads 'his heavenly sphere' for 'this hemisphere'.

51 Q8 omits the first 'he'.

60 Nectanebus, the last Pharoah, was alleged to be Alexander's father, having seduced Olympias (Alexander's mother) by magic.

67 Learning or wisdom (*sophiā* in Greek) was divided into seven branches: grammar, rhetoric and logic (the trivium), and arithmetic, music, geometry and astronomy (the quadrivium).

81 Q8 reads 'kepe' for 'depe'. Avernus is a term for the underworld.

86 Q8 reads 'pusshes' for 'quishes'.

87	Q8 reads 'trailed' for 'reyled'.
102	Q8 reads 'wilde' for 'wailde'.
110	The Camenae were goddesses of a spring outside Rome, treated as sources of inspiration and therefore sometimes identified with the Muses.

279

[Q1: 166] Blank verse. The source of the poem is Beza's *Silvae* 2, 'Mors Ciceronis' (for Beza, see headnote to poem 273). The politician and orator Marcus Tullius Cicero (106–43 BC) was a staunch supporter of the republican cause in Rome, and was executed on the orders of Mark Antony while attempting to escape by sea.

5	Q8 reads 'evill' for 'civill'.
8	Consul Marcus: i.e. Mark Antony.
14	Q8 reads 'cought' for 'rough'.
24	Antonius: i.e. Mark Antony.
29	Q8 reads 'sonne' for 'fone'.
30–32	Cicero had once successfully defended Gaius Popillius Laenas, and without payment, according to tradition.
34	Herennius was the centurion commanding the soldiers who killed Cicero. Q8 reads 'tyger' for 'eyger'.
38	Q8 omits 'attempt'.
44	Ravens, bird of ill omen, are associated with Phoebus.
46	Brutus and Cassius were strong supporters of the republican cause, in the service of which they assassinated Julius Caesar.
47	Q8 omits 'all'.
74	Presumably a reference to the *Philippics*, the fourteen orations Cicero made against Antony.
78	Q8 reads 'Graces' for 'Grayes'.
80	Peitho was the goddess of persuasion. Q8 reads 'here percing Picho' for 'hertpersing Pitho'.
82	Q8 reads 'foode' for 'soote'.
86–8	Cicero's head and hands were displayed in Rome on the Rostra, the platform in the Forum from which speeches were made. Perhaps this is what is meant by 'Antonius

boord', unless it simply means that the story or the body-parts were actually brought to Antony at the table, as Beza's Latin implies – Antony's feasting tables are also mentioned by Beza in the poem translated as 274 above.

280

[Q1: 167] Pentameter; two rhyming couplets. Its source is a poem about Livy by Beza, 'T.Liuij':

> Tumulum Tito nuper parabam Livio,
> Quum sic Apollo iussit ut desisterem,
> Haec mortuos, inquit, decent, vivit Titus.

[I was preparing a tomb for Titus Livy, when Apollo ordered me to stop: 'Such things are for the dead,' he said, 'But Titus lives']. (For Beza, see headnote to poem 273). An epigram.

1, 4   'Tullie' is Marcus Tullius Cicero.

2   'Cynthie': i.e. Cynthius, an epithet of Apollo.

APPENDIX: POEMS FROM Q1 EXCLUDED FROM Q2 AND LATER EDITIONS

A128

Poulter's measure. Various elements in the poem may be traced to Virgil or Theocritus, perhaps via neo-Latin poetry. See W. P. Mustard review of Merrill in *Modern Language Notes*, 41 (1926), pp. 202–4, for a discussion. A celebration of success in love.

12   Mars was the Roman god of war and Pallas Athena a war-goddess.

14   Venus was goddess of love.

15–16   Zeus/Jupiter (Jove) was father of the Muses and of the Graces (see notes to poem 271), but the reference appears to be to appointment rather than begetting by Jupiter here.

A129

Pentameter rhyming couplets. The poem's source is Beza, Elegia III (misnumbered as IIII). Grimald's translation is quite literal (for Beza, see headnote to poem 273). A love complaint. It has been suggested

that the 'Carie' addressed in lines 12 and 46 might have had the sur-
name 'Day' (see poem A130), and it has also been suggested (see
Rollins) that she may have been Grimald's fiancée, although according
to *ODNB* there is no evidence that he ever married or had children.

1	That is, two months had passed (Phoebe is the moon)
7	Having angered Jove, the immortal Titan Prometheus was condemned to be chained for ever to a rock in the Caucasus with an eagle pecking out his liver every day and his liver regenerating every evening so it could be eaten again.
13	Where Grimald refers to a jealous father ('sier'), Beza's original refers to a husband ('coniugi').
17	'olds' may be a mistake for 'woods' ('sylvae'), which is what Beza refers to.
24–5	Daphne, trying to escape the amorous pursuit of Apollo, called for help, and the river-god Peneus turned her into a bay tree (see Ovid, *Metamorphoses*, I. 452–567).
27	Callisto was raped by Jupiter disguised as Diana, and subsequently transformed into a bear by the jealous Juno. To save the bear Callisto from being killed by her own son, Jupiter turned them both into stars (*Metamorphoses*, II. 409–507).
31	Actaeon accidentally stumbled on the goddess Diana (also named Dictynna) bathing, and as a punishment was turned into a stag and hunted by his own dogs (*Metamorphoses*, III. 138).

A130

Pentameter rhyming couplets. The source of the poem is Beza, Elegia
VI, in *Poemata*. Grimald's translation is quite literal (for Beza, see
headnote to poem 273). An apology to a lady. 'Day' may be 'Carie
Day', Grimald's putative fiancée; see headnote to poem A129.

7	The speaker sees roses and/or anemones, which recall Adonis. Aphrodite fell in love with Adonis when he was hunting in the woods. He was killed by a wild boar and roses sprang from his spilled blood, and anemones from Aphrodite's tears of grief.
9	Narcissus rejected the nymph Echo, who loved him. He was punished for his cruelty by Aphrodite, who caused him to fall in love with his own image in water. Because he

could not reach his beloved, he wasted away and died, and the gods transformed him into a flower.

10   Hyacinthus was loved by Apollo and Zephyrus (the west wind). Jealous because Hyacinthus preferred Apollo, Zephyrus caused an accident which killed Hyacinthus, and a flower sprang from his blood.

13   The allusion 'dame Ceres ymp' probably refers to Proserpina, Ceres' daughter, taken to the underworld by Pluto. Merrill thinks it refers to Dionysus, Ceres' child by her brother Zeus. 'When Dionysus grew up, Hera, who was jealous of Ceres and hated her son, threw him into a state of madness, in which he wandered about through many countries of the earth' (Merrill, p. 419). However, the presence of Pluto and his horses in the following line suggests Proserpina, as does the fact that the speaker has been describing walking in gardens among flowers (Proserpina was snatched while picking flowers), and the fact that Beza's Latin refers to a female child of Ceres.

18   Cupid is 'Venus chylde'.

32   The goddess Venus bore Aeneas to the Trojan Anchises.

A131

Pentameter rhyming couplets. The source of the poem is Beza's epigram, 'Ponticus Cornelio de uxore non ducenda' (for Beza, see headnote to poem 273). The identities of Vincent and Blackwood are unknown; according to Merrill (p. 419), neither appear in the student lists at Oxford or Cambridge. Rollins suspects Vincent, 'whoever he may have been', was the author of poem A131, not Grimald, but the names here and in A132 may be personae, as equivalents of Beza's Ponticus and Cornelius. A condemnation of marriage/women.

6   The phrase 'flower of frying pan' is proverbial (Tilley F385). It has connotations of ugliness and squalor.

A132

Pentameter rhyming couplets. Its source is Beza's epigram, 'Cornelius Pontico de uxore ducenda' (for Beza, see headnote to poem 273). Rollins suspects the author of this poem was the unknown Blackwood rather than Grimald, but see headnote to A131. A defence of marriage.

A135

Pentameter rhyming couplets. An epigram. For Cato, see poem 139, line 17 and note. The younger Cato is intended here.

A136

Pentameter rhyming couplets. The source of the riddle is Diogenes Laertius, *The Lives of Eminent Philosophers* (Life of Cleobulus), II. 91: 'There is one father, he has twelve sons, and each of these has thirty pairs of daughters with different looks; some of the daughters are white, the others are black; they are immortal, but they all die.' Cleobulus (*c.* 628–*c.* 558 BC) was one of the Seven Sages of Greece. The solution to the riddle is a year.

10   Oedipus was able to solve the Sphinx's riddle.

A137

An English sonnet. An encomium.

2   Lysippus was a famous sculptor in bronze; he worked in the second half of the fourth century BC. Apelles was a great painter, who was working earlier in the fourth century.

A138

Poulter's measure. An epigram.

8   See Proverbs 15: 15.

12   Titan is a personification of the sun. (The sun-god shared the name Titan with his grandfather, Kronos' elder brother and ancestor of the Titans.)

A139

Fourteener couplets. The initials in the title may indicate 'Lady Jane Seymour', the daughter of Edward Seymour, Duke of Somerset; see headnote to A144. The learning with which Grimald credits the lady in lines 7–8 was not unusual among aristocratic women, with Elizabeth I a good example. An encomium of a lady.

1   'Charis' is the singular of 'Charites', and hence one of the three Graces; 'Pieris' similarly is the singular of 'Pierides', a

term for the nine Muses. 'Cypris' is Venus, who was associated with Cyprus. Rollins comments: 'A graceful compliment: Lady Jane was the fourth Grace, the tenth Muse, the second Venus.'

2   The 'assemblies thre' are the three groups mentioned in line 1 (Graces, Muses, Venuses). Jane is adjoined to all three. Phoebus and Diana (with her retinue of nymphs) were siblings.

3   The 'Nymphs Oreades' are nymphs of the mountains.

4   This suggests the addressee of the poem might have been in Queen Mary's circle, but as Rollins notes, there is no record of Lady Jane Seymour being one of Mary's maids of honour, although she was one of Elizabeth's subsequently.

5   Terpsichore is Muse of dancing and associated song.

A140

Fourteener couplets. Poems A140, A141 and A146 all appear by their titles to have been addressed to the same person ('Mistress D. A.'), identified by the acrostic in A141 as Damascene Awdley. Merrill points out that there was a noble family called Awdley in Staffordshire, and that since Grimald was licensed to preach in Eccles, in one of the county's most important churches, he may well have known members of this family. There are no records of a Damascene Awdley, however, although it is possible that 'Damascene' (Damask) was a nickname: cf. poem 175, 'A praise of Audley', perhaps written on the death of John Tucket, Lord Audley, who died before 30 January 1557/8 (Merrill). An encomium of a lady.

3   The 'lady Mnemosynes dere daughters' were the Muses.

7–8 A cestus is a girdle; the term is used particularly of the girdle of Venus, Jupiter's daughter.

19   The goddess Pallas Athene was associated with war, virginity, urban arts and crafts (including spinning and weaving) and consequently wisdom.

29   'The Romans used a white stone or piece of chalk to mark their lucky days on the calendar. Those that were unlucky they marked with charcoal' (Merrill).

A141

Pentameter lines in the irregular form ABABABCDCDEFEGG. For the identity of the addressee, see headnote to poem A140. An encomium of a lady.

6	Cyllene was the birthplace of the Roman god Mercury, who is often therefore given the epithet Cyllenius.
8	Minerva was goddess of crafts and trade guilds.
10	Venus is often called 'the Cyprian' in recognition of the importance of her sanctuaries on Cyprus. The 'Spartan bright' is presumably Helen of Troy, who was married to Menelaus, king of Sparta.

A142

Fourteener couplets. Merrill suggests that the addressee is Lady Margaret Seymour; cf. A143 and A144. An encomium of a lady.

1	Phoebus was the sun-god.
4	Janus (after whom the month January was named) was the god of gates and hence new beginnings.

A143

Pentameter couplets. For the identity of 'l[ady] M. S.' see headnote to A142. An encomium of a lady.

A144

Fourteener couplets. Merrill suggests that A139 and A142–5 were addressed to the daughters of Edward Seymour, Duke of Somerset, and his wife, Lady Anne Stanhope (cf. A264), namely Jane, Margaret, Katherine and Elizabeth. When the Duke was released from the Tower in 1550, Grimald addressed his 'Carmen Congratulatorium' to the Duke's daughters.

2	Deborah was an Israelite judge and prophetess, known for independence and strength; see Judges 4 and 5. In the name of God, Judith enticed Holofernes, leader of the enemy Assyrians, and killed him; see the Apocryphal Book of Judith. Mary Magdalene was a follower of Jesus, and was the first to see him resurrected (see e.g. John 20: 11–18). St Anne was the

mother of the Virgin Mary; her distinctive 'chere' may be due to her conceiving after many years of childlessness.

3   The Sibyl (or prophetess) of Cumae was offered a gift of her choice by Apollo. She asked for as many years of life as there were grains of sand in a pile of debris, and was granted a thousand as a result, but unfortunately she forgot to stipulate continued youth.

A145

Fourteener couplets. The poem may be addressed to Lady Elizabeth Seymour; see headnote to A144. An encomium of a lady.

1   Janus stands for January here.

3   The epithet 'dame Tellus' means the earth.

A146

A sonnet with the scheme ABABACACCDCDEE. The source of the poem is Beza's epigram 'Xenium Candidae' (for Beza, see headnote to poem 273). For the addressee, see headnote to poem A140. An encomium of a lady.

4   'This time of Janus Calends' i.e. it is the beginning of January.

9–10   Minerva being the goddess of wisdom, Grimald is presumably asking her to retain his gift of verse in her brain.

11   Mt. Helicon is one of the homes of the Muses.

13–14   This may be a key poem in understanding why the Grimald section was so radically cut in Q2: in printing these gifts to patrons in Q1, he has risked destroying their rarity value.

A147

Fourteener couplets. The identity of Mistress Susan H. is unknown. An encomium of a lady.

A148

Fourteener couplets. The poem is based on an epigram by Marc-Antoine Muret, or Muretus (1526–85), beginning 'Non tibi pro Xeniis fulvi, pretiosa metalli'. The poem is quite close to the Latin. An epigram on friendship.

A153

Fourteener couplets, although the first two lines appear to be hyper-metric. Merrill suggests that the poem is about the rebellion of Thomas Wyatt, son of the poet, in 1554. He conspired to prevent the marriage of Mary and Philip II of Spain, leading men of Kent to Southwark, but was separated from them and executed, after which the rebellion fizzled out. An epigram.

A155

Poulter's measure. Based loosely on a Latin poem *De Laude Horti*, in Scaliger's *Catalecta Virgilii* (1617 – see Mustard, review of Merrill, p. 203). An epigram.

1   Jupiter (Jove was the father of the Muses (see notes to poem 271).

A156

An English sonnet. An elegy/epitaph. For Sir James Wilford, see head-note to poem 151. In 1547 he was provost-marshal of the army which routed the Scots at the battle of Pinkie near Musselburgh (often referred to as the battle of Musselburgh). Later in the same year, he also served at the capture of Haddington; his action here is mentioned in Holinshed, *Chronicles of England, Scotland and Ireland* (1577). The battles of Musselburgh and Haddington were particularly import-ant because they gave the English control of Scotland almost up to Edinburgh. See also A157, 151 and 158.

11   'The French city of Montreuil [sometimes found with the Anglicized spelling Muttrel] was besieged by the Duke of Norfolk (the poet Surrey's father) in July–September, 1544' (Rollins). Laundersey is an Anglicized spelling of Lan-drecies, another French city. Wilford was evidently among the English forces attacking these cities.

A157

Pentameter couplets. The poem's source is an epitaph for the great scholar Guillaume Budé by Beza (for Beza, see headnote to poem 273). An elegy/epitaph. See headnotes to poems 156 and A156 for information about the knight in question.

A158

Poulter's measure. An elegy/epitaph. Lady Margaret Lee was Wyatt's sister, and the wife of Sir Anthony Lee. According to Merrill, she is thought to have been one of the four ladies in attendance on Anne Boleyn in the Tower, and to have been present at her execution.

A159

Rhyme royal. An elegy/epitaph. The identity of 'A.W.' is unknown. Rollins presents some possibilities very doubtfully; Merrill suggests Lady Anne Wentworth; poem 183 is an elegy to her.

A160

Pentameter couplets. The subject of the elegy is W. Chambers, brother of the Nicholas Chambers of A161.

1   Thalia was the Muse of comedy and bucolic poetry.

10   For Nestor, see note to poem 243.

15   Plautus, who wrote comedies between 205 and 184 BC, was the most important and influential of Roman playwrights.

A161

Pentameter couplets. The subject of the elegy is Nicholas Chambers, whose brother is the subject of A160. He may be the Nicholas Chambers who was awarded a BA from Christ Church, Oxford in 1547/8 (this was Grimald's college).

A162

Pentameter couplets. An elegy. 'Annes is, of course, a popular corruption of Agnes. As appears from [lines 53–4], Mrs. Grimald died sometime after January, 1552, when her poet-son left Oxford' (Rollins). For an excellent discussion of this poem see G. W. Pigman, *Grief and Renaissance Elegy* (Cambridge: Cambridge University Press, 1995), pp. 47–52.

9–10   Gnaeus Marcius Coriolanus was a general who gained his name from his capture of the Volscian town Corioli in 493 BC. On the pleas of his mother and wife, he later withdrew from an attack on Rome.

11–12   Quintus Sertorius (died 73/72 BC) was a distinguished
         Roman general and statesman. His father died when he
         was young, and he was warmly attached to his mother who
         arranged his excellent education.

13–14   The Sicilian brethren are Amphinomus and Anapus, who
         rescued their parents during an eruption of Mt. Etna by
         carrying them away on their shoulders.

15   The putative children of Tyndareos, king of Sparta, were
         Castor, Pollux, Clytemnestra and Helen of Troy, though the
         major mythological tradition is that Jupiter was their true
         father, having raped Tyndareos' wife Leda in the form of a
         swan.

16   Cleobis and Biton were sons of Cydippe, an Argive priest-
         ess of Hera. They were celebrated for their affection for
         their mother, and once drew her chariot some distance to
         the temple of Hera when the oxen were not brought in time
         (Herodotus, *Histories*, I. 31).

19–20   Caieta, nurse of Creusa and Ascanius, Aeneas' wife and son.

21–2   Acca Laurentia, who nursed Romulus and Remus after they
         had been taken from the she-wolf, hence the term 'lupa'
         (wolf). She was the wife of the shepherd Faustulus, and in
         some versions of the story was a prostitute, called 'lupa' by
         the shepherds. Rollins quotes Sir Thomas North's translation
         of Plutarch's *Lives* (1579): 'The Latines doe call with one
         selfe name shee woulfes *Lupas*, and women that geve their
         bodyes to all commers: as this nurce . . . dyd use to doe.'

23–4   Amalthea was one of Zeus' foster mothers; in early ver-
         sions of the story she was a goat who suckled the infant
         Zeus, and in later versions a girl who fed him with goats'
         milk. Zeus turned her into the constellation Capra (mean-
         ing she-goat).

25–6   The Hyades were the daughters of Atlas, nurses of Bacchus
         ('Lyai'); Zeus later turned them into a group of stars near
         to (and in some versions including) the Pleiades. Grimald
         has Bacchus rather than Zeus turning them into stars.

45   Minerva was goddess of crafts and hence skill and wisdom.

46   Phoebus was the god of music.

47   'Browns hold' is the name of the village north-west of
         Huntingdon where the Grimalds lived (records attest to the

family's presence from at least the mid-fifteenth century). It is now called Leighton Bromswold.

49–51 The Granta is the Cam, the river running through Cambridge, here a metonymy for the university, where Grimald attended Christ's College from 1536 until he graduated BA in 1539–40. The 'ladies nyne' are the Muses.

52 That is, Grimald was at Cambridge for five years. Titan is the sun; see note to A138, line 12.

53 The epithet 'that fayr foord' refers to Oxford. Grimald transferred from Cambridge to Oxford in 1541, and was made a probationer Fellow at Merton in May 1542. He was awarded his MA in 1544, and was employed at Christ Church after 1547. In 1552 he was granted a licence to preach at Eccles, and in 1553 he was made chaplain to Nicholas Ridley, the bishop of London. He left Oxford at the beginning of 1552, having spent around ten years there, 'twyse as long' as he was at Cambridge.

59 For Clotho, see note to poem 108, lines 1–4.

85 Mausolus, governor of Caria in Asia Minor in the mid-fourth century BC, was famous for the grand tomb built for him by his widow. This is the first instance of the adjective recorded in *OED*.

89 Hercules, great hero famous for strength and courage, was worshipped as god of commerce and victory. Achilles was the chief soldier of the Greeks in the Trojan War.

90 Hector was son of Priam, king of Troy, and the leading Trojan soldier. 'Ene' is Aeneas, who escaped from the defeated Troy and was ultimately responsible for the founding of Rome.

A163

Fourteener couplets. The source is a Latin poem by Walter Haddon (1516–72), in *Poemata* (1567 – see Rollins) a scholar and respected churchman. An elegy. There are inconsistencies in the records about Henry Fitzalan, Lord Maltravers, but he was born in the 1530s, was married to Anne Wentworth (cf. poems 183 and A159), and died of a fever while serving as an ambassador to the king of Bohemia in 1556, aged 18 or 19.

11   Queen Mary was on the throne when the poem was written
          and when the *Miscellany* was first published.

12   'Cesars broother' refers to King Ferdinand of Bohemia,
          brother of Charles V, Holy Roman Emperor.

35   The Roman emperor Titus died young (at the age of around
          41) having ruled only briefly (AD 79–81); he was a popular
          and successful leader, and a fine musician.

36   The 'yong prince Edward' was Edward VI (1537–53,
          reigned 1547–53), who succeeded to the English throne at
          the age of 10, and died six years later.

40   The identity of 'Shelley' is uncertain; Rollins presents a
          number of possibilities and concludes 'The name Shelley
          seems in the first half of the sixteenth century to have been
          almost synonymous with fighting.'

44   See note on line 36.

A164

Pentameter couplets. The source is an epitaph by Beza, beginning
'Extincto nuper Respublica moesta Valente' (for Beza, see headnote to
poem 273). For Lord Maltravers, see headnote to poem A163.

List of Poem Genres

As a supplement to our list of poetic forms, here we give a list of poetic genres/topics. Some of these may be disputed, and some poems belong to more than one genre or deal with more than one topic, but we hope it will be useful to the student and general reader who wishes to cross-reference the diverse kinds of poem contained within this very various collection.

apologies to ladies 59, 79, 95, ?174, A130

beast fables/allegorical narratives 29, 142, 206, 213, 220, 230, 265

celebrations of success in love 60, 90, 155, 233, A128

complaints (on subjects other than love) 2, 11, 15, 39, 41, 50, 96, 105, 106, 112, 126, 130, 195, 255, 256

condemnations of women 26, 187, 190, 239, 243, 245, 251, A131

condemnations of the world/poems on the vanity of life 141, 144, 191, 218, 234, 257

defences of women 27, ?194, 214, 240, 244, 246

dialogues ?87, 113

dream visions 47, 149

ekphrasis 158, 178

elegies 15, 34, 35, 36, ?106, 139, 151, 158, 175, 183, 197, 215, 223, 241, 242, ?270, ?279, 280, A156, A157, A158, A159, A160, A161, A162, A163, A164

encomia (praising men) 36, 188, A137

encomia (praising women) 8, 20, 168, 188, 189, 221, 264, 266, 269, A139, A140, A141, A144, A145, A146, A147

epigrams 31, 40, 61, 68, 72, 73, 76, 77, 78, 83, 92, 97, 114, 118, 119, 121, 124, 125, 127, 131, 132, 133, 148, 162, 173, 186, 187, ?196, 198, 199, 200, 201, 211, 224, 272, 273, 275, 276, A135, A138, A153, A155

female complaints 17, 19, 159, 192, 225, 259

fortune poems 86, 128, 146

Index of Verse Forms

other:

Index of first lines with poem number

Where a poem is otherwise known by a different first line, the better-known first line is also included below with a direction to the correct poem.